A POWER AMONG THEM

KAREN PASTORELLO

A Power among Them

BESSIE ABRAMOWITZ HILLMAN
AND THE MAKING OF THE
AMALGAMATED CLOTHING
WORKERS OF AMERICA

UNIVERSITY OF ILLINOIS PRESS

URBANA AND CHICAGO

Frontispiece: Kathleen Hermesdorf and
Angie Hauser of the Bebe Miller Dance
Company, © Lois Greenfield 2004

Library of Congress Cataloging-in-Publication Data

Pastorello, Karen, 1956–
A power among them : Bessie Abramowitz Hillman and
the making of the Amalgamated Clothing Workers of
America / Karen Pastorello.
p. cm. — (Working class in American history)
Includes bibliographical references and index.
ISBN 978–0–252–03230–1 (cloth : alk. paper)
1. Amalgamated Clothing Workers of America.
2. Hillman, Bessie. 3. Clothing workers—Labor
unions—United States—History. 4. Women clothing
workers—United States—History.
I. Title.
HD6515.C62U57   2007
331.88'1870973—dc22   2007035934

In memory of my grandmother,
Antoinette Elizabeth Barricelli Piarulle
(1906–1993)

To Labor!

Shall you complain who feed the world,
Who clothe the world, who house the world?
Shall you complain who are the world,
Of what the world may do?

    As from this time you use your pow'r
    The world must follow you!
    As from this hour you use your pow'r
    The world must follow you!

The world's life hangs on your right hand,
Your strong right hand, your skilled right hand,
You hold the whole world in your hand,
See to it what you do!

    Or dark or light, or wrong or right,
    The world is made by you!
    Or dark or light, or wrong or right,
    The world is made by you!

Then rise as you ne'er rose before,
Nor hoped before, nor dared before, and show
As ne'er was shown before
The pow'r that lies in you!

    Stand all as one, till right is done!
    Believe and dare and do!
    Stand all as one, till right is done!
    Believe and dare and do!

— Charlotte Perkins Gilman
   (*Source: Women's Trade Union League
   Convention Handbook*, 1911.)

Contents

Preface

One of the earliest and perhaps most prophetic memories I have of my childhood is accompanying my four-foot-ten-inch grand-mother to her "shop" to retrieve her final paycheck upon her retirement from Timely Clothes in Rochester, New York, on an overcast day in the fall of 1962. As we approached the box-like red brick building, my grandmother asked me if I would like to see where she worked. Jump-ing at the chance, I had no idea what to expect once inside the confines of the building where she had spent the last thirty years. Instead of entering the intimidating building, however, my grandmother hoisted me up to the level of the first-floor windows so that I could see inside. Peering over the window frame, in the dim light I saw what seemed to be hundreds of women sewing, sitting in neat rows of chairs, all intensely focused on hand-finishing the garments they held. Not one looked up to see my awestruck eyes. Nor, in the many years that have passed since, has that image slipped from my mind.

As the oldest child of Italian immigrant parents, my grandmother, Antoinette Piarulle, was forced out of her parochial school classroom and into the workplace in 1920, at the age of fourteen, so that she could make a financial contribution to her large family. Like other daughters of the immigrant generations, Antoinette worked in more than one of the factories that began to dominate the urban landscape of industrial Rochester at the turn of the century. After working for less than a year at Eastman Kodak Company, she spent a significant portion of her young adult years working in the same shoe factory as her father did. Upon her marriage to my grandfather, a semiskilled Italian immigrant laborer five years her senior, she ended her stint as a wage laborer in 1926. Her sojourn into marriage and full-time motherhood proved to be only temporary. Shortly after the birth of my mother in 1932, my grandfather lost his job. The next year the country sank into the depths of the worst economic times it had ever known. Since my grandparents found it too difficult to support two young children on whatever part-time work my grandfather could piece together, at the height of the Depression my grandmother returned to work. After learning on the job at both Hickey Freeman and Bond Clothing, she found permanent employment at Timely Clothes, one of the nation's leading manufacturers of men's suits.

I was born just as Antoinette's three decades as a hand button sewer were drawing to a close. By the time I was six years old, she could no longer grasp a needle, because rheumatoid arthritis had so gnarled and deformed her fingers as to render intricate tasks impossible. My grandmother's phone number was the first one I ever learned. Family history has it that I dialed Congress-6–3246 on a daily basis to instruct her not to "dare to thread those needles anymore." I must have worried about her as she labored every night over her "homework," which entailed hand-threading (later, threading with the aid of a contraption that my grandfather built) and waxing with round clumps of beeswax 250 to 300 needles per night. This unpaid preparation was necessary so that her time in the factory could be used exclusively to sew and thus earn her piece rate in the most efficient manner possible. Button sewing had been mechanized for decades, but the high-quality suits that Timely Clothes produced demanded hand-finishing.

I spent more time at my grandparents' house than my own. Broken Italian phrases intermingled with praise for "the savior" Roosevelt, "that God-blessed" Hillman, and "the Amalgamated" (Amalgamated Clothing Workers of America) became the cadences of my younger years. I often wondered why, after her own children were married and my grandparents were financially secure, my grandmother continued working. Years later, I realized that she found a sense of community within the workplace that mattered more than the income. Because close friends and even some relatives surrounded her, for my grandmother this monotonous work proved fulfilling. The union afforded protections that drastically altered the work environs she encountered on her first jobs. The answer to my question was simple: She enjoyed going to work. Although I never remember her discussing it, I'm sure too that she appreciated the autonomy that most women associated with work outside the home. What she did repeatedly articulate was the sense of satisfaction that membership in the Amalgamated Clothing Workers of America provided. The social and recreational opportunities available at the weekly union meetings carried the cherished camaraderie among the women workers to the world outside the workplace. The union gave a multifaceted meaning to the work that my grandmother, and thousands of women like her, performed.

Intrigued by both women's history and labor history, at the onset of my doctoral work I decided to explore women's participation in what I knew as the Amalgamated. A cursory glance at the history of the largest union of workers producing men's clothing in this country revealed that the Amalgamated Clothing Workers of America was officially established in 1914. If one person is synonymous with the founding of the ACWA, it is Sidney Hillman, a young Russian-Jew who ascended from the ranks of semiskilled apprentice cutters to assume the presidency of the union in the first year of its existence. During Hillman's tenure, the union grew to more than 250,000 members.

His influence extended past the labor arena into national politics. For more than a decade, he served as an adviser to the Roosevelt administration, becoming directly involved in the creation of New Deal labor policies. His political career culminated during the early years of World War II when he was named associate director of the Office of Production Management. By the 1940s, Sidney Hillman helped to achieve state support for workers' concerns, thus earning an indelible reputation as a labor statesman. The workers revered Sidney Hillman. His death was marked by banner headlines and a funeral procession befitting a head of state.

As I examined the guide to the official union papers more closely, only one woman's name appeared among the many men's names. Concern gradually displaced the sense of anticipation I felt as I delved into Bessie Hillman's papers for the first time. The traditional sources historians rely on, such as diaries, journals, and significant correspondence, were not only lacking, they were virtually nonexistent. The folder labeled "personal papers" that initially seemed so promising yielded no more than scattered household receipts and intermittent property tax records dating back to the 1920s. As I considered surrendering to the paucity of evidence, I began to realize that even these fragments could be joined together to tell an important story. The clues were subtle but compelling. At the very least, Bessie Hillman kept the Hillman family records and saw to it that Sidney "had the best circumstances for his work"; at most, she purchased property and managed the household while she pursued her own career interests outside the home.[1]

The more I contemplated reconstructing Bessie Hillman's life, the more determined I became. The multiple challenges I faced were largely due to Hillman's own disposition. As her daughter, Philoine Fried, aptly observed, Bessie Hillman was "a doer not a writer."[2] For Hillman, actions spoke louder than words—her life was a flurry of activity, but she never took the time to write any of it down. She typified working-class women activists of her generation, who rarely made space in their hectic lives to record what their days held. Early-twentieth-century conventions further discouraged them from acknowledging the historical implications of their activities. Hillman is representative of a group that class, race, and gender have relegated to the shadows of history. These women were oppressed in their homes and in their workplaces. A few did try to write about their lives, but due to the lack of support and conflicting demands imposed on them by their families, they found it impossible. Others were simply overcome by sheer exhaustion.

Although several accounts have survived, many in the form of oral histories or anthologies, early-twentieth-century sources regarding working women's labor activism are scarce.[3] One of the most difficult parts of this project has been to try to reconstruct the complex and vital life of a major historical figure using only shreds of evidence. Admitting that the dearth of the historical record allows certain silences to prevail became less problematic once I followed Janet Zandy's suggestion: to affirm "not only what is not spoken, but how and why it is not spoken." Whenever possible, I replaced the private silences in Hillman's life with the more public sounds of Amalgamated women.[4]

Although Bessie's life was not well documented in the Amalgamated's papers, insights into her life surfaced in the form of official publications, correspondence, and remnants of speeches. Personal interviews with relatives, colleagues, and friends lent meaning to the text of her work. Compilation of these various pieces revealed that this lone woman's work, catalogued under "Papers of Other Executive Officers" and simply listed as "Bessie Hillman," was more instrumental in the founding of the Amalgamated Clothing Workers of America than that of her future husband, Sidney Hillman.

Even though Bessie Abramowitz Hillman's labor activism spanned the course of more than sixty years and touched the lives of countless workers, she is rarely mentioned even in official ACWA histories. Sidney Hillman biographer and union historian, Steven Fraser, contends that "the nearly complete male domination of a union at least half female was never seriously challenged."[5] Fraser was not the first to discount women's participation in the organized labor movement.

Male-centered interpretations of the situation in the needle trades prevailed at the expense of female recognition for more than half a century. One-sided accounts, such as Benjamin Stolberg's *Tailor's Progress: The Story of a Famous Union and the Men Who Made It*, do more than subtly hint at the prominence of men over women unionists. Historians chronicling the ACWA have consistently ignored women's contributions to the union.[6]

This study places Bessie Abramowitz Hillman at the center of the historical events that marked the founding of the Amalgamated Clothing Workers of America. Empowered by her connection to the social feminist reform movement centered at Chicago's Hull-House, the young immigrant was one of the first to walk off the job as a button sewer at Hart, Schaffner, and Marx in September 1910 to protest an arbitrary reduction of wages. Within weeks, more than 35,000 workers followed the lead of Abramowitz and her cohorts, resulting in a massive strike that both paralyzed the Chicago men's clothing manufacturers and paved the way for the organization of the entire men's garment industry.

Bessie Abramowitz Hillman is seldom credited with being much more than an honorary official who assisted Sidney Hillman with union business after their marriage in 1916. However, John E. Williams, *Streator Independent-Times* editor and later Hart, Schaffner, and Marx arbitration board chairman, recognized Bessie's extraordinary character early in her career. Paying tribute to her in a 1913 article, Williams wrote, "Earnest and sincere in word and act, she is a power among the women workers, and a friend and counselor to the young girls in the industry."[7] One year later, Abramowitz and a handful of other delegates broke away from the exclusionary United Garment Workers convention to regroup as an independent union—the Amalgamated Clothing Workers of America. Bessie enjoyed the distinction of being the first woman appointed to the General Executive Board of the newly created organization.

Her efforts on behalf of women workers add another dimension to the history of the Amalgamated Clothing Workers and to women's labor history in general. During the union's earliest years, Bessie Hillman and her contemporary, Dorothy Bellanca of Baltimore, aggressively pushed Amalgamated leaders to offer women more than economic protections or token leadership positions. Together they compelled their male colleagues to recognize that women comprised the majority of workers in the clothing industry and played a crucial part in the mass strike movement responsible for the union's founding. The union could not survive without women's full participation. Once the ACWA was established as a permanent organization, Hillman and fellow female activists worked from within to facilitate the entry of women into the Amalgamated's ranks. In large part because of Hillman's efforts to infuse meaning into the organization, by having it offer more than economic benefits, members found the union experience both supportive and enriching. The collective solidarity Hillman helped them to achieve encouraged their involvement in the union and other realms of activism.

Hillman's quest for the organization of workers was rooted in her Russian-Jewish heritage. She was one of the few who, as Alice Henry noted in 1915, "stood above the rest" as a leader in "making the fight for higher wages, shorter hours, better shop management, and above all for the right to organize."[8] In more recent decades, scholars of immigrant women's labor activism have turned their attention to the emergence of working women's consciousness in the United States. Alice Kessler-Harris, Sarah Eisenstein, and Nancy MacLean were among the first to demonstrate how Jewish women's culture enabled unionization.[9] Later works by Susan Glenn, Annelise Orleck, and Elizabeth Ewen suggest that though Old-World traditions encouraged labor activism, New-World work experience was the primary force shaping women's consciousness.[10] Analysis of Bessie Abramowitz's life benefits from this new approach by emphasizing the intersections of her eastern European Jewish ethnic culture with her New-World experiences as they converged at a vulnerable time in her life. Abramowitz's story presents a case study of a working woman whose encounter with the women's political culture based at Hull-House transformed her entire life. The middle-class women reformers, specifically Jane Addams, imparted strong impressions of American women's values on working-class girls like Abramowitz and helped them formulate collective strategies that advanced women's interests.[11]

To date, the work by women's labor historians on garment workers concentrates on immigrant women leaders within the International Ladies Garment Workers' Union (ILGWU), situated on New York's Lower East Side. The majority of this scholarship comes in the form of comparative studies contained in collective labor biographies. This book contributes to the extant interpretations by illuminating a single immigrant woman's life experience in the men's garment union, the Amalgamated Clothing Workers of America, in Chicago (and later in New York). Although the union's institutional history provides a backdrop for this project, my primary goal is to demonstrate how the activism of Hillman and the Amalgamated women helped to build the character of this new industrial union.

Nancy Gabin, Ruth Milkman, and Dennis Deslippe were among the first to provide stories of labor women's political and economic reform efforts in specific unions.[12] In *The Other Women's Movement*, Dorothy Sue Cobble weaves parts of the stories they tell into a cohesive history to demonstrate how black and white women operating within the context of the labor movement "helped keep feminism alive from the 1930s to the 1960s when it had been all but abandoned by middle-class women."[13] Cobble does an outstanding job of describing this previously neglected generation of labor women, whom she calls "labor feminists"—women who prioritized the needs of working-class women. In chronicling Hillman's life and the lives of the women who surrounded her, I rely heavily on Cobble's definition of labor feminists as a multi-class group that "recognized that women suffer disadvantages due to their sex and sought to eliminate sex-based disadvantages" using the labor movement as the vehicle for betterment.[14] Descendents of the social feminists of an earlier era, labor feminists left the limited maternalist goals of the suffrage years behind to seek a more comprehensive form of social and economic equality. Cobble, borrowing from the first director of the United States Women's Bureau, Mary Anderson, terms this expanded vision "full industrial citizenship." Working-class women perceived equality and citizenship in broad terms that emphasized entitlements encompassing more than women's job rights and wage justice. Cobble credits labor feminists inside the unions with being the first to demand maternity leave, childcare provisions, and recognition of household labor and domestic-related occupations.[15]

In tracing Hillman's evolution from an immigrant worker to a labor feminist, I came to understand that her story diverges from the majority of Jewish women labor activists of her time. Her life course did not follow the conventional path that Susan Glenn refers to as the Jewish New Womanhood, "where teenage girls emigrate to this country, work in the garment industry, go out on strike, become brief union members, marry and settle into domestic life."[16] She did not relinquish her work upon marriage, nor did she trade her family life for union life as her husband did. Instead, she negotiated the boundaries of her public and private worlds to combine activism and family responsibilities throughout her life.

While her children were young, Hillman traveled to rural Pennsylvania, Connecticut, and upstate New York to organize shirt workers in sweatshops that had moved away from unionized metropolitan areas. As one of labor's earliest civil rights advocates, throughout the 1930s Bessie strove to bring black laundry workers into the Amalgamated.

In 1937, she simultaneously became education director for the New York Laundry Workers and cultural activities director for the ACWA, writing a regular column for the union newspaper, the *Advance*. Both positions reinforced her union leadership during this period. During World War II, she directed the Amalgamated's War Activities Department and served on the New York Advisory Board of the Office of Price Administration. As a member of the Child Welfare Committee of New York, Hillman utilized her expertise to help open childcare centers and recreational facilities for the children of war workers.

Politically active for the better part of her life, Hillman participated in the American Labor Party during the 1930s and 1940s and after the war affiliated with the reform wing of the Democratic Party. In 1951, she was appointed to the newly formed United States Department of Defense Advisory Committee on Women in the Armed Services. She represented American women's labor interests as a delegate to the International Confederation of Free Trade Unions and also through her work on the Protective Labor Legislation Committee of the President's Commission on the Status of Women in the early 1960s under John F. Kennedy. Concerned with paving the way for women of future generations, in a 1962 essay, "Gifted Women in the Trade Unions," Hillman encouraged women to become more involved in organized labor activities.[17] As an advocate of social justice, throughout her life she championed the causes of civil rights, education, and child welfare.

Although during Sidney Hillman's lifetime Bessie worked unwaveringly at her husband's side, following his premature death in 1946 she carried on alone for the next twenty-five years. Bessie bridged the gap between progressive-era social feminists and labor feminists of the post-1940 era by persistently demanding equal pay for women, an end to sex and race discrimination, passage of protective labor legislation, and enactment of reforms to end class injustice and improve the quality of life for working women. Later, as a widow reflecting on her own life experiences and encouraged by the nascent feminist climate of the 1960s, union vice president Bessie Hillman expanded her vision from one of industrial democracy that included female unionists to one that demanded "full industrial citizenship" encompassing "the right to market work for all women" and "social supports necessary for a life apart from wage work, including the right to care for one's family."[18]

From her first job to the last days of her life, Hillman possessed the ability to draw workers into the labor movement. Her early exposure to socialism and progressive ideology enabled her to create an enduring, pragmatic program that combined class concerns with racial and gender issues. She organized as a wife, mother, and widow. She learned to be comfortable in the public eye, first as "the first lady of the Amalgamated" and later as a union vice president. Hillman used her heavy Yiddish accent to her advantage, endearing herself to workers with her uncanny ability to tell a good joke. Although some rank-and-file workers may have considered her personality overbearing, for most workers, such as my grandmother, she exuded an inspiring charisma.

For more than half a century, Bessie Abramowitz Hillman helped to shape the centrifugal forces of the American labor movement. In her own right, she worked first to found the Amalgamated Clothing Workers of America, and then, acting on the principles of labor feminism, turned toward industrial democracy by demanding broader reform goals for workers through political and economic action.[19] She modeled her politics on the progressive women's political culture and firmly believed that feminism was best served by a trade-union organization that included all workers. Her affiliation with labor feminists outside the Amalgamated Clothing Workers in the early 1960s pushed her to lash out at the sexism of the labor movement. In essence, Bessie Hillman proved to be a quintessential social and labor activist who countered class, race, and gender discrimination by waging a lifelong battle for "workingmen and working women, especially working women, for equal liberty, and equal power as human beings."[20]

Acknowledgments

In any work of this breadth, the author incurs many personal and professional debts of gratitude. Chris Smith at Arizona State University pointed me in the direction of labor history more than two decades ago. His gentle guidance and friendship have been an abiding source of support. Kitty Sklar welcomed me into her women's history seminar at Binghamton University at an important time in my life. She introduced me to the vibrant women's political culture centered in progressive Chicago and, in doing so, helped shape the organizational framework of my study. Mel Dubofsky's willingness to contribute his expertise in all aspects of labor history is truly appreciated.

Certain archival staff members also deserve special mention for their efforts to assist with my research. Jeff Flannery at the Library of Congress Manuscript Division, Lynn Bassanese and Robert Parks at the Roosevelt Library, Tab Lewis and Janice Wiggins at the National Archives, Sarah Springer at the National Labor College, John Olson at Syracuse University, and Bob Kibbee at Cornell's Olin Library all offered their services to facilitate my research. The Kheel Labor-Management Documentation Center at Cornell University has been my home away from home for the majority of the research conducted for this book. Richard Strassberg, Hope Nisly, Paulette Manos, Barbara Morley, Patrizia Sione, and Melissa Holland have shared their enthusiasm for this project in the form of resources and knowledge over the years.

Laurie Matheson at the University of Illinois Press helped guide me through the twists and turns of the publishing process. I am also grateful to those who have read all or parts of this work. Laura Tate, Frances

Benson, Brigid O'Farrell, Sue Cobble, Nancy Dafoe, Benita Roth, Ken Teitelbaum, and Chae Ran Freeze have given their time and their insights to improve the quality of this study. Suzanne Parmiter, Karla Tracy, Pamela Auble, Judy VanBuskirk, Claire Parham, Mary Shanahan, Kirk Deutrich, and Elaine and Al Spaziano helped me see this through in a multitude of ways.

My colleagues at Tompkins Cortland Community College have offered tremendous support. I am especially grateful to the sabbatical committee for granting the leave from my teaching position, which enabled me to bring this project to completion. Phil Tate helped me answer a number of questions and Bruce Need copyedited this book, both while in the midst of full academic schedules. The librarians at the College are always ready to answer my reference questions and grant interlibrary loan requests. Thanks to the generous donations of Nick Salvatore, we now have a substantial labor history holding that I consult on a regular basis.

Three people I have met along the way deserve special recognition. Alice Kessler-Harris took time out from her busy schedule to read and critique the manuscript more than once. Her kind insistence that I view Hillman as part of a much larger labor feminist picture makes this work much more historically meaningful than the biography I originally set out to write. Tom Dublin, chair of my dissertation committee and longtime advisor, spent many hours reading numerous revisions of this work. He is the one who pushed me the hardest to expand my research base and refine my writing. One of my greatest debts is to Bessie's oldest daughter, Philoine Hillman Fried. She consented to numerous interviews and always made herself available to answer any and every question. She graciously opened her home and her heart to share family memories of Bessie with me, including portions of her personal papers and photographs, before donating them to the archives at Cornell University.

To countless family members, friends, and students, I offer my sincere appreciation for your companionship and ever-ready words of encouragement. My father, Ron Griffith, assisted with many of the photographs that appear in this book. I am most grateful to my children, David, Dominique, Chris, and Jamie, for keeping me grounded in the present. I hope that at least a small part of this work has touched their lives in a positive way. My husband, Jim, in his own unique way, is as committed to this project as I am. His pride in this accomplishment means more than I can say.

A POWER AMONG THEM

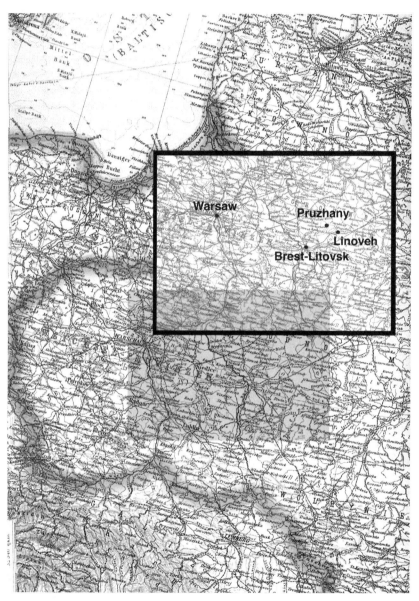

Detail from map of Belarus showing a section of Grodno province. Bessie Abramowitz's birthplace, Linoveh, is located about 30 miles northeast of Brest-Litovsk and a few miles southeast of Pruzhany. Source: Stieler's Hand-Atlas (Gotha: Justus Perthes, 1914). (Courtesy of Bird Library, Syracuse University.)

1 *Bound but Determined* *(1889–1908)*

Despite the turbulent times that increasingly characterized Jewish life in late-nineteenth-century Russia, Bessie Abramowitz enjoyed a relatively carefree childhood shaped to a large extent by the traditional patterns of *shtetl* (small-town) life. Perhaps her birth during Passover, the most generous season of all, in 1889, foretold her good fortune. Sarah (Rabinowitz) and Emanuel Abramowitz named their fourth daughter Bas Sheva (Bessie).[1] Eventually the Abramowitz family would include ten children: eight girls and two boys, all educated at home by a private tutor. Emanuel Abramowitz worked as a commission broker buying provisions from merchants on board trains passing through their tiny village crossing on the way to and from Minsk.[2] At the time of Bessie's birth, the Abramowitzes seemed to enjoy a fairly comfortable lifestyle.

The Paradoxes of the Pale

Like thousands of other Jewish families, the Abramowitzes resided in the Pale of Settlement. Linoveh, in Grodno province, with its approximately 150 inhabitants, was among the smallest of the hundreds of shtetls that dotted the Russian countryside in what is now Belarus.[3] A letter from Bessie's niece, Luba Aten, indicated that the Abramowitzes' house, with its five bedrooms and huge dining room, was one of the largest homes in the town. Aten described Linoveh as extremely tiny, lacking a police station, hospital, doctor, dentist, or midwife. It did not have a sewer system, electricity, or gas.[4] Comprised of only one unnamed road, at first glance tiny Linoveh typified in miniature the shtetls where, throughout the nineteenth century, the majority of Russian Jews resided. In every shtetl at the center of the unpaved roads and back alleys was the locus of spiritual life: the synagogue.

Community life, often viewed as an extension of the family, revolved around the synagogue. Rabbis were the most respected of all community members, although even their authority, after being challenged by the Haskalah (movement for secular enlightenment), had begun to wane by the late nineteenth century. Bustling marketplaces, where peddlers hawked foodstuffs, clothes, tools, and other necessities, enabled each shtetl to function as a somewhat self-sufficient, but often destitute, settlement. In spite of the impoverished and crowded conditions in these shtetls, they still retained remnants of the autonomous Jewish communities, the *kehillah*. Ostensibly abolished in 1844 by Nicholas I, the *kahals*, executive agencies of these self-governing entities, continued to function unofficially, assessing and collecting taxes, providing recruits for the tsarist army, and upholding rabbinical law in their own courts.[5]

The most redeeming quality of shtetl life was the assurance that "among Jews one was never lost."[6] *Tsodeka*, the religious act of giving charity to needy Jews and Gentiles alike, was firmly woven into the organization of the shtetls. With an enduring religiosity permeating secular life, the ideal of mutual responsibility evidenced itself in the tradition of giving charity on many levels, both public and private. This combination of individual benevolence and collective community service was an integral aspect of community function and an essential requirement for being a good Jew. As the primary dispensers of charity, women began to establish formal organizations to carry on and further their good works. Grodno and the other population centers housed a number of charitable societies founded and maintained by wealthy Jewish matrons. With the economic situation of Jews deteriorating throughout the nineteenth century, fundraising through house-to-house collections allowed these formal institutions to continue to provide for increasing numbers of poor and orphans. Thus, Abramowitz lived in a world where women provided for the needy. Young Bessie probably accompanied her mother as she gave food to the poor, cared for the sick, or watched over orphans, instilling in Abramowitz an early desire for social justice.[7] The knowledge that life could be improved by the collective actions of those more fortunate left a lifelong impression.

Seeking to assert control over autonomous shtetl communities, tsarist officials promulgated edicts that successfully disrupted Jewish economic activities, relegating many more thousands to the ranks of the needy than could be provided for by charitable institutions. In addition to restricting Jewish residence to the Pale of Settlement, stringent enforcement of Tsar Alexander II's 1882 May Laws prevented Jews from working on equal terms with the majority of the population. These harsh laws prohibited Jews from holding mortgages or property in their own names. Prior to this time, many Jews were successful merchants, liquor distillers, or tax collectors. Now state regulations outlawing their monopoly of the liquor trade jeopardized their livelihoods. Railroad construction facilitating transport of goods further displaced many Jews, since it undermined their earnings as middlemen.[8] Even though the Abramowitzes appeared economically secure, their supplemental income as innkeepers suggests that their family too began at some point to feel the economic pressure of discriminatory tsarist policies.

Linoveh's small size and relative geographic isolation offered the Abramowitz family protection from the more immediate upheavals that plagued the Pale. Massive construction of the Russian railroad system between 1895 and 1905 allowed thousands of Russian migrant workers to travel from shtetl to shtetl on the rail lines seeking employment. Bessie would surely have heard about these bands of discontented men, who vented their frustrations on Jews by inciting pogroms that more often resulted in the destruction of property than in the loss of life. Remarkably, Linoveh escaped the civil unrest and multiple pogroms experienced by other communities in Grodno province.[9] For a time, the Abramowitzes also avoided the increasing economic marginalization of the Jews. Yet, in all likelihood, family members could not help but be aware of the chaotic conditions that dominated life in many Russian shtetls at the turn of the century.

Bessie Abramowitz remained unscathed by the troublesome events that marked the decline of the Romanov dynasty. Surrounded by political and economic disorder, the young Abramowitz lived within a sheltered world that rarely deviated from tradition and was marked by the passage of the seasons and orthodox holidays. Although social critics denounced the custom-based provincialism of shtetl life for impeding progress, for the Abramowitzes, as for many other Jewish families, surely the unwavering routines of daily life served as a haven from the disorder outside Linoveh.

For the majority of women in eastern Europe, the domestic patterns of orthodox life—where women bore the brunt of familial responsibilities—continued virtually uninterrupted until the end of the nineteenth century. Girls like Bessie Abramowitz were expected to spend their childhood preparing to imitate their mothers as housewives. If a mother left home to work, her oldest daughter, who might be as young as seven or eight, was expected to run the household. Working mothers were a common sight in the shtetl marketplace, where they were keepers of small shops or peddlers. In many cases, all the financial concerns of the family fell upon the women, as their husbands fervently pursued their Torah studies or traveled away from home on business.[10] As was common in many shtetl families, Bessie helped her mother run the family inn while her father trekked through the countryside selling his wares to Russian peasants.

Because they shouldered the financial responsibilities within their orthodox families by working outside the home, women who became breadwinners gained a sense of autonomy in the domestic sphere that extended into the commercial marketplace. However, as a group, women continued to suffer from patriarchal notions of inferiority that excluded them from positions of religious or communal authority. Women's economic independence and participation in community life failed to offset their subordinate position in the traditional Jewish family. Paradoxically, their lives were constrained by a system of patriarchal obligation, but their world in large part created the social cement that assured cultural continuity.[11]

With the family essential to Jewish survival, marriage was a focal point in the lives of women. It was the most festive occasion in Jewish life. Bessie had to have been acutely aware that a sense of obligation rather than love usually lay at its foundation. Arranged marriages, where the future mother-in-law assisted by a *shadkhan* (matchmaker) selected the bride, were commonplace. In traditional households, the newlyweds lived in a matrilocal arrangement called a *kest*, in which the groom's new in-laws agreed to support the young couple for a period of up to four years so the husband's Torah study could advance.[12] For some young couples, this proved to be a nurturing and supportive relationship. For others, however, it was the most miserable period of their lives. Once married, women achieved full family status only upon the birth of a child. Failure to produce a child in the traditional period of ten years was considered the fault of the woman, and a man could divorce his wife for this alone.[13] Marriage clearly defined women's inferior place in Jewish society. For Abramowitz, as for an increasing number of Russian-Jewish daughters, the prospect of following in her mother's footsteps seemed dismal.[14]

The Woman Question

Critical of the prescribed place of women in Russian society, nineteenth-century writers presented alternatives to traditional shtetl life. One of the most significant questions emerging in the latter half of the century concerned the problem of what to do about the inferior status of Russian women. N. G. Chernyshevsky, one of the first Russian writers to expound on "the woman question," promoted education for women as a means of overcoming their ignorance. The assumption was that women should enjoy the same autonomy as men in all aspects of life. Furthermore, liberation through education from traditional roles would allow women to assert their special moral qualities while working for the good of society. Perhaps more effective because of their appeal for social justice, radical writers began to convince many Jewish parents that secular education, whether by private tutor or at the university level, would at the very least enhance their daughters' status as brides.[15] By the latter part of the nineteenth century, the government was allowing Jewish children to attend Russian schools, in an effort to assimilate them into the general population. The Abramowitz children were tutored at home because of their geographic isolation.

By the 1870s, middle-class Russian-Jewish daughters as well as sons became university students. In addition to their course work, these students frequently involved themselves in political movements and labor activism. Although no evidence survives indicating that Abramowitz belonged to any radical associations, her tutor, Schmeryl Pomerantz, introduced her to the writings of Karl Marx.[16] One can imagine a scene in which a young Abramowitz, staying up late with a small lantern casting a dim light on the book in her lap, eagerly peruses Marx's work, hungry for new ideas. Perhaps, despite knowing that Marx would not allow a woman to lead a workers' revolution, she thereby derived a temporary escape from her "dreary, boring and hopeless" shtetl world.[17] Although the paucity of evidence makes it difficult to determine the exact impression this early exposure to Marxism made on Abramowitz, it did provide a potential new way of thinking that enhanced her concern for social justice and would gradually alter her entire perspective on life.

Abramowitz's formal education suggests that the rationalistic Haskalah movement had affected the family. Originating in Germany, by the early 1820s the Haskalah movement had spread to the Russian

Empire. Followers of the movement, called *maskilim*, tended to be educated but still Orthodox Jews who believed that the key to emancipation and equality was the reconciliation of Judaism with modern Western ideas and practices. Prior to this time, even though religious education of men was a priority in Jewish families, women were not encouraged to study religion; nevertheless, they often educated themselves through any available means.[18] One of the most important books for Jewish women was *T'sena Ure'ena (Come Out and See)*. First published in the sixteenth century, for the next two hundred years it drastically influenced the education of European Jewish girls who could read and study the Talmudic sources and accompanying commentaries at home. Because women lacked formal Hebrew education, religious writings aimed at them were written in Yiddish. Women often prayed in Yiddish, too, which explains why it eventually became known as "the women's language."[19]

Enlightened Haskalah followers, influenced by Russian writers such as Chernyshevsky, Belinsky, and Dostoyevsky, bore witness to profound changes in Russian political and philosophical thought. Novelists criticized what they considered the backward conventions of Jewish life, including early and arranged marriages (especially where the husband was economically unproductive), the general oppression of women, and superstitions.[20] Gradually, these alternative ways of thinking began to erode the traditional lifestyle of even the most observant families. In the Abramowitz family, secular learning provided a source of excitement.

Crossing Borders

For Bessie Abramowitz, the boundaries of Linoveh slowly succumbed to the world beyond the Pale, as travelers staying overnight at the family inn shared their stories of America after the dinner dishes were cleared away. Further informed by letters from relatives who had emigrated, and perhaps even by local newspapers and immigrant guides touting the image of a promised land, Abramowitz devised a plan to travel to America. Bessie envisioned a life unrestrained by a cultural tradition that defined women as daughters, wives, and mothers, so she abruptly ended her carefree childhood, leaving her village to seek work, possibly in the nearby town of Pruzhany. This move, along with her actual emigration, is indicative of Abramowitz's desire to assert her independence; during this time, it was uncommon for young girls of her socioeconomic status—whose family did not depend on her income—to seek factory work.[21]

Away from home, Abramowitz encountered a rapidly industrializing Russia where many Jews who had migrated to urban areas found work. In this transitional world, women began to work outside the home and local marketplace for wages. Most Jews considered work in the needle trades respectable occupations for women. According to an 1898 investigation by the Jewish Colonization Association, a private philanthropic agency, more than 50,000 women in the Pale were engaged in some type of work in the clothing trades. Although the association did not provide exact statistics, the majority of these women were probably young single women from poor families. Jews who worked in urban centers tended to be employed in Jewish-owned shops. However, even Jews who had enjoyed the privilege of living in towns and cities outside the Pale of Settlement, such as master artisans, merchants of the first guild, university students, and professionals, had their privileges revoked by the tsarist government's 1882 May Laws.[22]

By the end of the nineteenth century, the province of Grodno had become a center for the garment industry. In eastern Europe, a specific craft structure developed. Garment workers fell into three categories: masters, apprentices, and hired workers, all of whom worked outside the guild system. Garment firms, like the one Abramowitz probably worked in, sold their products on the open market instead of producing items to order. Many of these craftspeople peddled their work in villages, much to the dismay of Christian crafters and guilds. By the turn of the century, approximately 250,000 Russian Jews worked in the garment industry, more than in any other industry. This severe competition among Jewish crafts in the Pale contributed to a specific way of life and even folklore among the masses of impoverished Jewish workers who, by the latter years of the nineteenth century, constituted the foundation for a Jewish proletariat.[23]

In the late nineteenth century, this craft system coexisted with the rise of factories. The only large-scale industries to employ Jewish men and women were the cigarette and match factories. One of the largest was the Shereshevsky Cigarette Factory in Grodno, employing approximately 1,800 by the outbreak of World War I. Workers encountered numerous hardships in this industry. In 1899, discontented women workers led 800 workers out in what became one of the first mass strikes in Russian history.[24] In sweatshops and factories, female activists initiated and promoted a sense of class consciousness among workers that easily transferred to the new world.

Grodno province rapidly became a stronghold of the organized Jewish labor movement. Among the first to become concerned with

workers' problems were young middle-class Jewish women from enlightened Haskalah families, many of whom had been radicalized by
their association with student radicals in Russia and Switzerland. After
being forced to leave the university centers of St. Petersburg, Kiev, and
Moscow by Russian police, these women returned to their hometowns
and founded new radical groups. As early as the 1870s, Vilna became a
center of these Jewish *kases* or "study circles," which included both intellectuals and workers. By the late 1880s, the tactics of the politicized
Jewish labor movement, the largest of which was known as the Bund,
shifted from propaganda to agitation. Accordingly, the workers began
to play a larger part in leadership.[25]

Abramowitz may have witnessed this intensified activism firsthand, as many of the young Bundist women broke with tradition in
more than just a political sense. Because the Bund was strongly anti-
clerical, members rejected orthodox religious practices, consequently
clashing with their families. Parents criticized young men and women
for studying together and attending meetings late into the night. Some
young girls ran away from home to escape marriages that their parents
arranged for them. Once the decision to break with the past was made,
the revolutionary group served as a surrogate family and proffered an
alternative but still communal lifestyle. Many Bundist women were
so strongly committed to the movement that they refused to marry
at all. Some set up households with male comrades for the purpose of
concealing revolutionary activities.[26]

Talented single women, many from middle-class families, pursued
activist careers not open to them in traditional orthodox society. These
"new Jewish women," including Sophia Perovskaya, Sophia Bardina,
Essie Helfman, Vera Figner, Maria Spirindonova, and Catherine Bresh-
kovskaya, became organizers, educators, and writers.[27] Women stocking
makers in Vilna organized the first of what would eventually become
hundreds of workers' *kases* within shops and factories. Initially designed
with charitable intentions to offset the costs of personal emergencies
such as illness and death, the *kases* evolved over time into the administrative organ of the Bund. Women contributed to the movement by
acting in whatever capacity the leadership deemed necessary, including
organizing other women, raising strike funds, writing and distributing
illegal literature, and acting as messengers and nurses.[28]

While working alongside its members and perhaps even joining
their expanding ranks, Abramowitz must have been intrigued by the
Bund, which was the first Jewish group to formally allow women to join
on an equal basis with men. Once admitted to membership, however,

women found that their problems were considered secondary to the success of the workers' revolution. In the weaving shops, for example, women were usually employed as assistants to the more skilled men and, along with mechanization, were viewed as a potential job threat. When the women went out on strike in one shop, the men responded with scorn and amazement, offering little if any support.[29] Although the movement expressed an interest in moving toward a position of sexual equality, in reality Bund women were relegated to a subordinate place in the kitchen. Despite their secondary status in Russia (as was later the case in the United States), single working women demonstrated the strongest devotion to the cause. In both countries, married women rarely went into the factory. Once married, women often deferred to their husbands' leadership and ideas. Nevertheless, single women workers were willing to sacrifice comfort, safety, and even their lives for a vision of the future in which all injustices would be erased.[30]

Exposed to a world different from and far more promising than their own, for some young women, including Bessie Abramowitz, emigration to America or Palestine became an alternative preferable to the transformation of Jewish life in the Pale. Returning from her factory sojourn after a matter of months, with money in her pockets and a newly acquired self-confidence, a further sense of urgency motivated Abramowitz. Her two older sisters had been married off and Bessie realized that she was next in line when she overheard the local matchmaker's conversation with her mother in the family kitchen.[31] At the prospect of an arranged marriage to a butcher's son—perhaps a boy of stable economic prospects, but almost certainly no match for Abramowitz's intellect—Bessie pleaded her case with her father. When she demonstrated the strength of her character by neither blinking nor turning away, Emanuel must have known that she was not like other girls in the Pale. She single-handedly convinced her father to allow her to reject the arranged marriage proposition. In the patriarchal world of shtetl life, where parents made the major decisions regarding their children, fifteen-year-old Bessie's instincts for survival prompted her to leave Linoveh regardless of her parents' wishes.[32]

Abramowitz was one of many young Russian-Jewish women who emigrated to escape an arranged marriage. Rose Pesotta, another notable émigré and later International Ladies Garment Workers Union leader, met the same predicament and decided, "come what might[,] no such marriage would take place." Pesotta took a more militant approach with her parents: after arguing with them for months, she threatened suicide. With the help of a married sister already settled in

New York, she too was able to leave the Pale and a pending marriage behind.[33]

With few possessions and a sense of self beyond her years, Abramowitz ventured outside the confines of the Russian Pale to take her place among the estimated 2 million eastern European Jews emigrating to the United States between 1880 and the outbreak of World War I.[34] Determined to create a life of her own, she left home in the late fall of 1905. With two young cousins acting as chaperones, Abramowitz clutched the passport endorsed by her father as she traveled across Europe. Shortly after arriving in Rotterdam, Bessie boarded the 2,350–passenger *Rotterdam* where, to be on the safe side, she listed her age on the ship's manifest as twenty-one years old.[35]

Although only a few of the details of Bessie's trip have survived, the description that Elizabeth Hasanovitz, a young Russian-Jewish dressmaker, recorded in her autobiography depicted a similar journey. According to Hasanovitz's account, the day of departure followed many weeks of preparation, including sewing and packing. Few Jewish activist women publicly acknowledge their mothers' influence on their lives, but Hasanovitz remembered her mother fainting as she prepared to leave home. She also described her siblings crying and her father "walking sadly back and forth across the living room" on that memorable day. Hasanovitz spent three days on a "bug and vermin infested" train to London, sleeping sitting up in her clothes. When she arrived at the immigration house, "not fit for animals," her luggage was opened and her "clothes were thrown carelessly together with the other passengers to be disinfected with steam and then replaced in [the] trunks all rolled up and wet." The transatlantic voyage was spent in steerage with "uncouth Russian peasants." Like Rose Pesotta and the majority of Abramowitz's contemporaries, Hasanovitz "found the road between the New York docks and the garment shops a short one."[36]

A New Beginning

Dubbed "Basche" by an immigration official along the way, Abramowitz landed at Ellis Island on December 14, 1905. She spoke only Yiddish and some Russian, but she did not let her lack of fluency in English deter her. Abramowitz immediately boarded a train to begin the final segment of her journey. Arriving in Chicago in a matter of days, Abramowitz moved in with relatives who owned a Halsted Street boardinghouse.[37] Due to her prior work experience in Russia, Abramowitz was probably already at least vaguely familiar with the complexities of urban life. On Halsted

Street in Chicago's Nineteenth Ward, she encountered a city in the process of transforming from a prairie transportation capital to the second largest metropolis in the country. Abramowitz's new neighborhood exemplified two fundamental aspects of life in the city: overcrowding and transiency. Newly arrived Russian Jews, Italians, and Greeks displaced more prosperous German and Irish residents in a densely settled, ethnically diverse neighborhood where, according to Hull-House founder Jane Addams, "the streets are inexpressibly dirty, the number of schools inadequate, sanitary legislation unenforced, the streetlighting bad, the paving bad . . . and the stables foul beyond description."[38]

Despite this difficult environment, young women often found support networks. Immersion in Chicago's Jewish-American community facilitated Abramowitz's acculturation into American society. Due to their meager incomes, as well as Old-World disapproval of young girls living alone, most immigrant working women like Abramowitz boarded with families rather than living independently. Since many of these young women were the first in their families to come to America, this type of living arrangement provided a family atmosphere as well as a way to guard respectability.[39] For the immigrant families who owned them, the boardinghouses offered a supplemental income.[40] Situated among her own kind in the predominantly Jewish section of Halsted Street, Abramowitz may even have felt at home.

Away from their own families, these women found a surrogate family in the boardinghouse and a springboard from which to integrate into the wider family structure of the immigrant community. Removed from parental scrutiny, these young people were also free to explore new ideas.[41] Reminiscent of evening hours spent at the Abramowitz family inn, after dinner the front room of the boardinghouse became a place for lively discussions about labor and political developments.

Abramowitz found promise in American life. She used the wages from her job as a button sewer at a nearby garment shop to sponsor the immigration of her two younger sisters, Pauline and Celia. It is likely that as the Abramowitz family finances declined, due to the political strife in Belarus, the girls' father, Emanuel, supported his daughters' emigration to Chicago in 1907. According to his granddaughter, Luba Aten, "Three daughters less meant a load off his shoulders, for without a dowry it was very hard to find decent sons-in-laws."[42]

The long-anticipated arrival of her siblings bolstered Abramowitz's support network. All three sisters lived at least for a time in the same Chicago boardinghouse. Pauline and Celia contributed to the family economy by making bow ties at home. Bessie protected her sisters from

the demands of factory life by discouraging them from working outside the home. The adolescent sisters hoped that their immigration to
America would allow them to achieve self-sufficiency and independence previously unknown.[43]

Influenced by the eastern European entrepreneurial system, and
in an attempt to permanently avoid involvement in the sweatshops,
the sisters considered opening a dressmaking shop together. A formal
photograph intended for advertisement purposes, taken prior to 1910,
reveals the three attractive sisters and their friends posing as shop owners attending to customers. Most striking is the Americanized appearance of the young women. Dressed in a long dark coat with a matching
straw hat, Bessie is formally positioned in a chair, pretending to be a
prospective customer with an order book in one hand and a handbag in
the other. In a country where "you don't go to work without a hat," for
the newly arrived immigrants like the Abramowitz sisters, "putting
on style" for the picture as well as in their daily lives represented one
of the first steps toward securing status as Americans. During the progressive era, "[d]ress became as ordered as other aspects of society," and
Americanization required conforming to a standardized, easily accessible style of clothing.[44] Young urban Jews, whose overall assimilation
outpaced that of most other ethnic groups, were particularly attuned
to fashion. One Chicago reporter observed that as far as the American
style of dress was concerned, no other immigrant was "so eager to become Americanized as the Jewish girl."[45]

Abramowitz's Americanization was also hastened by participation in recreational activities nonexistent in the Old World. Within
this new, exciting world of leisure, a climate of optimism colored an
otherwise dreary urban landscape, allowing young immigrant women
to seek relief from the workplace while asserting their personal autonomy. Burgeoning Chicago provided ample recreational opportunities for Abramowitz and others like her. By the turn of the century,
the city boasted an extensive and easily accessible municipal park system, complete with picnic groves where young people could spend time
together. Even the hardest-working immigrants found time for excur-
sions to dance halls, nickelodeons, amusement parks, or Abramowitz's
particular favorite—the theater. Impressed with Bessie's cultural pur-
suits, newspaper editor John E. Williams described her as "well-read
in modern literature" and taking "special interest in the drama and
music."[46] Attendance at the moving picture show one afternoon a week
afforded young immigrant women and men an opportunity to see what
life was like outside their insular ethnic communities.

In 1889, Jane Addams, along with Ellen Gates Starr, founded Hull-House. Addams and Starr hoped that the settlement house would fulfill its charter obligations: "To provide a center for a higher civic and social life; to institute and maintain educational and philanthropic enterprises, and to investigate and improve the conditions in the industrial districts of Chicago."[47] Young women viewed Hull-House functions as yet another form of recreation. With its wide variety of services, ranging from formal classes to staged presentations, the settlement became a school, social center, and source of moral support for foreigners. Like other young immigrants who planned to stay in this country, Abramowitz enrolled in night classes at Hull-House to begin formal English lessons; she became a naturalized citizen in 1913.[48] Women found numerous activities and facilities available at Hull-House, including classes offered through the University of Chicago, a coffeehouse, an opera house, concerts, music lessons, dancing lessons, suffrage speeches, union meetings, a gymnasium, a library, a labor museum, and numerous clubs. Many immigrant women regarded the settlement house "as an oasis in a desert of boredom and monotony," where one could be rejuvenated after a hard day of work in the factory.[49]

Exposure to progressive ideas concerning labor, education, politics, and suffrage at Hull-House eased the transition into American life and helped young women shape their future goals. Immersion in the community of middle-class women reformers centered at Chicago's Hull-House proved to be the greatest factor in the transformation of young immigrant women from passive victims into determined activists. At the settlement house, young immigrants with "restless minds" found something to interest them, to inspire them, and to absorb them.[50]

Rebellious from an early age, the spirited Abramowitz emigrated from a world where Jewish women maintained a tradition of work and self-sufficiency in the domestic arena. Labor, charity, and self-sacrifice for women, whether orthodox housewives or radical activists, dictated their life course. As a teenager, when most eastern European Jewish girls looked toward marriage as the next inevitable passage in their lives, Bessie Abramowitz decided to take a profoundly different course. As the economic and social order in Russia fell under attack, life in America offered an opportunity to the young Abramowitz—the opportunity to work and earn her own way. It entailed the right to react against abusive employers, authoritarian parents, arranged marriages, and the general constraints imposed on women of the rural shtetls in tsarist Russia. Like all immigrants who came before and after her, Bessie was willing to take a risk in the name of freedom.

Eastern European immigration history tends to focus on those who, accompanied by their immediate families, fled religious persecution and economic hardship. Abramowitz's circumstances, however, were significantly different. Leaving her relatively secure and supportive family behind, Bessie Abramowitz did not run from her homeland; rather, as an adolescent, she freely chose to emigrate alone to America in search of a better life. Bessie joined the thousands of "true immigrants" who planned to settle permanently and therefore quickly claimed many American customs for themselves.[51] Nevertheless, her Americanization process was tempered by her ethnic identity. Abramowitz selectively drew upon her Old-World tradition of self-sufficiency to purposefully negotiate rather than passively accept her position in American society. Empowered by a unique combination of their Bundist heritage and a sense of social justice refined at Hull-House, young Jewish immigrants like Bessie soon turned from discussion to action.[52]

2 "A Mighty Hard Struggle" in Chicago (1908–1911)

Although Abramowitz came to Chicago with limited material resources, she quickly found a job as a hand button sewer in a men's garment shop. Employment opportunities abounded for immigrant women in the turn-of-the-century Chicago workshops and factories. All a newcomer had to do was ask relatives, friends, or acquaintances if the shops they worked for needed help. Bosses reached into the ethnic enclaves to recruit immigrant workers as well. Abramowitz used this informal network to find work shortly after she arrived in the city.[1] Once inside the shop, she faced a new set of challenges that, along with her neighborhood and boardinghouse, defined her resettlement experience.

The Sweating Industry

Because of the high demand for ready-made clothing, the Chicago men's garment industry grew rapidly after the Great Fire of 1871. By the early 1900s, the city led the nation in the production of ready-made men's clothing. Garment factories employed more women workers than any other industry in the city. The Scandinavian and Czech workers who dominated the industry in the 1890s witnessed an influx of immigrants from southern and eastern Europe, who began to enter the trade in large numbers. Numbering more than 10,000, women constituted 55 percent of men's clothing workers in Chicago in 1905. Many of these young women were unmarried southern and eastern European immigrants employed in unskilled or semiskilled positions.[2]

An ever-increasing demand for high-end apparel and a plentiful supply of workers enabled manufacturers to begin to combine small shops into large factories. Shop owners often brought all the contractors already working for them together under one roof. These contractors, now known as "inside contractors," generally ran their own operations within the confines of a large factory.[3]

Simultaneously, small outside contract shops coexisting alongside factories continued to fill the demand for clothes of lesser quality. The division of production into self-contained operations meant that a man with fifty dollars and a basic knowledge of tailoring could open his own shop by setting up machines in his tenement and hiring his neighbors (often children and married women) as workers. To stay in business, the shop owner provided small orders directly to retailers and also took subcontracts from large firms that needed assistance, especially during busy seasons.[4] The outside shop owners were known as *sweaters* because during periods of fierce competition they lowered their bids and then sweated the difference out of their workers. The highly competitive shop was referred to as a *sweatshop*.[5]

The initial stages of garment production were similar regardless of where the production took place. Men designed and cut the material in the factory. In large Chicago factories, the garment was finished on site, with much of the work performed by female machine operators. Factory women performed the semiskilled finishing work by hand, making buttonholes and sewing buttons on garments. The job of pressing went to men in the large factories, who stood all day operating pressing irons. Outside contractors had the cut cloth delivered to their sweatshops, where a succession of specialized machine operators, each working on a particular piece of the garment, basted, sewed, or made buttonholes.[6]

The conditions that Bessie Abramowitz experienced on her first button-sewing job were typical of those that dominated the industry. Prevailing piece rates meant that Abramowitz earned only two and a half cents per coat, which at the end of a sixty-hour week amounted to three dollars. In addition to the long, monotonous hours on the job, to prepare for work—to maximize their production the following day— button sewers had to thread two hundred to three hundred needles at home. During rush periods, young women brought bundles of work home. If a worker refused, she lost her job. In slack times, employers demanded that the employees report to work and stay for the entire day even when the available work was finished in only a few hours.[7] Recent immigrants also found that tailoring skills no longer mattered very much in a world that prioritized speed and efficiency. The low pay and long hours these women experienced in their new world reminded them of the conditions they thought they had left behind.[8]

The most frequent grievances revolved around wage rates, tyrannical foremen, and unjust fines. Under the piecework system, prices were routinely cut a fraction of a cent or even a few cents at a time, and all the workers, regardless of their speed, suffered reduced incomes. Individual bosses in charge of each operation exacerbated the situation. In many of the shops, the foreman or forewoman received a bonus for all the work he or she could produce above a stipulated amount, and so inevitably became a slave driver. Some women in the same shop, doing exactly the same work, earned different piece rates in accordance with their ability to bargain for their labor. Long-time employees who were more fluent in English proved most successful in negotiating their own wages. The changing ethnic composition of the workforce thus enabled employers to continue a policy of arbitrary wage reductions.[9]

Lacking any semblance of job security, workers were often trained on the job as unpaid "learners" and commonly began to produce garments without knowing what rate they would be paid for each piece. Greenies or greenhorns (non-English speakers) were afraid to ask what they would be paid, because, as one worker admitted, "The bosses sometimes get sore about it."[10] Shop rules were strict, and pieceworkers who were allowed to socialize had that privilege revoked so that they would not distract other workers who were paid by the week. As the Chicago weekly, *Jewish Labor World*, put it, "piecework is one of the modern slaveries that blindfold and gradually murder workers." The article provided a graphic account of life for sweatshop workers: "The health of these sweatshop workers is very poor. The dust in these shops is so dense, the materials piled so high, the workers sitting so close together, that their sweat running down each one, everybody's perspiration is condensed in the air, mixed with the dust and each worker breathes everyone's perspiration into his lungs and possibly for that reason they are all slaves in the same manner with the same opinion."[11]

Resenting personal insults and abuses by their supervisors, the workers refused to surrender their self-respect. A system of unjust fines meant that the loss of empty reels, bobbins, or needles, failure to punch the time clock or punching it one minute late, and even a liberal use of soap when washing hands all reduced weekly wages. The practice of being fined for a spot on a garment, or being forced to purchase the damaged garment at the retail price, even though it may have passed through ten pairs of hands, further humiliated the workers.[12] Exorbitant fines coupled with individual bargaining for wages contributed to the workers' seething sense of outrage.

Beginning in the late nineteenth century, workers in the Chicago clothing industry made a number of unsuccessful attempts to organize. After the demise of the Knights of Labor, which had supported their early efforts, the workers tried a second time in 1896, but the strike ended in failure. In 1897, Swedish garment workers led by women established the Special Order Workers' Union and eventually won improved conditions for workers. Still, the union suffered a severe setback in 1905, when it was ordered by the American Federation of Labor (AFL) to affiliate with the United Garment Workers (UGW).[13] The union was renamed the Custom Clothing Workers, but its power was eclipsed by the domination of native-born male leaders in the UGW. Later efforts to unite garment workers were hampered by the massive influx into the workforce of immigrants whose linguistic differences made common understanding difficult.[14]

Labor's Allies

The workers' plight did not escape the attention of Hull-House founder Jane Addams, who became an outspoken advocate for the immigrant workers who suffered from "insanitary housing, poisonous sewage, contaminated water, infant mortality, the spread of contagion, adulterated food, impure milk, smoke-laden air, ill-ventilated factories, dangerous occupations, juvenile crime, unwholesome crowding, prostitution, and drunkenness."[15] From 1889 forward, Addams and Hull-House cofounder Ellen Gates Starr devoted their lives to aiding poor immigrant workers and their families in urban Chicago.

Despite opposition from some early settlement associates who equated the labor movement with anarchy, by the early 1890s it was "generally understood that Hull House was 'on the side of unions.'"[16] One example of support for labor was the Jane Club, founded in 1892 and named for its nearness to Jane Addams's heart. It offered cooperative-living arrangements so that working women would have a residence from which they could not be evicted in the event of a strike. Addams's escalating activism on behalf of the working class reflected her awareness of its mounting difficulties. She praised the "missionary work" performed by the working women who in 1893 founded the Eight-Hour Club "for the purpose of encouraging women in factories and workshops to obey the eight-hour law." Addams was especially impressed by the club's "enthusiasm [that] has carried them across a caste line." Their meetings at Hull-House united the well-to-do and the working women under the banner of a common cause.[17] Addams's work as an arbitrator, during the Teamsters' and 1905 garment workers' strikes, moved her to proclaim that the existing industrial system "thwarts our industrial demands, not only for social righteousness but for social order." In the name of social justice, Addams pledged to go "as far as possible" to alleviate "the evils of the sweating system."[18]

Working women whose lives intersected with those of middle-class reformers helped to organize women into trade unions by developing educational programs to increase working-class awareness. The reformers provided much-needed meeting space for early women's unions, and offered financial assistance to support their fledgling organizations. To Addams it seemed "perhaps natural that the unions organized at Hull-House [were] those in the sewing trades," where women "were sorely in need of help." Among the first to organize were the shirtmakers, who did so in the spring of 1891, followed by the cloakmakers in 1892, and the citywide Dorcas Federal Labor Union (later the Woman's Union Label League) led by Hull-House resident Alzina Stevens.[19]

While settlement residents directly aided union organization, Addams developed an ambitious plan embodying social democratic principles to ensure that industrial conditions would be democratic.[20] Alongside Illinois State Factory Inspector Florence Kelley, Addams pressed for labor reform, lobbying for state and federal protective legislation that dictated increased governmental responsibility for overseeing workers' welfare. New to immigrant ears was the implication that with the passage of such legislation, the state could serve as a protector of the people. Through their suggestion of government intervention on behalf of workers, progressive reformers headquartered at Hull-House restored what might otherwise have been a dwindling confidence in American institutions. In addition to championing organization to improve the lives of workers, campaigns for protective labor legislation (directed toward limiting hours and raising wages) were central to the combined activism of middle-class reformers and working women between 1880 and 1930.[21]

Some scholars accuse middle-class women's reformers of patronizing working-class activists as they pushed their own agendas forward. Others see a genuine cross-class relationship forged between the middle-class women "allies" and the so-called "girls," who worked in tandem to advance the causes of working women and the passage of the suffrage amendment.[22] To effectively analyze the cross-class relationships solidified in the first decade of the twentieth century, it is necessary to go beyond class generalizations and examine the individual personalities involved in the Chicago reform arena.

Jane Addams of Hull-House and Margaret Dreier Robins, the president of the Women's Trade Union League (WTUL), ranked as the most dedicated allies. On the surface, both women supported the idea of organizing women into trade unions, but their strategies differed. During labor conflicts, Addams, wary of male-dominated unions and seeking to avoid widespread "class warfare," advocated negotiation and arbitration with employers to settle industrial disputes. In contrast, Margaret Dreier Robins was less willing to compromise with employers, and worked to achieve the full realm of employee demands, including union recognition. Robins seemed less opposed to using the strike as a weapon against business owners.[23] The class tensions that existed in Chicago were unusual in that they were more often intra-class rather than inter-class in nature.

In 1907, when Robins arrived in Chicago to assume the presidency of the League, it was thriving under the leadership of Mary McDowell as president and Jane Addams as vice president. Shortly after meeting Addams, Robins described her as "the greatest woman I know"; still, the relationship between the two women suffered a temporary setback when, in 1908, Addams vetoed a proposal by Margaret's husband, Raymond Robins, and others to the Chicago School Board in support of the Chicago Teachers' Federation granting promotions to its members. Margaret Dreier Robins felt that she could no longer rely on Addams to defend trade unionism, and so made plans to move the League from its meeting quarters at Hull-House's Bowen Hall to "rescue [it] from none other than Jane Addams" herself.[24] Yet Robins, carefully discreet about the discord, presented a united front to the public. As a reporter for the *Chicago Examiner* noted, "not a breath of the undercurrent was permitted to escape the lips of anyone."[25]

Despite the controversy surrounding the vote on relocation by Chicago League members, Robins moved the organization to the Chicago Federation of Labor building on LaSalle Street. She hoped to draw the League closer to the labor movement by extending its reform activities into the male-dominated world of unionism. Robins explained the break from Hull-House as a consequence of the class division between the trade unionists and the social settlement workers, with Robins acting as the integrationist leader of the trade-union girls. However, her biographer, Elizabeth Payne, argues that the true motivation can be found in Robins's desire to dominate her own organization.[26] The division seemed to be superficial. Over the next few years Hull-House and the WTUL would work together, albeit sometimes using differing strategies, toward the same end.

Working women were sometimes skeptical about Margaret Dreier Robins's intentions. They respected Robins, but Pauline Newman, organizer of the International Ladies Garment Workers' Union (ILGWU), criticized Robins's efforts to influence women workers. In a 1910 letter to fellow WTUL member and organizer Rose Schneiderman, Newman disclosed her frustration with how "Mrs. Robins has made all the girls of the League think her way and . . . act the way Mrs. R. wants them to."[27] Robins attempted to impose superficial middle-class notions of femininity on the young women. To working women, Robins sometimes appeared arrogant and the aid she bestowed on them felt like charity. Nevertheless, these hard feelings were not enough to prevent the working-class women from joining the WTUL in their quest to organize.

Certain allies found fault with the working women. While collaboratively the reformers admired the eastern European Jewish women's political traditions that, like their own, encouraged collective activism, some (such as WTUL member Helen Marot) stereotyped them as too ideological and predicted that Jewish immigrants would be ineffective in trying to organize American workers. As a rule, middle-class women had little tolerance for the socialist sympathies of militant working-class leaders like Rose Schneiderman, who later became president of the WTUL; ILGWU organizer Pauline Newman; ILGWU educational director Fannia Cohn; and shirtwaist-maker Clara Lemlich, all New York–based Jewish labor activists who belonged to the Socialist Party early in their careers.[28] Abramowitz was less obvious than her New York contemporaries about her political persuasion. Unwilling to risk a rift with Addams and the other Chicago reformers, she kept her socialist leanings to herself.[29]

Working Women on the Edge

Sexist attitudes of national union officials contributed to working women's sense of marginalization. American Federation of Labor President Samuel Gompers and his fellow labor leaders rarely made sincere attempts to organize women. They viewed women as temporary workers who threatened men's jobs and reduced their wages by working for lower pay. Male unionists were ambivalent or openly hostile to women's labor activism, and perceived Jewish women as especially troublesome. The men regarded their ethnic activism as extreme and the women themselves as unstable and impulsive.[30]

Thus, almost without exception, women were excluded from the nation's male-dominated labor movement. In Chicago, however, the situation was different. Male labor leaders like Chicago Federation of Labor President John Fitzpatrick, "a leading proponent of unionizing working women," were receptive to women's organizational goals, and the coalition of progressive reform organizations in Chicago welcomed working women's membership and participation.[31] Hull-House's long-standing record of involvement with industrial workers in Chicago encouraged amicable relations between working women and middle-class reformers. As early as 1890, settlement residents joined with trade-union women in the Illinois Woman's Alliance to lobby against sweatshops and for protective legislation. Jane Addams applauded the "cultivated girls who . . . heroically cross[ed] the 'chasm' to join hands with [their] working sisters." In Addams's eyes, the cross-class bonds of sisterhood had even more potential than alliances between the men and girls of the same trade.[32] Despite their diverse methodologies, Chicago's reform coalition, including the WTUL, worked toward the same goal: to organize women into unions and lobby for the passage of laws to protect them in the workplace.[33] More than any other city, Chicago boasted a cohesive and effective reform network, with Hull-House at its center, complete with influential ties to labor, academic, and local reform organizations.

Empowered by their association with middle-class reformers in the highly charged environment of progressive Chicago, working women quickly became actors. Following the lead of their sisters in the East, who a year before had initiated a massive strike in the ladies garment industry, by 1910 many young immigrants in Chicago stood poised alongside their middle-class allies—ready, as Jane Addams asserted, "to take collective action, not only in the name of womankind, but in the name of democracy and social justice."[34] The alliances the working women enjoyed with the Hull-House reformers proved to be even more important than their alliance with the Chicago Federation of Labor.

Bessie Abramowitz's interaction with the Chicago reform community inspired her to act upon her principles. In tsarist Russia the rebellious Abramowitz had merely reacted against personal constraints, but the evolving political culture of early-twentieth-century Chicago enabled Abramowitz to redefine her vision from one that considered only her own well-being to a proactive ethic of social justice concerned with the general welfare of all working people. She combined the Jewish obligation of *tsodeka* with the middle-class reformers' goal of social justice aimed at improving the lives of workers.[35] Young Jewish women had another advantage. They "benefitted from a tradition of female participation in an urban labor force which began back in the Pale of Settlement." This cultural tradition of women's work enabled working women to "stake out a common identity with other workers in the shops against the boss."[36]

Abramowitz believed that in America, if nowhere else in the world, workers—including women—had rights. Defined in working-class terms, American citizenship encompassed the notion of entitlement, including female suffrage in a constellation of political demands aimed at empowering the working class. When, in 1908, her foreman deliberately altered the figures on her work sheet to reflect a rate of less than 2½ cents per coat, Abramowitz organized a group of workers to protest to management. As a result of her activism, she was fired and blacklisted.[37]

Forced to work outside of Chicago until the incident was forgotten, Abramowitz returned within the year and took a job under an assumed name sewing buttons on pants at Hart, Schaffner, and Marx (HSM), where her activism began in earnest. Until this time, local garment manufacturing firms had successfully resisted labor unions by establishing their own organization, the Chicago Wholesale Clothiers Association. Ostensibly founded to promote the sale of goods, the association discreetly affiliated with two of organized labor's staunchest opponents: the National Association of Clothiers and the National Association of Manufacturers. Hart, Schaffner, and Marx was not an official member of any employer association, but the firm refused to hire anyone suspected of organizing activities.[38]

Ironically, conditions at HSM seemed to be better than those at most other shops. Established in 1887 by a family of Bavarian immigrants, by 1905 the firm had purchased forty-eight sweatshops and become a model for industrialists. Producing a large volume of medium- to high-quality men's suits almost entirely on its own premises, HSM was the largest clothing manufacturer in Chicago, employing a labor force of more than 9,000. The firm pioneered standardized pricing and national magazine advertising. Along with other advanced factories in Chicago, Rochester, and Baltimore, it had developed an extensive task system requiring 150 separate operations to produce a single coat. These simplified tasks depended heavily on semiskilled labor.[39]

Hart, Schaffner, and Marx owners attempted to promote favorable employee relations by creating a labor department to deal with personnel issues. However, despite the appearance of a highly disciplined management system and a reputation for good employee relations, irregular practices such as arbitrary wage cuts and fining employees for the "so-called violation of shop rules" persisted at the firm. As in other factories that employed large numbers of immigrants, manipulative foremen turned ethnicities against each other by hiring the most recently arrived groups for lower wages.[40]

Starting a Fight

On September 22, 1910, Bessie Abramowitz, Hannah Shapiro, and their coworkers in Hart, Schaffner, and Marx Shop Number 5 shook their heads in disbelief at the news of another pay cut. The foreman's announcement that the women's wages for button-sewing would drop again, this time from 4 cents to 3–3/4 cents for a pair of pants, coupled with the company's failure to pay overtime wages and demands of more work for less pay, pushed the young immigrants to the breaking point. Faced with deteriorating conditions, Abramowitz, Shapiro, and several other young women finishers laid down their needles, picked up their hats, and walked away from their jobs and onto Halsted Street, refusing to accept this latest wage reduction.[41]

Spontaneous walkouts were almost a universal condition of the trade, but never before had a handful of immigrant women started a major strike in this manner. Abramowitz later recalled, "We all worked 90 to 100 hours a week for $8 or $9. Then we were threatened with a pay cut. It was too much for us so five of us girls started a fight to stop it." Accounts of this historic moment differ concerning the number of young women involved and who specifically was involved. Despite the fact that Sue Weiler and other historians who have chronicled the strike fail to acknowledge Abramowitz's presence during the initial walkout, there is no doubt that Bessie Abramowitz was at the center of the walkout.[42] This seemingly desperate, spontaneous protest sparked a four-month strike that eventually involved more than 35,000 workers and crippled the entire men's clothing industry in Chicago.

To observers, the origins of the strike at first seemed vague; however, Hull-House cofounder and labor activist Ellen Gates Starr succinctly explained why the men's garment workers struck: "if one must starve, there are compensations in starving in a fight for freedom that are not found in starving for employers' profits."[43] Undoubtedly the threat of starvation was a strong motivator. Others, like Chicago Federation of Labor President John Fitzpatrick, identified broader implications for workers in characterizing Hart, Schaffner, and Marx and other factories as "nothing more or less than slave driving institutions of the worst imaginable kind [where] the employees were compelled to go out on strike in order [to] be able to form organizations to protect their interests—and their lives in a good many instances."[44]

News of the uprisings in New York, Cleveland, and Philadelphia in the preceding months influenced the Chicago strikers.[45] Although these previous strikes had met with mixed success, they initiated a decade of labor unrest in the garment industry that ultimately led to the clothing industry emerging as a bastion of industrial unionism by 1920. The conflicts demonstrated that ethnic unionists led by Jewish women possessed the ability to organize for more than just immediate demands. All the strikes "linked shopfloor grievances with larger communal concerns for economic and social justice."[46]

The two New York strikes—the shirtwaist-makers' "Uprising of the 20,000," beginning in 1909, and the 1910 cloakmakers' strike— were significant in that they established the foundation for the ILGWU (which had been limping along since its founding in 1900) and the Protocols of Peace, respectively. The protocols were a series of collective bargaining agreements signed between the ILGWU and New York women's clothing manufacturers that increased wages, cut working hours, abolished inside subcontracting, and set the precedent for arbitrating grievances in the women's garment industry. The agreements were hailed by WTUL reformer Gertrude Barnum as a "high-water mark for the principles of industrial democracy."[47]

Seeking the same end, women in Chicago led the way. At first the strikers amused most of the other shop workers, who hesitated to join the young, inexperienced women. This initial reaction, especially on the part of male Russian tailors, was typical. Historically, skilled male workers had refused to support the sporadic female-led weavers and textile strikes in Russia throughout the 1890s.[48] Male workers at Hart, Schaffner, and Marx believed that the unorganized women were virtually powerless against the huge firm, and were therefore reluctant to support the strikers. Sidney Hillman and the other men who later became the leaders of the Amalgamated Clothing Workers of America went out with the first of the cutters three weeks after the strike began, but until then they crossed the women's picket line. Looking back on the strike, Sidney Hillman admitted that "at first we made fun of it . . . but somehow the girls managed to take out the men after awhile." Elaborating on the significant walkout at a union convention years later, Bessie Abramowitz quipped, "It is not always the men who lead the women. It was a mighty hard struggle for those eight girls to pull out the men."[49]

In dire need of assistance, Abramowitz appealed to the only union in the men's garment industry, the United Garment Workers. Accompanied by a small group of women strikers, she approached Chicago district president, Robert Noren, with a plan to unionize. After consulting the national union president, Thomas Rickert, the union leaders rejected her plea for support. Years later Bessie recalled her visit with Rickert, "who looked at us and laughed." He said, "You're crazy. The tailors cannot be organized."[50] The UGW represented primarily the elite male cutters, some of whom were native born and others of whom belonged to the older wave of immigrants from Germany and Bohemia who came to this country to learn a craft. Later waves of immigrants presented a threat to their privileges as skilled craft workers. Rickert's personal reluctance stemmed from a "lack of faith in the possibilities of organizing these people," some of whom he suspected of being socialists, and his belief that it was just an overnight strike.[51] Both Rickert's refusal to help organize the workers on an industry-wide basis and the continual attempts to break the picket lines by police and strikebreakers intensified Bessie's determination. She decided that if the strikers could not unionize through the UGW, she would chart her own course.

On October 11, 1910, more than 500 coatmakers, the majority of those from the Hart, Schaffner, and Marx shops, met in Hod Carriers' Hall and joined the union.[52] Before the ink on her union card had dried, the petite, dark-eyed Abramowitz stepped up on the makeshift speakers' platform and collected her thoughts. Reminiscent of Clara Lemlich's impassioned speech to the New York women's garment workers in 1909, Abramowitz's carefully composed speech reverberated through the hall. One can only imagine Abramowitz's intense, energetic presence as she attempted to persuade the strikers to adopt a deliberate course of action. Realizing that the workers' demands had not yet been formally stated, in her heavily accented English she outlined a procedure emphasizing negotiation rather than supporting the call for an immediate strike as Lemlich had done.

Contrary to the *fabrente maydlakh* (fiery girl) stereotype that male union leaders anticipated, Abramowitz remained level-headed as she cautioned the anxious strikers: "What folly would you men and women do here today? Have you thought of what it means to call a general strike? Do you know what responsibilities you would burden yourselves with? Stop and think!" All heads turned toward her as she continued her speech: "What we want to do now is to elect a committee of two workers in each of the shops on strike. Let this committee visit union shops in the city and draw up a comparative statement of wages paid, hours worked, and general conditions in Hart, Schaffner, and Marx and the other shops. Then let this committee draw up a wage scale, hour scale, and other demands, and then, we will be ready to call a general strike."[53]

News of the conflict spread through the city, and by mid-October approximately 8,000 HSM employees were out on strike.[54] Thousands of men and women in other plants and even college students began to join them. A core group of strikers, including many of the Jewish immigrant women who were among the initiators of the strike, began to meet at Hull-House to air their grievances.[55] The Old-World value of autonomy in the workplace inspired the young, unskilled women in poorly paid factory positions to chance joining the strikers' ranks. Their legacy of activism, with its concern for social justice, readily applied to new circumstances.

The workers elected the committee that Bessie recommended, with two members from each shop, each one representing a different craft. However, despite Bessie's warning, the most militant strikers demanded union recognition and on October 27 issued a call for a general strike. A massive walkout ensued as workers from Kuppenheimer's, Hirsch-Wickwire, and other large firms joined the Hart, Schaffner, and Marx employees already on the picket lines. By the end of the month, between 35,000 and 40,000 clothing workers had walked off their jobs—and more than half of them were women.[56]

Citadels and Support

Without any support from the United Garment Workers, Abramowitz and the other strike leaders turned to Jane Addams, who virtually overnight formed a committee of "women citizens" from Hull-House and the Women's Trade Union League to assist the strikers and "to outline the part women [would] take in the strike." Bessie later recalled how "Hull House became a citadel of hope and strength from then on." Addams's benevolence initiated an invaluable bond between the middle-class reformers and the labor movement in Chicago.[57]

In late October, the Women's Trade Union League officially offered aid to the strikers, who immediately accepted. The Executive Board of the WTUL, including its president, Margaret Dreier Robins, and her husband, Raymond Robins, as well as a number of other civic leaders, met at Hull-House to formulate a plan of action. Strategies employed in the 1910 strike were based on League experience gained during the historic shirtwaist strike in New York. League leaders realized better than the young strikers what they would face on the winter picket lines, as well as what the needs for strike relief funds, legal assistance, and bail money would be. Out of the meeting came the organization of an independent Citizens' Committee and the Strike Committee of the Women's Trade Union League. Chaired by Rabbi Emil Hirsch, the Citizens' Committee included businessmen and professionals who were concerned with the effect of the strike on Chicago's economy.[58] Both groups wanted to help end the strike as quickly as possible.

Jane Addams assumed the position of mediator so that she could investigate the dispute and then issue a report on existing sweatshop conditions. Along with Judge Julian Mack, Addams proposed the organization of workers as a remedy. Addams pushed Hart, Schaffner, and Marx owner Joseph Schaffner to recognize the importance of the public's stake in settling the industrial dispute. As a result, he willingly conceded to the union's preferential shop as long as it worked for "justice toward every interest connected with the institution and the highest economic efficiency . . . performing duty toward every body, inside and outside of the institution, employees, stockholders, customers, and the general public."[59]

Jane Addams also convinced Schaffner to go into the factories to witness the conditions firsthand. Although both Joseph Schaffner and his partner, Harry Hart, prided themselves on their modern, sanitary workshops, many of the oppressive conditions typical of the sweatshops persisted. Testifying before the United States Commission on Industrial Relations in 1914, though insisting that the strikers' grievances were minor in character, Schaffner realized that they had been allowed to accumulate to the point of creating in workers "a feeling of distrust and enmity toward their immediate superiors." He had been genuinely shocked by the outbreak of the strike. Schaffner went on to concede that he had been "so badly informed of the conditions . . . that he had concluded that the strike should have happened much sooner." He admitted that after his visit, he asked Earl Dean Howard, professor of economics at Northwestern University, to independently investigate the factories and report the findings back to him.[60] Addams's intervention and the pressure she exerted on the HSM owners were crucial to the outcome of the strike.

Although Schaffner characterized the list of grievances against his company as minor, the prolabor *Chicago Daily Socialist* considered HSM an anti-union shop. The paper accused Hart, Schaffner, and Marx of treading on the rights of labor: "First there was the decision that no union men or women would be hired. Then those who sympathized with organizations were dismissed. Spies were hired and placed among the employes and one person after another 'was fired.' Then a special policeman was placed in the various establishments and rooms. He was given a star and orders to keep his eyes and ears open. Later they began a gradual cutting down of the employes' earnings, instituted by the various processes."[61]

While Addams worked with members of her own class to raise employers' consciousness, WTUL President Margaret Dreier Robins remained skeptical of factory owners and took an alternate approach by encouraging striking women to appeal to public sentiment throughout Chicago. Following Robins's example, League leaders took the young women into the homes of the wealthy and let them tell their stories. On November 2, 1910, a formal breakfast meeting at the King's Stock Exchange Restaurant provided an opportunity for the League to "place before the public in clear and simple form the complicated number of grievances of which the strikers complained." Italian immigrant worker Clara Masilotti revealed that she had been coerced into "working faster for less pay." Abramowitz was one of the twelve striking women who "talked their hearts out," detailing a wide range of intolerable working conditions. She revealed that employers largely ignored the Illinois ten-hour law and, as a result, during rush periods she was forced to work twelve or thirteen hours without extra pay for overtime. In the years following the strike she would elaborate on the harsh conditions, explaining that when a worker fell ill on the job, the foreman refused to let him or her go home, and the worker was forced to "stretch out on the cement floor of the washroom and remain there until the bell rang at 6 p.m." Bessie recalled that "as a girl striker in Chicago in 1910, our first demand was for a women's rest room." These breakfast testimonials informed some Chicagoans for the first time of the exploitative conditions working women endured. Local papers featured reporters' stories about the event the following day. They also prompted Senator Henson to form a special state senate committee, chaired by Senator Johann Waage of Chicago, to inquire into the strike.[62]

Officially established on January 10, 1911, the senate committee consisted of five appointed senators and remained in session for more than two weeks. Holding daily sessions at the Hotel LaSalle, the committee summoned witnesses and recorded their testimony. Responsible for "educating the public into a fuller understanding of the strike," the committee's report to the full senate revealed the existence and operation of a labor bureau by the clothing manufacturers that maintained a blacklist "derogatory to the rights of the workers," and demanded that it be dissolved immediately. Many considered the mere exposure of this practice to be a victory in itself. Raymond Robins equated the revelation of the blacklist to striking oil.[63]

Local UGW officials followed the escalating strike. As the number of striking workers swelled into the thousands, Noren felt an obligation to at least offer a show of support. He notified the national office, and a reluctant Rickert traveled to Chicago to observe the events firsthand. Ill-informed, he stood on the sidelines, complaining that "for days and weeks no one—not even the people themselves—knew just what they wanted."[64] Shortly afterward, Rickert, and even some strikers, mistakenly perceived the most important demands to be union recognition and a closed shop (where workers would have to join the union before obtaining a job). Katharine Coman, Wellesley economics professor and chairperson of the WTUL's Grievance Committee, more accurately summarized the strikers' grievances. Relying on numerous interviews of young women workers from various shops, as well as on information gleaned at the breakfast testimonials, Coman concluded by early November that the most important grievances included arbitrary wage reductions, indefinite piece rates, and abusive foremen who levied unjust fines and demanded "top-notch speed" from the workers. Almost all the strikers agreed that they needed "some means of presenting their grievances to their employers, instead of being individually at the mercy of petty bosses, who might or might not be just."[65]

Women workers fought for bread and flowers. Signs that read: "Two Million Men Work Eight Hours We Want The Same," reflected an emerging gender consciousness. Other picketers' signs noted that "We Are Striking for Human Treatments," indicating that strikers sought remedies that transcended immediate economic issues.[66] For women workers in particular, "reasonable working conditions" included the right to "self-expression and self-government politically or industrially." The WTUL encouraged the strikers to seek the right to organize through demanding union recognition and union protection.[67] Working men and working women demanded higher wages and shorter hours, but they voiced additional fundamental demands, which eastern European Jews called *mentshlekhe bahandlung* (humane treatment). These demands assumed a new meaning in "the golden land of freedom," where it was especially difficult to reconcile this ideal with the cruel realities on the shop floor.[68]

Bessie Abramowitz maintained an almost constant presence on the picket lines, somehow avoiding arrest. She raised her voice in song as she paced up and down in front of her shop; she carried a sign that read, "We Want a Cot to Lie Down on—We Want Clean Washrooms—We

Want Better Conditions." Abramowitz preferred to maintain a presence in the middle of the lines rather than at the front. Stepping out from this inconspicuous vantage point to confront charging policemen, she fearlessly prodded the rear ends of their horses with her notoriously long hatpin, thus earning her nickname "Hatpin Bessie."[69]

Members of the WTUL Picket Committee, chaired by Emma Steghagen, as well as Hull-House residents, linked arms with the young women workers on the picket lines in an effort to provide respectability and protection for the strikers, as well as to familiarize themselves with the situation on the streets in case they were called to testify in court. Margaret Dreier Robins declared that this type of patrolling was perhaps "the most important service that any group of public spirited women can render their younger sisters in times of industrial struggle."[70] Although the strategies of Robins and Addams differed somewhat, the two leaders both helped in any way they could, and the working-class women were grateful for their assistance.

Women reformers also ensured a constant flow of favorable publicity throughout the strike. Appeals for money cloaked in contemporary rhetoric met with generous response. Postcards used to solicit funds bore the inscription "Sacred Motherhood," accompanied by Luther D. Bradley's classic drawing from the 1907 Chicago Industrial Exhibition's Committee on Women in Industry, depicting a nursing woman bent over a sewing machine surrounded by her small children. In addition to this obvious gender reference, strike literature also emphasized the age differences between the "girl" strikers and their middle-aged bosses. One popular drawing shows a very young girl hesitantly approaching her intimidating boss who is seated behind a desk, captioned by the question, "Is this an even Bargain?"[71] Middle-class reformers, determined to effect real changes in working women's lives, promoted labor organization as the best route to a more equitable bargaining position.

The WTUL contributed immense financial support, initiating a strike relief fund and eventually raising more than $70,000 in donations. The majority of the money went toward food and coal issued to workers and their families in six commissary stations throughout Chicago. Settlement workers and League women paid particularly close attention to the more than one thousand infants affected by the strike, starting a separate "babies milk fund" that delivered almost 125,000 quarts of milk to keep "strike babies" alive.[72]

Numerous organizations, including the Socialist Party, heeded the strikers' calls. The *Chicago Daily Socialist* was the only Chicago newspaper to offer coverage of the first three weeks of the strike. Rather than assuming leadership of the strike as they generally did, at the request of the Chicago Federation of Labor, the Socialists coordinated and built the logistical arm. Socialist women volunteered as speakers and conducted an extensive educational campaign, culminating in the publication of a special strike edition of the *Chicago Daily Socialist* for mass distribution. Enlisting the help of 400 striking girls as "newsies," they raised more than $8,000 for the strike effort.[73]

Throughout November, relentless intimidation of the pickets by the local police force continued. Local papers described the police as "Cossacks," who rode the streets of Chicago joining hired sluggers in attacking the workers. A *Chicago Daily Socialist* article, "An Army of Women," described a "sisterhood" where women were "pushing past the front ranks of battle and lifting their hands and their voices against the tyranny of might and carnage of the money mad capitalists of industry."[74] Scores of women were arrested. According to one reporter, "the club and society women fared no better than the men."[75] Labor supporter and lawyer Clarence Darrow defended those arrested.

Low Blows

Approximately 15 percent of the Chicago garment workers refused to join the strike. Some workers continued to work alongside strike-breakers recruited from outside Chicago. Most of these workers reasoned that they could not afford to be without work for any length of time, nor could they risk losing their jobs permanently. Nonetheless, strikers reacted severely against those who failed to support their efforts. In Abramowitz's northwest district, as late as November 1 the workers fought what the *Chicago Daily Socialist* reported as "another bloody battle" at 19th and Halsted Streets resulting from an attempt to get the remaining Hart, Schaffner, and Marx employees to strike. Two days later, police arrested nearly 100 as the strikers resorted to violence, dragging sewing machines into the streets and smashing windows in a further effort to halt production.[76]

Police brutality infuriated the strikers and provoked public sympathy for those in the picket lines. The official strike report issued by the Chicago Women's Trade Union League Strike Committee capitalized on instances of abusive treatment aimed at picketers. Under the subtitle "Police Brutality and Picketing," the report explained that "the brutality of the police is not merely the brutality of some of the men on the force, but it is the brutality of thugs, of the private detectives and the special agents hired by the employers."[77] This violence on the part of the police and private detectives hired to protect the strikebreakers swelled public sympathy for the strikers. Police brutality also persuaded some who had initially hesitated to strike. One woman striker recalled that as she and fellow workers were negotiating with their employer to end the strike, they heard "a terrific noise [and] rushed to the windows [where they] saw the police beating the strikers—clubbing them on our account, and when we saw that we went out."[78]

Ethnic diversity was more pronounced in the Chicago men's garment industry than in any other city. Strike leaders grappled with the monumental task of uniting different nationalities. They published literature in at least nine languages. Because so many strikers did not understand English, separate meetings became a necessity. In some halls the workers met in national or language groups: the Poles, the Bohemians, the Lithuanians, the Italians, the Jews.[79] When possible, workers formed groups based on the various branches of the trade: cutters, coatmakers, vestmakers, and pantsmakers. Ethnic-based locals that helped to alleviate ethnic differences operated well after the strike ended.[80] In halls throughout Chicago, striking workers met from early morning until late at night, listening to speakers like Abramowitz and others and discussing among themselves the complaints that brought them together. Meeting en masse for the first time, "these thousands of men and women, speaking many languages and believing diverse creeds, stood shoulder to shoulder . . . in their fight for a living wage, for just industrial conditions and the right to self-government."[81] The call for an industrial union was cast in many different tongues across Chicago.

Armed with communication skills refined by her association with Jane Addams, Abramowitz played an integral part in the course of the strike, speaking at the workers' meetings that convened on a regular basis in more than twenty halls around the city. She also led a largely Polish pantsmakers' group on Halsted Street. As one of seven worker representatives on the Strikers' Executive Committee, Abramowitz was charged with acting as a liaison between the Joint Strike Conference Board (which had assumed the leadership of the strike in early November) and the various strikers' locals.[82] As soon as settlement proposals came from the board's negotiating committees, strike leaders worked to translate and distribute them to all the meeting halls.

The strikers quickly learned that the UGW's offer of assistance lacked any substance. On November 5, Rickert and Addams reached an agreement with Hart, Schaffner, and Marx providing for arbitration of all issues, with the exception of union recognition. The agreement also failed to guarantee the rehiring of strike participants accused of violence.[83] The workers rejected the proposal, and this time their disgust with national officials was so obvious that Rickert had to leave the hall by a back door. Thousands of striking workers resolved to "repudiate the action of . . . Thomas A. Rickert in signing any agreement without presenting the same for approval."[84] Others who were outraged by this incident stepped in to help. The following day, the Chicago Federation of Labor's President John Fitzpatrick pledged his organization's unconditional support to the strikers' cause, instructing the Executive Board to "do all within their power to co-operate with the strikers, and assist the garment workers' organization wherever possible in helping the strikers financially, morally, and otherwise." The strike became the CFL's predominant concern until it ended three months later.[85]

Less than a week later, the striking workers suffered another blow when League members and officials of the Chicago Federation of Labor discovered that the treasury of UGW District Number 6 was empty. In fact, the union had issued worthless vouchers for relief to more than ten thousand people. Chicago Federation of Labor officials, WTUL leaders, and a few sympathetic UGW officers managed to raise enough money to distribute $3 worth of relief for each $5 voucher.[86] By that time, however, the strikers had lost confidence in the ability of the UGW to lead the strike. Now a vital strike ally, the CFL passed a resolution recommending a voluntary assessment of twenty-five cents per member per week to help finance the strike, while the WTUL actively solicited funds from its own members as well as from the community at large.[87] The people of Chicago came to the aid of the cold striking workers.

As the weeks turned into months, the strikers faced not only hunger but also police brutality and bitter cold. The strike grew increasingly volatile. Three hundred and seventy-four people were arrested and two strikers were killed. Nevertheless, the unremitting determination of the Chicago strikers represented the new spirit in the American labor movement. Immigrant workers refused to suffer in silence any longer. Their dedication inspired a number of sympathy strikes throughout the country.[88]

On December 8, the workers again rejected another agreement that would have sent them back to work without union recognition. The strike dragged on for five more weeks before Hart, Schaffner, and Marx employees agreed to return to work on January 14, 1911, with the promise that a board of arbitration would be established to adjust their grievances.[89] Providing at least some respite from the violence, the agreement guaranteed that there would be no discrimination due to membership or nonmembership in a union, and called for the establishment of an arbitration committee to settle current and future grievances.[90] Equally important, the hated "violence clause," which required any employees guilty of violence during the strike to be allowed to return to work only after approval by the arbitration committee, was finally deleted. The strikers did not win union recognition, but one of the first acts of the new board of arbitration allowed UGW representation. Hart, Schaffner, and Marx employees made substantial economic gains, thanks in part to the "socially minded" attitude of company owners who were willing to address the strikers' demands.[91]

Under the agreement, on January 16 Bessie Abramowitz, Hannah Shapiro, Sidney Hillman, and more than 10,000 of their fellow workers were greeted by their shop foremen as they returned to Hart, Schaffner, and Marx. On Halsted Street, where many of the affected strikers lived, jubilant men and women celebrated the news of the settlement. Although Hart, Schaffner and Marx employees had won a clear-cut victory, owners from the two "Association houses" (Hirsh, Wickwire, and Company and Kuppenheimer and Company) "refused to come to any settlement, claiming there was no strike and consequently nothing to settle."[92] Workers in those shops were forced to continue their vigil.

In the meantime, Margaret Dreier Robins began the new year trying to reinvigorate the remnants of the strike. When the newspapers mistakenly printed stories that the strike had been called off, Robins reacted by issuing a call to the women of Chicago.[93] She appealed to volunteers to conduct a house-to-house canvass of city homes to solicit donations for the financially strapped strikers who were "making an heroic stand for civilized working conditions and the abolition of the Sweatshop from Chicago's Garment Industry!" Coordinated by the Illinois Federation of Women's Clubs, "Sweatshop Sunday," held on January 22, 1911, was more successful in raising morale than in procuring funds.[94]

Conquered but Not Defeated

The remaining strikers solidly maintained their ranks until February 3, when, without consulting the strikers, the WTUL, or the officials of the Chicago Federation of Labor, Rickert and his lieutenants usurped the authority of the strike leaders and abruptly declared the strike over. Disregarding Rickert's declaration, at a meeting on February 5, Margaret Dreier Robins reported that "as far as the Chicago Federation of Labor and the Women's Trade Union League were concerned, the strike was still on."[95] Meanwhile, United Garment Workers officials told the strikers to return to work. Robins called the strike settlement a "hunger bargain," conceding to a reporter, "We are conquered, but we are not defeated."[96] Throughout the strike, Robins, unlike Addams, refused to make concessions or compromise with employers. With the notable exception of the Hart, Schaffner, and Marx workers, the strikers made no immediate gains. Some were not even allowed to return to their jobs. Raymond Robins accused the "UGW crooks" of selling the strikers short and preferring "their own arbitrary ends to the general welfare of all the workers."[97] In spite of these discouraging results, prolabor forces considered the strike, with its precedent-setting agreement for workers at Hart, Schaffner, and Marx, a success.

Abramowitz and thousands of her coworkers returned to work with a guarantee of improved working conditions and a board of arbitration to address workers' future grievances. Within a matter of months the HSM workers secured a fifty-four-hour work week, time-and-a-half for overtime, and double-time for holidays; in many departments, a minimum wage became a requirement. Union members did not receive a closed shop, but shortly after the strike ended, company owners conceded to a preferential shop—which would require employers to give union members hiring priority. Although it affected only about one in five workers, the agreement between HSM and the employees in its forty-eight shops provided the foundation for broader union contracts in the years to come.[98]

Chicago reformers overcame class tensions in the interests of the workers. Supported by extensive cooperation within the reform network, Chicago workers profoundly altered the course of labor history. Marking what few at the time realized was the beginning of industrywide organization, the cross-class, ethnic, and gender solidarity built largely by women was by far the most memorable strike achievement. Young immigrant women, some still in their teens, initiated a rebellion that gained momentum faster than they ever believed possible.

WTUL journalist Alice Henry described how the spontaneous enthusiasm of the young immigrant women effectively translated into a well-organized, disciplined campaign where at first "[f]ew if any strikers went into the strike with any clear sense of it being a social uprising. . . . The most we heard at first were personal individual wrongs. Amid that confusion and irritation and blind struggle rose the ideal of the union."[99] The sense of solidarity that emerged during the first major strike in the men's garment industry crippled production and stunned even the UGW.

Women effectively demonstrated their capacity both to ignite and to sustain the impulses of an Old-World revolt fueled by the American ideal of hope for a better life. Strike impetus came not from the union but from the immigrant workers themselves, who dreamed a "big dream of decent wages, decent homes, of dignity and democracy on the job—the dream of social, economic, and political justice."[100] Chicago immigrants turned to the strike as their major organizational weapon. Grassroots activism enabled women leaders to build the strike from the ground up, from local neighborhoods to a citywide effort. Organizational efforts in Chicago proved to be the training ground for the Amalgamated leadership.

Committed to a common cause, rank and filers rather than union officials initiated the strike. Though "affiliated with the UGW," the clothing workers in Chicago perceived themselves as acting "solely on their own" in organizing the strike against the largest tailoring firm in the nation.[101] From the beginning of the conflict, the women leaders exhibited a willingness to cooperate with male unionists and their leaders regardless of previous neglect of unskilled women workers. The rank-and-file women who initiated the strike were willing to submerge underlying gender tensions in the interest of solidifying ethnic working-class consciousness. Promoting gender solidarity, female strike leaders actively recruited rather than excluded their male coworkers. With their socialist ideology tempered by the moderation of mainstream progressive reformers, Chicago strike leaders in 1910 laid the groundwork for a new multiethnic industrial union.

Immigrant women and the male colleagues who eventually joined them readily assimilated into the cooperative environs of progressive Chicago from 1910 forward. Alliances among the women reformers from Hull-House, the Women's Trade Union League, and the young immigrant strikers continued to play a crucial part in the Chicago labor movement throughout the first half of the twentieth century. The middle-class allies riveted public attention on the plight of the workers, so that the concerns of labor became those of the city. These women also recruited speakers, directed strike aid efforts, and raised relief funds long after the UGW ran out of money. Their prestige in the community lent credibility to strike activities and induced many agencies and individuals to come to the aid of the strikers. Also, just as they had during the New York strike, the allies introduced a gender consciousness to the nascent class consciousness—and "the synthesis was electrifying."[102]

Years later, Abramowitz praised the cross-class alliances forged with women "who did not come from the ranks of working women, but were educators, social workers, writers, editors and even wealthy society matrons with a social conscience, who fought for the rights and welfare of the exploited and underprivileged. . . . These women actively organized, and most of them did not hesitate to walk a picket line, address a strike meeting or angrily harangue an employer or hostile government official. . . . [T]hey did more than merely encourage early trade union struggles; they became part of them."[103] Without the extensive relief apparatus coordinated by such allies, the strike would have failed.

Abramowitz's friendship with these women extended beyond the public arena. During the last months of the strike, Abramowitz and her future husband, Sidney Hillman, spent a considerable amount of time at Hull-House. Jane Addams acknowledged that "It is a matter of pride to the residents of the Hull-House that the first meeting which resulted in the organization, later designated as the Amalgamated Clothing Workers of America, should have been held in one of our rooms, offered as a refuge to a number of Russian Jewish men and women who had split off from a trades union meeting on the Northside of Chicago." The Amalgamated Clothing Workers of America was literally "born at the Hull-House."[104] A half-century later, Abramowitz expressed her gratitude for the nurturing that Addams had provided: "During the long weeks of the strike Hull-House was a home to me, and Jane Addams was like a mother. Many of our meetings were held there, and when they did not end until late at night, she would not let me go home alone so I slept at Hull-House. When she suspected that I had not eaten properly she would ask me if I had and see to it that I did."[105] Acting as a mentor, Addams was among the first to recognize Abramowitz's potential as a labor leader. During the strike, Addams personally schooled Abramowitz in labor-organizing tactics and helped her with her English.

Bessie Abramowitz and Jane Addams often expressed feelings of mutual admiration. Male labor leaders also appreciated the guidance that the women reformers offered. In a 1935 speech, Sidney Hillman praised Jane Addams's desire for industrial peace: "The agreement we entered into in 1910, through the efforts of Miss Addams has not only maintained peaceful and constructive relations between that firm and its thousands of workers but it laid a foundation for industrial peace and cooperation for over a hundred thousand workers in that industry."[106] The middle-class women and the young immigrants they befriended became the catalysts for the unionization of unskilled immigrant garment workers in Chicago.

While Hannah Shapiro and the other young women strikers who lit the first sparks of the great strike faded into the background, strike leader Bessie Abramowitz continued to occupy center stage. Although most accounts fail to detail or even mention Abramowitz's prominent part in the strike, in the beginning Bessie Abramowitz was more popular and widely known than Sidney Hillman. Abramowitz crossed paths with the middle-class allies regularly. She solidified the relationship between the women workers and middle-class women in Chicago. Sidney Hillman did not come to the reformers' attention until mid-November when, after a dramatic speech denouncing Rickert's betrayal, he was virtually adopted by the strike's progressive element.[107] At that point the strike began to evolve from a women's strike into a true cross-gender strike involving men as both leaders and participants. It was a memorable moment when men like Sidney Hillman, Samuel Levin, Frank Rosenblum, and Anzimo Marimpietri finally joined their female colleagues on the front lines.

With her vision of social justice enhanced by her close association with female reform leaders, Abramowitz emerged from the strike with a reputation as an indefatigable, capable organizer respected by workers and reformers alike. In 1940, Bessie Abramowitz Hillman recalled the "supreme sacrifices" that she and the other strikers had made thirty years earlier: "We did not have anything to eat but we were young and had idealism in our hearts, and we resolved that once and forever we must make a stop to slavery. . . . Despite all things we were victorious."[108] Initiated and maintained largely by women, the path-breaking strike in Chicago laid the foundation for the broader labor movement among workers in the men's garment industry.

3 The Founding of the Amalgamated Clothing Workers of America and the Search for Solidarity (1911–1918)

In the course of her first decade in her adopted country, Bessie Abramowitz catapulted from the ranks of unskilled immigrant labor to a position as a guiding force in the largest union in the men's garment industry. Her experiences illuminate the militance of Jewish women activists in the early part of the twentieth century. Her concern for the plight of the less fortunate reflected both her eastern European upbringing and her encounter with the American industrial system. The ideology of the social feminists at Hull-House and within the WTUL helped Abramowitz ground her political activism, and the bonds of cross-class sisterhood provided sustenance when she needed it most.

The Chief Woman Takes Charge

In the aftermath of the 1910 strike, Bessie Abramowitz worked fervently to lay the foundation for unionization in Chicago. The nature of Abramowitz's activism vacillated between a preference for partnership with male trade unionists and the separatist strategies of the feminist reformers, which, according to Susan Glenn, "fit uncomfortably in the class and ethnic frameworks of immigrant unionism." When the woman question "began to rock the boat of union politics," Bessie Hillman would be called upon to help decide how to advance the status of union women without compromising class solidarity.[1]

Abramowitz basked in the light of the hard-won strike concessions as she began her career as a professional labor organizer shortly after returning to Hart, Schaffner, and Marx. The respect and support she earned from the workers, progressive reformers, and even her employer increased the young woman's self-esteem. She was one of only four workers' deputies appointed to the Joint Executive Board of Hart, Schaffner, and Marx Employees in 1912, where she assisted in monitoring conditions within the firm and in outside shops. Abramowitz sat beside her male colleagues as the board adjusted complaints and enforced decisions on an individual basis before they were formally appealed to the newly instituted Board of Arbitration. Her responsibilities increased when she was elected business agent for the Chicago Vestmakers' Local 152. As the only woman on either board, Abramowitz undertook her work with the utmost seriousness. She retained her original union card, as well as active membership in Local 152, her entire life.[2]

Somehow Bessie juggled her tight schedule to find time for leisure activities. Attending the theater proved a favorite pastime and offered a respite from union business. When union duties intervened, though, they always prevailed over recreational activities. John E. Williams, the Hart, Schaffner, and Marx Arbitration Board chairman, recalled how one Saturday afternoon Abramowitz quietly sacrificed her two-dollar opera ticket to attend an arbitration hearing.[3]

In 1912, when Women's Trade Union League President Margaret Dreier Robins decided to appoint one female trade-union organizer "to be in charge of the Hart, Schaffner, and Marx girl employees only," she chose Abramowitz as the likely candidate.[4] Sidney Hillman, president of recently established Coatmakers Local 39, agreed with Robins; as a result, Abramowitz became an organizer for the United Garment Workers. Just as she had personally contributed to the 1910 strike, Robins took money from her own pocket to pay Bessie six dollars a week so that she could afford to leave the shop and become a full-time organizer. Robins, Addams, and other middle-class women firmly believed that organizing young women workers was crucial in promoting favorable relations with their employers. The reformers reasoned that when working women became union members, they would learn the importance of presenting their grievances through their appointed representatives. This strategy would prevent them from unsuccessfully going out on strike several times a week as they had done in the past.[5]

This more prudent approach held such promise that the firm of Hart, Schaffner, and Marx requested that Abramowitz come into their shops on a regular basis. Happy to comply, Bessie, sometimes accompanied by Sidney Hillman, went into the shops during lunch hours to explain the grievance system and encourage workers to join the union. Hillman, with whom Abramowitz was by now romantically involved, encouraged her activism, sharing with her some tips on effectively addressing groups. He gently took her hand and whispered in her ear, "Bessie, speak slowly. Take a deep breath before you start. Then say just what you have to say."[6] Abramowitz relied on the inspiring oratorical skills she had honed during the 1910 strike. Her words made a lasting impression on women workers. John E. Williams, *Streator Independent-Times* editor and later Hart, Schaffner, and Marx arbitration board chairman, fittingly described her as "the chief woman worker in the movement."[7]

Bolstered by the recognition she achieved as a working women's advocate, a confident Abramowitz followed Jane Addams into the political arena in the name of women's suffrage. Addams's political activism marked the next logical step on the progressive continuum. As a strong proponent of worker organization, Addams expanded her repertoire to include the ballot, which, she believed, "would afford the best possible protection to working women and expedite that protective legislation which they so sadly need and in which America is so deficient." She argued that if political rights were "given to women, if the situation were theirs to deal with as a matter of civic responsibility, one cannot imagine that the existence of the social evils like child labor and sweatshop conditions would remain unchallenged."[8]

For Abramowitz, political activity was directly linked to her responsibilities as a newly naturalized American. As a citizen, Abramowitz not only fulfilled her civic duties but also exercised her newly acquired rights by speaking at suffrage rallies and fundraisers. On November 5, 1913, she was one of three featured speakers at Lincoln Center discussing "The Attitude of the Different Racial Groups to the Recently Acquired Right of the Franchise of Women."[9] Only the announcement and not the text of her speech has survived; however, it serves as testimony to the increasing political participation of immigrant women workers. One can assume that her speech was devoid of the socialist underpinnings that characterized the speeches of Bessie's ILGWU contemporaries, Pauline Newman and Theresa Malkiel.[10] Perhaps because of her close ties to Addams and Robins, Abramowitz outwardly exhibited the politics of the social feminists who comprised the mainstream suffrage movement.

Abramowitz's speeches satisfied Addams, who consistently emphasized the reciprocal aspect of cross-class relationships, pointing out that once working-class women were "awakened to their nature," they would perform their obligations by participating in the public realm as conscientious members of a new ethical society where the welfare of the entire community concerned all its members. Addams also valued the traditions of mutual aid found in immigrant communities. While Addams visualized many immigrants joining the ranks of what she called "the transfigured few," who broke out of the dreary sweatshops (usually by getting an education), workers' problems also demanded more immediate action.[11]

Working-class women followed the lead of Abramowitz and other working-class members of the WTUL such as capmaker Rose Schneiderman.[12] These women activists worked to secure the ballot for working women so that they could free themselves "from the drudgeries and worries which come with long hours and low wages." Schneiderman believed that winning the right to vote was the first step toward this industrial citizenship. Only then, in Schneiderman's mind, could women win the full right to citizenship with the accompanying entitlements of "the right to be born well, the right to a carefree and happy childhood, the right to education, and the right to mental, physical and spiritual growth and development." This expanded notion of citizenship proved to be the basis for industrial unionism and, in a gender-specific version, the foundation for the new feminism of the 1960s as well.[13]

Abramowitz's stint on the suffrage circuit did not detract from her organizing efforts. Aptly demonstrating her talent for labor organization, during a six-week period she held fifty-six meetings of young women workers.[14] Successful recruitment attempts at the local level, however, could not compensate for internal conflicts at the national level. When the United Garment Workers failed to provide adequate support for its members during the Chicago strike and later in New York and elsewhere, it lost the support of the progressive tailors, who accused the union of being inept at leadership and collective bargaining.[15]

A Union Is Born

In October 1914, more than three hundred New York and Chicago delegates attended the United Garment Workers' biennial convention in Nashville, Tennessee. Bessie Abramowitz, the representative for Chicago Local 152, played an instrumental part in the convention, but Sidney Hillman did not attend the gathering. He was working as the chief clerk for the ILGWU at its offices in New York, representing more than 50,000 workers in helping to administer the Protocols of Peace.[16]

A group of militant East Side tailors traveled to the convention intending to replace the union's conservative leadership. To prevent a challenge to their authority, UGW leaders disenfranchised one-third of the New York and Chicago delegates by accusing them of belonging to locals that were in financial arrears. Amid protests from their fellow unionists, they were barred from the convention floor and sent to the visitors' gallery. A small group from Chicago, including Bessie Abramowitz, remained on the convention floor and battled to support the ostracized group. Male counterparts, such as fellow Chicago delegate, A. D. Marimpietri, immediately recognized Abramowitz's capacity for leadership for "even though she [was] not a boy she [had become] one of our very important delegates."[17]

On the second day of the UGW convention, Bessie stepped forward and requested that a committee of fifteen members be appointed to resolve the differences surrounding the question of recognition.[18] As the leader of the Chicago group, Abramowitz addressed the convention and fought to gain the sympathy of the women delegates, who had been told by Margaret Daley, a member of the UGW's Executive Board, that the dissidents were "anarchists and Jews who were determined to capture and disrupt the union." When Abramowitz's attempt to seek a resolution failed, 113 delegates, including Bessie and her Chicago group, abruptly left Capitol Hall in protest and reconvened in the nearby Duncan Hotel, declaring themselves the legal convention.[19]

Abramowitz acted quickly to nominate Sidney Hillman for the highest position in the new union, but some workers openly expressed their skepticism. Jacob Panken, a union member and later Socialist New York City municipal judge, initially rejected Hillman as a candidate on the ground of his visible absence. He felt that if Sidney were truly behind the emerging organization, he would have been at the Nashville convention. Panken told Bessie many years later, "I remember that night in Nashville . . . when you walked me up and down the streets of the city arguing that Sidney was the only logical person to be president of the Amalgamated. I did not know him as well as you did, but I deferred to your judgment and I'm glad that I did."[20]

According to his biographer, Steven Fraser, Sidney Hillman's selection was almost a "foregone conclusion," for he possessed all the qualities necessary for a union president. His accomplishments in Chicago were common knowledge in the men's clothing industry. Fraser elaborated on Hillman's additional qualifications: "His contacts with luminaries from the progressive movement were considered valuable in their own right . . . [and] at the same time, he was recently enough of the rank and file."[21] This description of Hillman could just as easily have been applied to Bessie Abramowitz. From the scant evidence available, however, it seems as though she never aspired to the position. Abramowitz believed that the poised and intelligent Sidney Hillman was the best person for the job. Despite the high regard in which the insurgents held her, in reality, the new organization reflected society at large: it was a man's world. Although Abramowitz campaigned relentlessly to bring women into the union fold, she knew that only a man would be a suitable and acceptable leader. Abramowitz recognized society's gender constraints and used her power and influence among the workers to support Hillman rather than promote her own leadership.

After successfully "making a fight" to nominate Sidney Hillman as the president of the new body, Abramowitz contacted him at the ILGWU headquarters in New York. On October 14, 1914, she released Hillman from a secret engagement promise, wiring him: "Understand that personal pledges must cease when sister organization at stake. To become a martyr, I urge you to accept the office." Others too, including fellow Chicago cutter Sam Levin, campaigned relentlessly to persuade Hillman. Levin wired Hillman twice that day to encourage him to accept the presidency. Following some deliberation, Hillman accepted and the Amalgamated Clothing Workers of America was born.[22]

Abramowitz returned to Chicago where, on October 21, 1914, at a mass meeting at Westside Auditorium, she vividly recounted her Nashville experiences. Executive Board member A. D. Marimpietri credited Abramowitz with "arousing great enthusiasm."[23] Yet, much to the disappointment of the ardent Abramowitz, Sidney Hillman hesitated to confirm the autonomy of the new union. He preferred not to jeopardize his relationship with the "dominant circles of Jewish radicalism" or the AFL.[24] Between the Nashville convention and the first official convention in New York City two months later, Abramowitz found herself "bombarded with questions about what we are going to do next." At a loss as to how to answer questions about whether the union would affiliate with the Industrial Tailors' Union or become a wholly independent union, an impatient Bessie Abramowitz ordered Sidney Hillman to "act at once in order to be able to do more effective work."[25] As a result of the prodding by Bessie and others, Hillman called a special convention in New York on December 9, 1914. At this convention, the newly created union overtly declared its independence by changing its name from the United Garment Workers to the Amalgamated Clothing Workers of America (ACWA).[26]

In keeping with the ideology of the progressive women's network, the ACWA advocated peaceful, orderly adjudication around the conference table, regarding "industrial warfare as a relic of uncivilized industrial practices." Strikes were to be a last resort. Most importantly, convention delegates echoed the strikers' banners that called for economic improvements and human treatment. Delegates and workers alike demanded "bread and flowers" in the form of an industrial union that would provide both immediate economic and long-term cultural benefits for its members.[27] Women would play an integral part in attaining those goals for its members.

Following the renegade convention in December 1914, Abramowitz traveled to New York to represent Chicago Vestmakers' Local 152 at the ACWA's first biennial convention. In an expression of appreciation for her union advocacy, Sidney Hillman appointed her to the Credentials Committee. He made special mention of this committee and saw to it that it reported first. In August 1915, Bessie became the union's first female General Executive Board member, appointed to fill a vacancy between national conventions. A few months earlier the board had arrived at the conclusion that "since there are large numbers of women in our organization and still more in the industry that are to be organized, it is therefore desirable that of the two members to be elected one should be a woman."[28] As a member of the Credentials Committee, Abramowitz continued to influence the union's national course of action while representing Chicago interests as the newly chosen secretary-treasurer of the ACWA's Chicago District Council Number 6.

In addition to her official union posts, Abramowitz continued her involvement in the Chicago reform community. Like Rose Schneiderman, "she kept one foot in each world."[29] In a 1915 letter addressed to "My Dear Hillman," she drew a clear distinction between her activities as a "social worker" and her "organization work," attempting to reconcile the two as best she could. In the realm of social work, she lobbied under the auspices of the Chicago WTUL for protective legislation to secure an eight-hour law for the women of Illinois, and later on a compromise bill providing for a nine-hour day. She described her work on the legislative subcommittee and teased Hillman about the picture she enclosed showing her "being the head of nine men."[30] The latter portion of the letter described what she regarded as her union or "organization work." In addition to helping plan the Chicago May Day parade and attending the Commission on Industrial Relations hearings,

Abramowitz detailed her trials with the WTUL leaders, who "took [her] name off the ballot, as a delegate to the [WTUL] convention." As their organization was still officially affiliated with the United Garment Workers union, WTUL leaders felt obligated to disassociate themselves from Abramowitz and the renegade ACWA. Because of her support for the break from the AFL-affiliated UGW, she was, in her words, "a se-ceder." Although she had served as a labor delegate to the WTUL na-tional convention in 1913, two years later she had to fight to have her name reinstated. Bessie warned Hillman that if "the Baltimore girls" tried to go to the convention, they too would have trouble being seated. Her keen sense of humor overshadowed what might otherwise have been taken as a sarcastic remark about the allies when, in closing, she asked Hillman, "How do you like these old maids? I am too young for them, so you can imagine their age."[31]

Judging by her correspondence, Abramowitz seemed to take her troubles with the WTUL in stride; however, within a matter of months, events in the labor arena forced her to suspend her involvement in progressive reform efforts and concentrate her energy solely on union work. For Abramowitz, as for the majority of workers, organization and union recognition took precedence over reform legislation—at least temporarily. She maintained a working relationship with the WTUL, but was probably troubled by the WTUL's failure to openly break with the AFL, an organization not entirely committed to organizing women or unskilled workers.[32]

In remaining unequivocally supportive, the Hull-House network ultimately helped shape both of the Hillmans' philosophies of a "mean-ingful role for labor" in a new industrial democracy. In their early years as labor leaders, both Bessie and Sidney were undoubtedly influenced by Marxist ideology and ultimately the Russian revolutionary movement, which demanded an activist state.[33] As garment workers in Chicago, it was sheer desperation that compelled them to act. The new union de-veloped a social consciousness and pragmatic approach that echoed Jane Addams's "new social ethic." In 1902, years before "new unionism" be-came a reality, Addams delineated her plan for a new social order in *Democracy and Social Ethics.* She advocated pushing social justice for-ward by establishing nobler and wiser social relations.[34] Although Sid-ney Hillman's biographer, Steven Fraser, asserts that "sorting out what 'industrial democracy' did and did not mean took years,"[35] Jane Addams and the Hillmans had an early and a clear vision of what it should be.

To democratize industrial society, the reformers also supported the idea of an expanded government whose purpose was to protect the workers. Addams believed that this social evolution itself would come from educated working people, as unions seemed to be the only entities moving in the direction of industrial democracy.[36] Her overt support of laborers and her speeches and writings defined the concept of industrial democracy embodied in the "new unionism" and helped to create an environment in which the ACWA could "transmute the idiom of the shop floor and the pragmatic designs of socialism into the modern grammar of the managerial revolution."[37] As Bessie Abramowitz and Sidney Hillman ascended into the national labor arena, these ideals were foremost in their minds.

Chicago Reprised

In the fall of 1915, the Chicago Amalgamated District Council 6 (later renamed the Chicago Joint Board) initiated a fifteen-week strike of more than 20,000 workers, mostly women and girls, who remained unorganized in the city's men's garment industry. Along with the primary demands for union recognition and the right to bargain collectively, low wages and long hours were included in the list of issues submitted to the Wholesale Clothiers' Association.[38] Bessie Abramowitz again played a significant part in the strike, this time as a paid organizer with full union support. She headed the northwest district, which was one of four districts, each with its own headquarters, meeting hall, and relief committee. This group of strikers, composed largely of Poles, Jews, and Lithuanians, established their headquarters in the Jewish Educational Alliance building on Division Street where Bessie Abramowitz and her compatriot Samuel Levin conducted meetings. Abramowitz walked the picket lines as she had during the 1910 strike, visited the wounded in hospitals, and acted as a messenger between the strike leaders and union lawyer Clarence Darrow.[39] One afternoon Bessie Abramowitz and Carl Sandburg, then a young reporter covering the strike, waited outside Darrow's office. When the lawyer came out, he asked Sandburg to serenade Bessie. Sandburg strummed his guitar as he sang: "Oh the times are bad and the wages low, Oh leave her, bullies, leave her. . . ."[40] Carl Sandburg clearly recognized the challenges Bessie faced.

    To avoid confrontation with the American Federation of Labor and the Women's Trade Union League, both of which officially still supported the United Garment Workers, Amalgamated leaders turned to Hull-House once more for assistance. Again, Jane Addams, Ellen Gates Starr, and other Hull-House associates unconditionally supported the union, as they had five years earlier, by helping on the picket lines, collecting funds, distributing clothing, and putting the case before the public in the press or before committees. Once exposed, the workers' plight attracted the attention of labor notable Mother Jones, who traveled to Chicago and vehemently urged a crowd of women strikers to continue to resist their bosses.[41]

Police blamed the violence that occurred on the striking workers, asserting that the men on the force were "in grave danger from these women."[42] Lawyer and labor supporter Harold Ickes observed that unlike the 1910 strike, the middle-class picketers (including his wife), who came from Hull-House, the University of Chicago, and the North Shore, were treated differently than those from the labor ranks: "The police were . . . careful to be duly respectful to those of us who were lending a helping hand. However, they made an extraordinary slip. They arrested Ellen Gates Starr, co-founder with Jane Addams of Hull-House. I undertook to defend her, and much to the distress of the authorities, I insisted that her case be tried even after the strike had been settled. . . . Despite the sworn testimony of three hefty policemen that they had arrested Miss Starr, who was a frail little lady, because she had put them in physical fear, she was triumphantly acquitted by judge and jury."[43]

Along with other women reformers, such as Grace Abbott, Harriet Vittium, Mary McDowell, and Mary Antin, Starr and Addams were members of the Citizens' Committee for Arbitration in the Clothing Industry. The *Chicago Tribune* reported on a meeting of the committee on November 1, 1915: "It was a quiet meeting on the whole, and the squad of policemen detailed to watch for 'incendiaries' found little to occupy their attention." Not one policeman was injured in the strike. Working-class women strikers fared far worse than their middle-class allies. As one local paper reported, "scores have had their heads broken." By the end of the strike, nearly 2,000 people had been arrested.[44]

After the shooting death of one of the strikers on the picket line, Addams organized a mass meeting to arouse the public conscience, and headed a delegation that appeared before Mayor William Hale Thompson to ask him to become chairman of an arbitration board to settle the strike. Forty-five years after the strike, Bessie Hillman lauded the efforts of Jane Addams and Hull-House workers, who "did all in their power to check police brutality and to obtain a just and lasting settlement of the dispute."[45] Addams assisted in successfully engineering an end to the strike that not only considered the immediate needs of the workers but also required a better method for settling industrial conflicts.

At the end of the strike both sides claimed victory. Many credited the leadership of Abramowitz, Levin, Marimpietri, and Potofsky with winning the campaign. Although the determined strikers secured a reduction of hours from fifty-two to forty-eight hours a week, along with a wage increase, shop owners refused to meet their principal demand: union recognition, including the right to bargain collectively.[46] It would take another four years before this demand would be met. In this instance, labor won only a partial victory. The most positive aspect of the strike was the systematic rather than spontaneous solidarity demonstrated by union strikers.[47]

What Is to Be Done?

For some, union solidarity appeared to be threatened when, in 1916 at the Amalgamated's Second Biennial Convention in Rochester, women drew attention to the "woman question" regarding the status of women in the new union. Although a resolution presented by Esther Graber of Philadelphia calling for the appointment of women organizers passed easily, the question of women's place in the union concerned convention participants for the next decade. As far as the feminists inside the union were concerned, recruitment of women was not an issue. Instead, the controversy was over whether women would be allowed to achieve parity in the union. To accomplish this goal, soon-to-be Vice President Dorothy Jacobs Bellanca unsuccessfully appealed to the Rochester convention delegates to establish a separate women's department within the union. Rather than explicitly demanding equality, Bellanca pursued a more moderate course, arguing that special women's meetings would attract the less receptive women.[48] Reformer Grace Abbott's front-page article in the first issue of the *Advance*, in March 1917, called for equal responsibilities for union women, asserting that "the girls are eager to carry their full share of the work, both as resourceful leaders and as part of a reliable rank and file." Women, both inside and outside the union, began to question the ACWA's reputation as a progressive union that was much more receptive to women than the UGW, one willing to recognize women as officials and organizers.[49]

Most male leaders, however, did not perceive the problem as involving gender equity, thinking rather that it revolved around how to keep women workers active once they were brought into the union fold. Short-sighted male officials believed that mere recognition of the women's efforts would surely serve this purpose. Leaders like Vice President Joseph Schlossberg reinforced the official union stance by emphasizing the importance of women in the ACWA, not only for the dues they contributed but also for their presence on the picket lines and for their committed activism for the union cause.[50]

Women, though, saw the situation differently. Token recognition of their accomplishments proved a far cry from attaining an equal place in the union they had helped to establish. The dilemma concerning the woman question was further complicated by the disapproving opinions of the leadership and rank-and-file men. Leaders were sometimes skeptical about recruiting or even retaining women, whom the men viewed as temporary workers. Some male unionists resented the presence of women in the ACWA, perceiving them to be threats to their own jobs. This apprehension on the part of union men meant that once women became union members, they were rarely appointed to leadership positions. Union feminists like Dorothy Jacobs Bellanca decried the lack of opportunity for women and waged an uphill battle not only against employers, but against male union leaders and resistant male union members as well.[51]

By opening the door to membership and focusing attention on maintaining women as active members, male leaders temporarily avoided the issues surrounding women's lack of leadership positions in the union. Many women agreed with Bellanca and Abbott: they were willing to participate in the ACWA on an equal basis with men as both members and leaders. They realized that the only way women members could "break the habit of submission to men was to start talking."[52] Bolstered by their strong numbers and a proven track record, union women began to demand equal opportunity. These aggressive women failed to make much progress, evidenced by the fact that even as late as 1923 nominations of women to local executive boards were still newsworthy items.[53]

Schooled in social feminist ideology by reform-minded Chicago women, Bessie Abramowitz firmly believed that women should be active in their unions—not only as organizers but as leaders, too. She served as a delegate at the 1913 WTUL convention, where leaders stressed the importance of women's union participation and conducted a comprehensive survey concerning the involvement of women in unions. The WTUL's "Report of the Committee on Organization" concluded that "too often the women [are] not even represented on the Executive Board or as officers." It recommended that the women in such unions "accept nominations to be members of committees and delegates to Central Bodies, and insist upon being represented in the administrative work of the Union, and insist upon further representation on Joint Boards as delegates, and demand a member of the Executive Board."[54] Action on this recommendation came the following year when the WTUL opened the Training School for Women Organizers in Chicago, the first full-time labor school in the United States. It was designed to train women organizers, "the best of whom," according to Margaret Dreier Robins, "without question are the trade union girls."[55] The two young women who attended the program the first year found a comprehensive program that included courses in trade-union organization, industrial organization, labor history, bookkeeping, and writing. Fieldwork, directed by Mary Anderson and Agnes Nestor, included visits to unions and street meetings and allowed the students to learn the duties of the union officers. Bessie attended the newly renamed Training School for Active Workers in the Labor Movement in 1915, the year before her marriage to Sidney Hillman and subsequent relocation to New York City.[56]

In the union's formative years, a number of colleges across the country initiated various worker education programs. Among the earliest and most notable were the Bryn Mawr Summer School for Women Workers, under the direction of progressive dean Hilda Worthington Smith; and Brookwood Labor College, a year-round coeducational institution, both opened in 1921.[57] Bryn Mawr's educational objective—offering working women the opportunity to expand their "influence in the industrial world and help in the coming social reconstruction"—seemed to echo the philosophy of the ACWA's educational programs, which were started at the local levels in 1916. J.B.S. Hardman, the ACWA's first educational director, believed that long-term education for workers would instill union loyalty and promote the social action needed to help participants change the social order. When workers failed to accomplish this lofty goal, the men of the ACWA abandoned the union education program, but continued to encourage labor college education for ACWA members.[58] In the meantime, the ILGWU retained a steadfast commitment to worker education, due in large part to the education department's executive secretary, Fannia Cohn. Male unionists, however, scorned her cooperation with the socialists and communists in the worker education movement. As they grew wary of her autonomy, they began to challenge the independence of the educational institutions that emerged from Cohn's efforts. By the late 1920s, ILGWU officials' support of worker education programs began to fade.[59]

Abramowitz's own experience within the union attested to the few opportunities available for Amalgamated women. Bessie believed that organization and education would create the solidarity necessary to improve the lives of workers. For most Jewish women activists, education was the driving force behind the transition from shop-floor worker to union organizer. Jewish culture promoted education, yet most young Jewish women suffered from a childhood deprivation of exactly that. In the cohort of Bessie's ILGWU contemporaries, only Fannia Cohn had been educated past the eighth grade.[60] Abramowitz had been tutored as a young girl in Russia, although it is difficult to infer the level of formal education she achieved. Once she came to the United States, her education took the form of English and citizenship classes, and then on-the-job training to become an organizer. The simultaneous mentoring by Jane Addams provided an informal education in the principles of social feminism at a receptive time in the young immigrant's life. In an era when many viewed women as difficult to organize, one of the most lasting accomplishments of middle-class reformers came in educating women for leadership positions.[61] For Abramowitz, as for most working-class women, dual identification as workers and politicized community members was an education in itself.

Once World War I erupted, union leaders were forced to confront the problems associated with wartime clothing production, thus providing another vehicle for women to call attention to their plight. Increasing numbers of women entered the workforce, as women job applicants were given preference "so unemployed men will seek war service," and women were recruited to replace those men already serving abroad. Despite the high demand for their labor, wages, hours, and working conditions again became problematic for women workers. National WTUL President Margaret Dreier Robins warned working women "to resist efforts of employers to increase profits by exploiting women during the war's hysteria." Attempting to remedy women's precarious position, Robins convinced her long-time friend Sidney Hillman that "protective legislation in the form of an eight-hour day, a living wage, one day rest in seven, and adult labor should be a condition in every contract made for government supplies."[62] Despite the fact that the ACWA was operating outside the confines of the AFL, cooperation between the WTUL and the Amalgamated grew during the war because of the attention that male union leaders like Sidney Hillman paid to women's concerns.

Issues concerning women's equity within the union became apparent when a separate column entitled "Special Department for Women Members" made its debut in the *Advance* in June of 1917; it ran for the duration of the war. One of the first articles, "Women War Workers," detailed the Department of Labor's reasons why women in uniform shops were paid less than men. The article stated that men and women had equal opportunity to earn the same wages because they were paid the same piece rates, but due to a variety of circumstances, including lack of training, self-assertion, and experience, women accepted lower wages than men. At the end of the war, there was little doubt that these "profit grabbing patriots" (employers) would allow the returning soldiers to starve in the streets before they gave soldiers their old jobs back at their former rate of pay.[63]

Provoked by a combination of factors, workers called for equal pay for equal work as ACWA President Hillman simultaneously condemned government awards of military uniform contracts to nonunion shops. He criticized the contractors who hired their work out "in great bundles being taken into tenements by poor women who slave 12 to 18 hours a day while [the uniforms] are made up in the midst of dirt and disease." In response to pressure from the union and its supporters, by August 1917, Secretary of War Newton D. Baker appointed a Board of Control to preserve labor standards and to prevent government contract work from being performed under sweatshop conditions.[64] The Amalgamated successfully regulated the industrial standards in the wartime clothing industries.

In the meantime, Bessie Hillman's close friend, Amalgamated activist Dorothy Bellanca, sought a more effective and lasting solution for women workers. She launched an organizational crusade and appealed to the Board of Control to assist with the organization of women workers. Bellanca argued that women were not just temporary workers waiting to marry and leave the industry, pointing out that more than two-thirds of them were breadwinners for their families. According to Bellanca, these women's earnings were necessary for their mothers, fathers, brothers, or sisters and would become even more so as men went off to war. She adamantly asserted that women could no longer work for less than men. They needed to organize permanently to achieve their goals.[65]

Mainly because of improved government-labor relations, workers in general made strides during the war years. This overall improvement was reflected in an almost 70 percent increase in union membership between 1917 and 1920, along with a rise in wages and the general achievement of the eight-hour day.[66] Women, however, did not fare as well as might be expected. Some, like Bellanca, mistakenly believed that women would be allowed to continue working after the war because they were cheaper than men. Nevertheless, despite renewed organizational campaigns and protective legislation on their behalf, as soon as the war ended women were forced out of their jobs.[67]

Hostility between male and female workers (especially those hired into nontraditional jobs) escalated during the war. One of the most extreme examples occurred in Cleveland in 1918, where 3,000 motormen and conductors successfully struck to force the company to discharge 150 women conductors who had been hired during the war. Discrimination against women workers was much more widespread than this isolated incident. Lacking any form of legal recourse, women were routinely dismissed to make way for returning servicemen. In May 1918, the "Special Department for Our Women Members," initially billed as a "permanent feature" of the *Advance,* was discontinued. In the spring of 1921, a "Women's Page" made a brief appearance, but was replaced in a matter of months by articles discussing international concerns.[68] For a short time, the woman question receded into the background.

Mixing Marriage and a Career

Working together closely from the time of the 1910 strike, Abramowitz and Hillman fell in love. Joseph Schaffner and others, who saw the young couple's common interests as admirable bonds upon which to build a personal as well as a professional relationship, encouraged their romance. Abramowitz, who had left Russia to avoid an arranged marriage, initially seemed the more enraptured of the two, speaking to others about "having her eye on Sidney" from the first months of the 1910 strike and caring for him when he was ill during the 1915 strike.[69] Preoccupied with union matters, Hillman devoted little attention to his personal life, but soon Abramowitz's love was reciprocated. For Bessie Abramowitz, choosing her own spouse symbolized a new form of power. The couple, however, chose to delay marriage for two reasons. First, Abramowitz and Hillman—like countless other immigrants who, in the Old-World tradition, honored their obligation to their parents—had been sending money back to Russia to support their respective families. Marriage and the expense of establishing a household meant that this aid would have to be sharply curtailed. Second, their union careers interfered, calling Hillman to New York and keeping Abramowitz in Chicago.

As soon as the union's future looked relatively stable, the couple began to voice their intentions. Initially Abramowitz announced her engagement only to a few close friends. Then, during the 1916 May Day parade, Bessie Abramowitz and Sidney Hillman publicly confirmed their engagement by linking arms and leading a contingent of clothing workers through downtown Chicago. On a day of individual triumph and celebration for Amalgamated members as well, the parade ended in a rally at the Auditorium Theater.[70]

Local papers romanticized the May 3 wedding that officially marked the Hillmans' partnership. Although the ceremony took place in a synagogue, Bessie in particular did not consider herself "a religious person." From her earliest days in the United States, she constructed her identity as a Jew not around a religious tradition, but rather in a cultural sense. After the ceremony, the exhausted newlyweds walked in a park, and after a long talk concerning union business they fell asleep on a bench. The culmination of more than two long years of waiting must have brought the new Mrs. Hillman a tremendous amount of joy. Now, after sharing common experiences, suffering, and comradeship, both could live under the same roof and deepen their bonds of affections for one another.[71] The fact that the couple chose to spend the days immediately following their marriage at the union's second biennial convention in Rochester symbolized the predominant place that the union would continue to occupy in both of their lives.

Whereas other women labor activists curtailed their careers once married, for Bessie Hillman marriage did not lessen her devotion; instead, it began a new phase of involvement in the union in which she played such an important part. Relocation to join Sidney in New York forced her resignation from her position as business agent for Chicago Local 152. Agreeing that only one of them should earn a union salary, Bessie also resigned from the General Executive Board and performed her work on a volunteer basis for the next three decades.[72] The union work that had brought the couple together would prove to be a sustaining factor throughout their thirty-year marriage.

4 Strong on the Outside: The Union, Women, and the Struggle to Survive (1918–1933)

In January 1918, within hours after addressing a mass rally, an exhausted Sidney Hillman wrote to his infant daughter Philoine from his Montreal hotel room. Bessie's eyes filled with tears as she read the letter addressed to the baby cradled in her arms. The president of the Amalgamated Clothing Workers of America poignantly recounted the revelation he had experienced as he spoke to a teeming crowd of Canadian workers whose "present is so colorless that their only joy lies in the future." Responding to the pleas for hope in their eyes, Hillman articulated his vision of a free new world where "Labor will rule." As he concluded his speech, he felt the presence of the Messiah in the hall "ready to do battle."[1] Bessie wished she could have been there to share her husband's joy.

Labor's Uncertain Future

Sidney Hillman's prophecy coincided precisely with the tide of optimism that swept the country at the end of World War I. Along with other labor leaders, the Amalgamated president anticipated a stellar future for American workers. Union workers' contributions to the war effort had won the support of business and government alike. The Amalgamated reaped benefits on a number of fronts. Just as it began to move into the international arena, the ACWA won what Bessie believed to be the greatest triumph of the twentieth century: the fight to unionize the Chicago market.[2] Unionization of New York followed soon thereafter. Woodrow Wilson rewarded women workers across the country with the creation of a federal Women's Bureau, headed by Mary Anderson, former bootmaker and longtime member of the Chicago WTUL. For a fleeting moment, as Steven Fraser observed, "the balance of power tipped in labor's favor."[3] Workers and their leaders had reason to believe that their good fortunes would continue. The reality of war's aftermath, however, quickly dashed these hopes.

In the wake of the postwar Red Scare, labor fell from grace. Prominent politicians and business leaders who, during the war, had considered labor officials their junior partners now condemned them as reds and anarchists. To make matters worse, the dissolution of the National War Labor Board left labor defenseless against escalating anti-labor sentiment. The year 1919 began with an unprecedented wave of labor unrest and ended with the deportation of labor supporter Emma Goldman and 248 others accused of being "enemy aliens."[4]

In a repressive postwar climate complicated by economic uncertainty, combative manufacturers and their associations thwarted attempts to unionize. Employers conducted open-shop campaigns, and a few created corporate welfare programs promising myriads of worker benefits designed to eliminate the need for unions altogether. Local governments did not hesitate to support manufacturers' efforts to defeat unions, sending in police forces to wage street battles. Union leaders also combated rising unemployment trends as the depression that "ravaged the clothing industry" set in. The consumer-spending spree that characterized the prosperous 1920s slowed by the end of the decade and, with it, the demand for ready-made clothing fell. Inventories piled higher in warehouses. First wages and hours were cut; then, clothing workers, accustomed to slack periods, lost their jobs permanently. A number of large and midsize companies closed their doors.[5]

In the face of these challenges, labor's resiliency waned. National union membership figures plummeted from more than 5 million in 1920 to less than 3.5 million by 1929.[6] The Amalgamated's membership numbers dropped from an all-time high of 177,000 in 1920 to 100,000 members by 1930. The most substantial decrease occurred between 1920 and 1921, when the Amalgamated lost more than 30,000 members.[7] The failing economy and dwindling membership figures alarmed union leaders. Although the most dramatic decline can be partially attributed to a major New York strike known as the Lockout of 1920–1921, a variety of circumstances contributed to the shrinking rosters.

In addition to the external circumstances that wreaked havoc with the union, its officials faced a mounting number of internal pressures as well. In the early 1920s, internecine battles between socialists and communists seeking to win the loyalty of the Amalgamated's rank and file erupted in a number of cities, including New York, Chicago, and Rochester. The disputes subsided as the insurgent groups slowly collapsed from within. President Hillman minimized the conflicts by presenting a united front and declaring in 1925 that the union had emerged from the contention "essentially unscathed." Shortly afterward, infiltration of the ACWA by organized crime rocked the union to its foundation. Racketeers (some of whom were local union officials) demanded "protection" money from members of the elite New York Cutters' Union. Hillman and his cadres finally acted in 1931 to expel the unsavory unionists from the organization,[8] but both of these occurrences forced union insiders to acknowledge the potential vulnerability of the organization.

Union Women Seek a Place

The "women question" emerged as one of the union's most pressing postwar problems. Like the internal tensions between political factions and the infiltration of the ACWA by criminal elements, the controversy over women's place in the union reflected the broader historical context. Although women gained the right to vote in 1920, men continued to exclude them from full participation in public life. Union men also employed a variety of arguments to undermine women's participation in labor organizations. ACWA Secretary Joseph Salerno appealed to popular sentiment by suggesting that women were "going into industry so fast that home life is very much in danger." Men clung to the decades-old "pin money" fallacy, insisting that women worked by choice, most often temporarily, and therefore were not entirely committed to the organization.[9] Male workers feared that in tough economic times they would lose their jobs to women. The sexually segregated structure of the industry invalidated this claim altogether, for women rarely, if ever, sought the same jobs as men did. Nevertheless, women's position in the Amalgamated remained tenuous at best.

To complicate matters further, following the ratification of the suffrage amendment, a schism emerged in the feminists' ranks over the question of how to achieve full equality for women. Alice Paul's

National Woman's Party (NWP) represented mainly professional women and held that women should be treated the same as men. The NWP began to pursue a constitutional amendment—the Equal Rights Amendment (ERA)—to guarantee full equality for women in all aspects of American life. Another, more numerous group of women (including Hull-House associates and WTUL members who were concerned primarily with the working woman's plight) opposed the ERA on the ground that its passage would invalidate the protective legislation already in place at the state level that the reformers had fought so long to secure. The WTUL legislative secretary, Ethel Smith, a leading advocate of this female-specific approach, argued that because women's work experiences differed substantially from men's, and because they lacked union representation, women workers needed protective legislation. In Smith's mind, cross-class alliances focused on the passage of protective labor legislation were essential to promote the best interests of women and the community as a whole.[10]

Nevertheless, NWP members insisted on passage of the ERA even at the expense of protective legislation. Seeking a more secure place in the Department of Labor and dependent on the support of trade unionists and women's organizations, the new Women's Bureau, under the leadership of Mary Anderson, along with its social feminist supporters, vehemently rejected the proposed ERA and vowed to continue the quest for protective legislation.[11] Working women, including Bessie Hillman, sided with the social feminists. They were not willing to risk hard-won legislation for an abstract commitment to equality. Furthermore, working women saw the ERA's proclamation of gender equality as a threat to their limited organizational position, and sensed that women still needed to acknowledge and protect their own special place. Protective legislation that would limit working hours, enact minimum wages, and address poor working conditions, rather than the economically destructive ERA, appeared at the time to be the best route to reform.[12]

Although both working-class and middle-class women worked toward the same end—to advance the cause of women workers by framing and legislating labor policy—working women's rationale differed distinctly from that of their middle- and upper-class allies. They realized that women were different but argued for protective legislation, not on the so-called maternalist grounds of women's frailty or their potential place as "future mothers of the race," but on the basis of women's entitlement. With their realities shaped on the shop floor, they demanded equal opportunity with working men. They sought empowerment as citizens rather than charity as refugees. In their minds, legislation was not a substitute for organizing but a catalyst for it.[13]

Ultimately, the cross-class alliances proved strong enough to overcome philosophical differences. For labor women like Hillman, ties with middle-class allies that dated back to the progressive era were solidified in the 1930s and endured for the rest of their lives, even as some reformers—Hilda Worthington Smith, founder of the Bryn Mawr Summer School for Industrial Workers and from 1933 to 1943 director of the Workers' Service Program in the Federal Emergency Relief Administration and the Works Progress Administration; Frances Perkins, former Industrial Commissioner of New York and, from 1933 to 1945, Secretary of Labor in the Roosevelt Administration; and Eleanor Roosevelt, First Lady and social justice advocate—went off to Washington to forward their mission in the New Deal cabinet. Elinore Herrick, president of the New York Consumers' League and a close friend of Bessie's, stayed behind to work with the New York office of the National Labor Relations Board as its regional director. Regardless of where these women were based, they perceived themselves as "part of a large family bound together by an almost mystical commitment to social reform."[14]

In addition to such Chicago connections as Grace Abbott and Mary Anderson, throughout the interwar years Bessie Hillman maintained an extensive circle of friends, including Pauline Newman, Elisabeth Christman (National WTUL secretary), and Rose Schneiderman.[15] These reformers shared her dual connections to the WTUL and to trade unionism. Some, like Newman and Schneiderman, shared Bessie's eastern European roots, were exposed to Marxism at a young age, spent their youth in the garment factories, witnessed or participated in at least one major strike, and linked education to reform. These women believed in self-determination and sought to organize working women into unions. Like Bessie, they combined strategies to survive in the element in which they operated.[16] By the 1930s, both Newman and Schneiderman seemed disillusioned with the progress they were making organizing women into unions and began to work more often for government agencies rather than for trade unions. Secretary of Labor Frances Perkins appointed Schneiderman to the National Recovery Administration's Labor Advisory Board; Newman held a number of temporary government appointments.[17]

Bessie retained an unrelenting commitment to trade unionism. Yet, even after she returned to labor organizing as her primary activity, she continued to fight for protective labor legislation. Labor activist and ILGWU education secretary Fannia Cohn voiced the sentiments of many, including Bessie Hillman, in a 1927 letter to her British counterpart, Dr. Marion Phillips, where she wrote: "[C]onsidering that very few women are as yet organized into trade unions, it would be folly to agitate against protective legislation."[18] Although Cohn distrusted the notion of a cross-class women's movement, Hillman, Newman, and Schneiderman recognized that allying with progressives of all social classes would be advantageous in the fight for protective labor legislation.

From her days as a union organizer based at Hull-House, Hillman and other labor women shared a conviction about developing industrial unions that empowered women.[19] These women were willing to make small compromises to win their larger goals. As one who shaped her feminist ideology in the aftermath of the 1909–1910 strikes, Hillman realized that the first step toward reaching any form of industrial democracy was the organization of garment women into the Amalgamated. Once women's loyalty was assured and their immediate demands were satisfied, female members would work toward the expanding vision of industrial citizenship or, as Hillman characterized it, the "big dream" of "decent wages, of decent homes, of dignity and democracy on the job—the dream of social, economic and political justice."[20] She believed that the new members could be educated and trained in the nurturing vein of Jane Addams's "useful citizens," who in turn could work for the good of the community. Only when unions like the Amalgamated won "absolutely democratic" industrial conditions would industrial peace become a reality.[21] The Women's Bureau under Mary Anderson's leadership and the 1930s Department of Labor with Frances Perkins at the helm presented these possibilities.

A Women's Department Within

While women activists across the country debated how best to advance the cause of working women, ACWA women, influenced by the creation of the national Women's Bureau, redirected their attention to internal affairs within the union and rallied around the creation of a separate women's department. At the Sixth Biennial Convention, held in Philadelphia in 1924, the lone female General Executive Board member, Mamie Santora, hailed the idea of a long-awaited women's department as a place "whereby women will be able to complain and to ask for things which will not be of benefit only to the women but which will be of benefit to the Organization and to all the workers." Proponents of the department viewed it as a way to increase activity and organize more women and perhaps even attain leadership positions.

After all, women like Hillman, Bellanca, and Santora had always been effective organizers of women.[22]

At the same time, however, Mamie Santora warned against the divisive aspects of the separate women's locals already established in some cities. Although women had founded these separate unions "because they don't get a chance," Santora urged a halt to the emergence of separate women's locals, arguing, "I don't think this would be the healthiest thing for the Organization. We are not an Organization of divisions, we want to amalgamate, we want to be with the men." Like her close friend Bessie Hillman, Santora identified herself as a worker first and as a woman second. A national women's department would be a compromise and "a way to bring women up to the high standards of the Amalgamated."[23]

In contrast to the more moderate stance of some of her colleagues, Dorothy Jacobs Bellanca, an outspoken feminist and ACWA vice president, pursued a separatist strategy in the search for women's equality within the Amalgamated. Bellanca considered the establishment of a women's department at the Philadelphia Convention a dream come true. Adding to her elation, the General Executive Board committee in charge of the new department invited "Sister Dorothy Bellanca to assume charge of the Women's Bureau."[24] While they supported the department, Santora, Hillman, and other old-guard unionists also spoke in favor of integration and, in the interest of solidarity, joined with the men "to march forward toward the ultimate goal" of industrial democracy, which seemed to imply equality for women. With the exception of demanding equal pay for equal work and advancing women into leadership positions, for the moment most union women did not press for status as equals. Linking class and gender concerns, they instead emphasized that a women's bureau would be beneficial to strengthening the entire organization.[25] Women organizers realized that progress often took years, so they learned to be very patient. For tactical reasons, Hillman and her contemporaries were often discreet about their feminism. Moreover, Hillman's close ties to the Women's Bureau coalition at the national level enabled her to hold fast to the hope that ultimately the state would intervene on behalf of women workers across the country, mooting the question of women's place within the union with a blanket of protective laws that would apply to women and eventually even men.

Women across the country, including Mary Anderson, director of the United States Women's Bureau, encouraged Bellanca as she "blaze[d] the way" for women to rise within the trade-union structure by organizing and creating "a closer means of organizing women members and the organization." Bellanca wanted to increase the numbers of women who operated within the trade-union network. She sided with the women workers who wanted to secure more than the immediate gains of higher wages and fewer work hours. They sought access to education and equitable relationships with the men who dominated the workplace and trade unionism. Bellanca also "hope[d] to create a closer relationship" between women union members and the United States Women's Bureau. Still, even Bellanca's feminism had its limits. Cognizant of prevailing gender expectations, Bellanca did not challenge women's dual burden in the workplace and in the home. Regardless of her efforts, she constantly found that "male trade unionists were alienated by separate women's organizations which they misunderstood."[26]

Despite her tactful diplomacy, union men, fearing women's power, voiced their objections to the autonomous department. Bellanca traversed the country trying to educate both men and women and "to sell the Women's Bureau as a way of serving the entire trade union movement." Even though the men held exclusively male meetings, they objected to the bureau's women-only meetings, entertainment, and procedures for women members, complaining that such practices hindered worker solidarity. When she discovered the potentially divisive qualities of the department, Bellanca proposed its dissolution, giving the organization's welfare priority over the individual's.[27]

Faced with unrelenting opposition from the men and her own increased family responsibilities, Bellanca's department dissolved only a year after its founding. Bellanca conceded, "Very often one has to do things against one's self for the benefit of the organization." She did not want to be considered an irritant to her male colleagues, many of whom continued to view her separatist strategies as potentially harmful to the solidarity of the organization. Her time as the bureau's director took a toll on Bellanca's health. She was exhausted from the constant travel necessary to promote her cause, and spending time on the road became even more difficult as her husband's health declined. Her domestic duties, which centered around caring for her ill husband, August, conflicted with her work. At the end of her tenure in August 1925, Bellanca confided to a friend that she felt depressed and anxious. Yet, despite her internal and personal struggles, her interest in aiding women never wavered.[28]

Settling for the Sake of Solidarity

The short life of the Women's Department reminded Amalgamated women of their unfulfilled expectations. In the years following the demise of the department, a debate in the *Advance* ensued around the question "Are Women Discriminated Against?" Members of Chicago Women's Local 275 initiated the debate when they wrote to J.B.S. Hardman, the editor of the *Advance*, summarizing earlier arguments. They complained that women were instrumental in winning strikes, yet their efforts and commitment invariably went unrecognized by union leaders, who continued to view women as temporary workers. Women members across the country responded to the letters and agreed that both employers and the union discriminated against women. One disgruntled writer pointed out that the union allowed them to take lower wages and bigger wage reductions than the men "that are married and have children to support." Once again, the underlying assumption was that women, regardless of their marital status, were not financially responsible for supporting families.[29] Without a women's department to recognize and protect their special interests, the women had little recourse.

Outside observers such as economist Theresa Wolfson advocated on behalf of female union members. Wolfson compared the treatment of women in the ACWA to that of workers exploited by capitalists, arguing that if male union leaders do not "serve the interests of their women members as assiduously as they do those of their men, they are in danger of creating their own competitors."[30] The union had only a few women organizers in the 1920s. Even ACWA insider Hardman acknowledged that "the absence of women in the leadership of our organization is deplorable," but he blamed the women themselves, "for if they wanted to be treated like men it was up to them to organize and fight their way to the front." Hardman, like many men and some women, felt that women should play the game by men's rules: "Women are up against the system as it is, and as it came to be in a world organized by men. . . . They will have to match power with power, and prove that they are stronger, before 'the others' will yield power to them."[31] Hardman articulated the entrenched sexist attitudes of many labor unionists at the time. Although it took some time for Bessie to win the respect of her male colleagues (with whom she did not always agree), for the sake of unity she consistently encouraged ACWA women to work in concert with their male colleagues.

Drawing upon social feminist doctrine that encouraged negotiation whenever possible, Hillman adopted a compromise position that emphasized women's similarities to men rather than their differences. Although she did not explicitly demand equal treatment for women, Bessie believed that women should have equal opportunities. In a 1927

Advance column entitled "May It Please Our Women Readers," women continued to protest the discriminatory attitudes that prevailed, claiming that women were vital to the union and had done the organizational work "but the men get all the credit." Women felt that they had fought long and hard only to be considered unnecessary in the end. According to one letter, this kind of discrimination "would not lead to strengthen the life of the organization." Some rank-and-file women argued, however, that the majority of union women would be willing to settle for special attention rather than seek leadership positions or power.[32]

In yet another attempt to address women's concerns, a committee presented Resolution 72 on the "Establishment of a Women's Bureau" to the biennial convention in May 1928, claiming that the prior bureau had been dissolved without any notice. By then, however, President Hillman—not known for his high regard for women's leadership abilities—had withdrawn his support on the grounds that women were already properly represented in the organization and that to approve a women's bureau would separate the union into two national offices, one for men and the other for women. Instead, he suggested voting for national officers, whether men or women, who would represent everyone in the organization.[33]

Bessie agreed with her husband. Attending every convention since the first but never before presented with an opportunity to speak, on the closing day of the 1928 convention Bessie Hillman, at Jacob Potofsky's request, stood in for her ill husband. Convention delegates greeted Bessie with a standing ovation and "tremendous rounds of applause" as she took the chair vacated by Sidney Hillman.[34] Comfortable on the dais, Bessie briefly reminisced about her early days in the Chicago union and then, after telling a joke, turned to more serious matters: the subject of a women's bureau. Bessie Hillman admitted that she had heard only part of the appeal for a separate bureau, but in an effort to repair any lingering rift she explained to the convention, "We don't need a Women's Bureau to work separately. I like to work with the men. I like to belong to the same organization with them and to transact the same business with them. There is no division among the tailors, as far as the women or the men are concerned. They are all one organization."[35]

As the union struggled to stand on solid ground, Bessie Hillman reaffirmed her commitment to organizational solidarity by urging women to avoid being the catalysts for internal dissension and to ally with the men rather than create an exclusively female department. The resolution was defeated, and a separate women's department was not proposed again in her lifetime. In a union that worked hard to recruit them to membership, the unresolved controversy concerning women's place in the union organization plagued Bessie Hillman and the Amalgamated for years to come.

The Head of the House

Even though Bessie often found the boundaries between union work and family life blurred, she defined her place in her own family with ease. Sidney Hillman had the highest regard for his wife's abilities and constantly relied on her support. Among the few surviving pieces of correspondence between the two is a 1921 telegram from Sidney, who was in Chicago, that illuminates the integral part Bessie played in union business. After directing Bessie to relay important union information to Jacob Potofsky, Sidney asked Bessie whether "all members vote for business agents in New York Joint Board or by trades?"[36] Clearly Bessie had more expertise about certain aspects of the day-to-day intricacies of union business than even Sidney did. In his diary, Jacob Potofsky articulated the thoughts of many when he wrote: "Hillman was fortunate in having married one who knew and understood him and his mission to a degree that made it possible for him to do his work unhampered by any restrictions."[37] Both Bessie and Sidney shared a commitment to act in the best interests of the working class as a whole. In Sidney's case, this commitment to the organization often took precedence over family responsibilities.

Bessie was also fortunate to be free from the worries of holding a major union office. She utilized this autonomy to her family's advantage. Not only did Bessie serve as Sidney's counsel while he traveled on union business for weeks on end, but she ran the household too. From the earliest days of the marriage, when she rented and furnished a small apartment in the Washington Heights section of New York on a $200 monthly budget, to her subsequent purchase of a house on Long Island, Bessie Hillman competently managed the family. This willingness and ability to take charge of domestic affairs is no surprise given the traditions of her childhood; where Bessie was raised, shtetl women often assumed such responsibilities.[38] In this she was like many immigrant women, who frequently carried traditions and values emanating from their rural past to their urban present.

Life for Bessie became more complicated with the births of the Hillmans' two daughters, Philoine in 1917 and Selma in 1921. Before the girls entered school, she did her best to balance motherhood and part-time union work. Surviving documents indicate that Bessie continued to walk the picket lines during the New York Lockout of 1920–1921. She also maintained her affiliations with the WTUL and the National Consumers' League, where she met first Elinore Herrick, director of the New York Consumers' League. Every two years Bessie traveled to the ACWA's national convention. In 1922, while Bessie was at the convention in Chicago, the union sponsored an opening banquet at the Congress Hotel, "in honor of Mrs. Sidney Hillman, formerly Bessie Abramowitz, one of the first deputies of the vest makers' local."[39] As the guest of honor, Bessie gave a short speech reminiscing about her early days as a union pioneer in Chicago, remarking that after visiting the Chicago shops she had found the "improvement in the conditions almost unbelievable." At the ACWA convention later that week, at a banquet honoring the thirty-three-year-old, Margaret Dreier Robins described Bessie as "the woman leader in the great strike of 1910."[40]

In 1924, shortly after Philoine entered grammar school, Bessie purchased the Hillmans' first home, on Union Place in Lynbrook, Long Island. Despite the relocation, there was no reduction of the centrality of the organization in the lives of the Hillman family. From their days as newlyweds, the Hillmans had included unionists in their extended family. First their small apartment kitchen and, later, when they moved to bigger quarters, their living room acted as a nightly meeting place for intense discussions. Union vice president Jacob Potofsky, whose personal life periodically suffered from problematic relationships, lived with the Hillmans intermittently for decades. Both Potofsky and his daughter, Delia, were considered part of the family. Every summer, extended vacations spent on the New Jersey shore included the surrogate union family. Philoine Fried remembered, "Not until we grew somewhat older were we able to differentiate between the relatives, the friends, and the union compatriots."[41]

For Bessie, buying property represented not only the family's upward mobility but also the attainment of her immigrant aspirations. Bessie signed the mortgage papers and oversaw all the expenses connected with running a home. The house itself was modest but comfortable, with four bedrooms: one for Bessie and Sidney; one for the two girls to share; a room for Jack Potofsky (who often stayed with the family), and a bedroom for Beatrice Cox, the housekeeper whom Bessie hired shortly after moving from the Bronx. Suburban life proved to be a mixed blessing. The mere purchase of property conflicted with Sidney's socialist convictions not to own any real estate, but apparently it did not cause any serious tension in the marriage. Perhaps Bessie felt isolated and too far removed from union business in Long Island. With the children situated with a full-time nanny/housekeeper in the suburbs, she felt comfortable commuting into the city to work. Philoine remembered that she was one of the only children in her class with a mother who worked outside the home.[42]

Philoine remembered that Beatrice Cox, who emigrated to the United States from her native England after her fiancé was killed in World War I, became a substitute mother while Bessie was away. Cox employed her "proper British ways" to discipline the children with a loving hand. The girls shared fond memories of the menagerie of pets that Beatrice introduced into the household. Bessie trusted Beatrice to raise her daughters, run the house, and generally "do the right thing" in her absence. Cox eventually became a member of the family.[43]

Although they appeared supportive of Bessie's union activities, the Hillmans' daughters had mixed reactions to their parents' penchant for union work. Both Bessie and Sidney were away from home for extended periods of time while their girls were young. Nevertheless, in keeping with the cultural dictates of the time, neither his wife nor his daughters ever questioned Sidney's more numerous absences or his neglect of domestic responsibilities. Philoine recalled that although Sidney "never even boiled a pot of water, he was a good father."[44]

Bessie also made time to unwind and be with her daughters. Philoine vividly recalled that Bessie stayed home during the summer months and "because she liked the ocean so much, she took us to the beach everyday by train."[45] This type of summer recreation was becoming increasingly common for immigrant families. When they could afford to do so, Jewish men, who worked all week in the city, sent their wives and children on vacation all summer. Eventually Bessie bought the family their own beach house.[46] While the Hillmans readily assimilated into American middle-class life, the multitude of dilemmas confronting union workers remained in the front of their minds.

Righting the Runaways

As soon as Bessie returned to work on a full-time basis, she became involved in the union's campaign to bring the "runaway shops" into the union fold. The errant shop owners posed a serious threat to union solidarity, by adding another dimension to an already dismal picture. During the postwar recession, struggling men's and women's clothing manufacturers sought "to solve their problems by running away from them."[47] They fled from union jurisdiction in production centers like New York to surrounding rural areas where the ACWA struggled to gain a foothold. Shop owners dismantled their operations (often under the cover of darkness) and moved to distant locations, where they reopened under new names. Capitalizing on cheap, unskilled, nonunion labor, garment shop owners relocated their urban factories to the agricultural towns and hamlets of Pennsylvania, New Jersey, Connecticut, and upstate New York. The low overhead and minimal investment required to resume operations facilitated the process. Promising work for the wives and daughters of local farmers and miners, the shops were a welcome addition to underdeveloped rural communities.[48]

Local Chambers of Commerce and boards of trade actively recruited needle-trades factories, but they rarely ascertained the standing of a company before it was "given a free hand" to operate. Community leaders desperate to attract industry enticed employers by promising to provide rent-free factories, pay moving expenses, and buy stock. In a *Virginia Quarterly* article, the chairman of a local northern New England Chamber of Commerce committee complained that all but one of the factory owners had demanded cash bonuses before they relocated. He concluded that "quite a good living could be made by a 'manufacturer' hauling some second-hand machinery and his industrial expectations from town to town, collecting cash bonuses and manufacturing nothing."[49]

Pennsylvania quickly became a haven for runaway shops. By the late 1920s, the state ranked as the nation's leading producer of cotton garments: shirts, pajamas, pants, sportswear, outerwear, and children's clothes. Those who did set up shop found an abundant supply of available laborers willing to work hard for meager wages. Within the next few years, the plight of the garment industry workers in the hinterlands gained national attention. Investigations into Pennsylvania shirt factories revealed that even during years of "normal prosperity," shop owners permitted abusive conditions, including child labor, excessively long hours, and low pay.[50] Girls as young as eleven or twelve worked in shops in Frackville, St. Clair, New Philadelphia, and Pottsville in Pennsylvania's anthracite region. Employers ignored state statutes prohibiting child labor. Frances Perkins observed that "while women of all ages are employed in the shirt industry, Pennsylvania and Connecticut are the only states in which child labor is extensively used."[51] Circumstances that prevailed there were replicated throughout the Northeast.

Ann Craton, one of the ACWA's "best organizers," who worked in the anthracite region as early as the winter of 1919–1920, found that initially employers offered comparatively high wages to the wives and children of miners. In families where the father or husband had been killed or injured in the mines, the runaway shops provided the families' only source of income.[52] Employers ultimately reduced the starting wages once the family members became dependent on their garment jobs. In 1933, Secretary of Labor Frances Perkins confirmed what federal inquiries had first revealed as early as 1927: that actual earnings diminished with the size of the community.[53] In other words, the smaller the town, the less the workers were paid. In all cases children made significantly less than adults. Declining profits became the manufacturers' excuse for further wage reductions.

Women and children worked side by side, hunched over their machines as many as seventy hours a week during the busy season. Foremen and higher officials used their positions to "take undue liberties" with female workers; however, these women rarely complained. Employment was scarce. Factory owners cooperated among themselves to create a blacklist system so efficient that "if a girl is discharged from a factory she cannot get work in any other in the neighborhood." Sanitary regulations were nonexistent, and thus the workers were continually exposed to diseases, gas poisoning, and fire hazards. Stubborn employers resisted any attempt to improve working conditions.[54] As the Depression tightened its grasp, conditions deteriorated still further.

For Bessie Hillman, these sweatshop conditions evoked grim memories of her early years in the Chicago garment district. Despite predictions that suffrage for women would alter their workplace conditions, within a decade after its passage, women were all too aware "that suffrage alone did not translate into equality and social justice."[55] Bessie Hillman and other labor leaders refused to ignore the situation any longer. Working women suffered more than men and, in an industry where they constituted more than half of the employees, the organization of women and children warranted another wholehearted attempt by the ACWA. Until the passage of the National Industrial Recovery Act in 1933, though, the majority of these efforts proved futile.

Union Feminism and the Advance of Industrial Democracy

Faced with numerous challenges to its solidarity, by the late 1920s, remarkably, the ACWA managed to emerge as a model industrial union with an all-encompassing concern for its members that, in many ways, anticipated the benevolence of the New Deal welfare state. Jane Addams explained that "even when it was weak in power, [the ACWA] was strong in upholding the principles for which it stood."[56] As garment workers, both Bessie and Sidney had witnessed the toll that strenuous and unsanitary conditions took on clothing workers. During Sidney's brief stint as a clerk for the ILGWU in 1914, the Protocol of Peace paved the way for the Union Health Center, which would later become a model for the Amalgamated's health care centers of the 1920s. Beginning with unemployment insurance inaugurated in 1923, the Amalgamated's comprehensive insurance coverage eventually included death benefits, accident and health insurance, surgical and maternity care, and retirement pensions. Union programs based on the progressive-era reformers' proposals for unemployment, old age, and health insurance, and for permanent relief programs such as public housing and public control of banking, provided a model for many of the New Deal reforms that followed.[57]

When the Committee on Economic Security, chaired by Frances Perkins, allowed the national health care insurance proposal intended for inclusion in the 1935 Social Security Act to succumb to pressure by the medical profession, ACWA members had little to worry about—their organization picked up the slack by building Amalgamated health centers across the country.[58] The union continually promoted an increased standard of living for its members. Bessie in particular empathized with the lack of affordable health care for workers. From their early days together, Sidney's health had concerned Bessie. Stress had a severe impact on Sidney. Its repercussions became more serious over time and resulted in chronic heart problems.

Sidney himself had little grounding in the difficulties workers faced when searching for health care or for housing for themselves and their families. Prior to his marriage, he had lived in Chicago boardinghouses and at Lillian Wald's Henry Street Settlement. Bessie clearly understood life from the workers' vantage point. After the Hillmans married, Bessie not only secured housing for the family, but also paid the rent, and later the mortgage and taxes, and all the bills associated with maintaining a home and family. She recognized the need for affordable family housing. The union began to address workers' needs beyond the workplace within its first decade of existence. Union leaders established "truly revolutionary" banks that provided low-interest personal loans and later mortgages to ACWA workers in Chicago in 1922 and in New York in 1923.[59] Health centers soon followed. In 1926, Bessie stood firmly behind the construction of the first cooperative housing project begun in New York to provide affordable residences for union members. Jane Addams praised "the sense of social obligation which preeminently typifies everything that the Amalgamated has done."[60]

Bessie Hillman remained loyal to her humane vision of industrial democracy organizing women at the grassroots level well after other network women had assumed positions of power outside the trade-union ranks.[61] She did not let her gender pose an obstacle to her activism. Bessie Hillman's refusal to bow to the strong public sentiment against married women (especially those with children) working outside the home inspired many future activists. Years later, Esther Peterson, former ACWA official and assistant Secretary of Labor under Kennedy, attested to Bessie's expertise on union affairs and her "intense and dedicated" approach to unionism, describing how workers, particularly women workers, gathered around her as she walked through the shops to ask "Miss Bessie" how they could personally contribute to the union cause. There was no doubt that "the women in the shops loved her."[62] Time after time, Hillman advocated for and with women so that they could share equal opportunities with men. She proved that women could become union leaders and influence union affairs. Acting as both an example and an advocate, Bessie undoubtedly pushed social welfare benefits, and thus industrial democracy, forward.

5 Enter Sister Hillman: The Runaway Campaign Years (1933–1937)

At the end of the 1920s, as production surpassed consumer demand, economists noticed a slow but steady decline in the national economy. The stock market crash in the fall of 1929 did not start the Depression, but it shattered Americans' confidence in the economy. What had begun as a gradual downward slope now spiraled out of control. By the spring of 1933, 15 million people, or one in four wage earners, were out of work. At one point, only 10 percent of Amalgamated members in New York City held steady jobs. According to Amalgamated General Secretary-Treasurer Jacob Potofsky, on the eve of Roosevelt's election the industry had regressed to the point that it was "in bad shape, again becoming sweatshop ridden: the workers were having a miserable time. . . . [T]he members needed relief; the local organizations needed help; new organizing campaigns had to be waged in old and new places."[1] Franklin Delano Roosevelt's election promised relief from the Depression, but Sidney Hillman waited until his organization could benefit from New Deal legislation to launch a full-scale organizing offensive.

New Deals and Old Discriminations

Sidney Hillman's wishes came to fruition with the June 16, 1933, passage of the National Industrial Recovery Act (NIRA), mandating a government-sanctioned system of business self-regulation, with provisions for state intervention to guarantee workers' rights to organize and bargain collectively—both also components of the later 1935 National Labor Relations Act, known as the Wagner Act.[2] This legislation triggered a national organizing campaign in which the forces of the labor movement converged in an offensive stance. The NIRA reenergized existing unions like the Amalgamated Clothing Workers of America, the United Mine Workers, and the International Ladies Garment Workers' Union and paved the way for the rise of a number of new unions in the steel, automobile, glass, and leather industries. The redemptive pulse of the New Deal intensified the drive for collective action on all fronts. The ACWA fortified its position when it affiliated with the American Federation of Labor in October 1933. In the midst of this prolabor climate, organizations like the National Consumers' League (NCL) renewed their campaigns to support working women.[3]

Founded in 1899, the National Consumers' League worked outside the parameters of the union "on behalf of labor rather than banding together to fight high prices or industrial concentration."[4] At the turn of the century, Florence Kelley and the women of the NCL pioneered the tactic of using consumer pressure on employers to raise labor standards by publishing "white lists" of fair employers, as a movement for "ethical consumption" spread to cities across the country. Outraged by the continued exploitation of women and child laborers, the League sought to coerce employers into fair labor practices, instituting "investigate, agitate, and legislate" policies in the early 1920s. NCL historian Landon Storrs demonstrates that despite a number of political and legal setbacks, by the 1930s the League had experienced a resurgence of power and taken the lead on legislative campaigns.[5]

Labor women embraced the opportunity to exact recognition as workers and as consumers too. Many social workers trained at the height of the progressive era began to enter the political arena supporting labor interests, believing as Frances Perkins did that "social justice was possible in an industrial community."[6] A more assertive League aided wage-earning women in protesting injustices and helped them organize into unions. Together they attempted to progress beyond state-level laws that affected solely women to help create a national labor standards policy that extended to women and men alike.[7]

Women's status in general surged ahead with FDR's inauguration. Roosevelt responded to feminist demands, including those of the Democratic National Committee's Women's Division director, Molly Dewson, by appointing Frances Perkins as the Secretary of Labor—the first woman Cabinet member in the nation's history. Other members of the women's reform network, from the National Consumers' League, the Women's Trade Union League, and various reform groups, also accepted government appointments in federal agencies charged with expanding social welfare programs, and went to work in Washington.[8] Many of these network women had close connections to labor. Among the most notable were Mary Anderson, who continued as the chief officer of the United States Women's Bureau until her retirement in 1944, and Hilda Worthington Smith, who directed the workers' education division of the Federal Emergency Relief Administration from 1934 to 1937. Some, like Bessie Hillman and her good friends Elinore Morehouse Herrick (with the National Labor Relations Board in New York), Frieda Miller (director of the New York State Bureau of Women in Industry), and Pauline Newman (with New York City's NRA Compliance Board), stayed behind to do important work from their local bases of power.[9]

Frances Perkins and Eleanor Roosevelt emerged as the most visible champions of women within the New Deal circle. Advocating women's rights in employment, in legislation, and in the development of institutional norms, both Perkins and Roosevelt recognized the need for gradual reform as they helped to set the stage for a wide array of New Deal programs.[10] Perkins and Roosevelt joined their contemporaries to confirm their dual commitments to women's issues and social reform. These women built lifelong friendships based on shared ideologies. Frances Perkins wrote in 1953 that the network women were "bound together by spiritual ties no one else can understand."[11]

Charged with coordinating the administration of the NIRA, the National Recovery Administration (NRA) attempted to represent both worker and employer interests by establishing a Labor Advisory Board and an Industrial Advisory Board to jointly formulate codes for fair competition. Women members, however, were conspicuously absent from both boards. The only exception was women's network insider Rose Schneiderman, who was named to the Labor Advisory Board by Frances Perkins in the spring of 1933.[12] Although the clothing industry codes entitled men's clothing workers to additional protection, because the codes did not specifically mention gender, women workers continued to operate at a disadvantage. For example, traditional male positions such as cutter had added wage increases guaranteeing $1.00 per hour, compared to the more general manufacturing category in which the majority of women worked and which paid only 40 cents per hour in the North and 37 cents per hour in the South. A coalition of women's organizations, including the National Consumers' League and the Women's Trade Union League, unsuccessfully protested the "Code of Fair Competition for the Men's Clothing Industry," which institutionalized the gendered wage gap and racism.[13]

Although the NRA codes did not treat gender or race equitably, women who worked in the industry's lowest-paying manufacturing jobs did benefit from the NRA code's minimum-wage provisions and its reduction of the work week from forty-four to thirty-six hours. Furthermore, Labor Advisory Board member Rose Schneiderman was thrilled at the prospect that the mere implementation of the code had the potential to accomplish what voluntary organizations in the women's reform network (such as the WTUL, the NCL, and the Women's Bureau) had been fighting for during more than thirty years: government regulation of working conditions for women as well as for men.[14] Reminiscent of the white lists of the National Consumers' League, firms that complied with NRA legislation were rewarded with a Blue Eagle.

Requiring a limitation of hours, establishment of minimum wages, and abolition of homework and child labor, the code, adopted on August 26, 1933, promised relief from the industrial depression.[15] ACWA Vice President Potofsky cautioned, though, that there was "a long journey between legal language signed into laws by the president and the jobs and paychecks of the workers. Someone, something had to translate the laws into hard reality, into jobs and decent wages. Someone had to police the shops to see that the laws were obeyed. For most workers, that someone was the union."[16]

Philadelphia: "A Thorn in the Union's Side"

The union had found its authority challenged in more ways than one in the past. As early as 1920, the ACWA had established an Out-of-Town Organization Committee to coordinate a limited campaign against runaway shop owners who had fled the New York metropolitan area. Rather than driving the renegade manufacturers back to the city, the union decided to save jobs by organizing the out-of-town shops throughout the Northeast. Sidney told Bessie that the ACWA's New York Joint Board of Shirt Workers blamed the runaway shops for causing their financial ruin, and continually pressured union officials to spearhead an extensive organizational campaign in the runaway cotton garment shops.[17] Because women and young girls constituted the majority of the workforce in the men's clothing industry, union leaders drew women organizers into the runaway campaign from the beginning. For a brief period, between 1919 and 1921, the ACWA sent male and female organizers to Pennsylvania's Appalachian territory, but the intense resistance they encountered dissuaded the ACWA from continuing its efforts there.[18] These early experiences foreshadowed the battles to come.

Following this unsuccessful drive, union leaders decided to delay the organization of the rural outposts while the organization tackled the stronghold of Philadelphia—the only major metropolitan clothing center in the country that had avoided organization. Sporadic attempts by the ACWA to organize Philadelphia's garment workers stretched back to 1917, but had consistently "met with discouragement and defeat." With only a skeleton organization surviving by the end of the 1920s, union leaders considered Philadelphia, with its organized anti-union employers, "a thorn in the union's side."[19]

The city was undeniably a refuge for runaway shops. Organizations like the WTUL, which could ordinarily make preliminary inroads into hostile territory, made little headway in Pennsylvania's adverse political climate. Politicians who requested several women's organizations allied with the Philadelphia WTUL to tone down their rhetoric, in exchange for continued support, outraged Philadelphia WTUL leader Pauline Newman.[20] Anti-union attitudes permeated local newspapers, whose articles openly attacked labor's efforts to organize. Members of the Philadelphia Clothing Manufacturers' Exchange, determined to keep their factories running full-time, used nonunion labor. Some employers resorted to requiring their workers to sign yellow-dog contracts swearing that they would not join any other union. Underpaid workers in Philadelphia produced low-cost clothing that invaded every major apparel market in the country. Diversion of work from New York shops to these Philadelphia subcontractors added to the already overwhelming unemployment problems. At the expense of the organized garment industry, Philadelphia manufacturers enjoyed an unrivaled growth spurt.[21]

Officials at the 1928 Amalgamated convention unanimously decided to launch a full-scale offensive in Philadelphia, using "all the resources at the disposal of the ACWA for the purpose of unionizing this important clothing market immediately."[22] Refusing to let the manufacturers' maltreatment of employees go unchecked, in late July ACWA President Sidney Hillman traveled to the city to address a mass meeting observed by local police. He demanded a return to higher wage scales, a forty-four-hour work week, and the abolition of contract shops. Organizers distributed circulars published by the Young Workers' (Communist) League and established a strike headquarters. They made a deliberate feint at an organizational campaign in the summer and fall of 1928 and then obvious union activities ceased.[23]

The lull in the campaign allowed the organizers to strategize. Groundwork began when a contingent of skilled organizers, including Bessie Hillman, who by then had situated her young family on suburban Long Island, converged in Philadelphia in the spring of 1929. They discreetly laid a foundation for what ultimately proved to be a vicious struggle. Union leaders quickly realized that since previous attempts to organize the area had failed, it was crucial to develop and employ a comprehensive strategy. They also reasoned that because many of the workers hailed from a "new generation who lacked a union tradition," organizing tactics that would have been effective fifteen years earlier would not do in 1929.[24] Above all, the situation demanded an innovative approach.

Bessie Hillman and the other organizers infiltrated from within. They referred to carefully constructed lists of workers employed in each shop, first educating individual workers and then small groups of them in their homes so that they could convince their fellow workers (some of whom were cynical, given the union's past failures in the area) of the advantages of joining a union. The majority of the 11,000 Philadelphia clothing workers turned out to be Italian immigrants or the children of immigrants, whom some labor activists considered less inclined to join a union than other ethnic groups.[25] Drawing on their experience in organizing diverse ethnicities (including Italians) dating back to the inception of the organization, Amalgamated leaders sent in Italian-speaking organizers. As was the case in turn-of-the-century Chicago, female organizers helped to break through cultural barriers that discouraged Italian women from speaking to male organizers.

Perceiving a once-remote threat now becoming a reality, Philadelphia manufacturers fought back. They lashed out at their competitors in New York, Chicago, and elsewhere who promised financial support for the Amalgamated's fight for control of the Philadelphia market. The manufacturers accused New York firms of being "unable to throw off union domination and lower their production costs."[26] Amalgamated leaders did their best to convince employers that although wages were higher in organized markets, greater efficiency ushered in by union practices actually cut production costs while improving the quality of the product. Labor activists fought to counter a barrage of attacks by manufacturers, who called unionists irresponsible troublemakers, bolsheviks, and radicals.[27]

Upholding labor's reputation became even more difficult when Philadelphia clothing manufacturers charged the union with conducting a "whispering campaign" against them, in which union agents allegedly told national distributors that an impending general strike would prevent the delivery of clothes for fall sales. Seeking to repair labor's damaged name, Bessie Hillman met with Philadelphia employers, newspaper reporters, municipal authorities, and public-spirited citizens. Due to the antagonistic nature of the campaign, Sidney Hillman maintained a vigilant presence in the city.[28]

Initially the union sought several small victories necessary "to inspire confidence in the power and genuine purpose of the organization and in doing so sacrifice color and drama to peace."[29] Rather than conducting a general strike involving all of the city's clothing workers simultaneously, the campaign proceeded on a shop-by-shop basis. This approach allowed the leaders to concentrate virtually all their organizers in one place at one time and thus more effectively coordinate the distribution of liberal strike benefits. Sidney Hillman's exhortation at the beginning of the strike campaign, to "[w]alk the picket line smiling [and] observe the law," encouraged an orderly campaign and averted harsh treatment by law enforcement authorities. Perhaps the most innovative aspect of the effort was the union's attempt to "mobilize the merchant's influence over the manufacturer, the authority of buyer over seller, on the side of the workers."[30] Retailers, concerned with the stability and integrity of the sources that supplied their clothing wares, encouraged manufacturers to settle with the union.

The campaign officially opened in the summer of 1929 with strikes at two small plants where conditions appeared favorable for success. Leaders settled both the Navytone and the Progressive strikes in a matter of a few weeks. The latter victory was particularly inspiring because the Progressive shop was located in the huge Kirshbaum clothing factory. Union members viewed the hoisting of the Amalgamated banner on this building as "an omen of success for the whole campaign."[31]

Winning the small houses bolstered the Amalgamated's confidence to the level necessary to confront the larger employers. Sympathetic workers in other cities donated their overtime pay to a strike relief fund. These contributions totaled between $800,000 and $1 million—an impressive amount given the economic circumstances of many American workers that year.[32] Organizers used the news of their successes as propaganda to entice others to strike. Workers at H. Daroff and Sons shocked company owners when they struck. Employees at the Jacob Seigel Company also "came out," followed by those at Pincus Brothers, where employers tried to force workers to sign yellow-dog contracts and locked the doors to prevent a walkout.[33]

Choosing to fight a legal battle in the courts rather than wage war on the streets, in August 1929 eight of the city's largest clothing manufacturers applied for a preliminary injunction against the Amalgamated in the Court of Common Pleas. On September 6, Judge W. H. Kirkpatrick, of the District Court of the United States for the Eastern District of Pennsylvania, responded by issuing a sweeping injunction against the union.[34] Three days later, and only hours after workers from Middishade Company and Makransky and Sons joined the strike, the injunction went into effect. It prohibited the union from interfering with the business of the manufacturers; from attempting "by threats, intimidation or otherwise to solicit, communicate or argue with any person or persons employed by the complainants; [and] from picketing on or near the premises of complainants or on the highways leading thereto in any manner with the purpose of intimidating, annoying, embarrassing or through fear exercising moral coercion over those lawfully employed by complainants."[35] Despite the potentially devastating legal ramifications of such a broad injunction, the union refused to be intimidated.

Clearly intended to cripple the Amalgamated's organizing activities, the injunction backfired. It did not break the solidarity of the strikers, but instead evoked a stronger sense of unity. To circumvent the binding injunction, union organizers told employees to quit their jobs rather than stage a strike. The court's decision fell prey to harsh criticism. Front-page headlines across the country encapsulated public outrage over the injunction.[36] A week later, heated discussions over this use of power by a federal court echoed in the halls of Congress. Calling it "a grave abuse of power" that denied thousands of workers "their basic right to organize to improve their condition through collective bargaining," Wisconsin Senator Robert M. LaFollette demanded an investigation by the Judiciary Committee.[37]

Succumbing to the barrage of criticism, Judge Kirkpatrick handed down a modification of his prior ruling that permitted the Amalgamated to enlarge its membership in "a peaceful and lawful manner," but still forbade the union from inducing employees to join a strike or to violate the yellow-dog contracts that the plaintiffs had required the workers to sign.[38] The union refused to compromise. In response to the ACWA's appeal, Kirkpatrick recorded a further opinion in early October. In a fifteen-page statement, he elaborated on his belief that the Amalgamated campaign in Philadelphia was intended to stop the production of nonunion clothing and in effect prevented interstate commerce, therefore violating the Sherman Anti-Trust Law.[39] With the appeal pending, LaFollette continued to push the Senate investigation, and eventually the union signed contracts with six of the eight plaintiffs involved in the case. By the end of October, all the plaintiffs had signed union contracts and striking workers returned to their jobs. In April 1930, Judge Kirkpatrick signed orders that discontinued the injunctions.[40] Pleased by the success of the campaign, in early November a beaming Sidney Hillman announced that after more than fifty strikes the job in Philadelphia was "more than ninety-five percent done."[41] A new joint board that organized at least 10,000 workers grew out of the effort. Through it all, Bessie's campaign contributions received little, if any, credit.

Although the 1929 campaign broke the solidarity of the Philadelphia manufacturers' association and overcame open shops and a hostile local press, it was not a complete success. A series of articles in the *Daily News Record*, entitled "Maladies of the Needle Trades," highlighted the strike and the unemployment problems that accompanied it. One optimistic reporter chronicling the situation agreed with Sidney Hillman's premature assessment, observing: "A small group of irreconcilables still stands out, but the market as a whole 'is in the bag.'"[42] Yet even after the campaign ended, 24 of the 324 Philadelphia firms stood fast outside the union. The ACWA waged a relentless campaign during the Depression years to rally these employees into the union fold.

Bessie Hillman became a familiar sight during the Philadelphia drives. Yet, in the midst of a 1932 Philadelphia strike, she met defeat for one of the first times in her life. She spoke at a number of mass meetings and rallies in the city praising clothing workers for "the magnificent campaign they [were] waging to better their conditions through union protection." However, while addressing a meeting of more than 4,000 hosiery workers who were seeking a closed shop, Hillman made an unprecedented move. Realizing that their employers would continue to refuse to concede to their demands, she "exhorted them to go back to work."[43] The situation forced Hillman to realize the limits of the union's power. Even in the face of Bessie Hillman's temporary retreat, the *Advance* predicted "One hundred percent organization of the Philadelphia market" in the immediate future. The Amalgamated would return to Philadelphia three more times in the ensuing years—in 1933, 1935, and again in 1937—in an attempt to accomplish that goal.[44]

Sent in once again to lay the groundwork for the momentous Philadelphia shirt organizing drive in the summer of 1937, Bessie Hillman faced one of the greatest organizational challenges of her life. She immediately impressed male union leaders with her organizational expertise when, after only a short time in Philadelphia, she "exhibited a complete knowledge of the peculiar problems of the situation and expressed an assurance that the organization would solve these in the typical Amalgamated manner."[45] Unlike prior organizational efforts, by 1937 Hillman's organizational efforts were aided by more receptive conditions.

Hillman attended a 1937 supper in her honor sponsored by the Women's Activity of the Philadelphia ACWA, where she gave "an enlightening talk on unionism and urged the girls to become active in their existing locals," rather than start their own local.[46] Like other "industrial feminists," Hillman believed that mixed rather than separate locals fostered solidarity and provided the most effective framework for permanent organization.[47] Shortly afterward, the *Advance* reported that only after "a concerted organizing drive led by sister Bessie Hillman was an advance made in organizing 20,000 workers." The six-month drive that Bessie directed in Philadelphia culminated in an agreement that ensured improved wages and working conditions.[48] Moreover, union organization in Philadelphia and later the rural runaway campaign of the 1930s provided a milieu to rally around. Eventually the war against the sweatshops and homework finishing in the men's clothing industry spread outside the city to related sectors, such as work clothing, children's clothing, and neckwear.

Setting the Stage

In the spring of 1933, just as the initial pieces of the New Deal legislation became law, the Amalgamated began to plan a massive assault on the rural runaway shops. This time "seasoned fighters," including Bessie Hillman, Dorothy Bellanca, Mamie Santora, and Gladys Dickason, assumed their places in the organizing brigade directed by Jacob Potofsky.[49] Just as the Women's Bureau coalition had proved instrumental in working with the nascent welfare state to formulate an effective labor policy, so would labor women be a major factor in the quest for industrial democracy through the runaway campaign. Throughout the Depression, "valiant soldiers" Bessie Hillman and Dorothy Jacobs Bellanca appealed specifically to women workers, who clearly worked not for pin money but to earn a living wage.[50]

While on the surface the campaign afforded Bessie Hillman a chance to reassert her organizational skills, the reasons for Bessie's return to full-time activism ran deeper. For Hillman, the runaway campaign was a prime opportunity to work with colleagues whom she loved and respected. Dorothy Sue Cobble recognizes that a sisterhood rooted in a shared commitment to women's workplace justice and social rights linked the social feminists of the women's network. Some of these women, such as Hillman, who had first met under the auspices of Jane Addams's Hull-House, worked together in New York throughout the 1920s. Dorothy Sue Cobble aptly labels these women "intellectual daughters and granddaughters" of progressive-era social feminists.[51]

Seeking the most expedient route to organizing women, these labor women combined the strategies of cross-class sisterhood with an integrationist approach, advocating a class-based struggle in which "working men and working women [would] have to work together to usher in democracy in industry."[52] Disillusioned with the meager political advances resulting from suffrage, Hillman remained convinced that despite labor's weak record, unions had made more real gains for women than any other type of organization.

Work as a full-time organizer dedicated to the cause of rebuilding the union she had helped to found also allowed Bessie Hillman to divert her attention from an increasingly troubled relationship with her husband. Her reentry into the full-time professional organizational arena coincided with her discovery of Sidney's intimate involvement with his longtime secretary, Tecia Davidson. Although the details are scant, putting the union above all else meant that Sidney was away from his family for extended periods of time. While Bessie remained closer to home raising their children, sometime in the early 1930s Sidney began a long-term affair with Tecia, who often accompanied him on business trips. Esther Peterson, later an ACWA official and close friend of the Hillmans, confirmed that Sidney Hillman "was involved with and went around with Tecia a lot."[53]

In Bessie's case, hardships at home enhanced rather than diminished her activist convictions. She seemed reinvigorated by the chance to assist in redefining the labor women's agenda as it moved into a new era, fighting hard for the rights of female unionists. While outwardly fighting to collectively organize and empower working women, Bessie Hillman fought for autonomy as an individual. In doing so, she intentionally changed the course of her own life as well.

Vigorously stepping onto the runaway campaign stage, Bessie and the organizers who joined her experimented with unconventional strategies: "moving over streets and into hall one day; and a quietly conducted drive from the grassroots up, another day—visiting homes, talking with circumspection and seeking to avoid rubbing anyone the wrong way; or an exercise in pressure on an employer's weak financial spot, or on the supply source of his orders, the day later."[54] Flexibility and the willingness to adapt to diverse situations were critical to the success of each new attempt. As the offensive proceeded from one locale to the next, organizing operations became more systematic.

With the Chicago and the early Philadelphia experiences under their belts, Hillman and her fellow organizers acted as diplomats upon arriving in a new city: making the initial contacts, assessing the terrain, interviewing labor groups, checking with city authorities about permits to distribute circulars, and seeking permission to hold meetings. Their pragmatic approach allowed them "to learn to do a big job by whatever means would lead to the end in view."[55] Once the groundwork was laid, Bessie Hillman relied on her past strike experience to develop organizing strategies specifically designed to win over the small-town rank and file. In the encouraging NIRA climate and with letters of introduction in hand, Hillman approached the police chiefs and mayors of each city, requesting their approval, before initiating organizing campaigns.

Then Hillman began the crucial campaign phase: appealing directly to the workers. Accompanied by local organizers, she went into the factories and contacted local church officials to gain their support and the backing of their parishioners as well. Hillman, always cognizant of ethnic and religious diversity, never failed to recognize that each situation required a unique approach. For instance, in especially strong religious communities, like those of the Catholics in Connecticut and the Mennonites in Pennsylvania, she met with the minister even before contacting local authorities.[56] Hillman had learned from Jane Addams to establish a presence through cooperation whenever possible. She tried to convince civic leaders that she was acting for the common good.

In one introductory letter, Reverend Francis Haas, the director of the National Catholic School of Social Service and member of the NIRA Labor Advisory Board, praised labor's newfound political strength: "Mrs. Hillman is contributing in a most vital way to effectuate the legislation passed by the last Congress and the plans for industrial recovery inaugurated by the President of the United States." Considering himself "honored . . . to introduce her to workers and employers," Haas applauded the union and Bessie Hillman's "splendid self-sacrifice." He detailed how "she has toiled tirelessly with her husband in building up the Amalgamated Clothing Workers of America to the point where it commands the respect and confidence of all decent and fair-minded manufacturers in American industry." Haas possessed a strong belief in the Amalgamated's ability to secure mass improvements for its members, concluding that "the success of the organization will not only help to realize the great objectives that President Roosevelt has set up in the NIRA but contribute most vitally toward building up a permanent and socially just order in society."[57]

In the runaway outposts, descendants of Slavic, Polish, and Italian immigrants had displaced the original wave of European settlers from Ireland and other parts of the British Isles. By the 1930s, many residents of the dilapidated anthracite towns were the American-born children of these immigrants from southern and eastern Europe, whose families still clustered in tight-knit ethnic enclaves like Paddy's Land, Dutch Hollow, Little Italy, Hunky Hill, and Polack Street.[58] Hillman spoke at countless public rallies, empathizing with workers suffering through the hard times of the Depression who sought nothing more than financial stability for their families. More often than not, she persuaded them that the union was the answer to their problems.

Peter Swoboda, a Lykens, Pennsylvania, shirt presser, who knew and worked with Bessie during the 1933–1934 campaign, remembered that although there were "few Jewish people in Pennsylvania and, in spite of her accent, she came across very convincingly." As in ethnic Chicago more than twenty years earlier, Bessie's sincerity endeared her to workers regardless of their heritage. Once she established herself as a formidable ally, workers listened. The most important aspect of every effort entailed recruiting and training a group of local workers who could maintain and expand upon the work of the national leaders after they left the area, so Hillman's ability to reach the masses made a tremendous difference.[59]

However, some, like Albany union member Frieda Schwenkmeyer, found Hillman's approach abrasive. She remembered that during the 1934 campaigns Bessie Hillman "talked too much and thought that because of her long experience in the union that she had all the right answers." Schwenkmeyer stated in no uncertain terms that Hillman "drove us crazy."[60] Yet even those like Schwenkmeyer, who faulted Hillman's assertive style, respected her leadership ability.

The First Offensive:
Babies Strike in Allentown and Northampton

The formal union campaign opened in the spring of 1933 in Allentown and Northampton, Pennsylvania, where conditions presented the worst-case scenario. Fearing the loss of jobs, economic and political leaders in both communities opposed efforts to organize workers. Resistant employers argued that the union "was out to close the factories and return them to New York."[61] Conversely, they claimed that if the union did successfully organize the workers, they would have to close their shops and go out of business. Some employers reacted by organizing company unions and forcing their employees to sign yellow-dog contracts.[62]

Pushed to their limit by poor working conditions, low pay, and long hours, in late March the workers, including many children, began walking off their jobs in Northampton, demanding higher pay and union recognition. Professional union organizers, often assisted by college students and even miners, rushed into the area to direct the strike. The National Child Labor Committee, a nonprofit agency established in 1904 to investigate and publicize the plight of child laborers in an effort to persuade Congress to pass protective measures, ascertained that there were more than forty sweatshops in the Northampton and Allentown areas, employing hundreds of boys and girls, more than a quarter of whom were under sixteen years of age.[63] Some children came to work because the shops were warm and lit, something their houses were not. Many came from destitute families where the father was unemployed for long periods of time. They knew beforehand that they would be categorized as unpaid "learners," but the learning period often went on for months. Employers constantly rotated employees to prevent them from becoming too skilled in a task where they could command higher piece rates. Even after Congress passed the NIRA in August of 1933, employers dodged the minimum wage and hour provisions by falsifying records.[64]

Influenced by the tactics of their social feminist predecessors, strike leaders exposed injustices to the general public. Publicity generated over the plight of the striking children helped the campaign gather momentum daily. Bessie Hillman no doubt compared the faces of these destitute children to those of her own two girls, now sixteen and twelve years old, who were well cared for in a comfortable home. The poverty and desperation of the young, largely female strikers reinforced the necessity of special protection.[65]

In the tradition of the progressive women's network, Hillman solicited the support of women's network dignitaries to lend credibility to the cause. Bessie involved her friends Cornelia Bryce Pinchot, the wife of the Pennsylvania governor, and Frances Perkins, former Hull-House resident and Secretary of Labor, in the strike efforts. Pinchot demonstrated her revulsion against sweatshops and child labor in emotional addresses to bristling crowds. As an ardent labor ally, she continued to assist the Amalgamated's organizational efforts throughout the decade.[66] Meanwhile, Perkins advocated for labor's cause at the national level. Reforms like social security, maternal and child welfare, health insurance, mothers' pensions, and minimum-wage and maximum-hour laws had been a top priority for network women.[67] Now they had a chance to implement these goals. During her tenure in Roosevelt's Cabinet, Perkins helped pen both the Social Security Act and the Fair Labor Standards Act, regarded as the most significant pieces of New Deal legislation.

To the pleasure of the labor women charged with organizing the strikers, state support for the strike surfaced in the Pennsylvania Department of Labor and Industry's official publication. The *Monthly Bulletin* "deplored the conditions of employment which have been imposed on minors between the ages of fourteen and sixteen." Many of the children on strike were sent back to school by truant officers once their circumstances were revealed. Ironically, their truancy had gone unnoticed while they were working for sweatshop wages.[68]

Headlines across the country referred to the striking workers as "baby strikers" and "slaves," and the accompanying articles found a receptive audience.[69] Union leaders argued that by paying "unspeakably low wages," employers had contributed to the misery of the Depression. Civic, political, and religious leaders immediately responded to the allegations. Due to the "seething unrest" in Lehigh and Northampton counties, Allentown mayor Fred E. Lewis initiated a local Anti-Sweatshop Committee that, like the Chicago strikers' breakfast testimonies in 1910, orchestrated a public hearing where one fourteen-year-old girl testified that she received a mere ten cents for two weeks of work. Other abuses began to surface. One shrewd employer withheld five cents from the pay envelopes of girls making five dollars a week for the ice water that they drank on hot days.[70] Impressed by Lewis's example, the Pennsylvania governor, Gifford Pinchot, formed a statewide Commission to Investigate Conditions in the Needle Trades Industry, headed by his wife, Cornelia. She informed this "sweatshop commission" that the average wage in the Pennsylvania shops was $7.54 a week for women, with half the workers receiving considerably less. The average wage in the cotton garment shops was nineteen cents an hour.[71]

Women's network insider and Pennsylvania Industrial Commissioner Charlotte Carr presided over the committee's hearings in Northampton, Allentown, and Bangor in late April and early May 1933. In its July report, the committee confirmed many of the strikers' accusations. In addition to deplorable working conditions, wages were found to be so low that it "was not possible for workers to maintain a decent standard of living." Further testimony exposed instances of women working more than ten hours a day and fifty-four hours a week, but employees stated that they were afraid to report the NIRA violations because "they feared the loss of their jobs." Among the various remedies recommended to correct these problems was the establishment of a "Bureau of Industrial Relations within the Department of Labor and Industry at the earliest possible date."[72] With public indignation aroused by the revelation of the horrendous working conditions, the Amalgamated demanded a permanent organization to protect workers. By the end of the strikes, the union had successfully negotiated settlements that improved the overall treatment of the workers by restricting child labor, providing higher wages, and granting union recognition. With the generous terms of these settlements in place and the union enforcing favorable federal legislation as Potofsky had predicted, ACWA ranks swelled and the organizers regrouped and moved ahead with their campaign.

Union campaign strategy initially dictated concentrating on one locale at a time. Organizers followed this plan meticulously, moving on after each individual victory and leaving the newly established locals to build the union. However, in August 1933 the shirtworkers' secretary-treasurer, David Monas, issued a warning against unstable locals, cautioning that it was not enough "to break the pattern of sweatshops through strikes." Instead, he believed that "the union should be so strong that they will forever deny to employers the power to re-establish such miserable conditions. . . . [L]ocals should enforce contracts and forever express the democratic needs and aspirations of the members."[73] Monas realized that occasionally, as in Allentown, where a local union branch existed, it was not always secure. In late 1934, the Morris Freezer Shirt and Blouse Factory formed a company union that discriminated against ACWA members, forcing the Allentown Amalgamated to wage a second battle.[74]

Connecticut and New Jersey

In the meantime, the drive to organize the runaways spread beyond Pennsylvania. Demonstrating their support for the campaign, but more importantly fearing the loss of their own jobs, the New York City Shirt Workers refused to prepare garments for out-of-town contract shops any longer. They planned a general strike that began on May 1, 1933, when the cutters, immediately followed by the pressers and operators, stopped working altogether. The work stoppage allowed union leaders to concentrate their efforts on the runaway campaign. General organizer Aldo Cursi enlisted the help of Mamie Santora,

Bessie Hillman, and Eddie Gill, who left New York and traveled to unorganized rural areas in New Jersey and Connecticut, where they made rapid progress.[75]

One of the first prongs of the offensive came when the manager of the New York Joint Board of Shirt Workers, Alex Cohen, convinced the small contractors in Connecticut to close their shops for a "holiday." This gave the union the opportunity to expand its initiative and launch a drive against Lesnow Brothers in New Haven, one of the largest shirt manufacturing companies in Connecticut. Employing approximately 550 workers, Lesnow Brothers appeared at the top of Bessie's "List of Shirtmakers in Connecticut." From the inception of the strike, Hillman performed a variety of duties. In addition to establishing local contacts and walking picket lines, she addressed the workers, handed out information cards, worked in the local offices, and generally did whatever was needed for victory. As in Pennsylvania, Bessie Hillman proved instrumental in coordinating organizing efforts in Connecticut, Massachusetts, and elsewhere.[76]

In New Haven and in many other northeastern cities, support for the strikes started with a small group of skilled workers, sometimes accompanied by sympathetic college students, and within a few days attracted massive public interest. The Connecticut State Board of Education sided with the strikers and formally notified the Commissioner of Labor that school-age children were employed in factories. A letter from the Connecticut State Board of Education described the case of "a little girl" working in the LeRoy Shirt Company who "received 37 cents for 24 hours work."[77] While the women in the shops were thrilled with the wage increases guaranteed by union contracts, others found different reasons for relief. Esther Peterson, who helped organize in Connecticut, remembered that "so many of these women and girls— many were merely teenagers—were sexually exploited on the job. A lot of the foremen wouldn't keep their hands off the women. Before the unions, the women couldn't stand up to their bosses or complain about inappropriate touching. If they objected, they knew they risked having their pay docked for some unfounded charge or they wouldn't get a good work assignment. With the union, the workers could hold their heads high and tell the foreman to go to hell."[78] When strikes began in other Connecticut cities, the Lesnow agreement, with its union recognition, wage increases, and arbitration provisions, served as a model for subsequent settlements, with strengthening clauses being added as the drive gained momentum.

The Anthracite Region

Despite mounting successes and cooperation from the members and locals of the United Mine Workers of America, the anthracite region in northeastern Pennsylvania proved the most difficult area to organize. One episode recounted by Theresa Pavlovak, a young garment worker in the anthracite region at the time, illuminates the complexity of the situation. Pavlovak remembered that one day in 1933 or 1934, while she was employed at Rosenau Brothers, she joined a group of women who were "picketing and walking up and down with signs and all" just as the coal miners were coming home from work. Her father, who was a miner, pulled her out of the line and instructed her to go home because she needed the job on which the family so desperately depended.[79] In principle the miners supported the union, but, in reality, striking wives and daughters meant the loss of wages. The extreme poverty of the region significantly hindered the runaway drive. These circumstances propelled Bessie to reformulate her strategy as one that relied heavily on the collaborative tactics of coordination and cooperation, calling a strike as a last resort only after all the possibilities for employer negotiation had been exhausted.

Bursting on the scene in August of 1933, Hillman met with Hazleton Mayor R. Alvan Beisel, quickly winning him over to her side. Peter Swoboda specifically recalled Bessie's meeting with the mayor and felt that she was not given enough credit for her successful coordination of this extremely difficult region.[80] In the meantime, other organizers forged ties with representatives of the United Mine Workers of America, some of whom were subsequently hired as organizers by the Amalgamated. Shortly afterward, S. Liebovitz and Sons, a large enterprise with more than thirty plants, one of which was in Hazleton, agreed to arbitration. By late August, approximately 1,500 garment workers from Hazleton and vicinity had signed with the new local there. In addition to Liebovitz workers, the Hazleton local included employees of the Janov-Abeles, Lakewood, Freeland, Shirtcraft, and McAdoo shirt factories.[81] Primarily because of Hillman's organizational expertise, Hazleton was the only major Pennsylvania garment center to unionize without a strike.

As the campaign accelerated, Bessie pursued as many rural outposts as was physically possible, including Meyerstown, the location of another Liebovitz factory. The drive in Hazleton coincided with and complemented a mass campaign of hosiery workers in Reading, where, after motoring down from New York with Jacob Potofsky and other union organizers and getting less than two hours of sleep, a rumpled Bessie joined the picket line. Undaunted by her lack of sleep, Bessie was "aflame with enthusiasm" when she met with the strikers in the Penn Pants Shop. By sharing her experience as a pantsmaker before any union existed, Bessie Hillman effectively established a sense of camaraderie with the rank-and-file workers. Eventually, 175 of the 290 workers at Penn Pants came out.[82]

Across the region, however, other shops adamantly resisted organization. Hesitant to entrust the job to others, Bessie stayed in Reading for more than two months, struggling to resolve what she described as "the most obstinate case in all the history of the Amalgamated." Runaway shop organizers in Pennsylvania experienced firsthand "the days of repressive working conditions, supported many times by local governments that did not hesitate to use shot-guns, bombs, tear gas, bullets and clubs against strikers of both sexes."[83] Hillman and the other organizers refused to be deterred.

Although Bessie tried to visit home whenever she could, more often her family came to her. Philoine, who maintained a lifelong affiliation with the labor movement, sentimentally recalled that though both Bessie and Sidney tried to make it home every weekend, sometimes the sisters, accompanied by the Hillmans' housekeeper, Beatrice Cox, traveled by train to Pennsylvania and other runaway outposts to see their mother on the picket lines. Philoine's childhood memories evoke pictures of "an exciting life" and having "a great deal of fun learning all the songs of the strikers." Selma, in contrast, was not happy about Bessie's absences from home and found nothing redeeming about riding for hours to share fragments of conversation with her mother in between the chants of picketers.[84] Her attitude probably resulted from the fact that she was still a toddler when her mother started to travel for extended periods. It also reflected the disapproving public attitude toward married women—especially mothers—working outside the home.

According to Bessie, "the life of an organizer was not so easy in those days." In the difficult anthracite region, union organizers were sometimes "turned out boldly."[85] The labor leaders persisted, but even their grueling work and intense dedication to the union cause were not always enough to overcome fierce anti-union sentiment. Employers referred to the strikers as "agitators." The owners of one shirt company wired the State Industrial Commissioner, Charlotte Carr, appealing to her in the name of patriotism to halt the strike against them. They demanded to know: "must this be tolerated in Free America?"[86]

In July 1933, a federal arbitrator intervened in the conflict. Judge Henry Moskowitz conducted a series of hearings where "workers and management in the Reading-Hazleton-Meyerstown-Pottstown-Newmanstown area told their troubles."[87] Testimony that included numerous recitations of long hours, low pay, racism, and six-week "vacations" without any pay surprised not only company lawyers, but even "an old hand at the mediation game" like Moskowitz. His decision in favor of the Amalgamated granted a 15 percent wage increase, time and a half for overtime, union recognition, the abolition of homework, and further arbitration concerning the issue of collective bargaining. Moskowitz recommended that his decision be applied to all of the Liebovitz and Sons shops, not just those involved in the hearing. He issued a statement that recognized the importance of this problem and urged both parties within the industry to stabilize conditions and "to establish firm foundations for the new deal."[88]

In spite of this glimmer of hope, skepticism and an anti-union climate lingered. As widespread unemployment problems intensified, workers became more difficult to win over. Cora Thomas, an unemployed Reading worker who had testified at the federal hearings, blamed her predicament on the union's attempt to organize workers, explaining in a letter to Bessie that "the [nonunion] shop was good enough for the last twenty-five years."[89] Cognizant of the plight of unemployed workers, Hillman reassured Thomas that "we are doing everything we possibly can to expedite the matter and we shall not stop until the girls are put back to work."[90] Labor supporters too tried to placate the dissension; Cornelia Pinchot had already asked "the girls to be patient under provocation."[91] Eventually the tide began to turn. In the late summer of 1933, the National Labor Board (NLB) intervened and began to arbitrate through its new industrial mediation board, which had already become involved in other difficult strikes such as those at Pottsville's H.D. Bob and Phillips-Jones Corporations.[92]

Though progress seemed gradual at best, behind the scenes labor leaders did everything within their power to swing a decision in their direction. In some cases the federal government's support drove a strike to victory. In September, Sidney Hillman telephoned his wife from Washington to tell her that the National Labor Board had requested that the Penn Pants officials appear before it within a week. Bessie was encouraged by the news. She knew that a call from the NLB in all likelihood indicated a positive outcome. As a result of a favorable board decision, Bessie Hillman and fellow organizer, Leo Krzycki, carried the shops to victory.[93] Success in the Reading district was tremendously significant for the entire clothing industry.

Greater Albany Area

With the difficult fight in the anthracite region drawing to a close, Bessie refused respite. In mid-April 1934, she obtained permission from the mayor of Albany, New York, John Thatcher, to distribute handbills advertising a meeting of shirt workers so that she could begin a campaign there. When Rotary Shirt Company officials failed to negotiate, Bessie Hillman called a June meeting for its approximately 200 employees. She explained, "We are not here to deprive you of your jobs but to regulate you in your jobs and to get you a decent living." A vote favoring a strike was taken and with the help of local organizers, Bessie led a strike against the company.[94]

Again union efforts received support from notables. Shortly after the strike began, Cornelia Pinchot answered a call from Bessie and came to Albany, where news of her speeches had already "spread like wildfire." She exhorted the workers to continue their fight for union recognition. Capitalizing on patriotic sentiment, Pinchot declared, "I believe in unions because I am an American." She also encouraged workers to help ensure implementation of the New Deal provisions, pointing out that "only where workers are organized had the NRA been enforced properly."[95] Bessie's oratory complemented Pinchot's wide-ranging appeals and engaged throngs of workers. "Militant, persuasive, and convincing," Hillman fueled the strikers' cause by generating positive coverage in the local papers.[96]

Bessie's diplomatic skills did not, however, always guarantee immediate success. In the early days of the strike, negotiations between Louis Cohen, president of the Rotary Shirt Company, and the union broke down. When Cohen cited escalating violence between strikers and nonunion employees as the reason for closing his plant indefinitely, Bessie accused him of being unresponsive to the demands of the girls who since April had tried repeatedly to reach an agreement to better their working conditions. Frustrated by Cohen's apparent lack of concern, Hillman toed a harder line, declaring that "now he must come to the strikers, they won't go to him."[97]

Hillman's tactic of putting Cohen on the defensive provoked an almost immediate response. With negotiations halted, picketing continued, and other union organizations in the Albany area pledged their support to the strikers. Hillman expanded her base by enlisting the support of local clergy. One local paper reported that a recently unionized taxi company had refused to give nonstriking workers at the Rotary plant a ride home. As support for the strike grew, in mid-June

Bessie took a short break from her Albany activities to head a delegation bound for the Cotton Garment Code hearing in Washington.[98]

Playing their New Deal trump card, union representatives announced, "NRA officials in Washington would be urged to withhold NRA tags for Rotary shirts in the event that the plant is reopened with strike breaker employees, until the strike has been settled."[99] The Rotary strike persisted for ten days, until June 28, when company management appeared before the regional Labor Board, which recommended that the union's demands be granted. Within a week both sides had approved an agreement. The settlement that resulted from the first strike in the Capitol area granted union recognition, wage increases in all departments, equalization of work, reinstatement of workers fired for not making the minimum, and back pay to those who had not received sufficient wages.[100] The celebration, however, was short-lived.

Heartened by the favorable outcome of the Rotary strike, in October Bessie commanded a central position as strikes erupted in Artistic Shirt Company plants in Albany, Troy, and Kingston, where, as ACWA organizer Mary Hillyer observed, company unions were already "dying . . . without really having lived."[101] Hillman coordinated an extensive educational campaign, distributing leaflets and quietly sending organizers into workers' homes to talk up unions and the Amalgamated. She urged local clergy to support the union drive openly and to speak at union rallies. National union officials were impressed by the orderly nature of the campaign. In late October 1934, Joseph C. Jacobson, for the Artistic Shirt Company, and Jacob S. Potofsky issued a joint statement: "The company has entered into a collective bargaining agreement with the Amalgamated Clothing Workers' Union, for the members of their Union. All differences are composed. Wage questions will be a subject matter for investigation and adjustments in the next couple of weeks."[102] Both sides expressed satisfaction with the outcome of the strike.

Workers celebrated the triumph for the 1,200 involved with a festive Victory Ball held at Kingston union headquarters. When the new cutters' Local 196 in Troy held its first meeting, newly appointed union Vice President Jacob Potofsky attended, but "Sister Hillman was barred because she was a woman."[103] At the time, men comprised the entire cutters' local, so the exclusively male guest list was accepted without question. Despite the fact that the majority of the workers and a number of the organizers in the Capitol district were women, the men-only rule stood unchallenged until the night of the cutters' union twenty-fifth anniversary dinner in 1958, where Bessie Hillman was, ironically, an honored guest.

On to Ohio

With her work in the Albany district complete, in the late fall of 1934 Hillman, assisted by organizer Josephine Kaczor, led the effort to organize the Kaynee Company, a major Cleveland employer. With the workers already out on strike, once again the Hillmans secured the support of Reverend Francis Haas, now an official for the General Code Authority of the NRA. Haas wrote to Reverend Theobald Kalanaja in Cleveland: "I am informed that the workers in the Kaynee factory are for the most part members of your parish. This fact places you in an unusually strong position to assist them, and I beg to repeat my request that you will help them publicly and privately in their struggle for better working conditions."[104] This time-tested strategy proved crucial in the vital ethnic neighborhoods of Cleveland. Parishioners and company officials responded positively to Haas's request. The National Labor Relations Board (NLRB) began hearings between officials of the Kaynee Company and leaders of the ACWA in October and late November, and those hearings revealed discrimination against married women. Only single women were hired back after slow periods; married women were not rehired.[105]

Adept at addressing mass meetings, Bessie Hillman, Jacob Potofsky, and Beryl (Ben) Peppercorn spread the strike from the three Cleveland plants to the nearby Bucyrus plant. Strikers, claiming that they had been discriminated against because they were union members, refused to work under existing conditions and demanded both union recognition and a 10 percent wage increase. In turn, the company claimed that wages were not involved and charged the union with striking before the NLRB had reached a decision.[106] Hired guards protected workers who disregarded the strike and continued to work in the plant. Local newspapers printed stories about the strike, accusing the union of driving factories out of Cleveland by initiating acts of terrorism against workers.[107] Strike leaders braced themselves against more vociferous attacks. Union organizers received another blow thirteen days later when a state judge issued an injunction that forbade picketing.[108]

During the winter of 1934–1935, Bessie Hillman temporarily relocated to Cleveland to lead the strike from a cramped downtown office while the picketers held their ground in the streets. Behind the scenes, Jacob Potofsky explored every possible angle in the quest for support. He urged Bessie to discuss the formation of a separate women's local and to employ a paid union representative to help "the girls win the non-union girls" to the side of the Amalgamated.[109] In the process of soliciting strike support, Hillman apparently won over even the Cleveland

Police Department: After a blizzard, policemen voluntarily shoveled the sidewalks for the picketers.[110]

William Dawson, field secretary for the Cleveland Federation of Labor, urged the community to support the strikers by appearing on the picket line and "then see to it that the demand for union labels, shop cards and buttons are pushed to a successful conclusion."[111] Unanticipated community support boosted the strikers' morale. On December 15, 1934, the National Labor Relations Board ruled that, in accordance with Section 7a of the National Industrial Recovery Act, which granted workers the right to bargain collectively with their employers through representatives of their choice, the employees of the Kaynee Company could hold an election by secret ballot under the supervision of an NLRB representative to determine whether they desired to be represented by the company's Employees' Council or by the Amalgamated Clothing Workers of America.[112] Ultimately, the workers chose to affiliate with the Amalgamated. Unwilling to relent, however, the Kaynee Company continued to dispute the issues until early in February 1935, when the NLRB forwarded a letter to the company advising Kaynee officials that the Amalgamated "is the exclusive agency which you have recognized and with which you should deal."[113]

Bessie and Sidney Hillman spoke to crowds of jubilant strikers as they returned to their jobs. The Hillmans' proud daughters recognized their mother's prominent place in the campaign. In the spirit of the victory they wired Bessie: "Did you doubt that good old ACWA would let you down? The union is behind us, Sidney Hillman is behind the union, and you ought to know who is behind him. More success to you in future endeavors. Will be happy to see you home again."[114]

Real Progress

The union experienced a number of successes during the NIRA years. Union efforts included policing violations of the NRA's cotton textile code. In the Albany area alone, the Rotary Company and fifteen other (nonunion) shirt and cotton manufacturers were "denied the NRA label because of their failure to observe the code labor requirements!"[115] Workers were routinely threatened with the loss of their jobs unless they signed an agreement to accept whatever wage the employer decided upon. Intimidation against those who joined the union was widespread. Companies continually warned workers that if they became union members, the firm would move out of town or go into bankruptcy. Under such circumstances the union campaign became imperative.

Although in May 1935 the Supreme Court abbreviated the ACWA's organizing campaign by declaring the NIRA unconstitutional, by then the union had already made great strides, bringing some 25,000 shirt workers into its fold between 1933 and 1935.[116] Women organizers were the mainstay of the Amalgamated's runaway shop campaign. Bessie's years of experience and proven ability to communicate her ideas to working-class men and women made her an exceptional organizer. Her efforts went largely unpublicized, but the successful organizing techniques she masterminded won over workers in the communities she visited and gained the respect of her male union colleagues as well. Even in the grip of the Depression, when work slowed to two or three days a week, union workers were grateful that agreements with their employers protected them from wage cuts.[117]

In some cases, union settlements with employers came only after bitter strikes; in others, proof of majority membership was sufficient to procure an agreement. By continuing to reach separate agreements with outside contractors in Philadelphia, the ACWA helped to eliminate abusive practices in the garment trades years before federal regulations like the Fair Labor Standards Act addressed the same problems. Organization of the cotton garment industry introduced the Amalgamated to hundreds of small communities. Dress shirt firms were the first to come under Amalgamated agreements, and the organization soon infiltrated the work clothing, washable service, nightwear, and miscellaneous garment and sportswear industries.[118]

Bessie Hillman in the Campaign Aftermath

Undoubtedly, labor suffered a setback when the demise of the NIRA and its minimum-wage provisions left northern manufacturers struggling to compete against the southern plants where wages were routinely cut. After 1935, employers again threatened to move—south this time—while those that planned to stay in the Northeast proposed lowering piece rates and restoring longer hours. In addition to the obstacles presented by employers, the union confronted renewed resistance from manipulated public opinion and physical violence directed against its organizers. Nevertheless, to labor's surprise, unlikely groups such as merchants occasionally stood behind the union's boycotts of goods produced by strike-ridden plants.[119]

Among the first to stand in the front lines to oppose the hostile anti-union climate of the late 1920s and early 1930s, Bessie Hillman expanded her profile and her power base, first in Philadelphia and then throughout the runaway havens. Initially her efforts were barely mentioned in union accounts, and were virtually ignored by the wider press. By the conclusion of the campaign, however, Hillman's "persuasive and engaging personality" drew attention. Mildred Jeffrey, a young organizer during the "baby strikes" in Allentown and Northampton who eventually headed the United Auto Workers' Women's Bureau, re members that, to her credit, the union president's wife, Bessie Hillman, "never put on airs."[120] Hillman was one of the most highly qualified women organizers involved in the campaign. With the experience of past battles etched in her mind, throughout the Depression she used her ability to "raise public interest in the labor movement."[121]

Under Bessie Hillman's guidance, the direction of the runaway campaign assumed a conciliatory approach whenever possible. In keeping with Addams's lessons, Hillman's philosophical preference was to negotiate with employers and to win the workers' demands through arbitration. ACWA leaders attempted to avoid violence if at all possible. In the face of vehement opposition, as in Philadelphia and in the anthracite region, Bessie's persistence paid off. Like her women's network counterparts, who worked with national leaders to formulate public policy for workers, Hillman worked in conjunction with union men to shape the overall character of the ACWA's organizational efforts. By 1937, even male union leaders recognized that "the story of the shirt workers is never complete without Bessie Hillman."[122] Hillman proved her worth as a leader while continuing to advocate for women.

Her most vital contribution was her ability to reach out to the entire community in presenting an educationally based organizing strategy that broke through multiple layers of resistance. The billing of the runaway drive as a fight for bread and roses, chronicled in a 1935 union publication—*Bread and Roses: The Story of the Rise of the Shirtworkers, 1933–1934*—successfully attracted workers into the ACWA. Hillman and the other organizers ensured that potential members were well informed about the plethora of benefits that the union provided for its members. As New Deal legislation finally began to address worker concerns dating from the progressive era, Hillman helped the union entice workers with an even more comprehensive program.[123] As her family's manager, Bessie knew what working-class families were up against when their income did not meet living expenses. With the establishment of union banks, workers could now aspire to home ownership. When the women reformers at the national level failed in some of their efforts to enact national health insurance and public housing programs, the union picked up the slack with its cooperative housing projects and medical care facilities.

Other examples of the advantages of union membership included the revitalized union educational programs offered at the local level. During the 1930s, the ILGWU and the ACWA capitalized on the Works Progress Administration's sponsorship of educational programs. The programs were designed both to attract new members and retain the old ones. Hillman consistently emphasized the lasting value of workers' education to ensure member loyalty. Local unions promoted lectures, circulating libraries, and scholarships to labor summer schools. The union supported cultural and recreational events, including plays, picnics, dances, and athletic teams for workers "learning how to play."[124] As they became more versed in union history and goals, the workers became politicized through these programs as well.

The reform spirit inherent in the New Deal assisted in merging political action with union education programs. Union organizers reinforced the concepts of unity and mutual support with messages that differed from those of the past. Many new members were uncomfortable with socialism yet interested in social and economic improvement. As the runaway campaign drew to a close, and the politicized ACWA moved toward mainstream politics, members were encouraged to embrace the New Deal and to reelect Roosevelt.[125] Union women easily related to Eleanor's political presence and social reform ideology and readily organized to ensure her husband's reelection. The entire union supported FDR at every turn. By 1936, union members like Hillman flocked to register with the American Labor Party so that they could vote for Roosevelt without falling under the Democratic Party's banner. Encouraged by state intervention on behalf of workers, many union members cast their first non-Socialist votes in the election of 1936.[126] In turn, the union's endorsement of Roosevelt was rewarded by the passage of the Fair Labor Standards Act in 1938. Politics and the rights of workers were intricately linked for the first time in union history. Political leaders recognized that workers, especially women workers, had interests to be protected. Once workers were inducted into the union, they anticipated doing more than paying dues and reaping benefits; they expected to vote and to participate as citizens. What JoAnn Argersinger concluded was the case in Baltimore can be extended to the ACWA in its entirety: The union used the hard economic times as a pivotal point from which to remake itself to continue its pursuit of industrial democracy.[127]

Hillman's support of the Roosevelt administration reflected the pleasure she took in the ability of the Women's Bureau appointees to influence New Deal policies. Even after the demise of the NIRA, both Eleanor and Franklin Roosevelt stood staunchly behind labor. By 1935, the Wagner Act (which upheld the worker's right to join a union); the leadership of the new Congress of Industrial Organization in organizing women; the efforts of the Textile Workers Organizing Committee with its focus on the unionization of southern workers, including large numbers of women; and the passage of the Social Security Act had attracted women into the union ranks.[128]

Bessie's activism undeniably benefited from her place as the "first lady of labor." From the 1930s until his death in 1946, Sidney Hillman's name was "a household word, appearing frequently on the front pages of the nation's newspapers and magazines."[129] Doors opened for Mrs. Sidney Hillman, and her status allowed her to avoid much of the criticism that other women activists experienced. However, the inclination of the press to conflate her identity with that of her husband meant that in more than one instance she failed to receive the recognition she had earned.

Hillman's increased visibility during this period offers insight into how she viewed her own work. Although observers were initially surprised at the sight of an international union president's wife "on the job doing picket duty," Hillman admitted that her prominent status in the union probably protected her from the dangers that plagued others. "I've never been struck. I've never been arrested. The police don't pick me up for some reason. I think my face is my affidavit."[130] Making optimum use of the spotlight, Bessie welcomed any publicity that furthered the union cause. As her command of English grew, her still-detectable Yiddish accent and colorful stories of life in the trenches impressed workers. At every opportunity she recounted—and, some might argue, self-aggrandized—her gallant version of the union's history, highlighting her own place in it. One New York newspaper reporter went to great lengths to point out that "Mrs. Hillman owes her present eminence to yeoman work in the pioneer days, rather than to the courtesy afforded the wife of the union's president."[131]

Although Sidney Hillman rarely praised his wife's accomplishments in public, his unqualified support of her work enabled Bessie to merge her public career with family life.[132] Her capacity to combine marriage, motherhood, and militancy complemented the working relationship that the couple sustained throughout their years together. They both frequently relied on this bond when "they faced severe problems that brought worries and distress."[133]

From the earliest years of the Depression, in her own union Bessie quietly guarded against the potential threat presented by division between union men and women or—worse yet—among the women themselves. Hillman's combined emphasis on class solidarity and community, as well as her integrationist approach, reflected her early socialist teachings, Hull-House mentoring, and trade-union affiliation. While their counterparts like Pauline Newman and Rose Schneiderman opted to forgo union organizing for government positions, Hillman, Bellanca, and Santora continued to move toward fusing industrial democracy into the "American way of life."[134] Regardless of their official affiliations, the network women remained committed to women's rights and social justice.

By the mid-1930s, buoyed by the creation of a welfare state partially shaped by their own hands and a prolabor presidential administration, Bessie Hillman and other labor women expanded their feminist goals from organizing workers within the framework of organized labor institutions to securing a broad agenda that sought "full economic citizenship," demanding and readily anticipating state intervention on behalf of women workers, often in the form of special protections. According to Dorothy Sue Cobble, these labor feminists "breathed new life into the social feminist" movement by linking it to the vitality and power of organized labor.[135] The fight they waged for full economic citizenship and "its associated entitlements," including the opportunity to work in one's chosen profession and access to key economic resources, proved to be the dominant force in the Women's Bureau network in the postwar era.[136]

An examination of the degree of cooperation among labor feminists explains why and how female institution-building survived in multiple venues after 1920. It also amplifies the place that working women played in welfare-state policy formation, from the grassroots level to the federal arena. Women's political participation and cooperation across class lines continued to grow after suffrage was won. While scholars fault middle-class women for failing to involve a substantial number of working women in their reform activities, Bessie and a multitude of others kept the tenets of their progressive faith alive, infusing it into American life. Hillman and her women's network contemporaries, including Dorothy Jacobs Bellanca, Mamie Santora, Frances Perkins, Eleanor Roosevelt, Mary Anderson, Elinore Herrick, Hilda Worthington Smith, Rose Schneiderman, Pauline Newman, Charlotte Carr, and Cornelia Bryce Pinchot, among others, deserve credit for the direction that industrial democracy took toward guaranteeing improved working and living conditions for workers. New Deal network women provided a crucial link to the 1960s and demonstrate that labor feminism is one of what Gerda Lerner calls the "long-unacknowledged sources" of the modern women's movement.[137]

6 The Power of Labor Feminism: Organizing the Laundry Workers and the Second World War (1937–1946)

By the late 1930s, Bessie Hillman could be counted among the nation's leading labor feminists. Hillman personified what Dorothy Sue Cobble calls "the other women's movement," a group that "put the needs of working-class women at its core" in seeking to better the lives of women.[1] Sustained by the camaraderie of women such as Rose Schneiderman, Pauline Newman, Elisabeth Christman, Dorothy Bellanca, and many others, Hillman seized the opportunity to advance the cause of industrial democracy. These leading labor women not only sought equality and justice for women in the workplace, but also fought to secure broader recognition in American society in general. By the end of the 1930s, federal policies incorporated, at least in part, the demands of the labor feminists who insisted that the reach of organized labor needed to be expanded, and called for a broad democratic social movement to combat fascism and function as a foundation for a new and different social and economic order in this country. This same agenda "contained the seeds of what came to be the early civil rights movement."[2]

The creation of an industrial democracy that encompassed both women's rights and civil rights loomed large on the horizon of Hillman's vision. A willing populace and influential associations with prolabor forces put these dreams within reach. To move ahead, Hillman used her Women's Bureau network connections, as well as those with civil rights organizations outside the realm of middle-class reform circles. As a young immigrant organizer, Hillman had learned from Jane Addams's example that multiple affiliations were the most effective strategies in building a framework for real social and economic progress. Now in her early forties, Hillman positioned herself to effect changes.

When her older daughter, Philoine, left home to enter Oberlin College in 1936, Bessie Hillman reconfigured her proximity to union headquarters with a unique solution: She traded residences with union vice president and close family friend, Jack Potofsky, moving her family out of the suburbs and into his apartment at 237 East 20th Street. This arrangement worked well for both families. Jack Potofsky and his second wife, Callie, wanted to raise their children away from the congestion of the city, and with the move Bessie and Sidney Hillman now lived within a matter of minutes from the action at union headquarters.[3] Bessie's resilient character enabled her to maintain a harmonious home life despite the tensions and anxiety generated by Sidney's continued involvement with his secretary, Tecia Davidson.

Organizing the Laundry Workers

The Hillmans' relocation coincided with the conclusion of the runaway campaign. The successes in the northeastern organizational drives, along with a number of developments in the labor arena, encouraged Bessie and other Amalgamated leaders to turn their attention to the plight of thousands of unorganized laundry workers—predominantly women—across the country. Passage of the National Industrial Recovery Act (NIRA) in 1933 had prompted the successful runaway strikes and pushed union membership to an all-time high. By 1936, the Amalgamated claimed 160,000 members.[4] At the midpoint of the decade, the passage of the Wagner Act ensuring workers' rights; the creation of the National Labor Relations Board's enforcement mechanisms; and the creation of the Congress of Industrial Organizations (CIO), for the purpose of organizing workers on an industry-wide basis, compelled the laundry workers to organize. Women's network insiders posted at the federal and state levels promised additional assistance. New Deal working women's advocates Eleanor Roosevelt and Frances Perkins collaborated with female leaders in the Democratic Party, such as Molly Dewson, to continue the work of progressive-era reformers in their quest for protective legislation.[5]

At the same time, feminists inside the ranks of labor were instrumental in convincing Amalgamated leaders to expand their efforts to include African-American women. Hillman's mentor, Jane Addams, and a number of other prominent progressive women were early supporters of the National Association for the Advancement of Colored People (NAACP) and the National Urban League, the primary agencies assisting blacks in the interwar years.[6] The Women's Bureau of the Department of Labor, under the leadership of Mary Anderson, also paid special attention to African-American women and to laundry workers, hiring Helen Brooks Irvin, an African-American economist, to advise the bureau on the needs of black women workers in 1919.[7] Bessie Hillman shared the long-standing commitment of WTUL President Rose Schneiderman and others in the League who heralded the inclusion of a laundry code in the short-lived NRA as "a basis for an organization in the laundry industry." After prodding Sidney Hillman for years to actively recruit laundry workers into the Amalgamated's ranks, in 1937 Schneiderman and her feminist colleagues finally turned the tide.[8] By that spring, the ACWA began making overtures to the tens of thousands of laundry workers.

National estimates regarding the total number of laundry workers in the 1930s varied dramatically. Some surveys took the large numbers of domestic laundresses and small (mostly Chinese) family-owned laundries into consideration, whereas others ignored them altogether. The 1930 federal census counted 310,379 laundry workers in the United States. More than half of these workers, or 175,641, were women.[9] An *Advance* article estimated that in 1930, there were 356,000 women who worked in private homes rather than commercial laundries.[10] A 1947 article, "Women in the Labor Force," published under the auspices of Frieda Miller's Women's Bureau, relied on 1940 federal census data to inform readers that, nationally, women constituted 77.7 percent of laundry industry workers.[11] Women also constituted the largest number of laundry workers in commercial laundries and private homes.

New York state reigned as one of the industrial centers, with 29,381 laundry workers in 1937. Close to 80 percent of New York laundry workers were women. Of these women, roughly 25,000 worked in New York City, home to the greatest number of commercial laundries in the country.[12] Other large cities, including Philadelphia and Chicago, also hosted large concentrations of laundry workers. A large segment of the urban industry consisted of workers in "family service" power laundries, which "relieve[d] several million housewives of much of the heavy task of washing and ironing household linen and family wearing apparel," and linen supply house workers, who laundered uniforms and linen for hotels, restaurants, hospitals, and barbershops.[13]

The organization of mostly black women laundry workers in New York marked the culmination of an arduous struggle over three decades to organize a diverse group of workers. From the turn of the century, the American Federation of Labor's International Laundry Workers' Local 280 (a shirt ironers' union) and Local 290 (a steam laundry workers' union) had officially welcomed both black and white members. In 1925, however, just as black workers began replacing immigrant workers in greater numbers, the Urban League's investigation of the laundry industry found that although "no discrimination was ostensibly employed[, black workers] are sometimes debarred by high initiation fees." Although black men "were on the same terms as white men," union leaders admitted that employers were "not looking for them."[14] Discriminatory hiring practices by employers plagued the industry even after World War II. Herbert R. Northrup explained: "Except for a few colored wholesale drivers, laundries rarely employ Negroes as routemen (truck drivers) on the grounds that white women object to their presence at the door." Employers, however, readily hired black women as workers because they were always willing to work for less than white women. By 1930, some 6,300 "Negro Females" represented the largest single group of operatives in the New York City laundry industry. Black workers, particularly black women, were concentrated in production jobs, especially in ironing departments. Routemen and mechanics were nearly all white men, and office help was the domain of white women workers.[15]

General racial prejudice against black workers, especially black women workers, stalled attempts to organize the laundry workers.[16] Interracial tensions between black and white female employees escalated in the years after World War I, when southern blacks seeking work migrated to urban areas in the North. In New York, the practice of replacing white laundresses with so-called "Negro 'girls[,]' because [management] could get more work out of them," caused resentment.[17] More desperate for work overall, black women were, as one woman put it, "nervous about our jobs," and less likely to complain to their employers about their situations lest they lose their jobs altogether. The bosses routinely told black laundry workers that they had to "work for less money than the white girls." The bosses then "incited one against the other and later they cut the white girls, saying they could get the colored girls cheaper."[18] Racially based wage differentials prevailed throughout the 1930s, despite the introduction of the NRA laundry code.[19] African-American women earned the lowest wages of all the workers in the industry. One laundry industry survey conducted by the Women's Bureau revealed that the median full-time wage for white women in eastern cities in 1938 was $17.80 per week, whereas black women earned $10.25 per week.[20]

Historically, unions led by white men showed little empathy for the problems of women or black workers, rarely reaching out to either group despite their promises to the contrary. An official history of the Amalgamated detailed the factors that these leaders believed hindered organization: "many workers considered themselves temporary, skilled groups showed no interest in organizing unskilled women workers, and the great diversity of races and nationalities presented difficulties."[21] Some, like former laundry worker Dollie Robinson, considered this rationale nothing more than a lame excuse. According to Robinson, "Laundry workers were easier to organize because their conditions were so bad that they were willing to make sacrifices to improve them."[22] Labor feminists concentrated their efforts in and around New York City, to change the direction for the majority of workers in commercial laundries: namely, black women in the lowest-paying positions.

Even as Bessie honed her organizing skills by tackling runaway shops in the mid-1930s, she stayed closely connected to the organizational problems in New York and the other industrial centers.[23] She joined the effort to organize the laundry workers as soon as she could. The immediate task of coordinating grassroots organizational efforts to encourage laundry workers to forge connections with the local labor movement fell to Bessie's longtime ally, WTUL President Rose Schneiderman. Despite the WTUL's failed attempts to organize the New York laundry workers in the early 1900s, Schneiderman and other League members resumed their work in the 1920s, this time with public opinion on their side.[24] They worked in conjunction with the Urban League to overcome the long-standing gender and racial differences among laundry workers that had previously discouraged them from organizing. Schneiderman and her friend Noah Walters, eventually general secretary of and organizer for the Negro Labor Committee, laid the groundwork. Attempting to resolve what Rose Schneiderman later referred to as "the Thirty Years War," they approached the laundry workers to seek a coalition between the two laundry workers' unions (Shirt Ironers' Local 280 and Steam Laundry Workers' Local 290), the Trade Union Committee for Organizing Negro Workers (sponsored by the Urban League), and the New York Women's Trade Union League (NYWTUL). Although Schneiderman resigned in frustration from the joint committee over the failure of a 1928 strike, the connections she helped to establish proved valuable once Roosevelt was inaugurated.[25]

The first year of the Roosevelt presidency presented an optimum time for organization efforts to resume. Given the Roosevelt administration's prolabor sentiments, the influence of the Women's Bureau on the New York State Department of Labor, and the presence of strong women labor leaders connected to trade unions and the WTUL, organizers working to unite the laundry workers faced fewer obstacles. In 1933, armed with a state minimum-wage ruling initiated by Frieda Miller, then head of the New York Bureau of Women in Industry, and the minimum-wage division of the state Labor Department, city laundry workers precipitated a series of strikes permitted under NIRA Section 7a.[26] Although some of the strikes ended within a matter of weeks, the owners of Colonial Laundry, a large linen supply company in Brooklyn, refused to settle.

Women's activism intensified strike publicity and attracted the attention of city officials. Not only did the 1934 strike garner publicity across the city, but the WTUL's New York branch also intervened on the side of the strikers, involving prominent women such as Cornelia Pinchot as picketers. Dollie Robinson, an African-American working at Colonial Laundry when the strike broke out, recalled that the conflict ended only after "Mayor LaGuardia turned off the water so that the clothes couldn't be washed."[27] Although strike activity ceased shortly afterward, within a few weeks it became apparent that the workers' victory was only a partial one. Acting on behalf of the Laundry Workers' Local 135, the NYWTUL submitted a "Memorandum on [the] Violations of Contract" to NRA authorities. The memorandum methodically chronicled complaints against Colonial Laundry. The most serious infraction concerned the continued employment of strikebreakers while former workers remained unemployed.[28] Nonetheless, the Brooklyn strike provided a "great impetus to growth" for the laundry workers' organization.

Workers continued to expose the unbearable working conditions that existed in the majority of laundries even after the strike ended. The Trade Union Committee for Organizing Negro Workers voiced complaints regarding the grueling nature of excessively long workdays, often ranging from "7:30 A.M. to 7:00 P.M. with but one-half to three quarters of an hour for lunch, and a full six day week, the wages were disgracefully low and utterly inadequate—from eight to ten dollars weekly."[29] After spending years in the wet environs of the laundries, workers, regardless of gender, came to expect arthritis and other ailments. A Women's Bureau publication contained the account of a woman in a hospital laundry department who lamented the rigors of her job: "I mangle [work with a steam roller] wet clothes and heavy spreads. I iron everything a person can think of. I operate a press machine which is hot like the devil, and after working in the heat of the laundry I have to sweep the whole place and wash the machinery."[30] Even male pressers at the top of the occupational hierarchy complained bitterly. For decades, they "earned their bread with sweat and hard labor . . . standing all day operating machinery that dries the marrow of one's bones and sets one's head reeling."[31]

The 1935 Wagner Act helped to transform the laundry workers' attitudes toward organization. The act guaranteed workers' right to select their own unions by majority vote, the right to strike, and the right to boycott and picket their employers. The act was put to the test in March 1937, when a strike by more than 1,000 laundry workers in the Brownsville section of Brooklyn finally united the workers. Shortly after that strike ended, a number of workers, led by organizer Helen Blanchard from the NYWTUL and assisted by African-American laundry worker Charlotte Adelmond, conducted another strike involving nineteen cash-and-carry laundries. In addition to the support of the Wagner Act, citywide contracts offered additional protection where the NRA and state attempts to regulate wages and hours had failed.[32] When the strikers approached the American Federation of Labor–affiliated International Ladies Garment Workers' Union for help, "they would not take them in, they did not want them."[33] Bessie Hillman later equated this experience with the clothing workers' rejection by the United Garment Workers in 1910, when the UGW "turned a deaf ear to us when we said the tailors wanted to be organized."[34]

Irate WTUL leaders announced that the "industrial organization of women becomes impossible within the framework of the AFL and because organization of women is the League's fundamental objective, the local leagues are free to extend their activities to aid in the organization of women workers wherever the opportunity offers."[35] When the United States Supreme Court struck down a minimum-wage law, leaving women in the laundry industry "at the mercy of unscrupulous employers," Rose Schneiderman recognized that "the time [had] come when the trade union movement must take a hand in helping to build the organization of the laundry workers." Schneiderman and a coalition of union leaders, including Maurice Firestone, the secretary of the United Hebrew Trades; Julius Hochman, the general manager of the Joint Board of the Dress and Waistmakers' Union; and Isidore Nagler, the general manager of the Joint Board of Cloakmakers, asked for the Amalgamated's assistance.[36]

Labor feminists, who had always ranked the laundry workers "among the most exploited of all groups of workers," would have to chart a different course.[37] For the first time since its inception, the WTUL formally supported the Amalgamated Clothing Workers of America—a union that by 1937 had severed its ties to the AFL to join the new Congress of Industrial Organizations, an organization committed to organizing workers on an industrial rather than a craft basis.[38] Now that the ACWA no longer had to compete for the laundry workers with its AFL rival, the ILGWU, the possibilities seemed limitless.

Dollie Robinson rejoiced because the workers had "finally found someone in the Amalgamated that would help them and give them a hand." According to Robinson, even before the strikes began, Charlotte Adelmond, a follower of black nationalist Marcus Garvey and an activist with the Harlem Labor Center, had started to organize women workers in her own home. Robinson believed that Adelmond, rather than the WTUL, "really started the laundry workers' union."[39] Meanwhile, Rose Schneiderman encouraged the continued use of white organizer Helen Blanchard, because she believed that "colored women had an inferiority complex and wouldn't give the same respect and attention to a colored as to a white organizer."[40]

Abraham Brickman, a laundry trade association worker with a background in social work, helped the League assemble an organizing committee, which included Schneiderman and Walters; the latter would act as the new organizer for Local 280, the shirt ironers' union. Only a multifaceted effort, assisted by "many friendly progressive individuals" outside the union, including the United Hebrew Trades and the Committee for Organizing Negro Workers, could effectively overcome persistent racism and result in a strong organization. Schneiderman sought out her longtime friend Sidney Hillman, and on June 16, 1937, laundry worker leaders began to confer with the ACWA with the intention of becoming part of an international "to give [the workers] strength and prestige in negotiating employer contracts."[41]

Fresh from their successes with the statewide runaway campaigns, in the summer of 1937 Amalgamated leaders Bessie Hillman and Jacob Potofsky joined the laundry workers' campaign, which was already running under its own momentum. Organization of the laundry workers presented the opportunity to add thousands of new members to the ACWA's rosters in the name of civil and women's rights. For Hillman, organization of the laundry workers also furthered her broader commitment to social justice. In her eyes, discrimination against blacks and women was symptomatic of a larger pattern of exploitation.

Members of the former AFL International Laundry Workers' Union (including the shirt ironers and steam laundry locals) joined with the members of the Laundry Drivers' Local 810, who had become dissatisfied with the leadership of the AFL's Teamsters' Union, to formally withdraw from the AFL and affiliate with the CIO.[42] Now called the United Laundry Workers' Local 300, on August 6, 1937, the workers began operating under the jurisdiction of the Amalgamated Clothing Workers of America's citywide agreement. WTUL organizer Helen Blanchard formally announced the affiliation.[43]

Within a few months, proud Amalgamated officials declared that the recently organized laundry employees now faced employers "not as a single union of 30,000 workers, but as one division of an army numbering over a quarter of a million, powerful in industry and respected throughout the nation."[44] Unionization proceeded unimpeded under the Amalgamated's banner. By 1938, roughly 80 percent of the Greater New York laundries were under contract. A total of twelve separate locals, built around the various sections and location of the industry, fell under the jurisdiction of the Laundry Workers' Joint Board (formerly United Laundry Workers' Local 300).[45] By 1944, the Laundry Workers Union included 45,000 members, with membership in locals in Chicago, Philadelphia, and San Francisco and smaller cities as well.[46]

Affiliation with the Amalgamated strengthened the laundry workers' position in their battles against uncooperative employers. Contracts assured recognition of the union's right to negotiate on behalf of members. ACWA representatives established specific clauses dictating grievance mechanisms. When employers in the now-closed shops refused to hire blacks, the union "would take up the matter as a grievance."[47] Collective bargaining helped to win a minimum wage of 35 cents an hour, with overtime guarantees of 44 hours a week for women and 48 hours a week for men; shorter hours; and better conditions overall, including vacations, sick leave, and daily rest periods. Contracts promised employment for eleven months of the year. Because the laundry workers were excluded from coverage under the Fair Labor Standards Act (passed in 1938), unionization was crucial.[48] ACWA feminist Bessie Hillman, and African-American laundry worker turned union activist Dollie Lowther Robinson, remained in the vanguard of the fight to extend coverage to laundry workers under the Fair Labor Standards Act—a struggle that lasted for more than twenty years.[49]

Questions about why the AFL failed to support the laundry workers persist. Although the obvious explanation is that the craft-based AFL did not want to organize an industrial union, some, like historian

Arwen P. Mohun, contend that racist AFL leaders had no interest in organizing the large numbers of African-Americans (particularly women) in the industry. Thus poised to organize, but abandoned by the AFL, the laundry workers welcomed the overtures of Sidney Hillman and the Amalgamated.[50] The Amalgamated also benefited from the laundry workers' alliance. Branching out beyond clothing workers to encompass service workers, especially black women workers, not only strengthened its numbers but also supported the Amalgamated's 1938 "Resolution on Race Tolerance," which denounced race hatred. For the moment, the ACWA's organizing efforts transcended the discriminatory standards maintained by the more conservative unions that favored the needs of skilled white male workers, and the Amalgamated adhered to its broad civil rights platform opposing "discrimination on the basis of race, creed, color, political or religious belief."[51] This empathy for black workers, urgently in need of protection from discriminating employers and racist union leaders alike, brought the union closer to industrial democracy.

At the union convention in May 1938, laundry workers' organizer Meyer Bernstein boasted that "the unlimited cooperation of our national office made it possible to organize 30,000 laundry workers." Keynote speaker New York Mayor Fiorello LaGuardia recognized Bessie Hillman "for her fine work" in leading the Laundry Workers' Organizing Committee. Under her guidance, the committee pledged to continue its national drive to educate and organize all laundry workers, including between 5,000 and 6,000 in New York City alone who still toiled in hot, humid, unventilated conditions where "hearts and spirits were mangled along with the sheets."[52]

Some laundry workers believed that once they affiliated with the ACWA, union leaders would ignore racial and gender inequities. These doubts proved well founded, as official Amalgamated publications overlooked the importance of women and minorities in organizing commercial laundry workers, instead focusing on a later effort to organize the white duck (uniform and apron manufacturing) industry.[53] The union contracts accepted distinctions based on gender, including sexual division of labor, gender-based wage differentiation, and the notion of a family wage for men but not for women.[54] For example, the family and wholesale laundry workers' contract ranked jobs in order of perceived skills and corresponding pay scales, with the men's jobs appearing at the top of the list and women's job categories at the end of the list. In rare cases where both women and men held the same job, like "flatwork packers," men made 65 cents an hour and women 52 cents an hour.[55] As long as racial and sexual discrimination were accepted in mainstream American society, male union leaders rarely worked to challenge racism in hiring practices and on the shop floor. Seeking to offer "as much assistance to them as possible," Bessie Hillman would be the first to intervene on behalf of the "half white and half Negro" laundry workers.[56]

In 1938, Sidney Hillman bypassed Noah Walters for the position of the Laundry Workers' Joint Board manager and instead appointed Walter Cook, a white accountant with no laundry business experience. After nine months as joint board manager, Cook had thoroughly offended the rank and file, who criticized his inept negotiations with laundry owners, leaving Noah Walters, the assistant joint board manager, to resolve contract difficulties. When Bessie Hillman invited the members of the women's chorus to her home, Cook spoke for an hour and a half "denouncing his fellow officers and exalting himself." He was trying to give a repeat performance at a business agents' meeting when Bessie Hillman took the floor to declare that he "was out of order." Articulating rank-and-file demands, at Bessie's insistence, Gus Strebel, "one of the best loved and most highly respected men in the movement," replaced Cook as the joint board manager.[57]

Directing Educational Activities

As was the case in the runaway shop campaign, Bessie Hillman's ability to appeal to rank-and-file workers was instrumental in bringing the laundry workers into the union ranks. As a result of her efforts, in early 1937 she was appointed the educational director for the laundry workers, taking an office in the Laundry Workers' Fifth Avenue headquarters. Hillman immediately began to create a comprehensive program of social and cultural activities whereby laundry employees could seek solace from the material and psychological demands of their jobs.[58] Bessie Hillman went out of her way to ensure that the New York locals conducted union-sponsored educational and recreational programs "without any discrimination."[59] Her efforts with the laundry workers in New York served as a model for educational programs in ACWA locals across the country.

In March 1938, Bessie Hillman initiated the "Laundry Workers News" column—the only regular *Advance* feature written by a woman.[60] These columns announced upcoming activities and highlighted workers' achievements. "Dolly Lowther Gets Honor from Hudson Shore Labor School" headlined the September 1940 page, the first issue to dedicate an entire page to laundry workers' news.[61] Bessie Hillman took her work very seriously. When asked by a New York reporter why she did not relocate to the nation's capital with Sidney, when he began his wartime job as associate director of the Office of Production Management in 1941, Bessie replied, "I have a job to do and I can't take time out to leave the job and become a society woman in Washington."[62]

From Hillman's first days as an organizer in the WTUL's Training School for Women Organizers in 1914, education had been an integral part of the organizing process. She spoke to numerous audiences of workers regarding her philosophy: "Education work in a union cannot be separated from the rest. . . . It is part of the whole working community. As workers organize, they also learn. You do not stop learning when you have finished formal schooling."[63] As the labor movement evolved, so did the goals of worker education, moving from socialist-influenced "workers' education" (which concentrated on changing society, as exemplified by the WTUL training school and Bryn Mawr Summer School for Women Workers) to the more narrowly focused "labor education," which trained workers in the fundamental aspects of how to run a union.[64] In the attempt to attract and retain new and more diverse members, the revitalized ACWA education programs of the late 1930s were similar to the ILGWU's programs initiated by Fannia Cohn. Cohn, along with her colleague Rose Schneiderman, had been making an effort to organize black women workers since the 1920s.[65]

As education director, Hillman realized that she had to continue to recruit new members and help them to assimilate into the Amalgamated. Bureaucratic pronouncements by male union leaders, though they had galvanized ethnic workers in the past, no longer attracted significant numbers of union members. This new generation of members was more inclined to respond to localized grassroots efforts, so Bessie constructed what she hoped would be an appealing program. Relationships forged across race and gender lines seemed best effectuated by the union's wide-ranging educational and recreational programs for workers and their children. New union members, more comfortable with popular forms of entertainment than with intense indoctrination, appreciated Hillman's effort to combine labor education with leisure activities.

Like Fannia Cohn, Hillman wanted to meet the needs of as many workers as possible and to foster unity and solidarity among workers of various racial and ethnic backgrounds.[66] Though at first Cohn distrusted collaborations with the middle-class women involved in the worker education programs housed at both Bryn Mawr and Brookwood Labor College (beginning in 1921), she soon relented and "allowed herself to be drawn in." Unlike Cohn, Hillman routinely welcomed cross-class efforts, including those that involved the Women's Trade Union League, trade unions, and students. When these schools condensed their courses into one- or two-week-long programs or closed their doors altogether, because of diminished funds during the Depression, garment industry unions intervened and resurrected worker education.[67]

By 1935, Fannia Cohn "had been relegated to the background," because of ideological differences with the ILGWU leadership, particularly international President David Dubinsky. Cohn's rigorous approach centered on overcoming class struggle and promoting interracial solidarity rather than on minimizing various ethnic cultures as the ILGWU leaders preferred.[68] Bessie Hillman's union experienced less internal dissension regarding educational matters. In the Amalgamated, education directorships were viewed as apolitical positions. As Sara Fredgant, an ACWA education director in Philadelphia in the 1940s and 1950s, explained: "An education director loses the effectiveness and becomes a politician when they become part of the decision making process."[69] Hillman maintained affable relations with a union leadership that allowed her to forge a vital place for worker education in the ACWA.

Hillman helped to erect labor education programs and recreation centers at strategic locations so that members across Greater New York had access to the numerous activities offered. The centers offered classes in English, public speaking, parliamentary procedure, and trade-union problems. Cultural activities included a union chorus, a drama group, and dancing lessons. Basketball, baseball, swimming, and bowling ranked among the most popular sports.[70] Group activities also helped to foster worker camaraderie. She encouraged participation in the chorus and in plays, such as *The World We Make*, where three laundry workers portrayed themselves in a Broadway play.[71] The multiple opportunities these neighborhood centers created for workers, especially those that addressed the workers' immediate needs, were reminiscent of what Hillman experienced as a young immigrant under the guidance of the social feminists of Hull-House. The increased cultural awareness and expanded knowledge of trade unionism assured member loyalty while simultaneously encouraging a sense of community.

Education that dispelled prejudice and encouraged tolerance became a crucial link in the process of achieving industrial democracy and elevating the workers' collective consciousness. Hillman believed that "the white workers begin to understand the problem of their Negro colleagues and the Negro begins to taste the fruits of non-discrimination."[72] By the 1930s, the majority of union recruits were native born, so Hillman's priorities concentrated on alleviating racial prejudice rather than on Americanizing workers. Racially mixed locals and their accompanying activities helped her achieve this goal. Sara Fredgant recalled that educational conferences that included both black and white male and female workers helped whites "realize how intelligent [blacks] were." When black men and women began to speak and ask questions, Fredgant observed that the whites became cognizant of "dealing with real human beings who have their problems and who understand what's going on." These conference interactions were a vast improvement over the "isolation and provincialism" that whites were used to in the workplace.[73]

During her eight-year stint as the education director of the New York Laundry Workers' Union (from 1937 to 1945), Hillman devoted herself to "broadening the worker's horizon" through education. She carefully crafted programs that extended well beyond immediate economic goals, promoting spiritual as well as material well-being in the union. Her sensitivity to workers' needs and desires meant that large numbers of workers, especially black workers, derived emotional satisfaction from their union membership. In the case of black laundry workers in particular, Hillman prioritized class solidarity and racial justice, to empower minority workers by heightening their awareness of union entitlements, and encouraged their participation in recreational and educational activities. Although it is difficult to judge the level of integration the various aspects of the education programs achieved, some pictorial evidence survives indicating that certain groups, such as the ACWA chorus, were racially mixed.[74] Nevertheless, as many of the educational and recreational programs were neighborhood based, demographics often limited opportunities to mingle with workers outside of a single racial or even ethnic group. Occupational segregation in the workplace further restricted interactions between races.

The Laundry Workers' educational programs aided in the organizational quest by informing workers how to reduce the number of hours worked, increase wages, and attain other protective measures. More importantly, they helped sell the union to workers who were not yet entirely convinced of its necessity, by introducing them to the additional benefits union members enjoyed. The Hillmans were convinced that member loyalty should be a high priority. Proponents of workers' education agreed with Bessie Hillman, who felt that new workers needed to become familiar with and enjoy the advantages of union membership before their loyalty could be ensured.[75]

Workers who came of age during the Depression had only minimal knowledge about the advantages of union membership. Union leaders like Hillman hoped that once they were briefed through education, this new generation of union recruits would seek the economic advances, cultural benefits, and sense of workplace empowerment made possible by union activity. Bessie Hillman contended that only when membership figures were secure could a national program of education be instituted "that will not only bring to the new members the past struggles and progress of our great union, but . . . will make them active participants in activities of their communities, becoming more useful citizens."[76] Promoting both gender activism and civil rights, Hillman applied her philosophy equally to all union members, regardless of gender, race, or ethnic background. She invited all to participate in union-sponsored activities, and whenever possible Hillman supported the advancement of black women workers to union leadership positions. In locals where the majority of members were black women, as in Philadelphia Local 170 and Local 791, members elected black women to the presidency.[77]

Hillman's union duties were virtually doubled by her appointment, in 1937, as director of the new Department of Cultural Activities (later renamed the Department of Education). The creation of this department attempted to accommodate the flood of new members driven into the Amalgamated during the Depression. Maintaining her title of Educational Director for the Laundry Workers' Union, Hillman worked to centralize the union's educational programs. A November 1937 article in the union's official periodical, the *Advance*, explained that the Department of Cultural Activities enabled workers to "gain opportunities for education on the economics of the clothing industry or learn how to argue against a wage cut by emphasizing the worker's role as a consumer." Drawing from tactics of the National Consumers' League, the Amalgamated department promoted consumer consciousness by encouraging women to use their purchasing power as a political weapon. In all respects the Department of Cultural Activities ran programs modeled after those of the Laundry Workers' Union. Department workers dispensed advice for local unions on how to plan a dance, organize a drama group, or develop any number of athletic teams. Leaders hoped that these activities would "engender the Amalgamated Spirit" by creating a working-class consciousness.[78] Although the union education department performed important functions, its offices were staffed primarily by women who were not regarded as part of the upper echelon when it came to leadership positions in the union.

J.B.S. Hardman, one of the first directors of the ACWA education department, member of the General Executive Board, and eventually editor of the *Advance*, disputed this comprehensive approach to education. Despite the fact that during his tenure in the ACWA education department, his efforts to "transform study into social action" were less than successful, he felt that by failing to encourage immediate and direct political activism through its current educational programs, "the union neglected to exploit a rich learning situation."[79] Hardman viewed the members who joined the ACWA during the Depression as "NRA babies" who needed immediate instruction regarding the union's political stance. Some hardliners saw the Amalgamated's existing educational program as too peripheral to the long-term goal of fortifying labor's economic and political power. Hardman and a few old-school socialist sympathizers held out for an independent labor party even after the Hillmans transferred their political allegiances to Roosevelt and eventually the Democratic Party.[80]

Union member Hyman Isovitz characterized the culturally based offerings as "a meaningless assortment of 'athletics, singing societies, and dramatic groups.'"[81] Echoing Hardman, Isovitz believed that this approach would fail to encourage effective political activism. He warned against what he perceived as the broader implications of this educational policy, arguing that it would produce a new breed of upwardly mobile and politically apathetic unionists "fit for bureaucratic routine."[82] Countering this sentiment, one official union historian voiced the opinion of the majority when he came down on the side of the Hillmans, asserting that "the formal education program has always reflected the needs of the union."[83]

With ACWA membership rising by tens of thousands and the union firmly entrenched in the Congress of Industrial Organizations, by the late 1930s officials paralleled the effort of other unions (such as the ILGWU, the International Association of Machinists, and the United Mine Workers) and turned toward the dual tasks of training union leaders and meeting the rank and file's demand for general education.[84] The ACWA's educational activities, like those of the ILGWU, were indeed influenced by long-standing leftist factionalism. Daniel Katz has observed that as the ILGWU attempted to construct a singular working-class identity, "[t]hese activities, including coursework, social activities, recreation, and political and cultural pageantry[,] served as the medium through which workers from distanced racial and ethnic groups formed a militant union consciousness." The coming of the war in the 1940s hastened this transition, as "multiple cultural identities" were assimilated or even displaced entirely by patriotism.[85]

Deflecting criticism, the 1938 General Executive Board biennial report contained a section entitled "Education Publicity and Research," which focused on "Intellectual Mobilization of the Membership." The report outlined the intended goals for new members who needed to be dedicated to the union's ideals, organizational needs, and purposes.[86] As the majority of participants in cultural activities were women, the logical solution was to expand workers' education and to design it with women's desires in mind.

To accommodate women-centered needs, in 1939 Sidney Hillman recruited Esther Peterson to work with Bessie as assistant director of the Department of Cultural Activities. Peterson's credentials included a master's degree in teaching and five years of experience as the recreational director at the Bryn Mawr Summer School for Women Workers. Interacting with workers and meeting women like Rose Schneiderman, Fannia Cohn, Bessie Hillman, Hilda Worthington Smith, and Eleanor Roosevelt at Bryn Mawr transformed Peterson's professional direction completely. From the mid-1930s forward, she cast her lot with the labor movement.[87]

Embracing the longtime progressive goal of training women to be leaders, Hillman and Peterson appealed to female union members to rise from the ranks for promotion. Together the two instituted summer programs and taught classes where union representatives with potential leadership qualities from across the country could learn about union history, organizing, and political problems.[88] Union members attended weekend institutes and took correspondence courses. Hillman, Peterson, and other labor leaders encouraged workers to attend the WTUL-sponsored, interracial Hudson Shore Labor School (formerly Bryn Mawr), established in 1935 under the direction of Hilda Worthington Smith, the former dean of Bryn Mawr.[89]

WPA Workers' Education Program instructors trained future rank-and-file leaders at the school. The way instructors incorporated the workers' experiences into their courses impressed Dollie Lowther Robinson, a student at Hudson Shore in 1940. In English, science, and economics classes, they created an atmosphere that "encouraged students to bring their work and life experiences to bear on what they read and heard there." With course and living expenses and even child care provided by the union, the students wrote papers, performed skits, and received their diplomas. In effect, the combination of courses in theory and advocacy offered tools for practical application. Students who completed the program went back to their locals to present reports. Women summer school graduates who attempted to advance occasionally found positions within their union locals.[90]

Perhaps to placate the large number of women in the union, male union leaders paid lip service to the concept of workers' education at the national level, but never provided sufficient funds to satisfy the actual demand. Programs that had anticipated paid staffing were forced to rely on volunteers. Without substantial backing, women who were training to be leaders could not afford to wait for an opportunity to present itself; most were forced to resume their old jobs rather than pursue leadership positions. Despite the efforts to empower women through education, the number of women in upper-level administrative posts remained few throughout the 1930s. Union men failed to subscribe to a new gender consciousness, and consequently Bessie Hillman, Dorothy Bellanca, and Mamie Santora were the only female members of the Executive Board for the first forty years of the ACWA's existence. Although Bessie Hillman worked as an unpaid volunteer, the two directorships she held in the 1930s and 1940s were both important jobs staffed by full-time paid workers in other unions.[91]

Women Workers on the Home Front

To demonstrate support for the United States entry into World War II, by early 1942 union leaders transformed the Department of Cultural Activities into the Department of War Activities. Labor feminists in the union, like Bessie Hillman, used the war to recruit women and black workers. True to the union's motto, "To touch the worker from cradle to grave," Bessie Hillman continued to develop a wide range of educational programs even after she became immersed in the war effort. Hillman made a special effort to extend activities to the laundry workers, inviting them to bring their children on free outings to Palisades Amusement Park and Bear Mountain. She also saw to it that free music lessons were available throughout the year to support singing, as well as dramatics, dancing lessons, and an orchestra comprised of children aged eight to sixteen. One of Hillman's proudest moments was the Laundry Workers' Children's Broadway production of *March to Victory* in the spring of 1944.[92]

Wartime organizing provided additional opportunities for white and black workers to interact. While organizing the laundry workers in the late 1930s, Bessie Hillman had gained "valuable experience" as she interacted with black workers for the first time in her life. Reiterating her impressions about "how well they worked together, in the factory as well as in union meetings," Hillman consistently reaffirmed the union's commitment to the organization of blacks, promising to work for them "to the best of our power."[93] By 1939, the East Midtown Committee for Religious and Racial Tolerance listed Hillman as a supporter, and by 1950 she was devoting "much of her time" to the CIO's Committee to Abolish Discrimination (known as the Civil Rights Committee when Bessie first joined it in 1940). Throughout her career, she remained a contributing supporter of the NAACP and the National Council of Negro Women.[94] In 1945, she attended a discussion led by Lillian Smith, southern civil rights activist and author of the best-selling novel *Strange Fruit*, designed "to create a better understanding between racial and religious groups."[95] Whereas many other union leaders, particularly those in the AFL, hesitated to affiliate openly with the civil rights movement, for Bessie Hillman (an early supporter of the black-only March on Washington movement), Rose Schneiderman, and other labor feminists, civil rights and labor rights were synonymous.[96]

Bessie Hillman personalized her public commitment to civil rights by mentoring Dollie Lowther Robinson, a promising young black laundry worker. With Hillman's encouragement, Robinson began to pursue formal education as a union leader in 1940. Bessie Hillman acted on her principles in appointing Robinson as the assistant educational director for the Laundry Workers' Union in 1941. Working closely with her mentor, Robinson witnessed Hillman's attributes firsthand. Characterizing Bessie with her "wonderful accent" as "honest to a fault," Robinson and her coworkers appreciated Hillman's straightforward manner. "She would tell you if she thought you were wrong or right, you knew where you stood. All the workers knew that whatever she did, she did it from the heart."[97]

Hillman's friendship with Robinson evolved during the early years of labor's involvement in the civil rights movement. Their camaraderie extended well beyond the boundaries of the workplace. Bessie took Dollie under her wing and together the two women went out into the field to organize. All too aware of the cultural disapproval of most interracial friendships, a grateful Robinson recalled that Bessie supported her unconditionally. "I know it must have been hard on her at times to really champion me. But she helped me survive."[98] Decades later Dollie Robinson recollected, "In the forties when we made trips to Washington she would sit on a park bench and eat a sandwich with me for lunch. Bessie Hillman could have eaten any place but the restaurants were not serving blacks in those days. In later years we returned to Washington to attend inaugural balls of presidents and to any and all of the restaurants. We shared and enjoyed it together."[99] Bessie Hillman transcended racial barriers long before it became acceptable to do so. Civil rights became her "deepest interest."[100] Eventually, thanks in part to Hillman's unwavering assistance, Robinson earned her law degree from New York University, obtained a number of administrative posts within the union, and went on to serve as the New York State Secretary of Labor and as Special Assistant to the Director of the Women's Bureau of the United States Department of Labor.[101]

When Robinson's daughter, Jan, was born in 1951, Bessie asked, "What is it 'you people' [and you never worried about Mrs. Hillman's 'you people,' because she'd say it for everyone. It had no racial connotation. It was 'you people,' and she meant 'you people.'] 'What is it you people do when children are born? Do you take them to church?'" Robinson answered affirmatively and Bessie replied, "We're gonna do that then." Direct and to the point, Bessie became a godmother to Robinson's daughter, a role she took very seriously. Hillman was very close to Jan, who spent every childhood summer at the Hillmans' Point Lookout, Long Island, beach house. Hillman's ability to conduct her personal and professional activities devoid of discrimination became one of her greatest legacies.[102]

With the union's organizational drive interrupted by the outbreak of the Second World War, black and white workers joined "in the common determination to do their utmost" for the war effort.[103] For many women on the home front, contributing to the war meant working in the defense industries. Although a small number of union workers sought higher-paying jobs in heavy industry, for the majority of garment workers mobilization brought "almost no discernible change."[104] As was the case during World War I, some apparel manufacturers converted their factories to produce military supplies, including uniforms, mattress and parachute covers, and knapsacks, but for most ACWA workers the jobs they had held in peacetime were the same ones that they worked during the war. Women's Bureau Director Mary Anderson observed that women in stores, laundries, restaurants, and garment factories were "still faithfully doing the work they had always done," though on a national level black women laundry workers may have been more likely to abandon their jobs to seek higher-paying work in wartime production plants. Some black women did find employment in wartime plants; however, evidence suggests that the U.S. Employment Service referred white women to clerical jobs and low-paying, unskilled work in manufacturing and channeled black women into domestic service and laundries.[105] Regardless of their race, women remained marginalized in the industrial sector and underrepresented in all professional careers.

In January 1941, President Roosevelt appointed Sidney to the post of Associate Director General of the Office of Production Management. Hillman invited his daughter Philoine, a student in economics at

Washington Square College (now New York University), to accompany him and his staff to Washington, suggesting to her that she would learn more there than she would in school.[106] Philoine Hillman flew with her father and his staff to the nation's capital, where she worked as a secretary in the wartime Office of Public Relations. Hillman, his staff, and his daughter shared an apartment during the week and flew back home to New York every weekend to be with family. While her husband and older daughter were in Washington, Bessie remained in New York with her younger daughter, Selma, who was attending a local drama school.[107]

Bessie stayed behind in New York to champion the defense effort from her position as the director of the War Activities Division of the Amalgamated, which she did from her newly relocated office in union headquarters at 15 Union Square. Assisted by longtime ACWA members Esther Peterson, Dollie Robinson, and Bess Blumberg (wife of ACWA Vice President Hyman Blumberg), Bessie Hillman galvanized defense activities in New York City: drawing up lists of blood donors, taking up collections, selling war bonds, and conducting salvage drives. She served on local price-control committees where, in an attempt to halt inflation, she encouraged women consumers to abide by the Office of Price Administration regulations, admonishing women not to purchase products above ceiling prices.[108]

In a time when most husbands opposed their wives' working outside the home, Sidney Hillman was an exception, in that he supported his wife's union activities. Furthermore, his union salary allowed Bessie to pursue an unpaid career in the union—a two-for-one deal that was most likely crucial to the union, especially in its early days. Although she held a union card all her life and consistently identified with the working class, thanks to Sidney's salary as ACWA president, the family maintained a comfortable middle-class lifestyle. Even as the Hillman daughters enjoyed the privileges of a middle-class childhood, Bessie and Sidney were able to imbue their children with Jewish traditions and culture, including a high regard for education. Philoine graduated from Washington Square College with a degree in economics, and Selma eventually graduated from the American Academy of Dramatic Arts.[109] Bessie's activism and her labor feminist colleagues left a lasting impression on her daughters. Philoine remembers that when it came to the reinvigoration of the women's movement, she "didn't know what all the fuss was about." All the women who surrounded the Hillman children were already professional women, working in their chosen fields as labor organizers, lawyers, or politicians. Philoine later realized that "that was not how the rest of the world was."[110]

Despite the fact that her own daughters were grown, Bessie Hillman readily identified with the difficulties that working mothers encountered. She was especially concerned about the children of women war workers. To her dismay, the War Manpower Commission, composed entirely of men, assumed that a woman's primary job was childrearing. In an effort to discourage mothers of young children from entering the labor force, the federal government kept childcare facilities to a minimum throughout the war. Although Women's Bureau leaders realized that "a number of young mothers who will provide the sole support for their families" should have access to "the essential facilities for child care," the bureau's official policy toward employing women with children under the age of sixteen read: "Except as a last resort, the Nation should not recruit for industrial production the services of women with such home responsibilities." To this end, even Secretary of Labor Frances Perkins sought to "prevent the spread of the day nursery system."[111] Even after 1943, when the Federal Works Agency finally began to fund daycare centers for defense workers, through the Lanham Act, and New York State was forced to provide funds for local communities, these combined endeavors failed to meet the demand. The number of childcare facilities remained insufficient, and the inaccessibility and limited hours did little to alleviate the high need.[112]

As a member of the wartime Child Welfare Committee of New York and the CIO's representative to the Governor's Committee on Child Care, Hillman waged a "worthwhile fight for adequate child care." Confronting state CIO officials, she argued that "there is more than enough money available . . . for the building of adequate child care centers for working mothers in great numbers in every community in the state of New York."[113] Within the Amalgamated, she supervised the establishment of comprehensive childcare centers, complete with dancing, singing, dramatic, and orchestra lessons. Reasoning that "if expanded child care and recreational facilities were available, more women could assume greater work responsibilities and undertake training for jobs at higher levels," Bessie Hillman and the Amalgamated led the fight for child care in the postwar years. By 1968, the ACWA had become "the first union in the country to initiate labor-management sponsored childcare centers."[114]

Until the end of the war, Bessie, in her own words, was "busily engaged at the General Office with war activities."[115] Yet, in spite of her preoccupation with her union responsibilities during the war years, Sidney Hillman's precarious health weighed heavily on her mind. Sidney's physical well-being had concerned Bessie since her days as a young organizer in the Chicago shops. He had a tendency to be too intense and to work himself into the depths of physical and emotional exhaustion. Whenever he was under severe stress, Sidney's health suffered. While still a relatively young man in 1924, he underwent major stomach surgery. Following the organization of the laundry workers, in the late fall of 1937, he contracted double pneumonia, and his doctors ordered a period of "prolonged convalescence" in Florida. Bessie stayed at his side for months, keeping him informed about union business (with the help of daily correspondence from Dorothy Bellanca) and trying to bolster his sagging spirits. Bessie clearly worried about her husband's emotional state as he grew apprehensive about events unfolding during his absence.[116]

In the spring of 1942, within weeks after his position in the Office of Production Management was discontinued due to an administrative restructuring, he suffered a third and severe heart attack that left him "flat on his back" for weeks in Doctors' Hospital in Washington. Sidney sank into a deep depression. In an effort to lift her husband's low spirits, in May Bessie met with David Niles of the War Production Board to request that President Roosevelt "send him a special message or take a minute to say hello to him on the phone . . . to give him the incentive that he needs [to get well]." Apparently Roosevelt had done this once before, when Sidney was "in a similar neurotic condition," and "the family was convinced that that telephone call saved his life." Bessie's appeal worked, and within a matter of days, FDR sent Sidney a letter wishing him well. Hillman was released from the hospital in July.[117]

Both during and after Sidney's convalescence, Bessie's union post allowed her to shape the ACWA's wartime domestic policies with his whole-hearted support. In her *Advance* "Education Department" column, she shared advice and information with the rank and file about coping with the daily hardships imposed by the war. By August 1943, the name of the column was changed to the "Amalgamated Civil Defense Committee News." Hillman used the reconfigured column to ask union leaders to recruit workers as volunteers for civilian defense activities such as teaching first-aid classes. Requests for wartime assistance accelerated when Bessie Hillman assumed the vice chairmanship of New York's Municipal Labor Committee of Civilian Defense in the fall of 1942. She shouldered an additional responsibility when, in November, Chairman James G. Blaine of the federal Civilian Defense Volunteer Office designated Hillman a labor representative and called upon her "to act with us in helping formulate our general policies and in carrying them out." Upon accepting the office, Hillman asserted that "labor is eager to serve the nation not only in the shop or factory, but in every phase of war activity on the homefront."[118] During the final year of the war, Amalgamated members donated more than half a million dollars to the war effort.

Every day Bessie Hillman enthusiastically appeared at her downtown union office to direct the Department of War Activities' efforts by conducting book drives, coordinating Russian clothing drives, and sponsoring blood donor days. Women garment workers volunteered at home while their male family members made their sacrifices on the battle lines. One of the most popular programs undertaken by the War Activities Department was the "Hostess Course" for young women members. Course graduates were awarded certificates entitling them to serve as guest partners to sailors and soldiers at union-sponsored dances and events. From "the gray ladies" rolling bandages for the Red Cross to Sidney Hillman's official post in Washington, union members' wartime participation assumed gendered meanings.[119]

Despite Bessie Hillman's persistent advocacy for workers' civil rights, racism continued to be one of the most difficult problems facing the Amalgamated on the home front. Prejudice pervaded even the blood donor program, in which, in compliance with Red Cross standards, workers separated donor blood according to race. Dollie Robinson was in charge of obtaining blood from blacks, but found that because of their resentment of the segregation policy, "it was hard to get." In the spring of 1943, as Hillman was leaving for a meeting at the National Red Cross headquarters in Washington, Robinson urged her to expose the problem by telling those attending the meeting "how much trouble it is to separate black [blood] from white [blood] and how senseless segregation is for slowing us down." Eventually the agency heeded Hillman's calls. Robinson recalled that as the war progressed, "no one stopped to segregate the blood as long as it was red."[120] More determined than ever, Bessie pushed for education to help ease racial intolerance.

The most obvious change for Amalgamated women war workers occurred among black women. Wartime labor shortages generated the possibility of upward job mobility for black women. While future Secretary of Labor Arthur Goldberg pushed for sweeping legal reforms to end American segregation, Sidney Hillman and Eleanor Roosevelt sought to advance civil rights in the context of the workplace by advocating federal policy changes directed toward securing defense jobs for black workers.[121] However, even though employers were willing to hire black machine operators and pressers, white union members resisted sharing the workplace with them. Jennie Matyas, an ILGWU Executive

Board member, concurred with her black coworker Maida Springer's account of the white workers' response, explaining "that the rank and file was like any cross section of society. As the number of black workers increased in the industry . . . whites developed a fear that blacks would take over."[122] Bessie Hillman and Esther Peterson, codirector of the Department of War Activities, refused to be dissuaded. They went into the apparel shops to help integrate them. Winning the women over through sheer determination, the two women "paved the way for every new minority hire."[123]

For previously unorganized black women workers, unionization not only provided opportunities to learn new skills at increased wages, but also allowed oppressed workers to achieve some measure of control over their lives.[124] Fannie Allen Neal, a great-granddaughter of slaves, was hired at Reliance Shirt Company in Montgomery, Alabama, during the war. To ensure her own job security, she mastered the only pattern-marker job in the plant. This upset other workers, who chided Neal because she held a "white man's job." Certain that she would not be fired, Neal retorted, "This is my job!"[125] Neal was paid fifty-six cents an hour, when all the workers knew that the white man who had held the job before Neal had made a dollar an hour. Thus, despite the efforts of people like Hillman and Peterson, blacks had a difficult time getting jobs in large numbers in wartime.[126] Cases like Neal's, which involved both race and gender discrimination, persisted even when union war contracts guaranteed equal pay.

Labor feminists backed the African-American civil rights leaders' use of the war as an opportunity to protest employment discrimination. A. Phillip Randolph, of the Brotherhood of Sleeping Car Porters, issued a 1941 "Call to Negro America to March on Washington for Jobs and Equal Participation in National Defense," arguing that if a democratic America continued to discriminate in the workplace based on race, it "belies the principles for which it is supposed to stand." Before the march could occur, the Roosevelt Administration responded to Randolph's pressure and the accompanying support from the CIO by issuing Executive Order 8802 in July 1941. Intended to end discrimination in industries vital to war production, the order created an independent agency, the Fair Employment Practices Commission (FEPC). In spite of its weaknesses with regard to women workers, the FEPC "legitimized black protest" for the first time within the federal government. Nevertheless, black workers realized few major gains, especially after the attempt to establish a permanent FEPC and a full-time employment policy after the war fell flat, "breaking the tenuous hold of the black working class on industrial work in the postwar era." However, the campaign for a lasting agency united trade-union leaders and the NAACP and a conference on civil rights evolved out of this coalition. Despite these advances, historian Eileen Boris maintains that the nation still suffers from an FEPC that "came too late" when it was finally re-created as the Equal Employment Opportunity Commission (EEOC) by the Civil Rights Act of 1964.[127]

As international leaders decided the terms of the postwar peace, soldiers displaced women workers across the country as they returned to their homes and the jobs they had held before the war.[128] For the most part, though, the increasing number of unemployed women did not include ACWA members. They remained largely unaffected by the demobilization because the needle trades were predominantly female.[129] In the Amalgamated, men still held the more skilled, higher-paid jobs as cutters and pressers. Because these positions tended to be held almost exclusively by older men who had spent years as apprentices, they remained in their positions during the war. In the hard-goods defense industries, such as the auto industry, women entering the plants in large numbers during the war disrupted the prewar sexual division of labor.[130] For the majority of Amalgamated women, however, their wartime experiences reaffirmed rather than challenged prewar gender differentiation, instilling in labor feminists a further sense of purpose.

On a personal level, wartime work enabled Bessie Hillman to solidify some of the friendships she had forged in previous decades. Union insiders Bess Blumberg and Dorothy Bellanca were among Bessie's dearest friends. From the 1930s forward, Esther Peterson and Dollie Robinson joined the extended union family, which often gathered at the Hillmans' home and seaside cottage. When the Hillmans visited friends, their daughters often accompanied them. Philoine recalls many happy times spent in the company of union officials and political leaders and their families, especially at the home of Pennsylvania governor Gifford Pinchot and his wife Cornelia Bryce Pinchot. Bessie spoke to Rose Levin, wife of longtime Chicago union leader Sam Levin, at least once a week by phone. She had befriended Rose in the early 1930s when Sam had experienced an extended illness; Bessie had "left her home and became the constant companion of Mrs. Levin."[131] She also continued to correspond regularly with noted WTUL leaders and political activists Mary Anderson, Pauline Newman, Elisabeth Christman, Rose Schneiderman, and Frieda Miller.[132] Eleanor Roosevelt, who immersed herself in, and eventually became a premier leader of, American women's political culture, also exerted a major influence on

Bessie Hillman. The two friends shared many of the same progressive ideals.[133] Education, civil rights, and women's rights were paramount concerns for both women.

The Politics of Labor Feminism

Amalgamated women expanded their political goals in a variety of ways during the Roosevelt years. As working women across the country mobilized to serve the war effort, the patriotic propaganda encouraged political activism. As Dorothy Sue Cobble explains, "labor women represented organizations with millions of members, ample treasuries, and an impressive degree of political and economic clout."[134] In the summer of 1936, garment unionists, including Rose Schneiderman and Fannia Cohn, created the American Labor Party (ALP) to enable socialists to vote for FDR without registering with the Democratic Party. Bessie Hillman actively participated in the ALP's Women's Committee from 1936 until 1944.[135]

During the Roosevelt campaigns, Bessie Hillman worked tirelessly to reelect the president. She combined her knowledge of education with politics to enlist support for Roosevelt. Along with the Hillmans, labor leaders overlooked the support that FDR garnered from Dixiecrats (southern Democrats), who vehemently opposed civil rights, in return for a promise to enact the platform of progressive reformers for the first time at the national level. In 1944, with Franklin Roosevelt's election to a fourth term crucial to labor interests, Bessie Hillman and other union leaders held countless meetings to discuss their strategies for the upcoming election. With large numbers of male voters serving overseas, Hillman drew on her political acumen and appealed to the women of America, "who now held the balance of power in their votes to work together to get as many women as possible to the polls." She also worked in conjunction with the New York Chapter of the National Council of Jewish Women to increase the number of eligible female voters, by helping members to obtain their citizenship papers, and with the League of Women Voters to coordinate a six-session course designed to assist women unionists in understanding "our present conflict and to realize our stake in the future."[136]

In an aggressive reelection drive, ACWA women and men canvassed neighborhoods and organized parties and parades. Activists warned minority women about the consequences of political apathy. Funded by the union's political action committee, Bessie Hillman organized several rallies complete with popular speakers and entertainers, including Sam

Jaffe and Zero Mostel, in the last weeks before the election. Gender-based activism by female union members culminated in late October with a "Special Women Voters' Edition" from the *Advance*.[137] Amalgamated efforts paid off. Assuming a large part of the credit for the election outcome, union members celebrated Roosevelt's victory.

Even while simultaneously involved in the war effort and Roosevelt's campaign, Bessie Hillman remained active in the Laundry Workers' Union. In April 1945, at a dinner in her honor, she welcomed new members of the Laundry Workers' Joint Board to the union. With the cessation of the war, Bessie devoted the last few "Department of War Activities" columns in the *Advance* to discussions of leisure activities for laundry union members during peacetime and a fall symposium, entitled "The Union Tomorrow," held at the Hudson Shore Labor School. After the war, the formal educational activities of the ACWA resumed, and by 1946 the Amalgamated established a refurbished educational department under the direction of Robert Levin, who intended to "unite political education with action and New Deal leaders."[138]

The Hillmans shared in the jubilation that marked the end of the war, yet the loss of numerous friends and relatives in Europe cast a shadow over the victory celebration. Bessie was distraught to learn that seventeen of her family members, including three of her sisters and one brother, had perished in the Holocaust. Her other brother lost his life fighting in the Far East. All of Bessie's in-laws, with the exception of one of Sidney's brothers, were lost as well.[139] In April 1945, FDR's death dealt a severe blow to the couple who, besides being staunch political supporters, counted themselves among the inner circle of Roosevelt associates. In May 1945, Bessie faced yet another sad occasion when Mary Dreier called on her to present a eulogy at Margaret Dreier Robins's memorial service.[140]

The innumerable losses she experienced in the course of less than two years failed to dim Hillman's spirit. She continued to function even after the most devastating loss of her life. On July 10, 1946, Sidney Hillman succumbed suddenly, at the age of fifty-nine, to a massive heart attack. With his passing Bessie lost her partner of more than thirty years. Although their marriage was sometimes difficult, for Bessie the loss was profound. Later that year, the death of one of Hillman's dearest friends, Dorothy Bellanca, compounded her grief.

With Sidney gone, internal conflicts erupted among union officials, threatening the cohesion of the ACWA. Even before Sidney's death, Amalgamated officials had been divided into two camps: one was the "Hillman-Potofsky faction," the other was the "Rosenblum faction."[141]

Now both Jacob Potofsky and Frank Rosenblum sought the top union position. While Bessie was still in mourning for Sidney, a group of union leaders approached her to ask her opinion concerning his replacement. She answered that Sidney would have preferred Jacob Potofsky to take the presidency. How much weight the widow's opinion carried is difficult to assess; however, the outcome seemed to reflect her late husband's wishes. In a show of solidarity, on July 13, 1946, the General Executive Board of the Amalgamated Clothing Workers of America unanimously elected Jacob Potofsky to the presidency.[142] Bessie Hillman filled the vacancy resulting from the election of Frank Rosenblum to the post of Secretary-Treasurer, and thus became one of twenty-one vice presidents of the Amalgamated. One of the few women ever to hold an executive union position at the national level, she refused to abide by the wishes of the male union leaders and act solely in a dignitary capacity.[143] From that point forward, fifty-one-year-old Bessie Hillman began to recast her career to firmly secure a position of responsibility in the union that she had helped to create and had done so much to further and support over the years.

Portrait of Bessie Abramowitz taken shortly after immigration. (Courtesy of Philoine Fried.)

Chicago Men's Garment Workers' Strike, October 1910. Women workers and allies picketing Hart, Schaffner, and Marx shops. Male workers who have not yet joined the strike observe from the sidelines. Bessie Abramowitz is the second person behind the woman in the white scarf. (Courtesy of Philoine Fried.)

Bessie Abramowitz's parents, Emanuel Abramowitz and Sarah Rabinowitz Abramowitz, early 1900s. (Courtesy of Philoine Fried.)

The Abramowitz sisters and friends in 1908 dress shop advertisement. From left: Bessie Abramowitz, Celia Abramowitz, unidentified woman, Pauline Abramowitz, and Sima Shauiro. (Courtesy of Philoine Fried.)

Rumanian Vestmakers' Chicago Local 152, 1912. Top row: Sam Bagut, Charles Diamond, Nathan Garkut, Sam Margolis, F. Nitowsky. Bottom row: Joe Gleckoneau, Ann Wagner (chairman), Bessie Abramowitz (business agent), Sam Diamond. (Courtesy of Kheel Center Archives, Cornell University.)

Hart Schaffner & Marx   Form 271

VEST SHOP NO.

No. ___

Name ___

Week Ending ___

Price ___

Lot | Shop Lot No. | Quantity

Task	No.
Trimmer	1
Sew out Welts	2
Sew out Flaps	3
Turn out Welts & Flaps	4
Stitch Welts	5
Stitch Flaps	6
Press Welt, Stretch Sh.	7
Trim Welts	8
Sew on Welts	9
Sew on Collars	10
Cut Open Seams	11
Press Seams	12
Turn in Pockets	13
Cut around Pockets	14
Tack Pockets	15
Sew around Pockets	16
Press Pkts. by Machine	17
Baste Canvas	18
Shaper	19
Lining and Breast Pkts.	20
Back Maker	21
Back Presser	22
Lining Presser	23
Lining Baster	24
Edge Sewer	25
Tape Feller	26
Tape Presser	27
Edge Trimmer	28
Edge Baster	29
Edge Stitcher	30
Basting Puller	31
Side & Shoulder Baster	32
Edge Presser	33
Put Vests in Back	34
Full Dress Lin. Baster	35
Lining Finisher	36
Backer	37
Turn out Vests	38
Neck Finisher	39
Buttonhole Marker	40
Buttonhole Serger	41
Buttonhole Maker	42
Off Presser	43
Button Marker	44
Cleaner	45
Button Sewer	46
Ticket Sewer	47
Collar Tacker	48
Brusher	49
Buttonhole	50
	51
	52
	53
	54
	55

Lincoln Centre Fellowship

Chicago

The first meeting of the second year of the Fellowship will be held in Emerson Hall, Wednesday, November 5th, 1913.

Dinner will be served at 6:30 as usual. Members may bring guests.

The subject of the evening is:

"The Attitude of the Different Racial Groups to the Recently Acquired Right of the Franchise for Women."

The speakers will be Mrs. Amelia Napieralska, Mrs. E. L. Davis, Miss Bessie Abramovitz.

Dinner 50 Cents

Hart, Schaffner, and Marx Task List, 1910 and suffrage talk announcement, 1913. (Courtesy of Kheel Center Archives, Cornell University.)

"Sacred Motherhood" by Luther Bradley. This drawing was originally displayed at Chicago's 1907 Industrial Exhibition. During the 1910–1911 Chicago Men's Garment Workers' Strike, the Women's Trade Union League sold it as a postcard to raise milk money for the strikers' babies. (Chicago Daily News negatives collection, DN-0004658. Courtesy of the Chicago History Museum.)

This Cartoon was contributed by Mr. Frank Hazenplug of Hull House and was extensively used as a poster and on circulars

"Participants in the Strike" by Frank Hazenplug, used as strike propaganda during 1910 Chicago Men's Garment Workers' Strike. (Contained in Women's Trade Union League, Official Report of the Strike Committee, Chicago Garment Workers' Strike, Rare Book Collection, Kheel Center Archives, Cornell University.)

Chicago workers on Sunday picnic, 1915. Bessie Abramowitz, bottom row, far right. (Courtesy of Philoine Fried.)

Amalgamated Clothing Workers Biennial Convention, 1916. Seated from left: Fiorello LaGuardia, Bessie Abramowitz Hillman, Sidney Hillman, Joseph Schlossberg, Abraham Miller. Standing, from left: Jacob Elstein, Sam Levin, David Wolf, Isadore Kantowitz, A. D. Marimpietri, Harry Cohen, Elias Rabkin. (Courtesy of Kheel Center Archives, Cornell University.)

Chicago ally Mary Anderson and Bessie Hillman, 1922. (Courtesy of Philoine Fried.)

The Hillman family, 1921. Bottom row: Selma Hillman, Bessie Abramowitz Hillman, Philoine Hillman. Sidney Hillman standing. (Courtesy of Kheel Center Archives, Cornell University.)

Bessie Hillman on break during Pennsylvania runaway shop campaign. (Courtesy of Philoine Fried.)

*Bessie Hillman with
her daughters, Selma
on left and Philoine on
right, 1937. (Courtesy
of Philoine Fried.)*

*Laundry Workers, 1940s. Dollie Lowther Robinson second from right.
(Courtesy Kheel Center Archives, Cornell University.)*

Reelect Roosevelt Rally, 1944. Sam Jaffe seated at far left. Pennsylvania Industrial Commissioner Charlotte Carr, third from left; Bessie Hillman seated fourth from left. Zero Mostel standing. (Courtesy of Kheel Center, Cornell University.)

Supporters of the Hudson Shore Labor School, 1948. From left: Eleanor Roosevelt, Bessie Hillman, and Hilda Worthington Smith. (Courtesy of Schlesinger Library, Radcliffe Institute for Advanced Study, Harvard University.)

Sidney and Bessie Hillman conferring at union convention, 1940s. (Courtesy of Philoine Fried.)

"The Distaff Side." Photograph of ACWA vice presidents Bessie Hillman and Gladys Dickason appeared in the Advance *on June 1, 1952. (Courtesy UNITE/HERE Archives, Kheel Center, Cornell University.)*

Bessie Hillman reunited with sister Feige Itka after forty-seven years, Israel, 1952. Bessie on far right, Feige Itka second from right. (Courtesy of Philoine Fried.)

Bessie Hillman with Southern workers, 1950s. Hillman is seated on far left with Jacob Potofsky next to her. (Courtesy of Philoine Fried.)

Trade Union Women's dinner, 1960. Seated from left: Dollie Lowther Robinson, Rose Schneiderman, Esther Peterson, Pauline Newman, unidentified woman, Bessie Hillman, and Bess Blumberg. (Courtesy of Kheel Center Archives, Cornell University.)

Bessie Hillman with Golda Meir in Israel, 1952. (Courtesy of Kheel Center Archives, Cornell University.)

Members of the President's Commission on the Status of Women, with
Lyndon Johnson, 1964. Bessie in bottom row, third from right. (Courtesy of
Philoine Fried.)

CIO convention committee meeting, 1952 or 1953. From left, Henry
Fleisher, Mike Ross, (unidentified), (unidentified), Haywood, (unidentified),
(unidentified), Joe Curran (?), Emil Mazay (?), rest unidentified. (Courtesy of
Kheel Center Archives, Cornell University.)

Bessie Hillman with first great-grandchild, Kathryn, late 1960s. (Courtesy of Philoine Fried.)

George Meany, Bessie Hillman, and A. Philip Randolph at Randolph's eightieth birthday party, 1969. (Courtesy of Kheel Center Archives, Cornell University.)

7 Union Women in the Postwar Years: Separate but Not Equal (1946–1961)

In July 1946, newly elected Amalgamated Clothing Workers of America Vice President Bessie Hillman stepped out of the shadow of her late husband and onto the podium to join her colleagues on the union's General Executive Board. Reentering the formal leadership ranks after a thirty-year hiatus not only provided a steady income for the newly widowed Hillman, but also allowed her to be recognized as a leader of the union that she had initiated.[1] By all accounts, Hillman had more years of experience in the Amalgamated than any other union official. Union member Lillian Poses reminded Bessie "that this recognition came not only because you were Sidney's wife, but more than that because of the outstanding contribution that you have made in the trade union movement in your own right all these years."[2]

Standing on Hope

Although Hillman may not have been aware of it at the time, Sidney's death liberated her from the constraints imposed on her while she reigned as first lady of the Amalgamated. She could think and act more freely, no longer obligated to clear her activities with Sidney. More importantly, on a personal level, regaining her rightful place in the organization that she had helped to found began to fill the gaping void left in the wake of her husband's death. Expressions of sympathy from cherished friends like Pauline Newman were a source of great comfort to Hillman.[3] Bessie considered the chance to busy herself with union work and fulfill the vision for the union that she had shared with her husband "a Godsend." Her work, as always, reflected her dedication to the organization, but now, in her own way, she could also thereby pay tribute to her late husband. Seeing the faces of union members and friends gave her "renewed hope and strength to go on."[4]

Though she anticipated the best, Hillman soon began to feel like an outsider looking in. Despite the fact that in the postwar years women constituted 66 percent of the ACWA's total membership, union policy remained driven from above, so that major policy changes and initiatives originated in the upper echelons of the male-dominated union hierarchy with the general president, general secretary-treasurer, and executive vice president, rather than with the numerous vice presidents. Moreover, unions functioned like men's clubs, accomplishing much of their work outside union meetings. Sara Fredgant, a Philadelphia union leader, remembered, "Because decisions regarding union business were made after rather than at the meeting, the women were misinterpreted by the men."[5]

A 1952 *Advance* photograph, captioned "The Distaff Side," demonstrated union men's perception of the women within their ranks. The two female union vice presidents, Gladys Dickason and Bessie Hillman, were pictured sitting side by side discussing a resolution for women's rights, implying perhaps that only women were concerned with this issue and thus further separating them from the men. Rather than using the opportunity to build solidarity with union women, male leaders continued to regard them with suspicion.[6] For Hillman and Dickason, the only female members of the Amalgamated's twenty-five-person executive board, gender distanced and even excluded them from the decision-making process. Adding to this sense of isolation were the internal divisions that erupted in the months after Sidney Hillman's death. Despite his failure to secure the presidency, Secretary-Treasurer Frank Rosenblum continued to vie for power in the ACWA. At least initially, Rosenblum and his supporters, rather than union President Jacob Potofsky, worked to amass an influential following.[7] Thus, in spite of what on the surface appeared to be an ideal situation for achieving her vision of an industrial democracy that championed both civil rights and women's rights, Hillman's opportunities for leadership were limited by internal union politics and the secondary roles prescribed for the female officials.

Evaluating Hillman's status during these early years in office, Philoine Fried suggested that her mother "wanted to do more but they wouldn't permit her to."[8] Internal dissension and a patronizing attitude on the part of male union leaders toward women prevented Bessie from achieving any real power. Hillman openly acknowledged that women were "seldom in a position to create policy, capable as they may be of interpreting it or carrying it out." Laundry worker organizer Dollie Robinson also believed that she was excluded from decision making based on gender: "We were shut out of decisions made by the president and the vice presidents." Ironically, union membership granted job-related rights to women, but their rights as union members were restricted within the organization.[9] The sexism of male leaders not only cast women workers in supporting rather than decision-making positions in the union (and often in the workplace as well), but also contradicted the principles of industrial democracy. Although Bessie could do little to allay the strife that rocked the union from within, she hoped that her close relationship to Jacob (Jack) Potofsky, who had lived with her family intermittently for years, might be advantageous in circumventing the obstacles posed by the chauvinistic union hierarchy. In her transition from a union organizer to an executive officer, Bessie Hillman gathered her resolve to rectify the ACWA's discriminatory practices.

Despite Bessie's attempt to participate more fully in union affairs, male leaders continued to relegate Vice President Hillman to ceremonial service. Her visit to Germany in the summer of 1947, "to see firsthand some of the problems of the displaced persons," marked the beginning of a series of diplomatic trips. Hillman was one of a number of American educators and female labor leaders who traveled to Germany under the auspices of the United States government after the war.[10] As she toured survivor camps, Bessie certainly could not have avoided thinking of her own siblings and extended family members slain by the Nazis in Poland and Russia. Experiencing such tragedy firsthand encouraged Hillman to support the work of the American Labor Organization of Rehabilitation Through Training, as it integrated, resettled, and retrained refugees and displaced persons all over the world in the 1940s and 1950s. Immediately after the war, the Hillmans sponsored the immigration of their niece, Luba Aten, who had survived Auschwitz. Later Bessie appealed to the State Department on behalf of two European cousins, Boruck and Etla Rutenburg, who faced deportation from the United States after migrating across the Canadian border.[11] Notwithstanding the importance of her European trips, the time she spent on the road away from union headquarters in New York meant that Bessie missed important union meetings.

Taxed by the constant motion of an extensive foreign and domestic itinerary, Hillman found ways to combine business with pleasure, thus lending a new perspective to her work. While on a 1952 trip to dedicate the Sidney Hillman Hall and Museum in the Amalgamated Technical School in Jerusalem, she visited her daughter and son-in-law, Philoine and Milton Fried, who were living in Israel. As was the case during her earlier trip to Germany, Hillman experienced VIP treatment, including escorted visits to trade-union sites and an opportunity to spend time with her friend Golda Meir, then Israel's Labor Minister. Meir shared Bessie's interest in advocating for working women, respected Hillman's opinions, and often discussed "vital problems" affecting Israeli labor with her. Meir concluded her speech at the dedication of the school with a compliment to Hillman: "I am pleased that she arranged her visit to this country in a fundamental manner, in the way that she and Hillman always did their work throughout their life together."[12]

The treatment of women in Israeli society impressed Bessie. The government provided maternity benefits and daycare centers for their children. City mayors also honored women on Mother's Day. Hillman made a second trip to Israel in 1961. The treatment she received, the observations she made about women, and the friendships she cultivated with influential women like Meir when she traveled abroad contributed to her intensifying activism upon her return.

Both as a consequence of the war and as part of the process of defining her own identity, Bessie Hillman, like her ILGWU contemporary Pauline Newman, gravitated closer to her Jewish roots as she grew older. In a 1952 speech to an Israeli audience, she conveyed her pride in "seeing my people from all corners of the earth working together to establish a dignified life of security and freedom."[13] In her work Bessie evidenced values that she had learned as a child in a Jewish household. Traditionally, the charitable virtues of progressive-era reformers are attributed to what one unionist termed "their Christian social responsibility."[14] However, it can be argued that Jewish female activists demonstrated a similar sense of responsibility rooted in their own religious culture.

In addition to the Jewish religious mandate of *tikkun olam* (repair of the world), Jewish women activists related *tsodeka*—charity, caring and "right action"—to helping others experience justice. Jewish feminist Letty Cottin Pogrebin explains that "the highest of the eight degrees of *tzedakah (tsodeka)* is that form of assistance we give to enable the weak to raise themselves." To be Jewish is to help not only yourself but also to help others around you.[15] These concepts bear a striking resemblance to Jane Addams's efforts to empower Hull-House neighbors so that they could improve their lots. In Hillman's case, both her cultural ties to Old-World Judaism and her early Chicago experiences definitively influenced her promotion of social justice.[16]

Although Hillman eventually resisted her travel duties, her work abroad paved the way for opportunities on the domestic front. In July 1951, Secretary of Defense George Marshall appointed Bessie to the Defense Advisory Committee on Women in the Armed Services, where she became one of a group of prominent women appointed "to furnish guidance to the Department of Defense on problems relating to women in the Services."[17] With the country in the midst of the Korean War, committee members were charged with actively recruiting young women—in Bessie's case, working women—into the armed services. Hillman accepted on the premise that she "could make suggestions to the military regarding the care and guidance of these young girls."[18] To more effectively pursue her goals, Bessie began to use a speechwriter, Catharine Williams, a member of the ACWA research staff. Speaking to large national audiences, Hillman may have been somewhat self-conscious about her lack of education and thick accent. She had always used handwritten, phonetically spelled notes scribbled on the backs of index cards, but as her professional speaking commitments extended to the world beyond the union, she prepared herself well in advance with neatly typed speeches that often incorporated Williams's research material.

While attending numerous parades and speaking to working women about joining the women's divisions of the military, Hillman articulated doubts about the effectiveness of her efforts, realizing that "although these women are very patriotic, because they are supporting themselves and their families, their economic circumstances prevented them from joining."[19] She was all too aware that the majority of women worked primarily out of economic need, which meant that they could not afford to serve their country if it meant jeopardizing their families' survival by leaving the workforce. Despite the military's strong dose of patriotism, Cold War propaganda could do little to alter this hard reality. In a letter to southern organizer Hazel Bankston, she grudgingly summarized her experiences in a single sentence: "Most of the time, I travel around."[20] Thus, even though Bessie Hillman found the work "extremely fruitful and rewarding," by March of 1954 she had grown tired of traversing the country. Citing the pressure of her duties with the ACWA, an exhausted Hillman quietly resigned from the Defense Advisory Committee.[21]

Labor Organizing and Civil Rights in Dixie

Bessie Hillman preferred to concentrate on more fundamental union work: in particular, shaping the union's position on civil rights. United States involvement in World War II had blatantly exposed civil rights abuses on the home front, and Americans had an increasingly difficult time justifying the fight against fascism abroad while endorsing racism at home. Hillman delved into the civil rights arena within months after the war ended. In October 1945, even before Bessie's election to the union vice presidency, Congress of Civil Rights President Quentin Sheean invited her to speak at a dinner launching a nationwide campaign to unseat Mississippi Senator Theodore Bilbo, an infamous Klansman.[22]

As a union vice president, Hillman jumped at the chance to participate in "Operation Dixie"—the "all out drive" the CIO initiated in 1946 to organize workers in twelve southern states. The drive targeted the textile industry, which CIO leaders believed was the key to organizing the South. Because women constituted more than half of the industry's workforce in most southern states, Operation Dixie concentrated specifically on advertising union benefits for women workers. The ACWA contributed both funding and leadership, in an attempt to put an end to the exploitation of both "poor whites and Negroes."[23] Throughout the late 1940s and early 1950s, Hillman used her expertise to work with union organizers as they tackled the anti-union South. From the onset of her involvement, Hillman realized that she faced a dual struggle both to organize workers and to combat racism among them.

Cotton manufacturing employed more workers than any other southern industry. Because mill owners tended to hire poor whites instead of blacks, the racial composition of the southern textile workforce had remained almost unchanged from the beginning to the midpoint of the twentieth century. Black men were only occasionally hired to perform the most menial tasks, such as sweeping floors or working in carding rooms where cotton dust permeated the air. In the case of women workers, evidence abounds to support Jacqueline Jones's assertion that "New South cotton lords hired virtually no black women as mill operatives or even menial laborers on a sustained basis." In 1910, there were only 883 black women textile workers in the South, employed mainly as seasonal scrubwomen.[24] As late as 1950, when southern mills employed close to 200,000 women workers, only about 3,000 of them were black women operatives.[25] The southern whites who readily filled the notoriously low-wage openings scorned black workers. In the summer of 1944, the owners of a large Virginia cotton mill surrendered to the "collective protest of white women and dismissed the few black women [they] had recently hired."[26] Rank-and-file workers and mill owners held fast to deeply embedded racist attitudes.

The Amalgamated had a long-standing interest in organizing southern workers. Although it had tried to organize in the South in years past, only one "small and weak" southern local (in Louisville, Kentucky) existed prior to 1933.[27] When the CIO established the Textile Workers Organizing Committee in 1937, Sidney Hillman became its chairperson. Two years later he oversaw the formation of the Textile Workers Union of America (TWUA). That union made early efforts in the South, but its progress was "depressingly slow."[28] By the time the Amalgamated joined the renewed southern campaign under the auspices of Operation Dixie in 1946, according to TWUA President Emil Rieve, mills in the region employed more than 80 percent of the nation's approximately 1 million textile workers.[29] Only 16 percent of the southern workers were covered by union contracts. Four-fifths of these unionized workers were in large mills in North Carolina, South Carolina, and Virginia.[30] Because intergenerational prejudices were not easily altered, southern textile mills remained the domain of whites until the 1960s.

These tensions tested Bessie Hillman's expertise; organization of the textile mills necessitated the formulation of a strategy that would combat class, race, and gender injustices. As she helped to coordinate the efforts to organize southern workers, Hillman devised a plan that encompassed both interracial cooperation and education. She connected with black women leaders and organizations in the North so that black and white women could work collaboratively toward racial equality. Hillman became the only woman on the CIO's Committee to Abolish Discrimination (later the Committee on Civil Rights) and served as the chair of the Urban League's Labor Relations Committee. In keeping with her civil rights advocacy, she made a number of financial contributions to the National Association for the Advancement of Colored People and to the Congress of Racial Equality.[31]

In the early 1950s, Bessie Hillman implemented an education program for southern workers. Her educational efforts expanded the ACWA's union label campaign southward to inform the consuming public. The campaign framework was initially established to combat the recession in the men's clothing industry in 1950 and 1951. Hillman considered the label campaign "the third link in the chain of labor's strength," right behind "labor's power at the bargaining table" and "its power at the ballot box."[32]

A portion of Hillman's union label duties involved surveying retail stores to make sure that the suits they sold were union-made. Her major focus, however, concentrated on addressing audiences. The almost instantaneous rapport that she enjoyed with the women members made her an ideal spokesperson for the union label drive. Bessie honored national campaign coordinator Fred Sard's request to make a "human presentation" about the benefits of the union label and to use her expertise to "help the field-man by making sure his press release is simple, modest, and effective." Sard suggested, "It would help if you meet with their [women's groups'] officers to acquaint them with the social and economic values of the work we are doing."[33] Bessie and other officials drew on time-tested tactics initiated by the National Consumers' League to conduct a massive public relations effort designed to encourage consumers, particularly those who were female union members, to buy only union-made garments.[34] By visiting locals, distributing literature, and advertising in area media, campaigners appealed to manufacturers, retailers, and consumers to maintain labor's position in a challenging postwar climate.

Hillman traveled throughout the South to spread "the gospel of the union label" and to continue to organize southern workers.[35] Hillman cast her message in simple rhetoric, informing the workers that the union's primary purpose was "to raise the standard of living, to increase purchasing power, to help make the workers useful members of the community." She reassured listeners that the union was "no longer suspect" and only out to stimulate production by increasing the sale of goods. Georgian Annie Belle Swaney wrote to thank Bessie for coming to Atlanta. She explained the show that the workers had staged in Hillman's honor: "In our crude way we are trying to show you and the other great leaders that you were our inspiration."[36] Bessie Hillman reveled in the demonstrative affection characteristic of the southern unions. By her own choice, she returned to the South many times.

Despite the large number of women textile workers, the ACWA and the TWUA were the only two unions involved in Operation Dixie that employed women organizers. Gladys Dickason formally directed the southern drive and Bessie Hillman assisted her. Hillman sought out black women to help organize the black women workers.[37] Although Hillman's ethnic and cultural background differed dramatically from those of the newest union members, the few southern black women organizers reminded Bessie of herself forty years earlier.[38] As a one-time Russian immigrant who had fought for survival on the fringes of American society, Hillman readily related to black workers who shared some of the disadvantages she had worked so diligently to overcome. Hillman displayed a penchant for championing the causes of those on the margins.

The cause of civil rights, fueled by the effort to organize workers in the racist South, tapped the potential of the official position Bessie held. Awed by the 1948 convention and in particular by Hillman's address to southern delegates, offering them "hope to stand on and courage to press forward," delegate Isabelle Jones, a black member of Atlanta Local 365, like many other members, developed a close relationship with Hillman. An inspired Jones informed Bessie that she was no longer afraid of picket lines, jails, or the Ku Klux Klan. Though some, like labor journalist Len DeCaux, criticized the Amalgamated conventions for being overly emotional, many in attendance, including Jones, experienced them as motivational events that generated the impetus they needed to become active leaders within the union.[39] Hillman's support of black women workers encouraged their activism.

Hillman assigned Dollie Robinson to the deep South to determine which shops would be receptive to organization. Robinson conducted "house to house visits each night" with workers from a very cooperative Tampa shop. She reported her experience to Hillman: "They are all Negro workers and I have enjoyed talking with them. They have been good for my soul." The time spent with the workers in Florida reinvigorated Robinson, who recounted: "I find myself remembering all the good things and forgetting all of the unpleasant things. In fact some days I don't remember that there was ever anything unpleasant about the 'cause.' That is as it should be."[40]

From afar, Hillman kept in close touch with the other southern organizers, encouraging them to address as many meetings as possible, "small or large." Hillman often reassured those like Hazel Bankston, who campaigned for the union label but sometimes felt defeated. Bankston shared her frustration about trying to attend as many union meetings as possible. Often, Bankston told Hillman, she had to "hunt them up," only to find that there were two or three on the same night. Bankston sought Hillman's counsel, plaintively writing, "I wish you were here with me, I miss you and could ask you a thousand questions a day." Hillman replied empathetically, "Please don't despair if things don't come your way. Union work is not easy—it always has been and always will be a great struggle. Yet through the years we keep on constantly making more progress because of [the] determination of people like you who stand by their belief."[41]

Nevertheless, the battle for civil rights proved to be an uphill struggle, despite Hillman's suggestion that "the Amalgamated never deviated from the principle that there must not be discrimination on the basis of race, creed, color, or national origin." Hillman could point to the more recent affiliates in New York City, like the Laundry Workers' Joint Board, to show how the union fulfilled its promises of equality. Hillman noted that "there is a Jewish manager and a Negro co-manager. On the staff of business agents there are Jews, Negroes, and Puerto Ricans—the three groups who comprise the majority of the members."[42] Still, white garment and textile workers refused to work alongside black workers in both the North and the South well into the 1960s. Corrine Lytle Cannon remembers that in 1962, she was the first black woman hired at Cannon Mills in Kannapolis, North Carolina.[43] Hillman realized that the condescending attitudes demonstrated by white union leaders toward black workers reflected the prevailing racist sentiment in American society. She was also aware of the fact that such attitudes were not necessarily confined to rank-and-file workers, which is the reason that throughout the 1950s and 1960s, the ACWA stood at the forefront of the movement to pass an all-inclusive civil rights bill.[44]

An Alabama shirtworker and a great-granddaughter of slaves, Fannie Allen Neal recalled that white business agents who were sent to the South in the postwar years often fraternized with company managers by taking them to dinner, even though it was a violation of the union contract to do so without someone from the factory present. Neal explained the business agents' lack of interest in the workers' well-being in straightforward terms: "They weren't concerned. They were white." Neal and her black coworkers "drove them" back to New York. The workers' assertiveness did little to endear them to ACWA vice president Gladys Dickason, who "got mad at us and wouldn't send us no business agents, and so we were mad at her." Dickason, a Columbia-educated economics professor born on a cotton farm in Oklahoma, had little patience with the black shirtworkers' behavior. Apparently, though she always commanded respect for her abilities, she was not always easy to get along with. Amalgamated leaders finally resolved the situation by sending in a more empathetic emissary in the person of Hillman's protégé, Dollie Robinson.[45]

By 1953, in spite of the efforts of Hillman and hundreds of other CIO organizers, Operation Dixie had failed to establish a strong foothold in the southern textile industry.[46] The report of the ACWA's Organizing Committee in 1954 attributed the lack of success of the southern campaign to "the reactionary climate engendered by the anti-union provisions of the Taft-Hartley Law and fostered by the present administration."[47] In her detailed study of the obstacles facing the Operation

Dixie campaign, Barbara Griffith concludes that "matters of race and religion, as well as the historical legacy of poverty and paternalism, all helped to weave the blanket of resistance that ultimately suffocated the C.I.O."[48] The demise of the campaign can be explained both by the failure of the mostly northern organizers to overcome white supremacy and by the negativity toward organized labor generated by the political climate surrounding the Red Scare. Segregationists used the fear of communism to cover their opposition to integration, and CIO unions had a difficult time convincing southern workers that the unions were not affiliated with communists.[49] Such accusations were not exclusively limited to the South, either.

Hillman refused to be dissuaded. In a 1957 speech to labor leaders gathered in Charleston, at the South Carolina Labor Council's second annual convention, she indicted the Eisenhower administration for its delay in producing antirecession action and argued that "greater efforts must be made to organize the nonunion laborers in the South." The ACWA vice president "termed it 'tragic' that workers don't realize the importance of joining together" to make their voices heard.[50] Union organizers could take some consolation in the fact that Operation Dixie, coupled with organized labor's pressure to amend the Fair Labor Standards Act (FLSA), eventually resulted in a series of wage increases granted by the southern mills in 1956, 1959, and 1960.[51]

Bessie Hillman raised the union's awareness of civil rights issues. Following the CIO's 1950 recommendation that its affiliates "create a Civil Rights Committee, or Department on Fair Practices," Hillman helped the Amalgamated to establish its own Department of Civil Rights to fight for an effective civil rights bill. She later explained, in 1968, that though she "didn't condone all the disturbance, looting, burning, and robbing, [the civil rights movement] was long overdue." Under Bessie Hillman's guidance, the union's Education Committee worked to eliminate the "gross inequality" manifested in the segregated facilities in the North as well as in the South. Ten years after the 1954 *Brown v. Board of Education* decision, the AFL-CIO's "Resolution on Federal Aid to Education" still found it necessary to demand that the Supreme Court desegregation order be properly implemented.[52]

Throughout the decade of the 1960s, Hillman held her ground, reiterating that the best way to abolish racial animosity was through education. She hoped that an intensified education program would ultimately increase political activism and that in turn, efforts to organize, especially in the South, would be more successful.[53] She affiliated with the Women's Activities Division of the AFL-CIO's Committee on

Political Education (COPE), and led a voter registration drive focused on southern workers. In 1966, Bessie became a life member of the National Council of Negro Women.[54] Hillman earned herself a national reputation as a staunch advocate for black workers. National Council of Negro Women President Mary McLeod Bethune was exceedingly grateful to Bessie for advancing the cause of civil rights. Following her first meeting with Hillman in 1949, Bethune wrote poignantly, "I found myself thanking God for you, for your interest and influence. I know that you will do all you can for us in any way that you can."[55] During her entire tenure as a union vice president, Hillman waged an educational and political campaign to secure civil rights.

Politics in the Postwar Years: Fighting to Keep Labor's House in Order

As she worked toward attaining civil rights for all, the postwar political situation dealt a series of defeats to Hillman and the labor movement in general. To many white Americans "obsessed with the threat of communism in the postwar period . . . efforts to promote racial equality portended the country's imminent takeover by foreign agents." Even labor unionists succumbed to the hysteria. In the late 1940s and early 1950s, labor organizations like the CIO "scrambled to prove [their] patriotism" by disassociating themselves from communists. In 1949, the CIO expelled eleven of its unions whose leaders were suspected of sympathizing with communists. Despite this, taken together, these unions had the best records for black advocacy, particularly for black women workers.[56]

In 1951, Esther Peterson wrote to Bessie from Sweden (where her husband, Oliver, was serving as a labor attaché), noting that the European "trade union friends" sought reassurance that "in the face of all the communist propaganda," American unionists were not becoming "tools in a Wall Street–government coalition."[57] As was the case after World War I, labor again assumed a defensive posture. On the national and state fronts, a series of anti-labor legislation, strike defeats, and declining union membership further weakened organized labor in the 1950s and 1960s.

While the Amalgamated helped to coordinate Operation Dixie, the CIO's Political Action Committee (PAC) conducted a Senate campaign in the South to improve conditions for workers through legislation. The outcome proved disappointing. Even with the combined membership of the AFL-CIO at 15 million, and despite Bessie Hillman's pronouncement deeming labor a "powerful force in politics," the political strength of labor could not divert the nationwide tide of postwar Republican ascendancy.[58] Wages in the southern states remained lower than in any other region of the country, and failure to expand the coverage of the FLSA hurt southern agricultural workers and nonunion laundry laborers, "the two leading occupations for minorities and a mainstay of the southern economy."[59]

Labor's waning political power in the immediate postwar years had other ominous implications. In 1947, deeply disturbed by the Taft-Hartley bill that threatened to reverse labor's gains under the Wagner Act, Hillman appealed to President Truman to exercise his veto. She adamantly asserted that "union security, national bargaining, social benefits, and the right to strike are not only essential to the everyday function of unions but are an integral part of our democracy." When the offensive bill was passed over the president's veto, it enraged labor leaders by outlawing compulsory union membership before employment and strengthening right-to-work laws that prohibited compulsory union membership after employment. Supporters of the Taft-Hartley Act sought to reduce organized labor's power, particularly in the South and West. Hillman waged her own war to discredit the Republicans by publicly denouncing their records.[60]

In 1949, shortly after Amalgamated leaders officially broke away from the American Labor Party, Bessie Hillman helped found the Coordinating Committee of Independent Democrats, which provided a channel for those Democrats "who cannot work in good conscience for Democratic candidates through Tammany Hall but who are in sympathy with the general aims and program of the Democratic Party."[61] With labor's political clout in jeopardy, at the ACWA's seventeenth biennial convention President Potofsky deemed the 1950 elections "a sober crossroad in labor's history, the final determination as to whether the New Deal was but a passing era in our national history or a permanent achievement in the expansion of the American way of life."[62] Bessie Hillman's accompanying declaration—that "unless we make the workers conscious politically as well as economically, we are not going to be able to elect people that protect organized labor"—foreshadowed the grim years to come.[63] Seeking to revive labor's political influence, Hillman worked in multiple venues.

With many union members discouraged from participation by the oppressive atmosphere of the McCarthy era, Hillman worked overtime to allay their fears. She urged Amalgamated workers to alert themselves "to what is behind all this hysteria." Encouraging education, she directed union leaders to "[g]et together with your members and find out the truth."[64] Hillman's political activism set an example. Esther Murray, newly appointed national representative to the CIO's PAC, looked to Hillman to give her "invaluable help" with the work she planned to do in the months preceding the 1952 elections. Based on advice received from Howard Samuel of the ACWA, Murray wrote to Bessie, stating that she believed Bessie was "the one person who can most effectively call together a group of political action leaders among women trade union members and wives of trade union members of the Amalgamated."[65] However, the Democratic Party lost the presidency to the Republicans despite labor's intense efforts.

Eisenhower's inauguration marked the first Republican presidential victory since 1929.[66] Disillusioned but still determined, Hillman addressed the Baltimore Joint Board, where she reiterated her philosophy that education was the strongest weapon to use in the political arena against the "anti-Communist hysteria" and to protect endangered civil liberties.[67] In 1956, Hillman worked for the election of former Illinois governor Adlai Stevenson. A member of the liberal and fervently anti-communist Americans for Democratic Action, she was invited to a number of political functions, including "a small off the record informal luncheon of labor leaders."[68] Nevertheless, Eisenhower's popularity proved "greater than his party's," and he swept the election, winning by a landslide even as the Democrats claimed victory in both houses of Congress.[69] Hillman refused to stop trying. In 1958, she served as a labor policy advisor for the Advisory Council of the Democratic National Committee, where she worked alongside Eleanor Roosevelt. The council recommended the passage of legislation to help organized labor "keep its house in order," including the repeal of the Taft-Hartley Act.[70]

A belated Kennedy supporter in the 1960 campaign (she had originally supported Adlai Stevenson), Hillman accused the Republicans of attacking every social welfare bill as wasteful, including bills that would provide more schools. She vehemently criticized the Republicans' vetoes of funding for depressed areas and housing legislation, their fight against the $1.25 minimum wage and their opposition to medical care for the aged—all items that Hillman adamantly supported.[71] Congressman Chester Bowles, chairman of the Platform and Resolutions Committee for the 1960 Democratic National Convention, solicited Bessie's opinion regarding "the policy points in your field which you would like to see covered in the platform."[72] Kennedy's support of social welfare benefits, coupled with a favorable record on race relations and labor issues, as well as Esther Peterson's praise for the young candidate, ultimately won Hillman and many other laborites over to the Kennedy camp.[73] Union members embraced the sense of promise embodied in the New Frontier's call for increases in minimum wages and funding for impoverished areas, along with improvements in education, medical care, and housing. After the election, Elinore Herrick, editor of the *New York Herald Tribune* and a close friend of Bessie's, wrote Hillman to say that she was "glad that Kennedy won." Herrick shared her hope that Kennedy would not make Arkansas Senator J. William Fulbright his Secretary of State, because of his segregationist convictions.[74] Almost one hundred years after the Civil War ended, the Democratic Party led a belated national drive for civil rights.

Courage to Press Forward

When Hillman ascended to the vice presidency of the largest men's garment industry union, in 1946, preoccupation with the postwar transition and the fight against growing anti-union sentiments obscured the organization's feminist consciousness. As Americans in general worried about another depression setting in, movies and magazines romanticized women's place as homemaking consumers.[75] American families tuned into television, where stay-at-home mothers like June Cleaver and Harriet Nelson displaced Rosie the Riveter and became the new national icons. These images propelled domesticity to unprecedented heights while at the same time they obscured the massive defense industry layoffs of women. Women unionists were among the first to confront the prevailing attitudes that minimized their contributions to the war effort and rescinded their wartime invitation into the workforce. Told that returning soldiers needed their jobs, women workers blamed employers, because unions had no control over job cuts.[76] Still, though many lost their jobs in heavy industry, women refused to leave the workforce altogether. The majority of women, with the exception of a small number of middle-class white women who had entered the workforce temporarily during the war, simply could not afford not to work.[77] Contrary to the impression the mass media and popular culture tried to create, women did not complacently leave the workplace to take up residence in suburbia; they kept working because they had no other choice. Minority women were hit especially hard when they were pushed out of their wartime jobs back into the low-wage service and domestic sectors.[78]

Women, married women in particular, entered the workforce in increasing numbers throughout the twentieth century. By 1960, one-third of married women earned wages. Overall, women constituted 25 percent of the workforce in 1940, 29 percent of the workforce in 1950, and 35 percent of the workforce by 1965.[79] These women workers were more inclined than ever before to join unions. By 1954, 17 percent of union members were women. In the ACWA, as in most other garment and textile unions, although men dominated the union hierarchy, the majority of union membership was comprised of women. The Amalgamated's ranks approached 350,000, and 66 percent of those members were women.[80]

While union leaders grappled with a host of problems, political and otherwise, at the national and state levels in the years following World War II, demands generated from within the union presented an entirely different dilemma. Hillman and other female leaders worked within the Amalgamated seeking social and economic advancement. Moreover, as the number of working women grew, women rank and filers reacted openly to their secondary status in the workforce. In the face of male opposition and a postwar reconversion process that further suppressed women, labor women collectively reasserted their reform agenda.[81] Male leaders in the ACWA seemed attentive to the discrimination problems facing women wage earners, but they failed to offer genuine access to the internal power structure, thus preventing any real change.

Women unionists presented a "Resolution for Women's Rights" at the ACWA's Sixteenth Biennial Convention in 1948, blaming employers for laying them off, cutting their wages, and discriminating against them in general. Although it was still possible for women to work after the war, their opportunities for employment were drastically reduced. The resolution further specified that "the deterioration of social and protective legislation which has accompanied this reactionary drive by employers has been injurious to women as workers, mothers, and citizens."[82] Ninety percent of women who worked earned less than they did during the war.[83] Many rank-and-file women considered the mere articulation of these grievances an advance in itself. In the earliest years of the postwar period, Bessie viewed the Amalgamated as the most promising avenue for altering this situation, boasting at a 1949 retirement ceremony for Rose Schneiderman that "American women have achieved greater economic equality and the dignity and protection of powerful trade union organization."[84] However, within a decade her optimistic perspective would be drastically altered.

Union women mounted a resistance movement against the "authority of gender hierarchy" to protest their subordinate status.[85] In the postwar decades, Amalgamated women demanded equity within the union and equal opportunity as full economic citizens, with a right to work for pay and a right to care for their families.[86] Although images and articles pressuring women to go back home and don aprons ran rampant once the war ended, the cultural dictates that surrounded them held little meaning for Amalgamated women who had always worked. When labor feminists rallied for women's workplace rights, they fought for those of working wives and mothers as well.[87] Frustrated by years of acquiescing to a male union hierarchy that thwarted women's progress, for the first time since the inception of the ACWA, rather than working with male union leaders, Hillman prepared to challenge them.

The foundation for the Amalgamated women's gender-based consciousness stretched back to the opening decades of the twentieth century, when Bessie and other young labor activists first affiliated with Chicago reformers. These women took to the streets to protest working conditions and demand women's rights. Enduring cross-class alliances generated a comprehensive program to provide protective legislation and seek social justice for the weak and unfortunate—particularly women and children workers. The combined efforts of these social feminists and working women activists influenced the labor agenda for the rest of the century.[88]

Middle-class allies led early struggles to enact protective labor legislation in the 1910s and 1920s, but by the 1940s trade-union women dominated the coalition, pushing for extended coverage and better enforcement of labor laws. Labor women relied on the categorization of women by social feminists as different from men and needing special protection. This encouraged the division of workers along gender lines, with women almost always assuming the lesser-skilled, lower-wage jobs. The analogous division of labor in the home that readily transferred to the workplace reinforced this gendered division. The needle trades in particular were viewed by employers as an extension of women's domestic duties within the home and the family. From the inception of the union, ACWA members subscribed to the notion that "women played a primary role as wives and mothers"; at the same time, however, they realized that many women were "obligated or wanted to lead productive lives outside their homes, and so they [went to] work."[89] Despite the fact that many women were the primary wage earners, the societal perception of motherhood, which viewed women mainly as the mothers of the future race, remained a deeply rooted justification for gendered wage and workplace discrimination and reasserted itself strongly in the postwar years.

For many Amalgamated women, wartime work had translated into a slight increase in wages. Still, a gendered wage gap persisted in the years immediately following the war, and sex segregation remained firmly entrenched. Women in the ACWA realized that differential treatment existed, but they accepted the sexual division of labor because they perceived it in terms of craft divisions where women's competition with men was minimal. They hesitated to undermine the family wage ideal, which espoused maintenance of male wages.[90] Working women overall accepted their situations because, as Alice Cook explained, "family, school, and society generally have imprinted the inevitability of these role differentiations upon both men and women."[91]

Even in a union with a reputation for being more liberal and progressive than most, from the beginning men's and women's wages varied due to differentials in sex-segregated occupations. Neither equal-pay legislation by the National War Labor Board nor special contract provisions for women workers during the Second World War permanently affected the attitudes that accounted for wage differentials. Technological advances did not affect the ACWA's gendered hierarchy to a great extent. Former Amalgamated Associate National Educational Director Connie Kopelov recalled that by the 1930s, "the advent of a lighter pressing machine in the shirt industry had resulted in the replacement of men by lower-paid women workers," but this practice had ended with organization. In other industries, such as automobile and steel production, automation often complicated the gendered structure of the workplace, but because of the general acceptance of sex segregation and the comparative lack of new technologies within the ACWA, the impact of technological advances was minimal.[92]

In keeping with Hillman's perception of feminism, most ACWA women did not want to displace men solely on the basis of their gender, but felt that they should earn the right to more skilled positions through hard work. They also sought to have more value attached to the jobs they already held. So, when it came to directly confronting the sex segregation of jobs in their own union, Amalgamated women stopped short. They pushed for expanding and upgrading their lower-skilled jobs rather than seeking more demanding work as cutters and pressers, jobs traditionally performed by men. In other words, they sought separate and what they considered fair treatment—or equity—rather than full equality with men. Dorothy Sue Cobble astutely observes: "They imagined ending gender hierarchies without necessarily ending all gender differences."[93]

In their struggle to gain just treatment for wage-earning women through organization and protective legislation, ACWA women leaders tried to ensure that their union offered an avenue for expressing gender-based aspirations. Relying on progressive tactics, including women-centered politics, they identified women's issues and then created educational programs and lobbying campaigns to advance their interests with regard to these issues. Disagreeing with ERA feminists, who demanded that "recognition be bestowed on them solely upon the basis of their sex," Hillman maintained that women "must earn recognition for ourselves on the basis of our ability."[94] In Hillman's mind, women had already successfully performed jobs that had previously been viewed as men's. Before World War II, women were viewed as too weak to do jobs like riveting and shipbuilding, but as a result of their nontraditional work during the war, "they have proven to the world that they can perform these duties" without getting sick or being injured.[95] Rank-and-file unionists also believed that they had been shortchanged. The 1948 Resolution on Women's Rights read: "Women have made great strides and have demonstrated the valuable contributions they can make to our economic, political, and cultural life. Yet they have not been accorded opportunities for full participation. On the contrary, they are widely discriminated against."[96] In light of women's wartime work experiences, Bessie and fellow labor feminists argued that women had every right to press for equal opportunities.

Feminist demands did not cease after the attainment of suffrage; labor women consistently worked toward reform away from the public eye. As Cobble notes, "Theirs was a vision of equality that claimed justice on the basis of their humanity, not on the basis of their sameness with men."[97] These labor feminists did not fold neatly into the category of "difference feminists," who sought special treatment for women on the basis of their sex, nor did they fit into the category of equal rights feminists, who proposed a constitutional amendment guaranteeing equality for women as individuals. Most labor feminists "never resolved the tension between equality and difference," but instead pressed for both equality and special treatment.[98]

By the late 1940s, Hillman realized that it was up to her and Gladys Dickason first to secure and then ultimately to use their leverage within their union to negotiate for women's rights on behalf of the Amalgamated's female membership. With women's position in both the labor movement and wider society rapidly eroding, Hillman, Dickason, and their contemporaries in other unions firmly committed themselves to a labor feminism that proposed equal treatment and social justice for women, first within and later outside their own organizations. For the next two decades, labor feminists in the ACWA attempted to "genuinely advance women's rights" by supporting the Women's Status bill, modeled after the 1947 Truman Civil Rights Commission, "which would set up a presidential commission to study and analyze specific discriminations against women and recommend corrective legislation to Congress," and the Equal Pay bill. They also urged "the adoption by state legislatures of more adequate protective legislation for working women."[99] By virtue of these women's activities, "labor ideologies and institutions had a powerful effect on the formulation and implementation of social and employment policy," not only during the New Deal but also in subsequent decades.[100]

By the 1950s, nearly all the states had enacted some form of protective legislation that went beyond wage and hour regulation for women to ensuring meal and rest periods and limiting both night work and the amount of weight women were required to lift.[101] The ACWA was only one organization in a coalition—including the National Consumers' League, the Women's Bureau, and former WTUL members, like Hillman—that continued to fight for protective legislation at the national level throughout the 1960s. Although Amalgamated women supported equal-pay legislation, they viewed the Equal Rights Amendment (ERA) as "a well-intentioned but misguided measure" that threatened to "open the door for the abolition of the large body of state legislation enacted for the protection of women." Nevertheless, many outside the union's ranks, who saw women competing for jobs with men, particularly in the heavy industrial sector, favored repeal of protective legislation.[102] Others, like Amalgamated women who faced sex segregation in the workplace, viewed protective laws as beneficial until the 1970s. As Alice Kessler-Harris has noted, though, "the price for protection was steep."[103]

Although Amalgamated women seemed comfortable with this "difference" categorization, it constituted a form of discrimination, because, in recognizing that women differed from men, it "shifted the discussion of women's 'rights' to the contexts within which men and women functioned." Conversations about equality that had occurred in Sweden and other European countries following the war did not take place in this country until much later.[104] Though some younger women in sectors like the auto industry were increasingly comfortable with moving away from distributing jobs on the basis of sex, most working women accepted the idea of differential (but equitable) treatment as a step toward achieving equality. Even when women integrated jobs that had traditionally been considered men's, a lack of opportunity and job rights persisted.[105]

By advocating for higher wage rates, often known as the "rate for job," labor feminists advanced the case for equal pay. Although the "rate for job" demand outwardly collided with "the older labor rationale for raising worker pay—the family or living wage," Amalgamated women found the idea appealing in that it could potentially provide equal wages for them as workers. Equal-pay lobbyists eventually incorporated the "rate for job" idea because women rarely performed the same jobs as men did.[106] In essence, the rate-for-job strategy enabled a continuation of job segregation by sex, while simultaneously fostering women's demands to receive the pay they deserved.

In the climate of emerging feminist sentiments, the immediacy of the equal-pay question took precedence. Union women viewed the legislation proposed in 1963, with its potential for increased pay, as directly linked to their daily existence. Like sex segregation, the equal-pay issue had a long history in the ACWA. With the passage of the Fair Labor Standards Act during the 1930s, the situation of women on the lowest rungs of the economic ladder improved. When New York State passed its minimum-wage law in November 1934, even unorganized laundry workers were granted a wage increase. For a short time, until they were declared unconstitutional on May 27, 1935, the NRA codes addressed the issue of minimum wages in major industries. Although equal-pay provisions were part of the clothing codes, because of their segregated position women as a group still earned less than men. In the New Deal years, working-class feminists pushed hard for extended coverage and more stringent enforcement of labor-related provisions. Their efforts were rewarded with the passage of the Fair Labor Standards Act in 1938, a law that instituted federal minimum-wage regulations that applied to both men and women, albeit in a limited number of industries.[107] Landon Storrs estimates that the Act covered only an estimated one-fifth of all workers at the time of enactment, and that the "vast majority of workers who earned below subsistence wages fell outside the law's scope."[108] Coverage fell short for large numbers of minority workers, including service, retail, and agricultural workers—unorganized workers who lacked political clout. However, at Sidney Hillman's insistence, it covered the garment and textile trades.[109]

Postwar promotion of the equal-pay cause proved popular because it did not threaten the elevated position of men in the workplace hierarchy. Labor feminists like Rose Schneiderman and Bessie Hillman spoke out against equal rights but endorsed specific civil and legal rights for women. The male-dominated CIO endorsed measures like the equal-pay bill, first introduced in 1945, because it both preserved the earning power of men and stabilized traditional gender roles.[110] Labor feminists, however, saw equal pay as a mandatory requirement for full economic citizenship. Women had proved their worth in the war by doing jobs that men had formerly done, but received only half the men's wages for their work. After the war, many women experienced job loss and lower wages. Declining power in the workplace motivated labor feminists' surge for recognition and equal treatment. Their efforts culminated in the 1963 Equal Pay Act.[111]

Despite the escalating push for equality, the immediate postwar political climate resulted in additional losses for women, both at work and at home. Eisenhower appointee Alice Leopold took the reins of the Women's Bureau from longtime women's network insider Frieda Miller in 1953. Under Leopold's direction, the focus of the agency changed from calling attention to and resolving women's problems to a bureaucratic function concentrated on collecting data to ensure the nation's best interests. Labor feminists criticized Leopold, with her business background and Republican sympathies, for neglecting the needs of working women.[112] Women's advocates were dealt another blow when the national Women's Trade Union League, which had been declining in the years after the war, formally disbanded in 1950.[113] With both the Women's Bureau and the WTUL losing ground, labor feminists in the Women's Bureau established the Labor Advisory Committee as a "think tank" for female labor leaders. In the end, this resilient network of women survived many of the agencies that they represented.[114]

After the loss of their wartime gains, including their brief experience in elevated positions, impatient working women demanded full economic citizenship.[115] In the postwar years, it was the labor feminists who lit the torch of gender equality. Dorothy Sue Cobble and Nancy Gabin, among others, have chronicled the gender-based protest these women ignited in their respective organizations.[116] The joint efforts of these women expanded the notion of justice from a limited one inside individual unions to equity in the world around them. Pursuing dual tactics, female union members both sought to add strong feminist components to collective bargaining activities in the workplace and joined their network colleagues in seeking protective legislation at the state level. During and after the war, women called attention to family issues.[117] Frieda Miller's postwar speeches expanded the notion of women's workplace rights to include the right to paid employment for all women—even for mothers of small children.[118] Regardless of their marital status, rank-and-file women refused to complacently accept gender-specific categories any longer. Union men, however, were not as amenable. Though a few male union leaders supported, or at least acquiesced to, the proposition of equal rights for women in their organization, their approval yielded few results.

Labor Feminists, Front and Center

The insidious undercurrent of gender tensions in the ACWA surfaced shortly after the war ended. Lack of male support had discouraged even assertive female labor leaders from challenging sex segregation on behalf of rank-and-file women. Moreover, due to the lack of female leaders and their exclusion from the decision-making process, women's interests had never been adequately represented during negotiations with employers. Amalgamated leaders relied instead on the women's dedication to class interests to influence them to accept the less-than-favorable terms. Many union men resented the women's request for special treatment, and had to be persuaded even to consider the issue of women's concentration or crowding in low-pay occupations. In the threatening climate of the Taft-Hartley Act and McCarthyism, male labor leaders reverted to narrowly focused economic goals.[119]

Postwar attacks on labor forced unions to retreat from social unionism and pushed many male leaders into a defensive stance as they struggled for the survival of their unions. If labor feminists saw room for opportunity to move their agenda forward during the AFL-CIO merger, their hopes were short-lived. On the eve of the 1955 merger with the CIO, AFL president George Meany noted that "beyond 'bread-and-butter' issues, the labor movement was now interested in automation, shorter hours, and racial equality as a way of protecting its members" from the ramifications of the Cold War. Meany failed even to mention women workers or their concerns.[120] Refusing to be ignored by unsympathetic male union leaders, Hillman and the union women forged ahead.

Even while they acquiesced to sex segregation in the workplace, working-class feminists in the ACWA demanded explanations from male officials concerning their lack of leadership positions in the union. With the advent of the Women's Department in the 1920s, union women had expected to move into union leadership positions, but it was not until the 1948 convention that delegate Dorothy Smiley from the Laundry Workers rose to address the "development of the women for leadership in the union." Smiley viewed Eleanor Roosevelt, Bessie Hillman, Dorothy Bellanca, Gladys Dickason, Esther Peterson, and Dollie Lowther as wonderful examples of what women could do if given a chance.[121] Smiley endorsed the resolution on women's rights, which passed unanimously following Potofsky's pledge that "as far as the Amalgamated Clothing Workers of America are concerned, women will have equal rights."[122]

Over the next few years, as their gendered consciousness evolved, ACWA women leaders, who had previously worked in conjunction with the men, began to rally for equal treatment in the union. Bessie Hillman led the charge. At a Pittsburgh District union dinner in April 1956, she urged women to "become as active as men in union activities" so that they could influence "decisions up to now made only by men, while we women stayed home."[123] Two months later, she addressed a union meeting in Ohio and directed women to "assume responsibility" in the union and to "strive for a position of leadership" in it. Hillman continued, "It is up to the women to prove through their activities in the union that they are entitled to a voice in determining conditions under which they are employed and to a voice in the conduct of the affairs of the union."[124] In 1957, approaching the age of seventy, she became a popular speaker on union women and a living symbol of union history. Professor Maurice Neufeld invited Bessie to Cornell's Industrial and Labor Relations School to share her legacy of union history with students who had "no concept of the degrading conditions under which workers lived and earned their living during the early days of the century and during the depression years."[125] By then, even union leaders outside the Amalgamated identified Bessie Hillman as a working women's advocate. United Auto Workers' International Women's Department representative Mary Francis invited Hillman to speak at a 1957 regional women's conference, asking her to "tell the women of the need for taking on their responsibilities in the trade union movement."[126]

The recognition Hillman earned from those in other unions reinforced her desire to be heard. The push came from labor feminists whose paths converged on both government and industry, including Women's Bureau leaders Mary Anderson and Frieda Miller, former ACWA activist and UAW Women's Bureau Director Millie Jeffrey, future Assistant Secretary of Labor Esther Peterson, and Katherine Ellickson from the CIO's Research Department, all of whom felt that women did and had done their share as workers, particularly during the war. Fifteen such women made up the Labor Advisory Committee established by the Women's Bureau in 1945 to serve as a "policy think tank" for top women labor leaders.[127] In prior years, Hillman had tended to view exclusively separate organizing strategies as a threat to class solidarity. She had always maintained that women "ought to be recognized because we work together with men in the shops, in the factories, in the mills; because we walk together on the picket lines, because we fight in the unions with them, because we suffer together and build together."[128] By the mid-1950s, though, Hillman had begun to reconsider that stance.

The male leadership's empty promises of equal treatment of women exasperated Bessie Hillman to such an extent that she became willing to step outside the parameters of her organization to adopt a separatist strategy demanding recognition, equality, and full economic citizenship.[129] Bessie Hillman had been instrumental in the birth of the union, had witnessed the rise and fall of the union's Women's Department, had organized shirt and laundry workers in the grips of the Depression, and had directed the ACWA's wartime activities. Now, as a union vice president assigned by the male leadership to a subordinate position that required nothing more than diplomatic duties, she had had enough. At this point, union women added leadership positions for women in the ACWA to their list of demands for full economic citizenship. Willing to risk a rift with the male leadership, Hillman believed that the playing field had to be equalized before the union could move forward.

Virtually the only surviving ACWA leader with ties to the turn of the century, Bessie Hillman personified the ideological continuity between early-twentieth-century progressive reformers and postwar labor feminists. In the postwar years, Amalgamated women constructed their own version of labor feminism, which acknowledged but did not openly contest occupational segregation and rejected the ERA.[130] Most importantly, Amalgamated women joined forces with other labor feminists who sought full industrial citizenship. Their demands included a federal equal-pay act, as well as state equal-pay laws and pay equity demands in collective bargaining; accommodation of family issues in union contracts and government policy; an end to all forms of discrimination; and a federal commission to study discrimination against women. These women sought changes in union policy as well as government policy.[131] In recognizing women's subordinate status, and in setting out both to change it and "to help younger women do the same," labor women were indeed feminists.[132]

Both labor feminists and the relatively small number of women in the National Woman's Party (NWP) embraced a firm commitment to the elimination of sex-based inequalities. The treatment of women in the workplace also troubled both groups, yet their strategies for resolving these problems differed. The NWP camp sought passage of the ERA as a comprehensive solution, even at the expense of sex-based state laws. Women who led the quest for ratification of the ERA, such as Alice Paul, felt that "women should enjoy the same freedoms as men." These women viewed unions as organizations that aimed at protecting men from competition rather than protecting women from the rigors of the workplace.[133]

Labor feminists often saw the equal righters as a group of elite women who did not truly understand the needs of working women. They also felt that the ERA was a class-based piece of legislation and that the NWP was overly concerned with legal rights and did not sufficiently promote social justice. Labor feminists agreed with occupational medicine pioneer and Hull-House worker Alice Hamilton's assessment of the ERA: "Women will lose more than they will gain."[134] By the 1940s, labor feminists generally agreed that many (but not all) of the sex-based labor laws were indeed discriminatory and unfairly disadvantaged women. Nevertheless, most labor women also realized that some protective laws did address sex differences. Laws concerned with maternity-leave clauses in union contracts and maternity benefits in union insurance plans, for example, were necessary to achieve equality. By 1947, Amalgamated women enjoyed a fifty-dollar maternity benefit and clauses in union contracts stipulating that their jobs would be held open for them while they were out on maternity leave.[135] The key for labor feminists was to amend sex-based laws so that women were not unfairly disadvantaged. Labor women worked within their unions and "looked to the state to help them transform the structures and norms of wage work and curb the inequalities of a discriminatory labor market."[136]

In addition to seeking legislation at the state and federal levels, whenever they could ACWA women assumed leadership roles in the workplace. According to Fannie Allen Neal, women took the lead in the union in the largely female shops. Despite their lack of official union posts, women were the backbone of the ACWA in its day-to-day affairs.[137] They voted more; attended more meetings, educational, and social events; and even filed more grievances than union men who held more skilled positions in the workplace. Women who developed leadership skills appreciated the agency they earned in locals at the grassroots level, even though the organizational hierarchy remained predominantly male. In the Amalgamated as in the United Auto Workers, gender segregation created a separate space for women that sometimes constrained them but could also be manipulated to build a power base for them.[138] Within the Amalgamated, women leaders, including Dorothy Jacobs Bellanca, Gladys Dickason, Esther Peterson, Dollie Lowther Robinson, and Bessie Hillman, led by example. They inspired other union women to speak up on behalf of women's rights. Delegate Dorothy Smiley found the courage to state to the full convention that "the development of the women for leadership in the Union is necessary."[139] Union activity created an opportunity for women's collective activism. Dickason realized that "[s]eeing each other at union meetings, working together on union committees," union women learned to know each other as people and to understand each other's problems. During the war, the union provided an opportunity for women to participate in organizations such as the Red Cross, women's clubs, and similar community organizations, which, as Dickason noted, "working-class women [did] not belong to as a rule." Women union members also actively worked on the CIO's political action committee, helping to "get out the vote, talk[ing] to their neighbors, and enlist[ing] support behind candidates with a good record on progressive legislation." Dickason asserted, "These activities have not only made them more alert citizens but have added to their general self-confidence and self-respect."[140] Involvement in the civil rights movement and political arenas refined the activists' skills and further opened the door to effective protest.

Demanding recognition, women shaped ACWA policies with their "female" model of collective action. Bessie Hillman had always found union work rewarding, but after reevaluating women's place in the union and in American society in the aftermath of the war, she had no choice but to react against the secondary status forced upon women by cultural dictates. Buoyed by a combination of a social-justice tradition from a previous era and heightened wartime expectations that, according to Dorothy Sue Cobble, "could not be buried," by the late 1940s labor feminists extended their demands from workplace equity to a quest for an industrial democracy with full industrial citizenship rights for all workers.[141]

Bessie Hillman, a vanguard member of the first generation of labor feminists, made women's issues, including education, health care, child care, and mandatory overtime, her first priority. Hillman's career as a vice president of a major union attests to the resilient nature of labor feminism. Joining others advocating for women and their families, Hillman helped to move "caring labor" to the center of the working women's platform.[142] At the same moment as middle-class feminists began to stagger under the weight of the Cold War era, the ACWA emerged as a crucial vehicle for gender-based protest.

8 Creating "A Sort of Revolution" (1961–1970)

On the surface, Bessie Hillman had always enjoyed amicable relationships with the men who comprised the union leadership. However, by the time she returned from her second trip to Israel in the spring of 1961, frustrated by women's lack of real progress and fortified by her recent experiences abroad, Hillman's patience had worn thin. Other women were also reaching their limits with the male hierarchies that pervaded all levels of the labor movement and politics. By the late 1950s, the discrimination complaints that flooded the Women's Bureau hinted at the dawn of a new mentality. Hester Staff, a stenographer from Michigan, wrote in and expressed her feelings bluntly, "The Roosevelt and Truman administrations made great strides in removing inequalities due to 'race, creed and color' but there seems to have been little improvement in the earning capacities of the female part of the population."[1] The ideology that assumed women's place was in the home (with the exception of during a national emergency) began to sway. At the behest of the labor feminists in the last half of the twentieth century, the American political agenda shifted toward a civil rights platform that incorporated women's rights. As women's labor historian Alice Kessler-Harris explains, "The freedom that had been demanded by a few daring women in the twenties and pursued by the persistent in the fifties became in the sixties an object sought by many."[2]

Doing the Job

Labor women who had worked behind the scenes became quite visible in June 1961, when the Industrial Union Department (IUD) of the AFL-CIO called a conference to formally address the problems of working women, who by then accounted for one-third of the workforce. Labor leaders who represented the interests of the former CIO unions, and currently constituted the IUD, coordinated a conference that turned out to be the first time in trade-union history that female trade-union leaders had met in a single location for the purpose of developing, discussing, and publicizing their agenda in a national forum. According to Katherine Ellickson, Assistant Director of the Social Insurance Department of the AFL-CIO, the conference was the "first and last conference of the kind held between the demise of the National Women's Trade Union League and the formation of the Coalition of Labor Union Women in 1974."[3] As the Women's Bureau began to fade, unions grew stronger.

United Auto Workers President Walter Reuther, whose union had experienced an influx of women into the auto plants during the war and in 1944 had established a Women's Bureau, opened the conference with a conventional keynote speech that supported civil rights and equal pay.[4] Agnes Meyer, noted journalist and social critic, took the podium next. Meyer struck a resounding chord for union women when she "turned her barbs against labor's male establishment." She encouraged women in traditional occupations to organize and then to seek leadership positions in their unions. Meyer also suggested that union women simultaneously initiate a separate women's movement from within their respective organizations.[5]

On the last day of the conference, plenary speaker Bessie Hillman added to its growing feminist tenor by going a step further and openly accusing male union leaders of being "the greatest offenders so far as discrimination against women is concerned." Amalgamated women had criticized their male leaders for this offense since the 1920s, but the dissension had stayed strictly within union quarters. Hillman's public chastisement broke that precedent. Hillman was one of the highest-ranking labor women in the country in the early 1960s, and her quest for equal economic opportunities for women dated back to the opening decade of the twentieth century; thus, the responsibility to speak out on behalf of working women rested on her shoulders. Never afraid to take a risk, and with seemingly little to lose, the seventy-two-year-old Hillman attacked the male dominance of the entire organized labor movement. Relying on her own union experiences to substantiate her claims, she stepped up to the microphone and announced, "I have a great bone to pick with the organized labor movement in this country. Women have advanced to higher positions of leadership in every other walk of life than they have achieved in the trade union movement." Without missing a beat, Hillman pointed out that there was not one woman on the thirty-one-person Executive Council governing the AFL-CIO; that no woman had ever been sent to represent labor at any international conference; and that despite staunch union support, not one woman had received a recommendation to the Kennedy Administration for a job.[6]

Hillman considered her audience the best proof of gender discrimination. Surveying the faces of the approximately 175 women in the audience, who represented more than 20 international unions, she observed, "Not one of you is on the executive or policy-making level of your union. Very few of you are even presidents of locals. They let you be shop stewards, business agents, educational directors." Hillman closed her speech without looking back: "You are three and a half million women who pay dues, pay assessments, walk the picket lines in your unions, and are a part of the organized labor movement. It's your job to participate in every activity, to rise within your union, to be responsible leaders, to get into those offices and jobs which will fit you for higher positions." Notably, she placed the responsibility on working women "to get these [jobs], not because you are women, but because you have shown that you can do the job." The conference, and Hillman in particular, forced male unionists to rethink the status of organized women.[7]

Exhilarated by the frankness of both Meyer and Hillman, the women in the audience cheered them on. Their speeches stunned the few men in the audience. At the conclusion of Hillman's talk, Jacob Clayman, administrative director of the AFL-CIO Industrial Union Department and one of the conference organizers, exclaimed, "Take to the hills, men. The dam has busted."[8]

One reporter, covering the event for the "Society-Home" page of the *Washington Evening Star*, referred to Hillman's address as a "Women's Revolt" and to Hillman herself as "one of the labor movement's heroes." Similar coverage appeared on the "For and About Women" page of the *Washington Post*—indicative of the times, newspapers assumed that Hillman's speech would be of interest only to women.[9] However, Hillman's words and the audience reaction to them impressed many, including Dollie Robinson, who, upon returning to Washington after a trip, noted that Bessie had "created a sort of revolution at the women's convention." Notes of congratulations came from other labor feminists as well. Mary Anderson wrote Bessie: "Good for you. I wish I had been there to hear you."[10] Despite the direct assault on male leaders, the *Advance* reported favorably on Hillman's address at the Industrial Union Conference, noting the lack of women's progress in an article entitled "IUD Conference Concludes: Women Still Have a Long Row to Hoe."[11]

Two months later, and again on the "Society-Home" page, the *Washington Evening Star* announced Esther Peterson's appointment to President Kennedy's "little cabinet" as an assistant secretary of labor. Dollie Robinson sent Bessie a copy of the article. Always one to appreciate humor, Hillman probably chuckled when she read Dollie Robinson's handwritten note attached to the article, referring to what "a hit" Bessie had made with the Washington reporters. Hillman's remarks did seem to have impressed the local media, but as Dorothy Sue Cobble notes, it would take years before the floodwaters Clayman predicted "would sweep through the labor movement."[12]

Hillman's landmark speech, however, proved to be an important first step in revealing the unresolved gender tensions between female unionists and the men in their organizations, which had long festered just below the surface of their organizations. These pent-up frustrations were not solely the result of women attempting to claim their postwar rights, but evidenced long-standing resentment of the discriminatory treatment by male union leaders and members that union women had endured for decades. Although their wartime gains were quickly slipping away, as the immediate postwar climate grew increasingly hostile to labor, union women had theretofore refrained from exposing the internal dissension to the outside world. In the interest of union solidarity, for years labor women internalized their grievances and maintained an oppressive silence. In the more comfortable climate of the Kennedy White House, they soon erupted.

Republican dominance under Eisenhower in the 1950s threatened the New Deal order, and the responsibility to promote social justice fell back upon the unions. Male labor leaders, now operating under the additional constraints imposed by both the Taft-Hartley Act and the Landrum-Griffin Act, struggled to maintain their eroding place in American society.[13] They moved slowly when it came to ensuring that women held an equal place in the union. Some men gave only lip service to women's demands, or protected their rights by default of expanding industrial democracy rather than because of any changed gender consciousness.[14] For example, most union men, including Walter Reuther, stood behind the idea of equal pay because it did not threaten men's workforce positions. Under the guise of protection, male trade unionists agreed with the idea of paying higher wages to women so that they would be less attractive to employers and thus male jobs would be protected.[15] Alice Kessler-Harris found that left-wing unions like the ACWA "tended to espouse more genuine egalitarian values." In the "grand synthesis" of his vision for postwar industrial democracy, Sidney Hillman had attempted to set labor's postwar reconstruction agenda by placing his union firmly behind the "People's Program of 1944," which called for equal pay for equal work as well as the defense of women's right to work and federally subsidized child care.[16] Nevertheless, occupational segregation and discrimination remained firmly entrenched throughout the men's clothing industry. In an environment where union men offered few, if any, concessions, by the early 1960s it became obvious that it was consistently labor feminists in the Amalgamated and elsewhere who advanced the cause of working women.[17]

In the late summer of 1961, just as labor feminists were closing ranks, Washington reporters solicited Hillman's response to Peterson's appointment as an assistant secretary of labor. She responded candidly: "Maybe, Esther, we will get some other women in important positions—now there is a hope!" Pauline Newman seconded Bessie's optimistic sentiments.[18] In addition to pioneering new paths for women, Peterson, a former ACWA employee, and by the late 1950s the first woman lobbyist for the Industrial Union Department of the AFL-CIO, had been instrumental in planning the IUD conference and firmly agreed with its recommendations, including the promotion of equal-pay legislation to halt discriminatory employment practices based on sex, stronger contract provisions to protect women workers' health and safety, federal assistance for childcare centers, and the condemnation of the ERA.[19] In Esther Peterson labor feminists found their leader.

Bessie Hillman as a Member of the President's Commission on the Status of Women

Social feminist allies in Congress, such as Mary Norton and Helen Gahagan Douglas, along with those in the labor unions, began pushing for a presidential commission to counter the ERA and, even more importantly, "to study and analyze specific discriminations against women and recommend corrective legislation to Congress" as soon as the war ended. The "Women's Status Bill," proposed in 1947, attempted to accomplish those goals. The following year the ACWA passed a Women's Resolution explicitly supporting passage of that bill. Despite the best efforts of its staunchest proponents, though, the Women's Status bill stalled and ultimately died in Congress in 1954.[20]

Devoid of a congressional mandate, Esther Peterson nevertheless got a commission off the ground within months of her appointment to the United States Women's Bureau. She had worked briefly with John Kennedy in the late 1940s on Capitol Hill, when he was a freshman representative from Massachusetts and she was an AWCA legislative representative. Most labor leaders were reluctant to support Kennedy's 1960 presidential bid, perceiving him as "born with a silver spoon in his mouth" and thus unable to empathize with workers' needs. In contrast, based on firsthand knowledge, Peterson saw him as one who "probably understood the issues a lot better than many people with working-class backgrounds."[21]

Although Kennedy boasted a strong labor record, only when his staff members persuaded him that it was politically expedient did women as a group get his attention. During his presidential campaign, the Massachusetts senator appealed to women voters by allowing his staff to establish two publicity and fundraising committees—the Committee of Labor Women and the Women's Committee for New Frontiers (to which Bessie belonged)—for the purpose of demonstrating the candidate's concern for women's issues. Even then, when it became obvious that a commission would help to offset his less-than-satisfactory record on women's issues, Kennedy had to be convinced to support and implement the idea.[22]

In one of his first official acts, Arthur Goldberg, Kennedy's Secretary of Labor and later Supreme Court Justice, chose Esther Peterson to head the Women's Bureau of the Department of Labor. Peterson assumed her position hoping to revive "the spirit of the bureau in the days of Mary Anderson and her successor Frieda Miller," and to assuage some of the class tensions that had characterized the "fallow years under Eisenhower." More importantly, Peterson wanted "to focus more energy on low-income women working in factories and service workers rather than exclusively the concerns of professional women working in offices and white-collar jobs."[23] Arguing that "special attention and special emphasis will be required to plan programs relating to women workers as they enter the labor force in ever increasing numbers," Goldberg secured congressional approval to elevate Peterson to the rank of an assistant secretary of labor.[24] Her influence within the Kennedy administration, coupled with her strong ties to labor, initiated and shaped what soon became the President's Commission on the Status of Women (PCSW). Hillman's close ties to Peterson promised potential access to this circle of power.

According to Alice Kessler-Harris, during Peterson's tenure the Women's Bureau "crept incrementally toward equal rights for women by trying to understand the factors that discouraged wage work among them and to increase opportunities for other work."[25] In February 1961, Peterson called a meeting of trade-union women to discuss discrimination against women. The women in attendance debated the exact purpose of the future commission. Katherine Ellickson, who would soon become the executive secretary for the President's Commission on the Status of Women, successfully suggested a more positive approach than had been considered previously: that the commission "be set up not to study discrimination against women but to study the status of women." Warning against adopting an explicit feminist message, she cautioned that it should be "cleverly set up . . . to win the respect of men."[26] Peterson drafted an outline for the commission, which she referred to as the Commission on Women in an American Democracy, and forwarded it to the Secretary of Labor. Arthur Goldberg immediately relayed the draft to the president.[27]

Despite Kennedy's hesitation, Peterson and a small core group of women (including Katherine Ellickson; Evelyn Harrison, Deputy Director for the U.S. Civil Service Commission's Bureau of Programs and Standards; and Dollie Robinson, Peterson's assistant) pressed forward with the business of creating a commission. Confidentiality took precedence during discussions so that "troublesome and futile agitation" from ERA advocates would be avoided.[28] Many of the women involved in the initial discussions regarding the commission belonged to a loose grassroots coalition of union members, civil rights advocates, and politicians who eventually helped to pass civil rights laws in the 1960s. Some women, like Pauli Murray, a PCSW member and one of the few black female attorneys in the country, fought to extend the Fourteenth Amendment to equate race and sex and, in doing so, to give women the same kind of citizenship that had been given to blacks.[29]

Bessie Hillman was in Israel from March until the end of May 1961, so she did not attend the commission's earliest meetings. Instead, Julia Maietta, also a friend of Peterson's, represented the ACWA at the national meeting of women's organizations, held on May 5, 1961, that helped to launch the commission. On a draft, dated August 11, 1961, generated at a meeting where Hillman's longtime friend and ACWA activist Dollie Robinson was present, Bessie's name emerged as a potential commission member. Upon her appointment to the Women's Bureau, Peterson hired Robinson "to bring into focus the concerns of Black and low-income women, the women in the sweatshops and laundries."[30] In all likelihood it was Robinson who suggested that Hillman be included in the labor category. To reaffirm Hillman's selection, Robinson penciled in two additional pieces of information on Hillman's brief biography: that she was a member of many organizations dealing with women's and children's issues and that she was also the widow of Sidney Hillman.[31] Bessie Hillman's nomination to the commission followed on the heels of her speech at the Industrial Union Conference, which in the minds of many unionists solidified her place as a nationally prominent spokesperson for working women. Undoubtedly, Hillman's good friend Esther Peterson wholeheartedly endorsed Bessie's appointment to the commission. Hillman's presence would help Peterson achieve her goal of filling commission slots to "create a commission that consisted of members of the power structure, people who could effect change." On December 16, 1961, President Kennedy signed Executive Order 10980, formally establishing the President's Commission on the Status of Women.[32]

In April 1962, commission chair Eleanor Roosevelt extended an official invitation to Bessie Hillman to serve on the Committee for Protective Labor Legislation. Given her long-standing involvement with working women's issues and civil rights, Hillman was perfectly poised to join the PCSW when the call came. Eleanor Roosevelt considered Bessie's experience "invaluable."[33] Already a member of the Women's Committee for New Frontiers, Hillman welcomed the chance to share her vision with a growing number of female colleagues.[34] Most importantly, as her IUD speech a few months earlier had demonstrated, she was not afraid to stand up for women.

From the onset of the commission, Peterson and the other members recognized that "the central problem which might tear the commission apart or prevent its functioning was the issue of protective labor legislation versus the equal rights amendment [ERA]."[35] For more than forty years the National Woman's Party and the Women's Bureau coalition had been at odds over how to attain the same goal, equality for women. The ERA, as supported by the National Woman's Party and the National Federation of Women's Clubs, mandated equality for women, but in doing so would eliminate much of the protective legislation passed on behalf of working women during the progressive era. On the other side of the fence stood the disciples of the social feminists, who were largely responsible for enacting the protective legislation that one labor feminist pointed out "took fifty years to get."[36] Thus, the Women's Bureau, the League of Women Voters, northern Democrats, and most labor feminists "believed that the sex-based state laws should be retained until they could be amended on a case-by-case basis." The latter group maintained that although the Fair Labor Standards Act had established the principle of equal pay, the government and the courts had failed to consistently apply it.[37] Worse yet, large numbers of workers were still excluded from the protection it promised. These opponents of the ERA hoped that protective legislation for women workers would inevitably spread to all workers—including men.[38] Peterson's sympathies lay with protective labor legislation; nonetheless, in the interests of the commission, she promised to take an objective look at the ERA.[39]

Bessie Hillman Takes a Seat on the Committee for Protective Labor Legislation

By the early 1960s, women held jobs in greater numbers than ever before: 34 percent of all workers (24 million in real numbers) were women. However, the majority of those jobs were "menial and subordinate," with the largest category of women holding factory jobs. Career opportunities for educated, middle-class women also remained scarce.[40] With labor women enjoying a strong presence from the inception of the commission, working women could rest assured that their interests would be represented. For Hillman, the President's Commission on the Status of Women served as a national platform from which to continue to protest the discrimination against women workers in the workplace. Addie Wyatt, a field representative for the United Packinghouse Food and Allied Workers, and Mary Callahan, Executive Board member of the International Union of Electrical Radio and Machine Workers, joined Bessie to represent the position of laboring women on the committee. Margaret Mealey, Executive Director of the National Council of Catholic Women, chaired the committee.[41] As was the case with most of the commission's meetings, the convening of the committee always evoked a series of "lively discussions" with "few disagreements about substance." With the majority of members committed to the idea of "adequate protection of all workers," many of the committee's discussions centered around what shape protective legislation should take.[42]

As a member of the commission, Hillman proved to be an avid contributor. Throughout the proceedings, other subcommittee members frequently deferred to her on labor issues. At the first subcommittee meeting, on June 6, 1962, Bessie Hillman articulated her preference that the committee adhere to "the question of protecting women." Whenever her colleagues veered away from that task, Hillman pulled them back by reiterating the stance she had held for decades: that for workers, the most important issues were minimum wages, maximum hours, and equal pay for equal work.[43] To better assess the situation of working women, the committee decided to send questionnaires to "leading national business and industry organizations and national women's organizations" to solicit opinions "with respect to protective labor legislation and its effects on women's status and future needs." The results were scheduled for review when the committee met for a second time in November 1962.[44]

Hillman's colleagues on the committee supported the early recommendation she made to extend minimum-wage coverage for both men and women not yet covered under the Fair Labor Standards Act by including workers in hotels, motels, restaurants, laundries, small retail establishments, agriculture, and nonprofit organizations.[45] Over the previous two decades, the Amalgamated had successfully helped to lead the drives to increase the minimum wage to 75 cents an hour in 1949 and to $1.00 an hour in 1955.[46] However, as Operation Dixie had demonstrated, forces sympathetic to labor could not defeat the alliance of southerners determined to preserve the racial order. The white supremacists consistently opposed the efforts to organize workers and to extend FLSA coverage in the South, leaving large numbers of workers unprotected. Hillman fought back. She continued to champion higher wage rates and the expansion of coverage under the Act. In 1959, she spoke at the Mississippi AFL-CIO State Federation of Labor Convention, where she campaigned for an increase in the federal minimum wage from $1.00 to $1.25 an hour and for an extension of coverage. Hillman reasoned that "certainly greater coverage under the higher minimum within the Wage-Hour Law will increase the purchasing power of the workers of the State of Mississippi as elsewhere, and contribute to the greater prosperity of the workers in the State as a whole."[47] This same rationale helped elicit support for Hillman's PCSW proposals.

Despite lingering questions complicated by traditional attitudes toward gender roles about who deserved a "living wage" and "maintaining women's primary commitment to the home," in 1961 Secretary of Labor Goldberg and his staff pushed through Congress a minimum-wage increase that promised to raise the minimum wage to $1.25 an hour by 1965.[48] For the first time since the passage of the FLSA in 1938, the legislation expanded statutory coverage. Now the amended act protected employees in large retail and service enterprises.[49] Still, even this latest amendment left approximately 17 million workers, including many women in agricultural and domestic work, unprotected. These were the workers that concerned Bessie. Injecting humor into an otherwise serious committee discussion regarding further extension of coverage to the workers still outside the reaches of the FLSA (including agricultural, domestic, and laundry workers), Hillman drew a laugh when she remarked, "I think we would all be in favor of this. I don't think there is anyone here who would object to this—they wouldn't dare!" The commission's final report supported both federal and state legislation to extend coverage to all workers.[50]

Hillman's position on the Committee for Protective Labor Legislation enabled her to articulate her demands on behalf of women workers in a national forum. Benefits for women workers were her paramount concern. Hillman wanted to extend the Amalgamated's model of industrial democracy by insisting that the government establish social welfare provisions for all workers. Bessie helped to lead the committee's (and ultimately the commission's) quest to seek maternity benefits and maternity leave that would be covered by social insurance or disability. She informed committee members that in the ACWA, "as long as a woman takes a leave of absence, her job is protected." "Pregnancy," in Bessie's words, "is a woman's business, not industries'."[51] She advocated the extension of medical coverage for women workers, but that idea met with the same ill fate as it did when Frances Perkins proposed it for all Americans as part of the Social Security bill almost thirty years earlier.[52] Daycare centers for working mothers were also something working women desperately needed. Throughout their careers, ACWA women leaders such as Gladys Dickason, Esther Peterson, and Bessie Hillman actively sought the construction of affordable childcare centers. When the funding for such centers evaporated after the war, these women joined with other AFL-CIO feminists in the 1950s to renew their efforts for public support of childcare centers.[53]

At the fourth meeting of the subcommittee, in March 1963, Hillman aggressively pursued legislation to guarantee the rights of all workers to join unions of their own choosing and to bargain collectively. To ensure women's opportunity to work and fair wages, she also supported the abolition of right-to-work restrictions in any states where they existed. When Loyola University economics professor and fellow committee member Doris Boyle suggested that wages were lower in right-to-work states because "they are agricultural workers who get low wages anyway," Hillman issued a firm rebuttal. Careful to preface her response with an acknowledgment of the "liberal-mindedness" of the committee members who "sympathized with labor," Hillman replied to Dr. Boyle, "Darling, I will tell you about myself. We have 7,500 members in the cotton garment industry in Mississippi, and where the union is, the difference in wages of—I will show you the documents—

from the non-union because of the right to work law, there is a vast difference, tremendous difference."[54] Hillman worked hard to convey the disadvantages of the right-to-work laws.

Although forty-hour-maximum provisions were part of the original Fair Labor Standards Act, Hillman dominated the discussions in her effort to convince the members of the necessity of covering all workers under the maximum-hour provisions of the Act. She reasoned that this legislation would help prevent unemployment by forcing employers to hire more workers, rather than having existing employees work excessive overtime that amounted to double shifts. She also believed that employees who worked more than forty-eight hours a week should be paid double time. Hillman cautioned the commission against making a great mistake "if we only spoke of the things recommended for women alone."[55] Protective labor legislation, in Hillman's mind, should protect all workers, thus rendering the ERA unnecessary. Her proposal provoked a controversial debate that carried over to future meetings. The Committee for Protective Labor Legislation finally agreed that protective laws applicable to both men and women (including the maximum-hour laws) should be supported.[56] In the end, the PCSW members favored Hillman's recommendation for "premium pay for overtime" in the maximum-hour regulations, but rejected Hillman's rationale when they applied it exclusively to women. Her PCSW colleagues put their faith in an inclusive FLSA with "the hope that gradually legislation will be developed that will afford similar coverage for men."[57]

By the time the President's Commission on the Status of Women finished its work, Hillman and the other labor feminists had successfully persuaded commission members of the urgency of expanding the FLSA.[58] By sharing her union's advocacy of maternity benefits and daycare centers, Hillman influenced the direction of the committee's recommendations. The commission's report, *American Women*, supported both "paid maternity leave or comparable insurance benefits . . . for women workers" and the establishment of subsidized childcare centers with sliding fee scales.[59]

Hillman realized that discrimination against women existed across the board in the labor movement and in wider society. Women who did not work outside the home also suffered from its repercussions. Although still a strong advocate of protective legislation, Hillman was selective. She warned against legislation that in any way limited women's workforce opportunities. Toward the end of the committee's work, the question of limiting women from working in dangerous occupations came up for discussion. Mary Dublin Keyserling asked Bessie if she would allow a woman to work in a pool room. In her response to Keyserling, Hillman came as close as she ever would to revealing her ideology concerning full equality for women: "If they want to they can as far as I'm concerned. If we are going to fight for equality we can't deviate from these things." Bessie went on to suggest that protective provisions regarding weight limits and dangerous occupations should be general and categorized under the health and safety codes—categories that were applicable to both men and women.[60]

In 1963, the same year that the President's Commission on the Status of Women published its findings, Betty Friedan's *The Feminine Mystique* topped the bestseller charts. Friedan articulated what the PCSW's *American Women* termed "old injustices imposed on women citizens."[61] Whereas Friedan concentrated her exposé on the reaffirmation of outdated roles that continued to pervade middle-class women's lives, *American Women* focused primarily on the dilemmas afflicting working-class and minority women.[62] Commission members reiterated the need for universal coverage under the FLSA for women, the need for maternity benefits, and the need for daycare centers, along with other long-standing progressive goals. Both publications acknowledged women's secondary status in American society and hoped to enlist the federal government to the cause of gender equality.[63] According to Katherine Ellickson, in grappling with "the woman question" on a national level, labor feminists operating within the realm of the President's Commission on the Status of Women indisputably "furnished the stimulus, institutional frameworks, and content for much of the subsequent women's movement."[64]

As far as African-American women were concerned, the commission's recommendations picked up where the Fair Employment Practices Commission left off, providing the first national assessment on the status of African-American women and laying "the groundwork for the creation of the National Women's Committee on Civil Rights."[65] Labor feminists reaped the benefits of a labor movement that had been strengthened by a civil rights platform that supported unionization and "challenged the notion of separate but equal and insisted upon equal treatment and equal access for all citizens."[66] Although the commission disappointed Hillman by failing to underwrite women's right to work, it initiated a dialogue about discrimination that linked women's rights to the larger concept of civil rights, and it ultimately linked these rights to the doctrine of full economic citizenship.[67]

Hillman made several important acquaintances while serving on the commission. Economist Mary Dublin Keyserling exerted an important influence on Bessie. At the initial meeting of the subcommittee on protective labor legislation, Keyserling remarked that she was "struck by the lack of progress" of women in American society. Bessie disagreed, stating that as far as union women were concerned, they had advanced "in the last ten or twenty years in the case of women being conscious of their roles and opportunities." Nonetheless, Hillman had to admit that women still lacked positions in the upper echelons of the unions. Keyserling pointed out that in American society as a whole, men were moving faster than women, particularly when it came to wage earnings. Bessie agreed with Keyserling's assessment.[68] Despite their occasionally divergent perspectives, Keyserling appreciated the "real contributions" that Bessie made to the committee's effort to improve protective labor legislation and its administration.[69] She recalled her work with Bessie Hillman on the Committee for Protective Labor Legislation "with great pleasure." Keyserling wrote to Bessie, "the nicest thing about the meetings was the opportunity to get to know you better." In 1964, when Peterson became a special assistant to President Johnson in the newly created Office of Consumer Affairs, Keyserling took over at the Women's Bureau. Upon taking office, Keyserling contacted Hillman: "I do hope that I will have the opportunity to see you soon and to talk over some of the plans and goals of the Women's Bureau. Your advice and counsel would be invaluable."[70]

By putting labor feminists' concerns, including maintenance of support for protective labor legislation, at the top of a federal agency's agenda, just as her predecessor had, Keyserling reaffirmed the idea that working women's interests merited national attention. Under her direction, as state commissions on the status of women and the resultant Citizen's Advisory Council on the Status of Women were established to fulfill the goals of the PCSW, the Women's Bureau tried "to organize trade union women to be more effective advocates for themselves."[71] Bessie was pleased that from her Women's Bureau post, Keyserling, who had encouraged Hillman's advocacy of both civil rights and anti-poverty measures, advanced a program that "gave priority to extending labor standards to low-wage workers and securing government income supports for childbearing and childrearing." To the dismay of both Keyserling and Hillman, however, business and professional women came to dominate the state commissions and later the Citizen's Advisory Council. These women pressed for strict enforcement of Title VII and by 1967 had turned toward the ERA.[72] Even after the passage of the 1964 Civil Rights Act, Keyserling and Hillman continued to prioritize civil rights. They linked their work to civil rights organizations, frequently interacting with black women activists within these organizations.

Both women's concerns "extended beyond the ranks of union members to poor and unorganized women."[73]

Hillman's work on the PCSW also gave her the opportunity to reconnect with some of the labor feminists she had met only briefly at the IUD conference in the summer of 1961. Bessie may have crossed their paths in Democratic political circles or in her work with civil rights organizations, but as a rule the opportunities for labor feminists to meet with one another outside their own unions were rare.[74] With the demise of the Women's Trade Union League in the early 1950s, and the obstruction of working women's progress during Alice Leopold's Women's Bureau tenure in the Eisenhower years, meeting on common ground for extended periods of time while serving on the protective labor committee was a welcome respite from the isolation these women sometimes experienced as leaders in male-dominated unions. Addie Wyatt and Mary Callahan spoke openly with Hillman about the racial and gender segregation that persisted in their respective unions. Hillman admired Wyatt's attempts to combat both sexual and racial discrimination in the Packinghouse Workers' union. Hillman could also identify with Callahan, who worked in and later led a local in an electrical union where job segregation was seldom questioned.[75] Mary Callahan remembered that toward the end of the 1960s, Esther Peterson called a meeting of labor union women at her Washington, D.C., home. Women from the auto workers', clothing workers', and laundry workers' unions attended. In the wake of the PCSW's work, the discussion revolved around getting "all the women in the unions together." Unfortunately, despite the best intentions of these women leaders, such a meeting never materialized.[76]

Labor Feminism Rising

If, as the PCSW proved, labor feminists' demands warranted consideration by the federal government, then they certainly deserved attention from male trade-union leaders. Like Hillman, most women commission members did not label themselves feminists even though they sought the advancement of women. Union women tended to be "a little bit suspicious" of women in organizations labeled feminist.[77] Esther Peterson explained simply that "we did not think in those terms." These women defined feminism narrowly and viewed self-proclaimed feminists as too self-serving in their goals and too militant in their tactics to be respected by the rank and file. Hillman agreed with Peterson's class-based analysis that "so many of these ardent feminists came from good families and held good jobs, if they worked at all, and they had not the slightest idea of the problems their sisters faced at the other end of the social and economic scale."[78]

As time went on, though, many women who had earlier disavowed the feminist label began to seriously consider the demands of the so-called "hardcore feminists," in order to push working-class feminism toward full equality for women. With the tensions between rising workforce participation and the denial of egalitarian demands exposed, women activists who had collaborated at the national level to work toward industrial citizenship for women staged a fight for women's equality within their unions. Hillman voiced support for protective labor legislation and opposition to the ERA, on behalf of her ACWA constituency, until the end of her life, but she never sought anything less than full equality for women. Bessie informed many of the middle-class members of the PCSW, for the first time in their lives, about the frustrations and unfulfilled promises women workers confronted. In turn, work on the PCSW served as an advanced training ground for Bessie Hillman and the other labor feminists who emerged in their own unions in the 1950s as champions for women workers. For many, this work within the upper echelons of a presidential administration enhanced their careers. Collaboration with middle-class women, many in high-ranking government posts, generated new cross-class alliances and broader reform vistas. Labor feminists expanded their horizons past their own unions and advanced their activism beyond the labor arena into the field of political and human rights.

Hillman's work on the PCSW changed her outlook. Meeting women leaders from all walks of life confirmed her suspicion that despite labor feminists' efforts to the contrary, the labor movement remained an essentially sexist entity. Her associates on the PCSW afforded Hillman the respect that she was sometimes denied in her own union. Seeing how far her PCSW contemporaries had come in their respective fields encouraged her to continue to demand women's rights within the labor movement. Her inclusion on the PCSW validated her own career and her union work attained a greater significance outside the ACWA. As a result of their work on the President's Commission on the Status of Women, labor women were impelled to lead the charge to challenge the "age-old barrier of women's traditional sex roles" through legislation.[79]

The equality promised under the 1963 Equal Pay Act was vital to working women and ranked at the top of the priority list for labor feminists. Union women, including Bessie Hillman, had fervently supported passage of an equal-pay bill, which had had provisions requiring wages to be paid on the basis of the job rather than the sex of the worker since it was first introduced in 1945. Appearing before a congressional committee in 1950, Helen Blanchard spoke on behalf of the Amalgamated women who wanted to be accepted as equals and demanded that Congress "abolish the horrible practice of discrimination purely on the basis of sex."[80] Testifying before a House subcommittee in 1963, ACWA Associate National Education Director Connie Kopelov advocated passage of the bill by construing the amendment as protecting *men's* jobs: "Such legislation is needed because the payment of a lower wage to women than to men for the same or similar work has invariably undermined the wages of the men or has resulted in the replacement of men with lower-paid women, thus also impairing the living standards of the families of male workers."[81] Male union leaders supported the reasoning that raising the standard of living and thus purchasing power would help prevent the spread of communism in the United States. Support for equal pay came from government officials as well. Applying Keynesian economic theory that she had learned while at the London School of Economics under Keynes, Mary Dublin Keyserling believed that increasing labor's purchasing power would strengthen the economy. Labor Secretary Arthur Goldberg tied economic opportunities for women directly to a healthy economy.[82]

Peterson considered the hard fight to win passage of the "equal pay amendment" to the Fair Labor Standards Act, in June 1963, one of her first victories as an assistant secretary of labor. Yet, to the dismay of Peterson and the other labor feminists—who had been fighting for legislation to equalize the pay of men and women since World War II—congressional wrangling left the act "gutted of language that required equal pay for 'work of comparable quantity and quality' that offered at least a restrained threat to labor market segregation."[83] An amendment exempting women in administrative, executive, and professional positions from coverage weakened the Act further. Once passed, the Equal Pay Act applied only to employees who were covered under the minimum-wage requirement of the FLSA; that is, those employees who worked in establishments that did business of at least $250,000 a year. Many employees, including those in small retail establishments, restaurants, and beauty shops, were not protected. Employees in agriculture, seasonal amusement or recreational establishments, motion-picture theaters, certain small newspapers, hotels, motels, and laundries were also excluded from coverage.[84] Nevertheless, in spite of its compromised language, the 1963 Equal Pay Amendment to the Fair Labor Standards Act marked the federal government's official entry into the fight for women's economic rights. The act offered "improved prospects for achieving gender equity in the workplace" by offering a legal basis upon which to contest gender-related wage discrimination through the courts.[85] A legal basis for protesting racial discrimination would soon follow.

Labor Feminists Stake Their Case

Interestingly, labor feminists experienced gains at the national level prior to advancing their status in their own unions. Although Bessie Hillman never formally aligned with the reinvigorated women's movement of the 1960s, she always insisted that women be permitted the same opportunities as men, and she decried the tokenism that women experienced. With a mounting sense of confidence instilled by her growing reputation as a spokesperson for working women's rights, in 1962 Bessie Hillman contributed an essay on the status of working women, entitled "Gifted Women in Trade Unions," to *American Women: The Changing Image*, reiterating the dearth of females in top labor positions and appealing to women of all ages to take steps to change this condition.[86] Refusing any longer to settle for anything less than leadership positions, Hillman advised young women to become active leaders in the trade-union movement. A record number of women were working in 1961. Of the 24 million women who worked for pay by the early 1960s, more than 3 million women, or about one in eight, belonged to unions.[87]

Rather than faulting employers for not hiring or for intimidating women workers, or even blaming working men for their lack of support for female coworkers and female family members, Hillman focused on the lack of representation for union women at the national level. While she admitted that men—especially male union leaders—were responsible for this dilemma, she pointed out that women were also guilty.[88] It was obvious that women members wanted more than a token woman on the General Executive Board, "but they couldn't agree on who and weren't aggressive enough in trying to get it." ACWA member Sara Fredgant warned that women "still have to fight for every inch of ground, if they don't it will be given as token representation again." Eula McGill agreed that women needed to assert themselves more. Echoing Hillman, she criticized those women who "sat back and whined and don't try."[89]

Hillman cautioned women who were already trade-union leaders: "You must not look to the men to choose you for higher executive positions because you are active in the union unless you deserve it. . . . Don't take it for granted that just because you're active you are going to be picked by men for higher jobs. You have to assert yourself by being worthy and by standing up to all the tests in the labor movement—and then you're going to be recognized." Hillman added words of encouragement: "You've got to do it, and I know you will." Hillman held "a deep conviction that given a more important function within the labor movement, women could do much to restore the union image as the indomitable fighter for social justice and enlightenment," an image that Hillman stressed had been "sadly undermined in recent years."[90] Nelson Lichtenstein lent insight into labor's eroding status, noting that "the solid quality of postwar U.S. unionism reflected the institutional constraints and legal structures under which the unions were forced to function." During the 1950s and 1960s, Lichtenstein argues, "[i]n the United States intellectuals, jurists, journalists, academics, and politicians came to see the unions as little more than a self-aggrandizing interest group, no longer a lever for progressive change."[91] Hillman, however, refused to give up on labor's reform agenda. She sought to tap the potential of union women, urging them to become leaders and make "a better world."[92]

In addition to a less-than-favorable political climate facing potential women activists, family circumstances often discouraged women from entering the public arena. Though they faced discrimination by union men and employers, an even larger obstacle to industrial citizenship for working wives and mothers was the burden of the so-called double day. ACWA member Sarah Barron realized that women's overwhelming responsibilities forced many women to refrain from activism. Barron pointed out that "a woman has a triple problem. She has the problem of her home; she has the problem of her children; and she has the problem of her job."[93]

Labor feminists pushed for "social supports for caring labor" that would aid working mothers as they raised their families.[94] Hillman, who had had both household help and a supportive husband, nevertheless empathized with the realities for women unionists. Working women did their best to accommodate multiple demands on their time. Even for some would-be activists, who were willing to shuffle their priorities so that they would have time for union activities, financial hardships created by their position as sole supporters of their families prevented them from becoming full-fledged activists. Most female labor activists tended to be young, single, and unencumbered by family responsibilities. Fannie Allen Neal was a divorced single mother for whom the "union took precedence over everything in my life." She refused "dates from fellows" and spent time away from her family so that she could attend union meetings instead. Like the few other women activists with families to raise, she relied on assistance from others. Her sisters helped to raise her daughter so that Neal could travel on union business and, later, on civil rights business. In Bessie Hillman's case, she hired household help even after her children were grown, so that she could concentrate on union business. Neal emphasized the importance of the union in her life and in the lives of other devoted women activists, admitting that "not all members were like this but we were loyal until the end."[95]

Family responsibilities did not always preclude women's activism, but many labor feminists felt that working women remained in secondary leadership positions due to the responsibilities associated with marriage and children. Marital status sometimes affected the way women were treated by male union officials. Most union leaders believed that women who achieved leadership positions were competent, but they berated those, like the ILGWU's Fannia Cohn, whom they considered "married to the union."[96] In union men's eyes, there was clearly something amiss with those who failed to conform to the cultural confines of marriage and family.

Some Amalgamated women, like laundry workers' organizer Charlotte Adelmond and men's clothing worker Sara Fredgant, did sacrifice family life for the sake of their unions. Fredgant substituted work for family, becoming so involved in the union that she "never thought of marriage."[97] However, Dollie Robinson warned that women could become "too enmeshed in the union and disappointed if things didn't go right." Robinson used Hillman as an example when she observed that women tended to stay active in the union longer if they had outside interests.[98]

One of the sustaining factors in Hillman's professional commitment was the balance she achieved between work and family life. Bessie's intense dedication to the union never wavered, but she thoroughly enjoyed her life outside the union, too. In addition to entertaining, Hillman loved the theater. One of Philoine's favorite memories of her mother is of going to see the Broadway performance of *Fiddler on the Roof* together. Hillman rarely talked about her childhood in Linoveh, but as she watched the musical, set in tsarist Russia, long-suppressed memories came rushing back. During the scene where a young shtetl girl becomes distressed over the prospect of an arranged marriage, Bessie jumped out of her seat and, pointing at the stage, exclaimed, "That's me! That is what happened to me!"[99]

Esther Peterson remembered that much of the support the union offered her "as a woman" came from Bessie. Whereas some union officials thought they could push women around, Hillman, whom Peterson considered "a practical woman," encouraged Peterson to continue to work while pregnant. "She inspired me to do what I wanted and needed to do, regardless of what other people thought. She helped me realize that I didn't need to apologize for having a baby and speaking at a union function." Hillman taught Peterson about "the genuineness of people who have strong feelings, to hell with the trappings."[100]

As other Amalgamated women began to follow in the footsteps of female leaders like Hillman and Peterson, they found their leadership positions very rewarding. Regina Urdaneta, Puerto Rican Joint Board president in the 1960s, enjoyed the recognition and respect of those she "took care of."[101] Urdaneta viewed her responsibilities as a union leader as an extension of her family duties. Nevertheless, it was difficult to recruit younger women as leaders. The obvious generation gap between union pioneers like Hillman and women members who came of age in the postwar decades offers a partial explanation. Rank-and-file members were not only significantly younger than union leaders, but they often belonged to different ethnic or racial groups as well. As the numbers of new members swelled, leaders had problems finding common ground from which to relate to new recruits. Urdaneta complained that the leaders distanced themselves from the rank and file.[102]

Even once-revered leaders did not escape criticism. Freida Schwenkmeyer, who met Bessie in the 1930s during the Albany campaign, remembered that her first impression of Bessie Hillman was that she was a "know-it-all." Hillman's style of dress probably also contributed to the generational gulf. She was always impeccably dressed in the latest style, including elaborate hats, furs, and accessories that most workers could ill afford. Schwenkmeyer readily admitted, though, that "all of the old timers," including Bessie Hillman, worked long hours and with little or no pay during the union's organizational campaigns.[103] Despite their differences, by the 1960s Amalgamated women closed their ranks and looked past their male coworkers and in search of their own tools to improve their status and to fight discrimination.

Where Industrial Democracy Ends, Industrial Citizenship Begins

In August 1963, blacks organized the largest protest in American history: the March on Washington for Jobs and Freedom. Hillman's friend A. Phillip Randolph led more than a quarter of a million marchers (including ACWA workers), and Martin Luther King, Jr., addressed the crowd with his memorable "I have a dream" speech. Twenty years earlier, Randolph's threat of a march on Washington had led to the creation of the Fair Employment Practices Commission; similarly, within a year the current movement culminated in the passage of the 1964 Civil Rights Act, hailed as a legal revolution for the black cause.[104]

Labor feminists disagreed about the potential effectiveness of Title VII of the Act, which prohibited employment discrimination on the basis of race or sex. Mary Callahan, of the International Union of Electrical Workers and former member of the Committee for Protective Labor Legislation, initially opposed Title VII, but later began to view it as a positive development for women.[105] Esther Peterson went on record as opposing Title VII. This was not, as she later explained, because she was opposed to the idea of prohibiting sex discrimination in employment, but because she feared that the "sex amendment" attached by Representative Howard Smith of Virginia "was just an attempt to defeat the Civil Rights bill." Peterson "didn't want anything to jeopardize the Civil Rights Act." In retrospect, Peterson realized that Smith's ploy had backfired entirely, and rather than hold minorities back, "the bill moved women forward."[106]

Still, ACWA President Potofsky hesitated to endorse the 1964 Civil Rights Act Title VII legislation, believing that "protective laws should not be discarded until adequate substitutions are passed." The Amalgamated president emphasized the difference between men and women, proposing that rather than lowering the standards of men, the standards of women should be raised. Hillman agreed with Potofsky and other union leaders who reacted negatively to Title VII, because of the "onslaught against state protection for women workers" that resulted from its enactment.[107] Ironically, Title VII, which in reality had little connection to the ERA, would indeed result in the systematic elimination of protective labor laws—on the ground of discrimination because they applied only to women.

The Equal Employment Opportunity Commission (EEOC), Title VII's enforcement arm, received an overwhelming number of workplace discrimination complaints immediately after its creation. In establishing the five-member bipartisan EEOC, the Civil Rights Act gave the commissioners power to investigate and attempt to resolve complaints voluntarily before bringing them to a hearing with the civil rights division of the Department of Justice, to seek court enforcement of the EEOC's decision, or to notify individuals that they could proceed to federal court to seek relief.[108] More than 25 percent of the cases filed by working-class women in the first year involved sexual discrimination. Although the first case of this kind was not prosecuted by the Justice Department until 1970, many labor feminists began to change their views of Title VII by the late 1960s.[109] At the ACWA's Twenty-Fifth Biennial Convention in 1966, Amalgamated women supported the passage of a "Resolution on Women Workers" that urged the EEOC to more effectively address the elimination of discriminatory practices based on sex while at the same time preserving the "long-standing and essential standards won through state protective legislation." In addition, the resolution "recommended the passage of equal pay legislation in those states which do not yet have it in order to protect those workers not covered by the federal law."[110]

By the end of the 1960s, unions began to change their stance on protective legislation. Some union women pinned their hopes on the rationale that, taken together, the Equal Pay Act and Title VII were a means for working women to contest both occupational segregation and discrimination.[111] After initiating a substantial number of discrimination suits with the EEOC, labor women changed the labor movement's stance on gender equality and began to move toward favoring the ERA. Auto and electrical unions containing women who wanted to perform men's jobs were among the first to support the ERA. Although not all the women in the UAW agreed, in 1967 it became the first union to formally oppose protective legislation.[112] Nancy Gabin contends that "those having the most to lose from the elimination of protective laws for women rejected the ERA in the fiercest manner." Women in unions with high percentages of women fell into this category.[113] Amalgamated women pressed for extending protective measures to all workers and did not support the ERA until 1974.[114]

Although, as Nelson Lichtenstein claims, by the early 1960s the term *industrial democracy* no longer figured in labor-movement rhetoric, the currents that sparked this aspiration remained vital. According to Lichtenstein, the ideology of industrial democracy both unified the working class and manifested "a particular appeal" for women.[115] Its inherent directive to fight for a humane society gave rise to a feminist consciousness that reacted to the gendered tensions in the labor movement and inspired a fight for workplace justice. As they grew stronger in mind and in number, labor feminists, who had shared their muted desires with one another in the union halls of the 1920s and publicly voiced their agenda in the workplaces and New Deal circles of the 1930s, began voicing their demands for full industrial citizenship to Congress immediately after World War II ended. By the early 1960s, with the return of the Democrats and Esther Peterson and the revival of the feminist movement, women finally began to make progress toward realizing their agendas.

Throughout the mid-1960s, as labor feminists actively recruited new members, the percentage of women in unions rose.[116] Labor feminists focused more attention than ever on opening leadership positions in the Amalgamated to women. They also made a concerted effort to help younger women move ahead, and mentored them whenever an opportunity presented itself. Hillman routinely assisted job-seeking women by writing letters of recommendation for them, as she did for Dollie Robinson for the New York State Department of Labor Secretary. As a member of the Women's Bureau coalition, Hillman acted in concert with other labor feminists to advance working women in all walks of life. At Pauline Newman's request, Hillman wrote a letter supporting Lucille Buchanan's bid for the directorship of the United States Bureau of Labor Standards. Hillman agreed with Newman's assessment that "it is high time that the Department considers women for higher positions."[117]

One of the lone female executives in her own union, Bessie Hillman drew strength from other social and labor feminists. Rose Schneiderman, whom Hillman had known "personally and intimately since 1911," remained one of her closest friends.[118] Throughout her life Hillman corresponded regularly with Pauline Newman and Elisabeth Christman. After Mary Anderson retired from the Women's Bureau and published her autobiography, *Women at Work*, Bessie Hillman wrote a note of warm congratulations, reminding Anderson that "your friendship means very much to me."[119] In 1962, Anderson's hastily written note to Bessie, informing her of Elisabeth Christman's heart attack, revealed the intimate connections among labor women. Anderson asked Hillman to "let Pauline and Rose know."[120] Not only did Bessie work closely with Dollie Robinson and Esther Peterson as they advanced in government posts throughout the 1960s, she counted them among her most intimate friends. Hillman's friends appreciated what Dollie Robinson described as her "priceless sense of humor." According to Bessie, "Things shouldn't always be serious and sober." Cherishing close relationships with her family and goddaughter Jan Robinson, Bessie invited them to stay at her Lookout Point cottage half a block from the ocean on Long Island. Spending time with her four grandchildren also brought Bessie great joy. She lamented that the oldest grandchild, Dorothy, was the only one Sidney had known.[121]

In contrast to many of her contemporaries, who ended their public careers by the mid-1960s, Bessie Hillman forged ahead, never seriously contemplating retirement. She found new causes to combine with the old. Sidney's extensive involvement in international labor issues, as well as the examples of women like Eleanor Roosevelt, Esther Peterson, and Mary Dublin Keyserling, encouraged Hillman's burgeoning interest in social justice and human rights in the international arena. Her experience on the President's Commission on the Status of Women and her travel abroad enriched her awareness of multinational women's issues. Hillman represented American women's labor interests as a delegate to the International Confederation of Free Trade Unions at the United Nations in 1962 and 1963. At one of the sessions, she praised "nearly all the new nations of Asia and Africa [that] have included clauses in their constitutions guaranteeing equal rights for women." The international confederation also worked to integrate women into the trade-union movement. Hillman sided with the proponents of political rights for women, the employment of women, and retirement and pension benefits for all workers.[122]

Septuagenarian Bessie Hillman kept a close watch on emerging labor issues. She became increasingly concerned with issues pertaining to old-age benefits. Speaking to retired Amalgamated members, Hillman learned that older workers often led "solitary lives" on fixed incomes and had difficulty finding retirement homes. Although the Amalgamated sponsored a number of programs for its retired members, including cooperative agreements between the Department of Social Services, settlement houses, and the union to run day programs for older people, there were no special provisions for housing for retirees. Hillman hoped for a more comprehensive approach to address the needs of retirees that went beyond recreation centers and subsidized day programs for retired members.[123] In October 1969, she wrote to Ethel Reilly, an ACWA retiree, to inform her that "the recent negotiations which attempted to increase the pensions of union retirees failed." Hillman urged Reilly to pressure politicians to increase Social Security benefits.[124]

In the early 1960s, Bessie Hillman reached beyond the clothing trades, taking an interest in the plight of agricultural workers like California organizer Maria Moreno, who corresponded regularly with her about organizing farm workers.[125] Even while she organized workers, Hillman recognized the pressing need to groom a new and educated generation of leaders. Although with the exception of her citizenship classes she had had little formal education herself, Hillman adamantly advocated free public education—a system she believed that labor had helped to establish. During the 1960s, Hillman spoke frequently at the graduations of the annual weeklong summer ACWA Training Institute at Bard College.[126] In her own community, she demonstrated her commitment to education by serving on the board of directors for the La Guardia House Nursery and the Fashion Institute of Technology.[127]

Hillman saw the potential to develop "a fuller and richer democracy" by promoting close relationships with colleges and universities.[128] Throughout the last decade of her life, she aptly served as the chair for the Amalgamated's Education Committee, which constantly pushed for educational benefits at the national, state, and union levels, including "the extension of tuition-free public schools beyond high school and community college, an increase in federal scholarships as a step toward a free college education," upgrades for vocational education, and the possibility of providing college education insurance for ACWA members' children.[129] With her steady drive for education, organization, and political action, Hillman served as an example and an inspiration to trade-union women.

Just as they had after the passage of the suffrage amendment in 1920, labor feminists remained politically active after the passage of the Equal Pay and Civil Rights Acts. During the Kennedy administration, many Americans learned to view change as a positive value.[130] Attitudes toward civil rights and women's place in society gradually began to change. Following Kennedy's assassination in November 1963, many feared that the vision for a better America would start to fade, but Lyndon Baines Johnson pledged to carry out the war on poverty and to back civil and women's rights in his Great Society programs.[131]

Hillman supported Johnson by working for the passage of the Medicare bill, federal aid to education, a higher minimum wage, the repeal of right-to-work laws, more quality housing, and anti-poverty measures. In an effort to effect change, Hillman simultaneously immersed herself in state politics. She rejoiced in 1964 when the Democrats won the majority of seats in the New York State Assembly and Senate for the first time in almost thirty years. She hoped that the letters she wrote to various state representatives, urging them to vote in favor of labor, would result in the passage of progressive labor legislation. Most importantly, Bessie Hillman trusted that, in the wake of its recent success, the Democratic Party "would discharge its responsibility to the people to achieve a better society for all."[132] Hillman's wishes came to fruition when Dollie Lowther Robinson was elected to the 1967 New York State Constitutional Convention. Robinson called on Hillman to submit "any suggestions she wished considered."[133] No written record exists to indicate what suggestions Hillman may have had.

By 1967, formal political education activities became a necessity for labor so that it could counteract the Ninetieth Congress's fiscal slashing of education, the war on poverty, and housing and urban renewal programs. Newspaper headlines chronicling the growing U.S. commitment in Vietnam disturbed Hillman. She blamed the escalating involvement for causing a "budgetary squeeze," which in turn prevented new legislation and caused cutbacks in crucial social welfare benefits.[134] The diversion of resources into the war effort threatened the postwar order. Short of formally allying with the anti-war movement, Hillman spoke out against the war even though some AFL-CIO leaders assumed what they considered a patriotic stance and supported the war.[135] Combining the proven progressive tactics of political action and community organization to exert pressure on individuals, Hillman addressed union audiences and conducted extensive letter-writing campaigns directed at politicians, attempting "in the tradition of the labor movement" to "bring dignity and well being to the poverty stricken."[136] Despite labor's mixed political record and the 1968 election of the Republican candidate Richard Nixon, in the long run Hillman judged her union's collective political activism on behalf of all workers a success, proclaiming, "I believe that we have played a major role in the social welfare legislation which American workers now enjoy."[137] With the workers' concerns over politics, education, and civil rights apparent at the 1970 ACWA convention, members of the Education Committee warned that the Nixon administration's educational cutbacks needed to be reversed so that programs such as Teacher Corps, Head Start, and vocational education could expand. The committee also demanded "that racial and economic bias be totally eliminated from all educational facilities, programs, materials, and textbooks."[138]

Despite labor's weakening political grip, the movement's political activism in the civil rights arena paid off. At the same time African-Americans gained job opportunities, because of the passage and enforcement of Title VII, labor feminists in the Amalgamated confronted discrimination. Between 1966 and 1970, Amalgamated women filed more complaints on the basis of racial discrimination than members of any other union.[139] Of the twelve complaints filed by Amalgamated members with the EEOC between 1966 and 1970, black women who alleged that their employers had discriminated against them on the basis of their race filed nine. The employers were charged with discrimination in three of the four complaints that progressed as far as the EEOC hearing process.[140]

Because of ambiguity and confusion over what constituted sexual discrimination, proven accusations of discrimination on the basis of sex trailed behind those based on racial discrimination. Feminists, including some in labor's ranks, such as United Packinghouse Workers leader Addie Wyatt and United Auto Workers leaders Caroline Davis and Dorothy Haener, demanded that sex discrimination be treated as seriously as race discrimination; many of these activists went on to form the National Organization for Women (NOW).[141] However, for the time being, ACWA women were satisfied by their version of labor feminism, which allowed occupational segregation to exist while they concentrated on civil rights. Labor women were at that point just coming around to questioning the root causes of job segregation.[142]

Laundry workers, many of whom were black, reaped the added rewards of the 1966 extension to the FLSA. That latest amendment extended coverage to the majority of women and minority workers. In addition to the guarantee of a minimum-wage increase to $1.60 by 1971, for the first time employees of hotels, motels, restaurants, laundries, public schools, nursing homes, and hospitals, as well as agricultural workers on large farms and those in the construction industry, would be covered. The 2 million domestic workers were the only major occupational group excluded from the scope of the FLSA. Although activists hailed the Act as "a major triumph for the civil rights movement as well as the labor and women's movement," as late as 1972, of the 11.3 million workers who were excluded from protective coverage under the FLSA, approximately 5 million were women.[143] Despite the mixed record of male labor unionists when it came to civil rights and women's rights, black and white labor women continued to fight in unison for women's equality long after the passage of the Civil Rights Act.[144]

Labor Women Find Their Place

The American Labor Education Service acknowledged in 1961 that, despite direct evidence of discrimination against women on union jobs, there was no question that "the chief support for women in the struggle against unequal treatment has come from unions."[145] With most of the top AFL-CIO leaders out of step with the multiple insurgencies of the anti-war protest, the rise of a feminist consciousness, and civil rights beyond the passage of the Civil Rights Act, women in the Amalgamated (and a handful of other unions with a notable labor feminist presence) reinfused the principles of social justice and introduced the feminist notion of "rights consciousness" into the labor arena. Examination of the Amalgamated's history in the 1960s reveals that while a number of unions substituted "caution, bureaucracy, and self-interest" for the quest for industrial democracy in the postwar years, the labor feminists within the Amalgamated, the Packinghouse Workers, and the United Auto Workers kept their organizations on a "dynamic frontier," influencing policymaking and expanding the labor movement's politics by supporting both the civil rights drives and anti-poverty efforts of those years.[146]

In March 1968, Bessie missed the General Executive Board meeting in Miami Beach due to illness. She did recover in time to attend the biennial convention, where she led the continued drive for childcare funding. Thanks in part to the efforts Hillman had initiated during World War II, in 1968 the Amalgamated Clothing Workers of America became the first union in the country to co-sponsor a daycare center with an employer. Advocating caring labor practices, the union gained national recognition for "taking the lead" in establishing model programs for more than 2,000 children in 15 centers in areas of Virginia, Maryland, Pennsylvania, Delaware, and North Carolina. Potofsky felt that this first step was "long overdue" and expressed the hope that the federal "government will assume the responsibility" on a nationwide scale. The Amalgamated sponsored a congressional bill to guarantee that collective bargaining would include the subject of childcare benefits. Eventually, a center for working parents in the state office building in Harrisburg, Pennsylvania, would be named for Bessie Hillman.[147]

Plagued by poor health during the last year of her life, Hillman nevertheless remained a committed activist, continually expanding her reach beyond the labor arena to the broader realm of humanitarian concerns. She traveled to Gloversville, New York, to assist President Potofsky with the presentation of the Amalgamated charter to a new local, and spoke on political action at an education parley in Maine. Rising to the occasion, Vice President Hillman infused her speech with her oft-repeated theme of promoting education to help answer larger questions: "We are all here to learn. To learn why there is no Peace, why war still exists or why innocent farmers and workers are killed by bombs and bullets they do not understand. We have to learn why there is still unemployment in this great land, why there are people who have been so long without jobs that they are almost without hope. We have to learn why many people in our country and in other lands are hungry."[148] The problem of preserving peace became a dominant theme in Hillman's later speeches. Her quest for industrial democracy expanded into a search for human rights in the international arena.

Hillman was resilient. Reporting to the office every day even in the eighth decade of her life, she never stopped educating or organizing workers. In the last year of her life she expanded her union's reach. When no other union would, she actively organized the production and maintenance workers at the Xerox Corporation in Rochester, New York.[149] In March 1970, she traveled with Esther Peterson and Jake Potofsky to San Juan, Puerto Rico, to meet with the Governor of Puerto Rico, Luis A. Ferre, and the Secretary of Labor, Julia Vicenty, to discuss the future of Puerto Rican labor organizing.[150] Bessie remained devoted to keeping the memory of Sidney Hillman's work alive. One of her last official acts involved the presentation of the Sidney Hillman Foundation Award for Meritorious Public Service to David Morse, director general of the International Labor Organization, in the fall of 1969.[151]

Hillman rallied from illness to attend the ACWA's Twenty-Seventh Biennial Convention in Atlantic City the following May, where she reported on the activities of the Education Committee and witnessed further discussion of women's rights.[152] Bessie faced the harsh fact that gender discrimination still existed. In her final year of life, she continued to oppose the advancement of women as a group based solely on gender. Hillman concentrated on helping women workers in the best way she knew how: by inspiring them to attain higher goals so that they would assume positions from which they could help themselves. She led by example, encouraging young women to "go as far as you possibly can" in college, "to read widely and intensively and to establish contacts with men and women functioning in union organizations on the job."[153] In part, Bessie traced her own life in anticipating the role that labor feminists could play in attaining full economic citizenship. "In the final analysis," she maintained, "there is only one essential requirement for a union leader; a sincere interest in the material well-being and the social, cultural and spiritual development of one's fellow human beings, together with a conviction that these goals can best be pursued by organization, education, and common dedication to a common cause."[154] As she had for the past sixty years, she stuck close to the social feminist lessons gleaned during her years in Chicago, combining education and organization with protective legislation to achieve labor's goals.

Although the changes resulting from Title VII persuaded many labor feminists, including Esther Peterson, to lean toward supporting the ERA, Hillman steadfastly held to her convictions.[155] In keeping with Hillman's stance, the Amalgamated endorsed the AFL-CIO's Resolution on Women Workers and pledged to join with "other labor organizations and liberal forces to safeguard and strengthen existing state protective laws for women, to make them applicable to men wherever appropriate, and to continue the struggle for improved state and federal labor standards legislation for all workers."[156] In the course of fostering workers' aspirations for workplace justice, Hillman helped women explore their place in a more caring labor movement with special protections. She concurred with Mary Callahan's plan to first extend these protections to men and then "go for the ERA."[157]

Bessie Hillman simply ran out of time. Her sixty-year career as a trade-union activist came to an end on December 23, 1970. She died in St. Vincent's Hospital in New York City at the age of eighty-one from complications following stomach surgery. When asked by her children if she had any regrets, Bessie wrote on a slate, "I'm only sorry to say good-by to my union."[158] To Bessie Hillman, the union was more than a means through which to accomplish her goals—it coursed through every fiber of her being.

Although the banner headlines that had reported the death of her husband twenty-five years earlier were missing from the nation's major newspapers, reactions to Hillman's death resonated from across the country. Philoine Fried remembers that Pauline Newman, Bessie's contemporary and longtime education director of the ILGWU health center, was "furious" when Bessie died, for now the eighty-year-old Newman was "left all alone," the sole survivor of an irreplaceable generation.[159] United States Secretary of Labor James D. Hodgson was one of the many dignitaries who sent condolences to Bessie's union family. One of the most fitting tributes came from Leo Perlis, Director of the AFL-CIO Department of Community Services, who wrote about Bessie's ability to fire others with "spirit and enthusiasm" and remembered how "she served with patience, good humor, and wisdom always attempting to improve the lot of workers, their families, and all citizens." Capturing the essence of Hillman's spirit, Perlis added: "She was a fine Jewish mother before Jewish mothers became famous. She was an active citizen at a time when active citizenship was considered a prerogative of the well-born, the well-placed and the well-to-do. And she was a liberated woman before Women's Lib. She was an original in an era of originals. Her death is not only our loss but marks the passing of that era as well."[160] But before the era was over, Bessie Hillman, and the labor feminists who surrounded her, had made their place as workers and as citizens in an expanded labor movement.

Epilogue: Lifting Their Spirits

At an age when most young Russian girls began to prepare for marriage, fifteen-year-old Bessie Abramowitz made a decision that dramatically altered the course of her life. Apprehensive about the future that awaited her as a shtetl woman, Abramowitz chose to leave home. Like the tens of thousands of immigrants who had gone before her, including her activist predecessors such as Emma Goldman and Rose Pesotta, she left behind all that was familiar to travel to a world that, from afar, seemed alive and full of promise.

Reaching the new land did not immediately translate to the good fortune Abramowitz had most likely anticipated; instead, the relatively comfortable circumstances she had left behind seemed lost forever. Nevertheless, though New-World hardships proved disenchanting, they were not entirely disheartening. Within a few blocks of Abramowitz's Halsted Street boardinghouse stood Hull-House—a bright spot in an all-too-dismal neighborhood. A gathering place for the nascent women's political culture, Hull-House nurtured the reform spirit that characterized turn-of-the-century Chicago.

Affiliation with Jane Addams, Ellen Gates Starr, Margaret Dreier Robins, and the other reformers based at the settlement house profoundly affected not only Abramowitz, but also the trajectory of the entire American labor movement for the next seventy-five years. In the first decades of the twentieth century, Bessie and her future husband, Sidney Hillman, frequented Hull-House, where they learned the meaning of industrial democracy and tools that included the art of arbitration. For this tutelage the Hillmans remained extremely grateful. Abramowitz's own union, the Amalgamated Clothing Workers of America, became "a citadel of progressive impulses which kept progressive activities alive" even after union activities no longer prevailed on the settlement's formal agenda. Labor historian David Montgomery noted that Hull-House cast a long shadow over the nation in this way.[1] Inspired by a combination of their Old-World convictions and New-World possibilities, the Hillmans adopted many of the goals of their middle-class allies, ultimately aligning with the Roosevelt administration to provide an enduring reform legacy within the New Deal.

Bessie Hillman's unending gratitude manifested itself on countless occasions. In the early 1960s, she came to the defense of Hull-House against its proposed demolition to accommodate the expansion of the University of Illinois at Chicago. Learning of the plan to destroy the building, an impassioned Bessie Hillman pleaded with Mayor Daley to do everything in his power to save Hull-House, an institution that she described as "not only hallowed and venerable, it is sacred to every American with the slightest understanding of the social forces that have given America its internal strength and vitality." In the fullest sense, Hillman wrote, "it is woven into the fabric of America." She cautioned, "If it dies, a vital part of America dies."[2] Two years later, thanks to the efforts of the Amalgamated, other labor organizations, civic organizations, and a number of prominent citizens, the University of Illinois established a fund to preserve and restore the original Hull-House mansion, fondly referred to by Amalgamated members as "the House of Labor."[3]

Working women cultivated an uninterrupted current of feminist activity from the progressive era that endured the conservative decades of the postwar years. Labor feminists incorporated broad social-justice goals, rooted in the progressive-era social feminist political culture, into a reinvigorated postwar agenda that entitled women to wage work, just compensation, and political participation, as well as to the right to care for one's family and community.[4]

For more than half a century, Bessie Hillman, after leading the pathbreaking Chicago strike in 1910 and pushing the insurgents toward independence at the United Garment Workers Convention four years later, worked first to help lay the foundations of the organization and then to assist in transforming the ACWA from a union primarily concerned with immediate gains to an organization that demanded equity for workers, especially women workers. In the 1940s and 1950s, despite the "absence of a feminist movement outside the plants," Hillman's gender advocacy evolved from carving out specific opportunities for women in her own union, by correcting inequalities in the workplace and ultimately in the union itself, to pushing for equality for all workers, regardless of gender, race, or ethnicity.[5] Hillman's life attests to the fact that working-class feminism not only survived the postwar era, it thrived.

Bessie Hillman's story enlightens the narrative of labor feminism. Her private and public life defied the conventions of "Jewish New Womanhood," according to which young Jewish girls followed a pattern of immigration, garment work, activism, and a routine domestic life after marriage.[6] In the ACWA, Bessie and Dorothy Jacobs Bellanca remained active after their marriages to high-ranking union officers. Bellanca's husband, August, was a union vice president who also supported his wife's work; the Bellancas never had children. Bessie Hillman, cloakmaker and socialist organizer Theresa Serber Malkiel, and Clara Lemlich Shavelson of the International Ladies' Garment Workers Union were among the few Jewish women activists who successfully combined union work, marriage, and children. Malkiel married a Socialist lawyer, had a daughter, and continued her activity in the Socialist Party after her marriage, focusing in her later years on adult education for women; Shavelson married a printer, had three children, and became a staunch Communist Party activist.[7] In contrast, many female union leaders followed the examples set by women like Rose Schneiderman, Pauline Newman, and Fannia Cohn, who were so strongly committed to the movement that they either remained single their entire lives or found same-sex partners who were equally involved in the labor movement.

Admittedly, Bessie and Sidney Hillman did have help with domestic duties. While their daughters were young, Beatrice Cox served as the housekeeper and nanny. Once Philoine and Selma were older, Bessie hired cleaning women on a weekly basis; most were associated with Father Divine, a Harlem minister. Bessie loved to entertain and to cook. The Hillmans' home was filled with music from the Victrola and the laughter that accompanied Bessie's punch lines. When company dropped in, they often played cards and sampled Bessie's baked goods, which ranged from Russian strudel to apple pie.[8]

Hillman, like other labor feminists, could not escape sexism in her own union. She fought an uphill battle to assert her place in the union and to gain the respect of the male union officers. In her early union years, when ACWA officials and journalists increasingly referred to Bessie as "Mrs. Sidney Hillman," she strove to maintain her identity as a union founder, chiding, "I was Bessie Abramowitz before he was Sidney

Hillman."[9] Despite these underlying gender tensions, where union affairs were concerned neither Bessie nor Sidney openly competed with one another. Their marriage was one of mutual cooperation, and they worked as one toward their shared vision. Bessie Hillman, however, received little credit for this joint effort. Decades later, Esther Peterson, a former assistant secretary of labor and longtime union insider, corrected this oversight: "Bessie built the union and Sidney [Hillman]."[10]

The death of her life partner released Bessie from domestic responsibility. Like other labor feminists of her generation, Hillman never questioned male hierarchy in the home. After his death, freer to act and speak with few restraints—and to get paid for it as well—she spent less time at home and more time in the office or traveling on union business. Hillman's multiple duties as a wife, a mother, and a union official provided a training ground for her postwar activities. Plagued by personal losses, yet driven by a quest for industrial democracy that included a commitment to both women's rights and civil rights, Bessie Hillman became more active than ever before in the labor organization that she had helped to create.

Although, as Dorothy Sue Cobble asserts, Hillman was only one of a number of women who fit the "pattern of working-class women's activism," by virtue of the length and breadth of her career her life in some ways was exceptional.[11] She was one of only a handful of union women who brought their early activist experiences to bear on a working-class feminist movement that connected the prewar progressivism of women reformers to modern women's activism of the 1960s. Her early vision of industrial democracy informed the labor feminist platform. Her position as the wife of a much-loved leader and her high office as a widow enhanced Hillman's status in the labor movement. As Jacob Potofsky put it, "Her simplicity and forthrightness earned her the love of several generations of union members: her energy, spent so unstintingly, was contagious and workers responded to her sincerity, many times participating more vigorously than they had intended to." From her organizing efforts in the runaway shop campaigns to her later crusades for civil and women's rights, Bessie Hillman's power resided in her ability to "lift the spirits of the rank and file" and persuade them to embrace the union cause.[12]

Bessie Hillman was an effective leader. She made optimum use of existing resources and when necessary she created circumstances that promoted activism. She led by example, always willing to guide and mentor. Esther Peterson ranked Hillman "among the fine women who helped me and influenced me most."[13] Hillman recognized and eventually acted on the gender tensions between male leaders and their female constituency, yet she did not consider herself a feminist and would have been uncomfortable being called one. As an advocate for working women, she never believed "that women had any different part in the trade union movement than the men."[14] Working in concert with men, she constructed her own version of feminism that emphasized both women's rights and obligations to family and community. Hillman practiced what she preached. She found great satisfaction in empowering others by "helping them find a formula through which they could help themselves." According to Bessie, "[t]he union leader usually needs to provide only a spark; the rank and file normally can be relied upon to catch fire and sweep forward under their own power and enthusiasm, often overtaking the leader and pulling him along behind."[15]

In many ways Hillman's activism succeeded. She lured many women away from the sidelines into the activist arena—one of the most notable being Dollie Lowther Robinson. Robinson found what she called "the Bessie Hillman charm and sincerity" hard to resist.[16] In the image of Addams's mentorship of Hillman a generation before, Bessie exerted a profound influence on Robinson, who eventually called for an "NAACP for women" a year before the inception of NOW—founded on this very premise.[17]

While Sidney was alive, Bessie worked as an educator and organizer, making her move to more full-fledged activism after his death. In the postwar years Bessie Hillman turned a corner. As her autonomy increased, she spoke louder, demanded more, and forced men to listen. Partially as a result of the articulation of women's demands, working-class feminists did enjoy some rewards, with the establishment of John F. Kennedy's Presidential Commission on the Status of Women and the passage of the Equal Pay Act. Bessie Hillman and several other distinguished labor women played important parts in these developments. Hillman's appointment to the International Confederation of Free Trade Unions and her organizing efforts abroad provide examples of her exceptional interests in the global aspects of working women's condition.

Hillman refused to succumb to the union's policy, which tended "to discard those who did the building and the organizing."[18] Her popularity with the voters in ACWA elections during her lengthy tenure as vice president evidenced the respect that she earned from the workers, who viewed her as anything but a token woman. Her demands for the overall improvement of working women's lives cut across racial and class lines. For her efforts in defining and advancing the distinct character of working-class feminism in the Amalgamated Clothing

Workers of America, labor activists praised Hillman for being part of the "advance guard" for women's liberation.[19] In the postwar era, union women provided a crucial link between the advocacy of the progressive reformers and the modern women's movement, and, in the process, made a significant contribution to the evolution of labor feminism. Bessie Hillman was by no means the only labor feminist; however, she was one of the most visible. Her enduring convictions unequivocally qualify her as one of the "midwives" of the wider women's movement.[20]

Although Bessie's tendency to do rather than to write makes the question of how she evaluated her own life difficult to answer, she did provide some insight at a ceremony in 1960, marking the fiftieth anniversary of the historic 1910 Chicago strike of garment workers. Bessie had an audience that included 100 of the surviving participants. She reflected: "I don't regret for one moment that God gave me the wisdom to walk out. If I had my life to live over again, I would not make any other choice. It enabled me to say I have led a good life, a rich life. If not for the strike, for one thing, I would not have met Sidney Hillman. . . . It was all so worth-while. . . . Sisters and brothers, oldtimers who walked with me on the picketline, I'm grateful to you for the privilege you gave me."[21]

Hillman did not live to see the founding of the Coalition of Labor Union Women (CLUW) in 1974, but her fellow women trade unionists did not hesitate to infuse Hillman's labor feminist principles into an organization committed to organizing women workers, fighting discrimination in the workplace, and increasing women's participation in union affairs by promoting them into the ranks of union leadership. Hillman believed that progress for women was best served by labor organization; she believed that the trade union, once men were cured of their sexism, would be the primary agent of women's freedom.[22] Echoing Hillman, Amalgamated vice president and later CLUW President Joyce Miller addressed the coalition a year after its establishment: "We are loyal to our unions. Within that framework, we want to advance the role of women."[23]

In the decades following Hillman's death, women organizers proved vital leaders in the drive to organize southern textile plants. In 1980, the union signed its first contract with JP Stevens, capping a string of victories in the "fight for stringent health and safety measures, contract enforcement and educational programs." By the early 1990s, the Amalgamated Clothing and Textile Workers Union played "a national leadership role in the battle for health care reform and guaranteed universal health coverage," and had joined with workers in Canada and Mexico to fight for international workers' rights as well as "environmental and social standards in all trade agreements."[24] By the end of the decade, the organizing tactics pioneered in the union's early years, which had relied on a "burgeoning student and consumer anti-sweatshop movement," made inroads into apparel plants in Guatemala and the Dominican Republic. In 1999, a Manhattan consumer–labor coalition provided crucial support for a successful eight-month campaign to organize Mexican immigrant greengrocery workers in stores on the Lower East Side.[25]

Faced with relentless foreign competition and a shrinking roster, in 1976 the Amalgamated Clothing Workers of America merged with the Textile Workers Union of America (ACTWU); then, in 1995, the ACTWU announced a historic merger with the International Ladies' Garment Workers' Union to form the Union of Needletrades, Industrial, and Textile Employees (UNITE). Although by 2001 the number of UNITE members had dropped to between 180,000 and 200,000, eleven of the thirty-one vice presidents are women. As one UNITE official observed that same year, women (who constitute roughly half of all union members) are still a minority when it comes to leadership positions, but they hold a higher proportion than at any earlier time, and UNITE is "moving in the right direction."[26] UNITE merged with the Hotel Employees and Restaurant Employees (HERE) in the summer of 2004 to form UNITE/HERE.[27] On September 14, 2005, UNITE/HERE Executive Board members voted to break away from the AFL-CIO so that they could organize new members and pursue a bipartisan political agenda. Part of a larger coalition called Change to Win, today UNITE/HERE represents 450,000 workers in the hotel, gaming, laundry, apparel and textile manufacturing, retail, and food service sectors.

Hillman and her labor feminist colleagues left an "unfinished agenda" behind.[28] Working women remain central to the continuing quest for gender equality. Despite the U.S. Department of Labor's claim that we have "a Secretary of Labor and a President who are true champions of working women," the last major advance for women came more than ten years ago with the 1993 passage of the Family and Medical Leave Act.[29] In the ensuing decade, the labor movement has been wracked by a series of upheavals, the most recent being the disassociation of a number of unions (including UNITE/HERE) from the AFL-CIO. Though the more optimistic labor leaders view this split as a necessary evil, one cannot help but recognize the lack of solidarity in an increasingly fragmented movement. Unionization rates have tumbled. In 1983, 20 percent of all workers belonged to unions, compared to 12.5 percent in 2004.[30]

What remains of the women's movement is on equally shaky ground. Some see women's presence in a "Third Wave" of feminism; others bill the movement as defunct. With both the labor movement and the women's movement struggling to stay afloat, there is little evidence of collaboration between feminists and labor unions. Cross-class cooperation is rare. Most Americans are not even aware that the Women's Bureau is still around. The Bureau exists in name only, operating under the guise of cooperating "with employers and other partners to improve the prospects for the 21st Century working women."[31] This is a far cry from its original mandate to investigate and improve the position of women workers.

One former Women's Bureau regional administrator points out that the Bureau has eliminated vital information from its website, including the data that compared women's workforce status to men's workforce status.[32] Women's wages have in fact increased over time, but as a group they consistently make less than men—the latest best estimates are that women make seventy-seven cents for every dollar men make. Deindustrialization means that working-class females are no longer as crowded into the semiskilled or unskilled industrial workforce as they once were; instead, women are now crushed into even lower-wage clerical, domestic, and service-sector jobs. Eighty-nine percent of all working women today are unorganized.[33]

The persistent lack of cohesive female leadership in the remnants of the organized labor movement and in American politics offers little solace. There is a need to repoliticize women's concerns such as subsidized child care, paid family leave, and extended job guarantees. The National Organization for Women is making an admirable attempt to prioritize women's workplace issues and to elevate these concerns to the national political level.[34]

Bessie Hillman's activism teaches us that complacency as we have known it is not acceptable, nor should defeat be an option. There is no choice for the working class but to regroup, with or without the support of the major political parties. Only when prevailing circumstances are confronted as challenges rather than accepted as obstacles too difficult to overcome can we begin to reach past our national borders to search for new forms of worker justice and human rights. Bessie Hillman's legacy of opportunity—her ability to let go of a portion of the old to take hold of what is good and possible in the new—coupled with the lessons of labor feminism and the movement's multifaceted, adaptable, and often cooperative resolution strategies, are ready for the taking so that constructive conversations can begin anew.

NOTES

Preface

1. Katia Mann, quoted in Tillie Olsen, *Silences* (New York: Delacourt Press, 1965), 218.

2. Philoine Fried, interview with author, December 28, 1997.

3. Autobiographies of working women include Rose Schneiderman and Lucy Goldthwaite, *All for One* (New York: Paul Eriksson, 1967); Agnes Nestor, *Woman's Labor Leader: The Autobiography of Agnes Nestor* (Rockford, IL: Bellevue Books, 1954); Mary Anderson, *Women at Work* (Minneapolis: University of Minnesota Press, 1951); Rose Pesotta, *Bread upon the Waters* (New York: Dodd, Mead, 1944; Ithaca, NY: ILR Press, New York State School of Industrial Relations, Cornell University, 1987).

4. Janet Zandy, ed., *Liberating Memory: Our Work and Our Working-Class Consciousness* (New Brunswick, NJ: Rutgers University Press, 1995), 6; Janet Zandy, ed., *Calling Home: Working-Class Women's Writings* (New Brunswick, NJ: Rutgers University Press, 1990).

5. Steven Fraser, *Labor Will Rule: Sidney Hillman and the Rise of American Labor* (New York: Free Press, 1991), 224.

6. Benjamin Stolberg, *Tailor's Progress: The Story of a Famous Union and the Men Who Made It* (New York: Doubleday, Doran, 1944), 338–39. Stolberg documents the history of the International Ladies Garment Workers Union and includes primarily sketches of men; however, he mentioned both Fannia Cohn and Rose Pesotta, whose leadership he described as "the romantic reform variety so characteristic of many women who rise in the social movement." ACWA histories that downplay women in the labor movement are Amalgamated Joint Board and Local Unions in New York, *The Book of the Amalgamated in New York, 1914–1940* (New York, 1940); Hyman H. Bookbinder, *To Promote the General Welfare: The Story of the Amalgamated Clothing Workers of America* (New York: ACWA, 1950). One exception is JoAnn E. Argersinger, *Making the Amalgamated: Gender, Ethnicity, and Class in the Baltimore Clothing Industry, 1889–1939* (Baltimore: Johns Hopkins University Press, 1999).

7. John E. Williams, "The Russian Jew in American Industry," *Streator Independent-Times*, June 28, 1913; reprinted in *Survey*, August 23, 1913, ACWA Papers, Box 228, Folder 4, Kheel Labor-Management Documentation Center, Cornell University (hereafter "ACWA Papers").

8. Alice Henry, *The Trade Union Woman* (New York: William D. Appleton, 1915), 137–38.

9. Alice Kessler-Harris, "Organizing the Unorganizable: Three Jewish Women and Their Union," *Labor History* 17 (Winter 1976): 5–23; Nancy MacLean, *The Culture of Resistance: Female Institution Building in the International Ladies Garment Workers Union, 1905–1925*, Michigan Occasional Papers in Women's Studies 21 (Ann Arbor: University of Michigan, 1982); Sarah Eisenstein, *Give Us Bread but Give Us Roses: Working Women's Consciousness in the United States, 1890 to the First World War* (Boston: Routledge & Kegan Paul, 1983), 12–54.

10. Susan Glenn, *Daughters of the Shtetl: Life and Labor in the Immigrant Generation* (Ithaca, NY: Cornell University Press, 1990); Annelise Orleck, *Common Sense and a Little Fire: Women and Working-Class Politics in the United States, 1900–1965* (Chapel Hill: University of North Carolina Press, 1995); Elizabeth Ewen, *Immigrant Women in the Land of Dollars: Life and Culture on the Lower East Side, 1890–1925* (New York: Monthly Review Press, 1985). See also Ann Schofield, *"to do and to be": Portraits of Four Women Activists, 1893–1986* (Boston: Northeastern University Press, 1997).

11. Donna Gabaccia, *From the Other Side: Women, Gender, and Immigrant Life in the United States, 1820–1990* (Bloomington: Indiana University Press, 1994), 117.

12. Nancy Gabin, *Feminism in the Labor Movement: Women and the United Auto Workers, 1935–1975* (Ithaca, NY: Cornell University Press, 1990); Ruth Milkman, *Gender at Work: The Dynamics of Job Segregation by Sex during World War II* (Urbana: University of Illinois Press, 1987); Dennis A. Deslippe, *"Rights, Not Roses": Unions and the Rise of Working-Class Feminism, 1945–1980* (Urbana: University of Illinois Press, 2000).

13. Alice Kessler-Harris, "Commentary: Labor Feminists and a Feminist Labor Movement," in "Roundtable on Dorothy Sue Cobble's *The Other Women's Movement: Workplace Justice and Social Rights in Modern America*," *Labor: Studies in Working-Class History of the Americas* 2, no. 4 (Winter 2005): 54.

14. Dorothy Sue Cobble, *The Other Women's Movement: Workplace Justice and Social Rights in Modern America* (Princeton, NJ: Princeton University Press, 2004), 4, 232n11. Cobble includes elite and nonelite women in her definition of labor feminists.

15. Cobble, *Other Women's Movement*, 4, 56–57.

16. Glenn, *Daughters of the Shtetl*, 238.

17. Bessie Abramowitz Hillman, "Gifted Women in the Trade Unions," in *American Women: The Changing Image*, ed. Beverly Benner Cassara, 104 (Boston: Beacon Press, 1962).

18. Cobble, *Other Women's Movement*, 4.

19. Fraser, *Labor Will Rule*, 170–72; J. M. Budish and George Soule, *The New Unionism in the Clothing Industry* (New York: Harcourt, Brace & Howe, 1920), 202–4.

20. Horace M. Kallen to Philoine Fried upon Bessie Hillman's death, December 23, 1970, private collection of Philoine Fried.

Chapter 1: Bound but Determined (1889–1908)

1. To avoid confusion I use the Americanized version of Bas Sheva: *Bessie*. Evidence suggests that Abramowitz adopted this name sometime shortly after immigrating to the United States.

2. Philoine Fried, interview with author, December 29, 1996; *The National Cyclopedia of American Biography*, vol. 56 (Clifton, NJ: James White, 1975), s.v. "Bessie Abramowitz Hillman."

3. The Pale of Settlement, first created by Catherine the Great in 1791, eventually consisted of twenty-five western Russian provinces where Jews were forced to reside. Gary Mokotoff and Sallyann Amdur Sack, *Where We Once Walked: A Guide to Jewish Communities Destroyed in the Holocaust* (Teaneck, NJ: Avotaynu, 1991), 187. Linevo (Linoveh) is listed with a population of ninety-six at the onset of the Holocaust.

4. Luba Aten to Philoine Fried, ca. 1970, private collection of Philoine Fried. Luba lived in a village about five miles from the Abramowitz family. For exact coordinates for Linoveh (also spelled Linevo or Linowo), see http://www.jewishgen.org/ShtetlSeeker/, which indicates that the hamlet was located approximately five miles southwest of Pruzhany, Belarus.

5. For more on autonomous Jewish institutions, see Shmuel Ettinger, "The Council of Four Lands," in *The Jews in Old Poland, 1000–1795*, ed. Antony Polonsky, 89–104 (New York: Institute for Polish-Jewish Studies, 1993); M. Stanislawski, *Tsar Nicholas I and the Jews: The Transformation of Jewish Society in Russia, 1825–1855* (Philadelphia: Jewish Publication Society of America, 1983), 9.

6. Elizabeth Herzog and Mark Zboroski, *Life Is with People: The Jewish Little-Town of Eastern Europe* (New York: International University Press, 1952), 193–205.

7. *Evreiskaia entsiklopediia* (St. Petersburg, Russia, 1991), 6:793–94.

8. Arcadius Kahan, *Economic History of the Jews* (New York: Schocken Books, 1976), 82; Simon M. Dubnow, *History of the Jews in Russia and Poland* (Philadelphia: Jewish Publication Society of America, 1918), 2:259–84; Ezra Mendelsohn, *Class Struggle in the Pale: The Formative Years of the Jewish Workers' Movement in Tsarist Russia* (Cambridge: Harvard University Press, 1970), 3–4.

9. Shlomo Lambroza, "The Pogroms of 1903–1906," in *Pogroms: Anti-Jewish Violence in Modern Russian History*, ed. John D. Klier and Shlomo Lambroza, 194–247 (New York: Cambridge University Press, 1992).

10. Sidney Hillman's mother, Judith, helped support the family by opening a small grocery/bakery business in the front room of the Hillman home so that Hillman's father, Samuel, could study the Torah. Steven Fraser, *Labor Will Rule: Sidney Hillman and the Rise of American Labor* (New York: Free Press, 1991), 3–10.

11. Elizabeth Ewen, *Immigrant Women in the Land of Dollars: Life and Culture on the Lower East Side, 1890–1925* (New York: Monthly Review Press, 1985), 47.

12. Pauline Wengeroff, "A Grandmother's Memories: Images from the Cultural History of the Jews in Nineteenth Century Russia," in *The Golden Tradition: Jewish Life and Thought in Eastern Europe*, ed. Lucy Dawidowicz, 160–70 (New York: Holt, Rinehart & Winston, 1967); David Biale, "Eros and Enlightenment: Love against Marriage in the East European Enlightenment," *Polin* 1 (1986): 49–67; Susan Glenn, *Daughters of the Shtetl: Life and Labor in the Immigrant Generation* (Ithaca, NY: Cornell University Press, 1990), 10–12, 78–79; Chae Ran Y. Freeze, "Making and Unmaking the Jewish Family: Marriage and Divorce of Jews in Imperial Russia, 1850–1914" (PhD diss., Brandeis University, 1997).

13. Naomi Shepherd, *A Price Below Rubies: Jewish Women as Rebels and Radicals* (Cambridge: Harvard University Press, 1993), 49.

14. Judi Miller, "Bessie Hillman: Early Labor Leader," in *Women Who Changed America* (New York: Manor Books, 1976), 122.

15. Barbara Alpern Engel, *Mothers and Daughters: Women of the Intelligentsia in Nineteenth-Century Russia* (New York: Cambridge University Press, 1983), 72–74; Richard Stites, *The Women's Liberation Movement in Russia: Feminism, Nihilism, and Bolshevism, 1860–1930* (Princeton, NJ: Princeton University Press, 1978), 88–99. Nikolay Chernyshevsky's *What Is to Be Done? Tales of New People* (New York: Vintage Books, 1961) is a fictional account written as government policy changes began to accommodate women's educational needs. He extolled education as a liberating force and mechanism for social change.

16. Philoine Fried, interview with author, December 29, 1996. Pomerantz eventually married Bessie's oldest sister, Feige Itka. The Zionist couple migrated to Palestine shortly after World War I.

17. Luba Aten to Philoine Fried, ca. 1970, private collection of Philoine Fried.

18. The classic work on the Haskalah is Jacob Raisin, *The Haskalah Movement in Russia* (Philadelphia: Jewish Publication Society of America, 1913).

19. Sydney Weinberg, *World of Our Mothers: The Lives of Jewish Immigrant Women* (Chapel Hill: University of North Carolina Press, 1988), 15–20. Weinberg examines the concept of "domestic religion" and the unique role piety played in the lives of Jewish women.

20. Herzog and Zborowski, *Life Is with People,* 161–64; Lucy Dawidowicz, *The Golden Tradition: Jewish Life and Thought in Eastern Europe* (New York: Holt, Rinehart & Winston, 1967), 40–41, 114–41; Harriet Davis-Kram, "The Story of the Sisters of the Bund," *Contemporary Jewry* 5 (1980): 29. Critical examples of secular Yiddish literature are contained in the many works of I. L. Peretz, one of which is "The Three Seamstresses," in *The Golden Peacock: A World Wide Treasury of Yiddish Poetry,* ed. Joseph Leftwich, 77 (New York: T. Yoselofs, 1961); see also S. Y. Abramovitch, *Tales of Mendele the Book Peddler: Fishke the Lame and Benjamin the Third,* Library of Yiddish Classics, ed. Dan Miron and Ken Frieden (New York: Schocken Books, 1996).

21. Miller, "Bessie Hillman," 123.

22. See Glenn, *Daughters of the Shtetl,* 16–33.

23. Arcadius Kahan, "Urbanization Process of Jews in Nineteenth Century Europe" and "Jewish Entrepreneurs in Tsarist Russia," in *Essays in Jewish Social and Economic History,* 205–8 (Chicago: University of Chicago Press, 1986).

24. Kahan, *Economic History of the Jews,* 205–8.

25. For more on the general labor movement in Russia, see Reginald Zelnick, *Labor and Society in Tsarist Russia: The Factory Workers of St. Petersburg, 1855–1870* (Stanford: Stanford University Press, 1971). On the Bund, see Henry J. Tobias, *The Jewish Bund in Russia: From Its Origins to 1905* (Stanford: Stanford University Press, 1972). Women labor activists are rarely treated separate from men, and consequently very little historical attention has been given to the participation of women in Russian strikes. One of the more detailed treatments in this area is Shepherd, *A Price Below Rubies,* 2–3, 142–43. For female university students' ties to the labor movement, see Engel, *Mothers and Daughters,* 133–34, 144–47; Stites, *The Women's Liberation Movement in*

Russia, 136, 141. Both of these historians mention the radical activists Berta Abramovna (Beti) Kaminskaya and Dora Aptekman.

26. Weinberg, *World of Our Mothers*, 72.

27. Elaine Leeder, *The Gentle General: Rose Pesotta, Anarchist and Labor Organizer* (Albany: State University of New York Press, 1993), 9.

28. Davis-Kram, "Sisters of the Bund," 36–37.

29. A. Menes, *"Di Yiddishe arbayter bavegung in Rusland fun onhayb bizn sof nayntzike yom,"* in *Historishe shriftn*, 1–59 (New York: Komitet fun Yidishe delegatsy es un Komitet farm Yidishn velt Kongres, 1939); Davis-Kram, "Sisters of the Bund," 39–40. This situation is similar to the Hart, Schaffner, and Marx strike that occurred under Abramowitz's direction in 1910. Older men in particular often refused to meet with women, for social and economic reasons.

30. Statistics on the number of employed married women in Russia are available in the 1897 census compilations by Andreas Kappeler, *Volkszahliny*. For related figures on immigrants, see also U.S. Immigration Committee, "Immigrants in Cities," vol. 2, Table 401, pp. 546–47, cited in Glenn, *Daughters of the Shtetl*, 66–67, 76–79.

31. Philoine Fried, interview with author, December 29, 1997.

32. Luba Aten to Philoine Fried, ca. 1970, private collection of Philoine Fried.

33. Rose Pesotta, *Days of Our Lives* (Boston: Excelsior Publishers, 1958), 218, 221. Both women completed the break from the practice of arranged marriage by choosing men for romantic rather than traditional reasons.

34. See Samuel Joseph, *Jewish Immigration to the U.S., 1881–1910* (New York: Columbia University Press, 1914), 179, cited by Alice Kessler-Harris, "Organizing the Unorganizable: Three Jewish Women and Their Union," *Labor History* 17 (Winter 1976): 6n3. The proportion of Jewish women immigrants between 1899 and 1910 was higher than any other immigrant group with the exception of the Irish.

35. Family History Immigration Center, Ellis Island Passenger Arrivals, "Manifest for Rotterdam," Basche Abramowitz, http://ellisisland.org/ (accessed February 2, 2006). Abramowitz's place of residence is listed as Linowo (an alternate spelling of Linoveh).

36. Elizabeth Hasanovitz, *One of Them: Chapters from a Passionate Autobiography* (New York: Houghton Mifflin, 1918), 12; Ann Schofield, *"to do and to be": Portraits of Four Women Activists, 1893–1986* (Boston: Northeastern University Press, 1997), 118.

37. Family History Immigration Center, http://ellisisland.org/; Philoine Fried, interview with author, December 29, 1996.

38. Jane Addams, *Twenty Years at Hull-House* (New York: Macmillan, 1910), 80–81. In the foreword of a 1938 edition, Henry Steele Commager remarked that "all the evils and vices of American life seemed to be exaggerated in Chicago." For a detailed description of Chicago's urban development, see Harold M. Mayer and Richard C. Wade, *Chicago: Growth of a Metropolis* (Chicago: University of Chicago Press, 1969).

39. Living and working conditions of young single working women are discussed in Joanne Meyerowitz, *Women Adrift: Independent Wage Earners in Chicago, 1880–1930* (Chicago: University of Chicago Press, 1988); Annie M. MacLean, *Women Workers and Society* (Chicago: McClurg, 1919), 88–89; Elias

Tobenkin, "The Immigrant Girl in Chicago," *Survey* 23 (November 6, 1909): 189–95.

40. According to the 1900 Census, almost 25,000 Jews resided in Cook County. Most of them settled in the area around Halsted Street. U.S. Department of Commerce, *Twelfth Census of the United States, 1900.* Vol. 1, *Population* (Washington, DC: Government Printing Office, 1902), 746, Table 34, "Foreign Born Population."

41. Glenn, *Daughters of the Shtetl,* 60–63; Kessler-Harris, "Organizing the Unorganizable," 5–23.

42. Luba Aten to Philoine Fried, ca. 1970, private collection of Philoine Fried.

43. Miller, "Bessie Hillman," 123–24.

44. Kathy Peiss, *Cheap Amusements: Working Women and Leisure in Turn-of-the-Century New York* (Philadelphia: Temple University Press, 1986), 63.

45. Andrew R. Heinze, *Adapting to Abundance: Jewish Immigrants, Mass Consumption, and the Search for American Identity* (New York: Columbia University Press, 1990), 93–94.

46. John E. Williams, "The Immigrant Girl in Industry," in John E. Williams, *An Appreciation with Selections from His Writings,* ed. Jacob Potofsky (Chicago: Chicago Joint Board, 1930), 46. Bessie attended the Yiddish theater in Chicago.

47. Jane Addams, *Twenty Years at Hull-House,* with a foreword by Henry Steele Commager (New York: New American Library, 1961), 89.

48. Biographical data on "Bessie Hillman" prepared for *Who's Who of American Women,* n.d., private collection of Philoine Fried.

49. Polacheck, *I Came a Stranger: The Story of a Hull-House Girl* (Urbana: University of Illinois Press, 1989), 97, 183. Polacheck's book is the only comprehensive account of life at Hull-House written by a neighborhood woman.

50. Hasanovitz, *One of Them,* 14.

51. Heinze, *Adapting to Abundance,* 93; Donna Gabaccia, *From the Other Side: Women, Gender, and Immigrant Life in the United States, 1820–1990* (Bloomington: Indiana University Press, 1994), 124.

52. Elinor Lerner, "Immigrant and Working Class Involvement in the New York City Woman Suffrage Movement, 1905–1917: A Study in Progressive Era Politics" (PhD diss., University of California–Berkeley, 1981); Glenn, *Daughters of the Shtetl,* 60–63; Kessler-Harris, "Organizing the Unorganizable," 5–23.

Chapter 2: "A Mighty Hard Struggle" in Chicago (1908–1911)

1. This type of networking often resulted in ethnic concentrations in certain jobs. Donna Gabaccia, *From the Other Side: Women, Gender, and Immigrant Life in the United States, 1820–1990* (Bloomington: Indiana University Press, 1994), 47.

2. Approximately 8,000 men employed in the trade held the higher-paid jobs as cutters, trimmers, and hand-finishers. U.S. Senate, *Report on Conditions of Women and Child Wage Earners in the United States,* 61st Congress, 2d Session, Senate Document #645 (Washington, DC: Government Printing Office,

1911), 2:18; Barbara Mayer Wertheimer, *We Were There: The Story of Working Women in America* (New York: Pantheon Books, 1977), 319.

3. Youngsoo Bae, *Labor in Retreat: Class and Community among Men's Clothing Workers of Chicago, 1871–1929* (Albany: State University of New York Press, 2001), 67.

4. Leo Wolman, *Clothing Workers of Chicago, 1910–1922* (Chicago: Chicago Joint Board, 1922), 18; N. Sue Weiler, "The Uprising in Chicago: The Men's Garment Workers Strike, 1910–1911," in *A Needle, a Bobbin, a Strike: Women Needleworkers in America*, ed. Joan M. Jensen and Sue Davidson, 115–16 (Philadelphia: Temple University Press, 1984).

5. Joan M. Jensen, "The Great Uprisings: 1900–1920," in *A Needle, a Bobbin, a Strike: Women Needleworkers in America*, ed. Joan M. Jensen and Sue Davidson, 85 (Philadelphia: Temple University Press, 1984).

6. Weiler, "The Uprising in Chicago," 115–16; Steven Fraser, *Labor Will Rule: Sidney Hillman and the Rise of American Labor* (New York: Free Press, 1991), 46.

7. Agnes Nestor, *Woman's Labor Leader: The Autobiography of Agnes Nestor* (Rockford, IL: Bellevue Books, 1954), 131.

8. U.S. Department of Interior, Census Office, *Twelfth Census of 1900, Special Report on Occupations*; Elias Tobenkin, "The Immigrant Girl in Chicago," *Survey* 23 (November 6, 1910): 189–95.

9. Illinois Bureau of Labor Statistics, *Fourteenth Biennial Report* (Chicago, 1906), 348, Table 35, "Working Women in Factories"; Annie M. MacLean, "The Sweatshop in Summer," *American Journal of Sociology* 9 (November 1903): 289–93. According to the Illinois bureau's report, weekly earnings for button-hole makers ranged from $5.61 to $18.99, hand workers from $2.39 to $15.55, and machine operators from $3.36 to $18.82.

10. Neva Kaye, "The Immigrant Woman and Her Job," *Advance*, May 2, 1930, 4–7.

11. *Jewish Labor World*, September 4, 1908, 2–3; Chicago Foreign Press Survey (WPA Project), Chicago Public Library, Chicago, Illinois.

12. Alice Henry and Miles Franklin, "Why 50,000 Refused to Sew," *English-woman* (1911), 297–308.

13. Wertheimer, *We Were There*, 322.

14. Wolman, *Clothing Workers of Chicago*, 19; Charles E. Zaretz, *The Amalgamated Clothing Workers of Chicago: A Study in Progressive Trades-Unionism* (New York: Ancon, 1934), 111.

15. Jane Addams, *Newer Ideals of Peace* (New York: Macmillan, 1911) (orig. ed. 1907), 182.

16. Jane Addams, "The Settlement as a Factor in the Labor Movement," in *Hull House Maps and Papers: A Presentation of Nationalities and Wages in a Congested District of Chicago* (Boston: Thomas Y. Crowell, 1895), 214.

17. Addams, "The Settlement as a Factor in the Labor Movement," 216. Two years after its passage, a state judge declared the Illinois eight-hour law unconstitutional.

18. Jane Addams, *Twenty Years at Hull-House* (New York: Macmillan, 1910), 166.

19. Addams, "The Settlement as a Factor in the Labor Movement," 188–89; Addams, *Twenty Years,* 155–58; Kathleen Banks Nutter, "Mary Kenney O'Sullivan," in *Women Building Chicago: A Biographical Dictionary, 1790–1990,* ed. Adele Hast and Rima Lunin Schultz, 650–53 (Bloomington: Indiana University Press, 2001); Ann D. Gordon, "Alzina Ann Parsons Stevens," in *Women Building Chicago,* 842–44.

20. Jane Addams, "The Subtle Problems of Charity," *Atlantic Monthly* 83 (February 1899): 163–78.

21. The Working-People's Social Science Club, "Programme of 1893," in *Hull House Maps and Papers: A Presentation of Nationalities and Wages in a Congested District of Chicago* (Boston: Thomas Y. Crowell, 1895), 216–17; Kathryn Kish Sklar, "The Historical Foundations of Women's Power in the Creation of the American Welfare State, 1830–1930," in *Mothers of a New World: Maternalistic Politics and the Origins of the Welfare States,* ed. Seth Koven and Sonya Michel, 43–93 (New York: Routledge, 1993); Kathryn Kish Sklar, "Political Cultures in the Progressive Era: The National Consumers' League and the American Association for Labor Legislation," in *U.S. History as Women's History: New Feminist Essays,* ed. Linda K. Kerber, Alice Kessler-Harris, and Kathryn Kish Sklar, 36–62 (Chapel Hill: University of North Carolina, 1995).

22. For details of this debate, see Ann Schofield, *"to do and to be": Portraits of Four Women Activists, 1893–1986* (Boston: Northeastern University Press, 1997), 14.

23. Addams, "The Settlement as a Factor in the Labor Movement," 199–204; Addams, *Twenty Years,* 163–68; Addams, *Newer Ideals of Peace,* 145–50; Nancy Schrom Dye, *As Equals and as Sisters: Feminism, Unionism, and the Women's Trade Union League of New York* (Columbia: University of Missouri Press, 1980), 103–4.

24. Elizabeth Anne Payne, *Reform, Labor, and Feminism: Margaret Dreier Robins and the Women's Trade Union League* (Urbana: University of Illinois Press, 1988), 63–65.

25. Quoted in Payne, *Reform, Labor, and Feminism,* 66.

26. Payne, *Reform, Labor, and Feminism,* 67–70.

27. Pauline Newman to Rose Schneiderman, December 1, 1911. R.S., A 94. Tamiment Institute Library, New York, New York.

28. Alice Kessler-Harris, "Rose Schneiderman and the Limits of Women's Trade Unionism," in *Labor Leaders in America,* ed. Melvyn Dubofsky and Warren Van Tine, 167–68 (Urbana: University of Illinois Press, 1987); Dye, *As Equals and as Sisters,* 53–59, 115–21; Annelise Orleck, *Common Sense and a Little Fire: Women and Working-Class Politics in the United States, 1900–1965* (Chapel Hill: University of North Carolina Press, 1995), 67–68.

29. Carolyn Daniel McCreesh, *Women in the Campaign to Organize the Garment Workers, 1880–1917* (New York: Garland, 1985), 197.

30. Orleck, *Common Sense,* 60; Alice Kessler-Harris, *Out to Work: A History of Wage-Earning Women in the United States* (New York: Oxford University Press, 1982), 153.

31. Payne, *Reform, Labor, and Feminism,* 64; "Extracts from the Minutes of the Chicago Federation of Labor," November 6, 1910, 1, Chicago Federation of Labor Collection, Papers of John Fitzpatrick, Chicago Historical Society, Chicago, IL.

32. Meredith Tax, *The Rising of the Women: Feminist Solidarity and Class Conflict, 1880–1917* (New York: Monthly Review Press, 1980), 65–90; Addams, " The Settlement as a Factor in the Labor Movement," 190.

33. Diane Kirkby, "'The Wage-Earning Woman and the State': The National Women's Trade Union League and Protective Labor Legislation, 1903–1923," *Labor History* 28 (Winter 1987): 54–74.

34. Quoted in Sklar, "The Historical Foundation of Women's Power," 73n103.

35. Letty Cottin Pogrebin, *Deborah, Golda, and Me: Being Female and Jewish in America* (New York: Crown, 1991), 237–39. The linguistic root of *tsodeka*, "*tzedek*," means justice.

36. Nancy MacLean, *The Culture of Resistance: Female Institution Building in the International Ladies Garment Workers Union, 1905–1925*, Michigan Occasional Papers in Women's Studies 21 (Ann Arbor: University of Michigan, 1982), 21–22.

37. Matthew Josephson, *Sidney Hillman: Statesman of American Labor* (New York: Doubleday, 1956), 44; "The End of the Struggle," *Life and Labor*, March 1911, 89.

38. Weiler, "The Uprising in Chicago," 119.

39. The number of Hart, Schaffner, and Marx employees at the time of the strike varies depending on the source. At the Senate hearing, Joseph Schaffner testified that there were 6,000 employees (in 1914) with "no contracting for a number of years." By eliminating the practice of subcontracting as a result of the HSM agreement, the number of employees may have decreased. See Commission on Industrial Relations, *Final Report and Testimony* (11 vols.), 64th Congress, 1st Session, Senate Document #415 (Washington, DC: Government Printing Office, 1916), 1:564. For a high estimate, see WTUL, "Chicago at the Front: A Condensed History of the Garment Workers Strike," *Life and Labor*, January 1911, 11, which approximated the number of employees at 10,000 in 1910.

40. "Extracts from the Minutes of the Chicago Federation of Labor," November 6, 1910, 1; "Chicago Strike," *Proceedings of the Seventeenth Convention of the UGWA*, August 26, 1912; Commission on Industrial Relations, *Final Report and Testimony*, 564–65. See also Tobenkin, "The Immigrant Girl in Chicago," 190–92; Stephan Skala, "The Great Organizing Campaign in Chicago, 1915–1919," *Advance*, May 5, 1922, 4–5.

41. "Hart, Schaffner and Marx Face Strike; Employes in Revolt against Wage Cut," *Chicago Daily Socialist*, October 11, 1910, 1–2; Women's Trade Union League, *Official Strike Report of the Strike Committee, Chicago Garment Workers' Strike, October 29, 1910–February 18, 1911* (Chicago: Women's Trade Union League of Chicago), 3.

42. For Abramowitz's involvement in the strike, see Donald Robinson, "Labor Leader's Wife Helped Form Amalgamated Clothing Workers 30 Years Ago," [from local Chicago paper, 1945] ACWA Papers, Box 120, Folder 4, Kheel Labor-Management Documentation Center, Cornell University (hereafter "ACWA Papers"). This statement was corroborated at various times in Abramowitz's life. See *Chicago Daily Socialist*, October 1, 1910 and November 4, 1910; *Labor Daily*, September-October 1910; *Chicago Record-Herald*, April 28, 1916; A. D. Marimpietri, *From These Beginnings: The Making of the Amalgamated Clothing Workers of America* (Chicago: ACWA, 1928), 7–8; "History and the

1910 Strike," *Advance*, February 1936, 3. See also Weiler, "The Uprising in Chicago."

43. Ellen Gates Starr as quoted in Allen F. Davis, *Spearheads of Reform: The Social Settlements and the Progressive Movement, 1890–1914* (New Brunswick, NJ: Rutgers University Press, 1984), 106–7.

44. "Extracts from the Minutes of the Chicago Federation of Labor," November 6, 1910, 1.

45. "Hart, Schaffner and Marx Face Strike," 2.

46. David Dubinsky, "The Meaning of 1910," *JUSTICE*, September 1, 1960; Gary Fink, ed., *Greenwood Encyclopedia of American Institutions* (Westport, CT: Greenwood Press, 1977), 121–22.

47. Quoted in Schofield, *"to do and to be,"* 39.

48. A. Menes, *"Di Yiddishe arbayter bavegujng in Rusland fun onhayb bizn sof nayntzike yom,"* in *Historishe shriftn* (New York, 1939), 1–59; Harriet Davis-Kram, "The Story of the Sisters of the Bund," *Contemporary Jewry* 5 (1980): 29–30.

49. When testifying before the Commission on Industrial Relations in 1914 and asked about the day the strike initially started, Hillman stated, "I believe it was sometime in October." See Commission on Industrial Relations, *Final Report and Testimony*, 566. For more on Sidney Hillman's belated strike participation, see Josephson, *Sidney Hillman*, 44–49; Samuel Lashensky, "I Was There at the Beginning," *Advance*, April 15, 1962, 11. Lashensky relates that it was not until months after the strike began that Sidney Hillman emerged as a leader.

50. *Proceedings of the Thirteenth Biennial ACWA Convention*, 1940, 566. In 1910 the UGW was the only men's garment makers' union recognized by the AFL.

51. In an investigation for the Commission on Industrial Relations in 1914, Dr. Leo Wolman estimated that by 1910 the UGW had organized less than 20 percent of all workers in the men's garment industry. See Francis J. Haas, "Shop Collective Bargaining: A Study of Wage Determination in the Men's Garment Industry" (PhD diss., Catholic University of America, 1922), 7.

52. "HMS Employees Rally to Union," *Chicago Daily Socialist*, October 12, 1910. The *Chicago Daily Socialist* was the first newspaper to print any reference to the upheaval.

53. Ibid.; "Chicago 1910 Strike," in *Anthology of Historical Documents*, ACWA Papers, Box 234, Folder 3. It is clear that Abramowitz viewed a general strike as a last resort. Scant evidence suggests that she and Shapiro complained to their foreman seeking a restoration of wages before actually leaving their jobs.

54. "Hart, Schaffner and Marx Face Strike," 1–2.

55. Jane Addams to Mary Rozet-Smith, October 17, 1910 and December 1, 1910, Jane Addams Papers, Swarthmore College Peace Collection, Series 1, 5–1300 and 5–1364; Jane Addams, "Immigrants under the Quota," *Survey Graphic*, November 1929, 139.

56. Estimates concerning the number of strikers vary from a low of 35,000 (*Chicago Daily Socialist*, October 28, 1912) to a high of 50,000 (WTUL, *Official Strike Report*, 3).

57. Bessie Abramowitz Hillman, speech on Jane Addams, March 1960, ACWA Papers, Box 228, Folder 6.

58. WTUL, *Official Strike Report*, 6. The report described how the WTUL Strike Committee performed its work through the following subcommittees: Committee on Grievances, Picket Committee, Organization Committee, Publicity Committee, Committee for Securing Speakers for Hall Meetings, Committee for Arranging Parlor Meetings, Committee on Theatre Benefits, and for Visiting Union Meetings for Funds, Committee on Cooperation of Women's Clubs, Committee on Church Cooperation, Relief Committee, and Rent Committee.

59. Commission on Industrial Relations, *Final Report and Testimony*, 565. See also Jane Addams to Mary Rozet-Smith, November 16, 22, and 24, 1910, Jane Addams Papers, 5–1323, 5–1332, and 5–1339; WTUL, *Official Strike Report*, 10. Both Hull-House and WTUL leaders consistently proposed the organization of workers as a remedy to labor grievances.

60. Jane Addams to Mary Rozet-Smith, November 16, 1910, Jane Addams Papers, 5–1323; Commission on Industrial Relations, *Final Report and Testimony*, 564.

61. "Hart, Schaffner, and Marx Face Strike," 1.

62. WTUL, *Official Strike Report*, 6; "The Girls' Own Stories," *Life and Labor*, February 1911, 51–52; ACWA Papers, Box 120, Folder 4.

63. *Chicago Daily Socialist*, January 28, 1911; WTUL, *Official Strike Report*, 31; Raymond Robins to Mary Dreier, January 24, 1911, Margaret Dreier Robins Papers in WTUL Microfilm Collection, Reel 22, Frame 36.

64. *Proceedings of the Seventeenth Convention of the UGWA*, 1912, 23–24.

65. WTUL, *Official Strike Report*, 6–9; Henry and Franklin, "Why 50,000 Refused to Sew," 299.

66. "Scenes in the Monster Parade of the Chicago Garment Strikers When Nearly 50,000 Were in Line," *Chicago Daily Socialist*, November 19, 1910, 2; "Bread and Flowers," *Advance*, May 30, 1924, 7.

67. WTUL, "Trade Union Organization the Way Out," in *Official Strike Report*, 6–9.

68. *Chicago Daily Socialist*, December 12, 1910; Susan Glenn, *Daughters of the Shtetl: Life and Labor in the Immigrant Generation* (Ithaca, NY: Cornell University Press, 1990), 174–75.

69. Philoine Fried, interview with author, December 29, 1996.

70. WTUL, *Official Strike Report*, 10–11. The WTUL distributed the same reference cards printed with the "Rules for Pickets" that they distributed to the picketers and allies during the 1909 New York strike. They read: "Don't walk in groups of more than two or three. Don't stand in front of the shop; walk up and down the block. Don't stop the person you want to talk to; walk right along side of him. Don't get excited and shout when you are talking. Don't put your hand on the person you are speaking to. Don't touch his sleeve or button: This may be construed as a technical assault. Don't call anyone 'scab' or use abusive language of any kind. Plead, persuade, appeal, but do not threaten. If a policeman arrests you and you are sure you have committed no offense, take his number and give it to your Union Officer."

71. WTUL, *Official Strike Report*, 10. This cartoon was contributed by Mr. Frank Hazenplug of Hull-House and was extensively used as a poster and on circulars. WTUL, *Official Strike Report*, 16–41. The report credits numerous agencies that donated time and money to the strike cause. Those that receive special mention include the Firemen's Association, the Jewish Workingman's Conference, the Industrial Committee of the Churches of Chicago, the Illinois Federation of Women's Clubs, the Women's Suffrage Party of Illinois, and the Chicago Teachers' Federation. See also ACWA Papers, Box 228, Folder 4.

72. "5,000 Babies Starve: Big Strike Is Cause," *Chicago Record Herald*, November 28, 1910.

73. See *Chicago Daily Socialist: Special Strike Edition*, November 19, 1910; Mari Jo Buhle, "Socialist Women and the 'Girl Strikers,' Chicago, 1910," *Signs* 1 (1976): 1042.

74. "An Army of Women," *Chicago Daily Socialist*, November 21, 1910, 9.

75. *Chicago Daily Socialist*, November 3 and 4, 1910.

76. "Small Shops Closed by Strike Order," *Chicago Daily Socialist*, October 28, 1910; *Chicago InterOcean*, November 3, 1910.

77. WTUL, "Police Brutality and Picketing," in *Official Strike Report*, 9–11.

78. "The Girls' Own Stories," *Life and Labor*, February 1911, 52.

79. For exact ethnic composition, see U.S. Senate, *Report on Conditions of Women and Child Wage Earners*, vol. 2, 47: "In the Chicago men's garment industry the Italians constitute 11.7 percent; the Hebrews, 11.6 percent; the Germans, 9 percent; the Scandinavians, 10.7 percent. The Bohemians, however, are 26.1 percent, and the Poles 22.5 percent; the Lithuanians are 2.2 percent. The Slavic races predominate, forming more than one-half the force. The Americans constitute less than 2 percent."

80. At the time of the strike, eight locals were operating in Chicago under the coordination of District Council No. 6. *Amalgamated Clothing Workers of America: A Documentary History* (New York: Amalgamated Clothing Workers of America, 1940), 45.

81. WTUL, *Official Strike Report*, 3–4; Henry and Franklin, "Why 50,000 Refused to Sew," 299.

82. Members of the Joint Strike Conference Board included CFL President John Fitzpatrick, CFL Vice President Edward Nockles, gloveworker Agnes Nestor, WTUL President Margaret Dreier Robins, and UGW President Robert Noren. See WTUL, *Official Strike Report*, 12–13.

83. "Garment Strike Over," *New York Times*, November 6, 1910; "Strike Will Go On," unidentified paper, Jane Addams Papers, Reel 53, Frame 495.

84. *Chicago Daily Socialist*, November 6, 1910. For Rickert's account of the incident, see *Proceedings of the Seventeenth Convention of the UGW*, 1912, 23–26.

85. "Extracts from the Minutes of the Chicago Federation of Labor," November 6, 1910, 1–2.

86. Henry and Franklin, "Why 50,000 Refused to Sew," 300; "Extracts from the Minutes of the Chicago Federation of Labor," December 4, 1910, 4, and February 19, 1911, 9–10; Jane Addams to Mary Rozet-Smith, November 28, 1910, Jane Addams Papers, 5-1351; WTUL, *Official Strike Report*, 13–14. Many single

girls gave their vouchers to married men so that their families could eat. Robins estimated that the cost of food for the strike amounted to about $1,500 per day.

87. "The Report of the Committee on Garment Workers' Strike" reported that the cost of the strike to the CFL and the WTUL was close to $54,000; of this amount, about $11,000 was raised through the efforts of the Socialist Press. Affiliated organizations donated a little more than $40,000, and the remainder was received from the general public, including the *Jewish Labor World*, which raised about $36,000 for meal tickets. See "Extracts from the Minutes of the Chicago Federation of Labor," February 19, 1911, 9.

88. Charles Lazinskas and Frank Nagreckis, both Lithuanians, were killed in separate incidents in early December. *Chicago Daily Socialist*, December 5, 1910, December 15, 1910, and December 16, 1910.

89. Weiler, "The Uprising in Chicago," 131.

90. *Proceedings of the Seventeenth Convention of the UGW*, 1912, 27–30. See Fraser, *Labor Will Rule*, 65, for the part Sidney Hillman played in convincing the workers to accept the agreement. Judi Miller, in *Women Who Changed America* (New York: Manor Books, 1976), 163–64, suggests that Abramowitz drafted what eventually became the agreement in the form of a passionate speech that she planned to deliver to Joseph Schaffner. However, due to her heavily accented English, it was Sidney Hillman who presented her ideas to the Joint Strike Committee.

91. Commission on Industrial Relations, *Final Report and Testimony*, 564–66; *Proceedings of the Thirteenth Biennial ACWA Convention*, 1940, 419.

92. "Extracts from the Minutes of the Chicago Federation of Labor," January 15, 1911, 7.

93. "Extracts from the Minutes of the Chicago Federation of Labor," January 1, 1911, 6, and February 5, 1911, 8.

94. Raymond Robins to Mary Dreier, January 24, 1911, Margaret Dreier Robins Papers in WTUL Microfilm Collection, Reel 22, Frame 36; WTUL, *Official Strike Report*, 30.

95. "Extracts from the Minutes of the Chicago Federation of Labor," February 5, 1911, 8.

96. "The End of the Struggle," *Life and Labor*, March 1911, 88; *Proceedings of the Seventeenth Convention of the UGW*, 1912, 27–30.

97. Raymond Robins to Mary Dreier, January 24, 1911 and February 4, 1911, Margaret Dreier Robins Papers in WTUL Microfilm Collection, Reel 22, Frames 36 and 51.

98. Commission on Industrial Relations, *Final Report and Testimony*, 565; Margaret Dreier Robins Papers in WTUL Microfilm Collection, Reel 12, Frames 262–74; ACWA Papers, Box 234, Folder 4.

99. Alice Henry, "50,000 Refuse to Sew," *Life and Labor*, June 1912, 11.

100. Bessie Hillman speech, no date, ACWA Papers, Box 189, Folder 8; Ann Schofield, "The Uprising of 20,000: The Making of a Union Legend," in *A Needle, a Bobbin, a Strike: Women Needleworkers in America*, ed. Joan M. Jensen and Sue Davidson, 174 (Philadelphia: Temple University Press, 1984); Melvyn Dubofsky, *When Workers Organize: New York City in the Progressive Era* (Amherst: University of Massachusetts, 1968), 3–4.

101. *Proceedings of the Seventeenth UGW Convention,* 1912, 26; New York Joint Board, "Needle and Thread" (New York, 1940), ACWA Papers, Pamphlet Collection; Raymond Robins to Mary Dreier, January 24, 1911 and February 4, 1911, Margaret Dreier Robins Papers in WTUL Microfilm Collection, Reel 22, Frames 36 and 51.

102. MacLean, *The Culture of Resistance,* 23.

103. Bessie Abramowitz Hillman, "Gifted Women in the Trade Unions," in *American Women: The Changing Image,* ed. Beverly Benner Cassara, 102–3 (Boston: Beacon Press, 1962). Bessie referred to Margaret Dreier Robins as "one of the best friends of the strikers."

104. Jane Addams, "Immigrants under the Quota," *Survey Graphic,* November 1929, 139, in ACWA Papers, Box 228, Folder 6.

105. Bessie Hillman, speech on Jane Addams, March 1960, ACWA Papers, Box 228, Folder 6; Philoine Fried, interview with author, March 15, 2002.

106. Bessie Abramowitz Hillman, speech on Jane Addams, March 1960, ACWA Papers, Box 228, Folder 6. Also cited in *Advance,* January 15, 1971, 3, and "Bessie Hillman to Take Part in Jane Addams Memorial," *Advance,* September 10, 1960, 10.

107. Davis, *Spearheads of Reform,* 107. Davis notes that Sidney Hillman was so strongly influenced by Jane Addams and the Hull-House group that when he moved to New York in 1914, he resided at Lillian Wald's Henry Street Settlement, one of the few places organized labor received support.

108. *Proceedings of the Thirteenth Biennial ACWA Convention,* 1940, 567. The *Chicago Record Herald,* April 28, 1916, reported that "in 1910 Miss Abramowitz attracted wide attention in labor circles in the city."

Chapter 3: The Founding of the Amalgamated Clothing Workers of America and the Search for Solidarity (1911–1918)

1. Susan Glenn, *Daughters of the Shtetl: Life and Labor in the Immigrant Generation* (Ithaca, NY: Cornell University Press, 1990), 228–29.

2. Records of the Joint Executive Board, ACWA Papers, Box 234, Folder 5, Kheel Labor-Management Documentation Center, Cornell University (hereafter "ACWA Papers"); "Trade Board Organized," ACWA Papers, Box 234, Folder 4; "Work of the Trade Board," ACWA Papers, Box 234, Folder 5; "Agreement Creating the Trade Board," Margaret Dreier Robins Papers in WTUL Microfilm Collection, Reel 12, Frame 263. Vestmakers Local 152 also admitted pantsmakers.

3. John E. Williams, "The Immigrant Girl in Industry," in John E. Williams, *An Appreciation with Selections from His Writings,* ed. Jacob Potofsky (Chicago: Chicago Joint Board, 1930), 46.

4. Margaret Dreier Robins, "Why Women Must Organize," *WTUL of Illinois Yearbook, 1907–1908* (Chicago, 1908), 2–7; Raymond Robins to Mary Dreier, February 4, 1911, Margaret Dreier Robins Papers in WTUL Microfilm Collection, Reel 22, Frame 51; Alice Henry, "The Hart, Schaffner and Marx Agreement," *Life and Labor,* June 1912, 170–72.

5. Robins, "Why Women Must Organize," 2–7; Bessie Abramowitz to Mary Dreier, September 28, 1950, ACWA Papers, Box 112, Folder 21.

6. Agnes Murphy, "At Home with Mrs. Sidney Hillman," *New York Post,* August 19, 1962; Mary Anderson, *Women at Work* (Minneapolis: University of Minnesota Press, 1951), 44; Agnes Nestor, *Woman's Labor Leader: The Autobiography of Agnes Nestor* (Rockford, IL: Bellevue Books, 1954), 131; Margaret Dreier Robins, "Some Results of the Hart, Schaffner, and Marx Agreement," Margaret Dreier Robins Papers in WTUL Microfilm Collection, Reel 12, Frames 272–73.

7. John E. Williams, "The Russian Jew in American Industry," *Streator Independent–Times,* June 28, 1913; reprinted in *Survey,* August 23, 1913, in ACWA Papers, Box 228, Folder 4.

8. Jane Addams, "Why Women Should Vote," *Ladies' Home Journal,* January 1910, 22–23; Jane Addams to the General Federation of Women's Clubs, ca. July 7, 1906, published in *Woman's Journal* 37 (July 7, 1906): 108; Jane Addams, *A New Conscience and an Ancient Evil* (New York: Macmillan, 1912), 73.

9. "The Attitude of the Different Racial Groups to the Recently Acquired Right of the Franchise of Women," private collection of Philoine Fried.

10. For a discussion of the cross-class political debate in the New York suffrage movement, see Annelise Orleck, *Common Sense and a Little Fire: Women and Working-Class Politics in the United States, 1900–1965* (Chapel Hill: University of North Carolina Press, 1995), 105–13; Ann Schofield, *"to do and to be": Portraits of Four Women Activists, 1893–1986* (Boston: Northeastern University Press, 1997), 92–94.

11. Jane Addams, *Democracy and Social Ethics* (Cambridge, MA: Belknap Press, 1964; original edition, 1902), 84–85; Jane Addams, "The Subjective Necessity of Social Settlements," in *Philanthropy and Social Progress,* ed. Henry C. Adams, 1 (New York: Thomas Crowell, 1893); Philip Davis, *And Crown Thy Good* (New York: Philosophical Library, 1952), 86.

12. Orleck, *Common Sense,* 6, 54.

13. Rose Schneiderman cited in Orleck, *Common Sense,* 88; Dorothy Sue Cobble, "Lost Visions of Equality: The Labor Origins of the Next Women's Movement," *Labor's Heritage* 12, no. 1 (Winter/Spring 2003): 6–23.

14. A handwritten note states that Bessie "took position as organizer of Chicago WTUL on September 18, 1911 and quit on December 11, 1913." ACWA Papers, Box 313, Folder 15.

15. New York Joint Board, "Needle and Thread" (New York, 1940), ACWA Papers, Pamphlet Collection.

16. Barbara Mayer Wertheimer, *We Were There: The Story of Working Women in America* (New York: Pantheon Books, 1977), 328. Sidney took the high-paying job in New York so that he and Bessie would be able to marry sooner.

17. A. D. Marimpietri to J. S. Potofsky, October 11, 1914, ACWA Papers, Box 234, Folder 9; A. D. Marimpietri, "Report of the Nashville Convention," ACWA Papers, Box 234, Folder 9.

18. *Proceedings of the United Garment Workers of America,* October 12–17, 1914, 69–72.

19. "Founding of the ACWA," ACWA Papers, Box 234, Folder 11; A. D. Marimpietri, "Report of the Nashville Convention," ACWA Papers, Box 234, Folder 9. Selma Goldblatt, a delegate from Rochester, was the only other woman besides Abramowitz in the insurgent group.

20. Jacob H. Panken to Bessie Hillman, July 14, 1946, ACWA Papers, Box 115, Folder 5.

21. Steven Fraser, *Labor Will Rule: Sidney Hillman and the Rise of American Labor* (New York: Free Press, 1991), 90.

22. Bessie Abramowitz to Sidney Hillman, October 14, 1914, ACWA Microfilm Collection, Reel 1, Frame 6; telegrams from Levin to Hillman in Hillman Scrapbooks (Red Books), vol. 1, 109, ACWA Papers.

23. See "Minutes of Mass Meeting of Garment Workers of Chicago," October 21, 1914, ACWA Papers, Box 234, Folders 3 and 9, and Box 235, Folder 3.

24. Fraser, *Labor Will Rule*, 88–93.

25. Bessie Abramowitz to Sidney Hillman, November 20, 1914, ACWA Microfilm Collection, Reel 1, Frame 7.

26. *Proceedings of the ACWA Founding Convention*, 1914, ACWA Papers, Box 119, Folder 6. The UGW, with its severely curtailed membership figures, did survive on its own until it merged with the United Food and Commerce Workers in 1994.

27. J. B. S. Hardman, *The Amalgamated—Today and Tomorrow* (New York: ACWA, 1939), 24; *Chicago Daily Socialist*, December 12, 1910; "Bread and Flowers," *Advance*, May 30, 1924, 3.

28. "ACWA Executive Board Minutes, 1915," ACWA Papers, Box 164, Folder 3; Bessie Abramowitz to Sidney Hillman, April 13, 1915, ACWA Papers, Box 160, Folder 8.

29. Orleck, *Common Sense*, 3.

30. Bessie Abramowitz to Sidney Hillman, April 13, 1915, ACWA Papers, Box 160, Folder 8.

31. Ibid.; *Proceedings of WTUL Fourth Biennial Convention*, 1913, National Women's Trade Union League Papers, Arthur and Elizabeth Schlesinger Library, Radcliffe College, 4.

32. For an analysis of the complex relationship between the WTUL and the AFL, see Elizabeth Anne Payne, *Reform, Labor, and Feminism: Margaret Dreier Robins and the Women's Trade Union League* (Urbana: University of Illinois Press, 1988), 100–08. After her move to New York, Bessie joined the local branch of the WTUL.

33. Fraser, *Labor Will Rule*, 124–27.

34. Addams, *Democracy and Social Ethics*, 12, 213; Jane Addams, *Newer Ideals of Peace* (New York: Macmillan, 1911 [orig. ed. 1907]), 211–13.

35. Fraser, *Labor Will Rule*, 124–27.

36. Addams, *Newer Ideals of Peace*, 30; Jane Addams, "The Settlement as a Factor in the Labor Movement," in *Hull House Maps and Papers: A Presentation of Nationalities and Wages in a Congested District of Chicago* (Boston: Thomas Y. Crowell, 1895), 203.

37. Fraser, *Labor Will Rule*, 171.

38. General Executive Board of the ACWA, "A Statement of Desired Working Conditions," ACWA Papers, Box 228, Folder 9. This "Statement" was an open letter to workers from Sidney Hillman explaining the refusal of manufacturers to arbitrate and the union's goal of eliminating sweatshop conditions.

39. Stephan Skala, "The Great Organizing Campaign in Chicago, 1915–1919," *Advance*, May 5, 1922, 4–5; *Advance*, May 12, 1922, 5–6; Sarah Rozner to Amal-

gamated officers upon the death of Bessie Hillman, January 19, 1971. Rozner was a union member and organizer who knew and worked with Abramowitz from 1910 until her death.

40. "A Sandburg Serenade to Miss Bessie," *Advance,* August 15, 1967, 11.

41. The majority of financial support for this strike came from the membership of the union's international. Skala, "The Great Organizing Campaign," 5–6; Jacob Potofsky to Ellen Gates Starr on her eightieth birthday, February 24, 1939, ACWA Papers, Box 227, Folder 7; Sidney Hillman at 1935 celebration of Jane Addams's seventy-fifth birthday and the twentieth anniversary of the Women's International League for Peace and Freedom, ACWA Papers, Box 228, Folder 6; Elliot J. Gorn, *Mother Jones: The Most Dangerous Woman in America* (New York: Hill & Wang, 2001), 238.

42. "Garment Workers Special Strike Edition," *Day Book,* November 6, 1915.

43. "Regular Cossack Methods Used by Police," *Day Book,* November 6, 1915, ACWA Papers, Box 228, Folder 6; "Striking Clothing Workers," *Chicago National News,* October 25, 1915.

44. "Garment Workers Special Strike Edition," *Day Book,* November 6, 1915; Hillman Scrapbooks, vol. 1, 136, ACWA Papers.

45. Bessie Hillman, speech on Jane Addams, March 1960, ACWA Papers, Box 228, Folder 6.

46. "Hart, Schaffner, and Marx Arbitration Agreement," ACWA Papers, Box 228, Folder 3; Sidney Hillman, Frank Rosenblum, and A. D. Marimpietri, "The Clothing Strike," September 16, 1915, ACWA Papers, Box 228, Folder 9; Skala, "The Great Organizing Campaign," 4–5; *Advance,* May 12, 1922, 5–6; "Jane Addams and the ACWA," in *Amalgamated Clothing Workers of America: A Documentary History* (New York: ACWA, 1940), 418.

47. Youngsoo Bae, *Labor in Retreat: Class and Community among Men's Clothing Workers of Chicago, 1871–1929* (Albany: State University of New York Press, 2001), 138–39.

48. *Proceedings of the Second Biennial ACWA Convention,* 1916, 100, 193.

49. Grace Abbott, "Amalgamated Girls Show Great Loyalty to the Union That Welcomes Them to Its Ranks," *Advance,* March 9, 1917, 1; Nina Asher, "Dorothy Jacobs Bellanca: Feminist Trade Unionist, 1894–1946" (PhD diss., Binghamton University, 1980), 285–86.

50. "Girls for Men's Jobs," *Advance,* April 27, 1917, 4. By the mid-1920s, dues for women, which had been lower than men's, were raised to the same rate. Wages, however, remained unequal.

51. "The Story of Twenty-Five Years," *Advance,* May 17, 1929, 7; Asher, "Dorothy Jacobs Bellanca," 17; Wertheimer, *We Were There,* 334.

52. Paul Blanshard, "Who Bosses the Women and Why," *Advance,* August 4, 1922, 10.

53. "Women Nominated for Local Executive Board," *Advance,* November 30, 1923, 7.

54. *WTUL Convention Proceedings,* 1913, 24–25, Margaret Dreier Robins Papers in WTUL Microfilm Collection, Reel 1, Frames 24–25; ACWA Papers, Box 235, Folder 2.

55. "The Fourth Biennial Convention," *Life and Labor* 3, July 1913, 210. Quoted in Joyce Kornbluh and Mary Frederickson, eds., *Sisterhood and Solidarity:*

Workers' Education for Women, 1914–1984 (Philadelphia: Temple University Press, 1984), 7. In 1915 the school was renamed the School for Active Workers in the Labor Movement. National Women's Trade Union League, "School for Workers Active in the Labor Movement" (Chicago, 1915?), Pamphlet 58–3026, State Historical Society of Wisconsin.

56. "Training School for Women Organizers," *Life and Labor* 4, no. 5, March 1914, 90–91.

57. Joyce Kornbluh, *A New Deal for Workers' Education: The Workers' Service Program, 1933–1942* (Urbana: University of Illinois Press, 1987), 16–19.

58. Kornbluh, *A New Deal for Workers' Education*, 45; Kornbluh and Frederickson, *Sisterhood and Solidarity*, 52–53; "Summer Schools," *Advance*, March 1, 1929; Hilda Worthington Smith, "Training Women Workers to Be Leaders," *Advance*, February 7, 1930.

59. Daniel Katz, "Race, Gender and Labor Education: ILGWU Locals 22 and 91, 1933–1937," *Labor's Heritage* 11, no. 1 (2000): 4–19; Kornbluh and Frederickson, *Sisterhood and Solidarity*, 52–53; Thomas Dublin, "Fannia M. Cohn," in *Jewish Women in America: An Historical Encyclopedia*, ed. Paula E. Hyman and Deborah Dash Moore, 254–56 (New York: Routledge, 1997).

60. Orleck, *Common Sense*, 38–39; Theresa S. Malkiel, *Diary of a Shirtwaist Striker* (Ithaca, NY: Cornell University Press, 1990), 49–50; Schofield, "to do and to be," 117. These women included Rose Schneiderman, Pauline Newman, Clara Lemlich, Theresa Malkiel, and Rose Pesotta.

61. Wertheimer, *We Were There*, 265–66; Alice Kessler-Harris, "Where Are the Organized Women Workers?" in *A Heritage of Her Own: Toward a New Social History of American Women*, ed. Nancy F. Cott and Elizabeth H. Pleck, 360 (New York: Simon & Schuster, 1979). Kessler-Harris maintains that obstacles to women's organization included limited labor-force opportunities, protective labor legislation, and the exclusionary practices of labor unions.

62. "Special Department for Women Members," *Advance*, June 15, 1917, 6.

63. "Women War Workers," *Advance*, June 29, 1917, 6.

64. "Hillman Scores Bad Conditions in Uniform Shops," *Advance*, July 6, 1917, 1; "Army Uniforms Are to Be Taken from Sweatshops," *Advance*, August 31, 1917, 1; "War Labor Board," *Advance*, January 25, 1918, 6. Members of the board included Louis Kirstein, manager of Filene's Department Store; Mrs. Florence Kelley, Secretary of the National Consumers' League; and Captain Walter Kruesi, of the Quartermaster's Corps, U.S. Reserves. Later, Agnes Nestor, President of the Chicago Women's Trade Union League, also joined the board for the purpose of representing women.

65. "Unorganized Women in Clothing Industry Biggest Menace, Warns Dorothy Jacobs Bellanca," *Advance*, August 24, 1917, 6; "Military Work National Policy for ACWA," *Advance*, August 24, 1917, 1.

66. Melvyn Dubofsky, "Abortive Reform and the Wilson Administration," in *Work, Community, and Power: The Experience of Labor in Europe and America, 1900–1925*, ed. James Cronin and Carmen Siranni, 211n4 (Philadelphia: Temple University Press, 1983).

67. "Women Forced Out," *Advance*, December 13, 1918, 8.

68. Ibid.; U.S. Department of Labor, "Women Streetcar Conductors and Ticket Agents," *Women's Bureau Bulletin* 1, no. 11 (Washington, DC: Government Printing Office, 1921): 7–15.

69. Anderson, *Women at Work*, 45; Matthew Josephson, *Sidney Hillman: Statesman of American Labor* (New York: Doubleday, 1952), 83–84; George Soule, *Sidney Hillman: Labor Statesman* (New York: Macmillan, 1939), 155.

70. Chicago Vestmakers Local 152 to Abramowitz, note of congratulations, Hillman Scrapbooks, vol. 1, 122, ACWA Papers; "Labor Heads Engaged; Met During Strike," *Chicago Record Herald*, April 28, 1916; Nestor, *Woman's Labor Leader*, 131; *Chicago Daily News*, May 1, 1916; Josephson, *Sidney Hillman*, 152.

71. "Love and Romance Interwoven with Strikers and Industrial Conflicts," *Chicago Record Herald*, April 28, 1916; Bessie Hillman to Morris Siegel, June 12, 1947, ACWA Papers, Box 115, Folder 21; Judi Miller, *Women Who Changed America* (New York: Manor Books, 1976), 168; Josephson, *Sidney Hillman*, 153; Fraser, *Labor Will Rule*, 94, 99.

72. "Biosketch," May 3, 1949, ACWA Papers, Box 112, Folder 5; Miller, *Women Who Changed America*, 169; Fraser, *Labor Will Rule*, 99; Josephson, *Sidney Hillman*, 154–55. Josephson explained that in regard to the material aspects of life, Hillman remained a socialist, never desiring to own anything of monetary value.

Chapter 4: Strong on the Outside: The Union, Women, and the Struggle to Survive (1918–1933)

1. Steven Fraser, *Labor Will Rule: Sidney Hillman and the Rise of American Labor* (New York: Free Press, 1991), 144.

2. Quoted in Fraser, *Labor Will Rule*, 146.

3. Fraser, *Labor Will Rule*, 125.

4. John Chalberg, *Emma Goldman: American Individualist* (New York: HarperCollins, 1991), 144–47.

5. Fraser, *Labor Will Rule*, 178, 243–52; JoAnn E. Argersinger, *Making the Amalgamated: Gender, Class, and Ethnicity in the Baltimore Clothing Industry, 1899–1939* (Baltimore: Johns Hopkins University Press, 1999), 122–25.

6. Alice Kessler-Harris, *Out to Work: A History of Wage-Earning Women in the United States* (New York: Oxford University Press, 1982), 262, 268.

7. "Membership of the Amalgamated Clothing Workers of America," ACWA Papers, Box 246, Folder 2, Kheel Labor-Management Documentation Center, Cornell University (hereafter "ACWA Papers").

8. Fraser, *Labor Will Rule*, 245–51.

9. Quoted in Alice Kessler-Harris, "Where Are the Organized Women Workers?" in *A Heritage of Her Own: Toward a New Social History of American Women*, ed. Nancy F. Cott and Elizabeth H. Pleck, 354 (New York: Simon & Schuster, 1979).

10. For an analysis of working women's position on protective labor legislation, see Amy Butler, *Two Paths to Equality: Alice Paul and Ethel M. Smith in the ERA Debate, 1921–1929* (Albany: State University of New York Press, 2002); Dorothy Sue Cobble, *Dishing It Out: Waitresses and Their Unions in the Twentieth Century* (Urbana: University of Illinois Press, 1991), 11–12; Dorothy Sue Cobble, "Recapturing Working-Class Feminism," in *Not June Cleaver: Women and Gender in Postwar America, 1945–1960*, ed. Joanne Meyerowitz (Philadelphia: Temple University Press, 1994); Dorothy Sue Cobble, "Lost

Visions of Equality: The Labor Origins of the Next Women's Movement," *Labor's Heritage* 12, no. 1 (Winter/Spring 2003): 6–23.

11. Barbara Mayer Wertheimer, *We Were There: The Story of Working Women in America* (New York: Pantheon Books, 1977), 274.

12. Alice Kessler-Harris, "Problems of Coalition Building: Women and the Trade Unions in the 1920s," in *Women, Work and Protest: A Century of U.S. Women's Labor History*, ed. Ruth Milkman, 132 (New York: Routledge & Kegan Paul, 1987); Alice Kessler-Harris, *Out to Work: A History of Wage-Earning Women in the United States* (New York: Oxford University Press, 1982), 208–10; Susan Lehrer, *Origins of Protective Legislation for Women, 1905–1925* (Albany: State University of New York Press, 1987), 182; Joan Hoff, *Law, Gender and Injustice: A Legal History of U.S. Women* (New York: New York University Press, 1991), 192–244; Kathryn Kish Sklar, *Florence Kelley and the Nation's Work: The Rise of Women's Political Culture, 1830–1900* (New Haven: Yale University Press, 1995), 258, 281–82.

13. Annelise Orleck, *Common Sense and a Little Fire: Women and Working-Class Politics in the United States, 1900–1965* (Chapel Hill: University of North Carolina Press, 1995), 123–24, 160.

14. Susan Ware, *Beyond Suffrage: Women in the New Deal* (Cambridge, MA: Harvard University Press, 1981), 33.

15. All these women were considered working-class leaders of the WTUL. Anderson eventually directed the U.S. Women's Bureau and Christman was the National WTUL's secretary until its dissolution. See Orleck, *Common Sense*, 126–27, 144, 149, 266.

16. Estelle Freedman, "Separatism Revisited: Women's Institutions, Social Reform, and the Career of Miriam Van Waters," in *U.S. History as Women's History: New Feminist Essays*, ed. Linda K. Kerber, Alice Kessler-Harris, and Kathryn Kish Sklar, 186–87 (Chapel Hill: University of North Carolina, 1995); Dorothy Sue Cobble, *The Other Women's Movement: Workplace Justice and Social Rights in Modern America* (Princeton, NJ: Princeton University Press, 2004), 56.

17. Orleck, *Common Sense*, 150–51, 167.

18. Fannia Cohn to Dr. Marion Phillips, September 13, 1927, Fannia Cohn Papers, Box 4, Rare Book and Manuscript Division, New York Public Library.

19. Orleck, *Common Sense*, 6.

20. Bessie Hillman, untitled speech, n.d., ACWA Papers, Box 189, Folder 8.

21. Jane Addams, "The Subtle Problems of Charity," *Atlantic Monthly* 83 (February 1899): 163–78; Jane Addams, *Democracy and Social Ethics* (Cambridge, MA: Belknap Press, 1964; original edition, 1902), xlix, 213.

22. "Mamie Santora," *Advance*, May 23, 1924, 10; "The Women's Department," *Advance*, May 30, 1924, 2; "General Executive Board in Session," *Advance*, August 8, 1924, 7; "Mamie Santora and Hilda Shapiro Speak at Mass Meeting in Philly," *Advance*, April 11, 1924, 2.

23. "Mamie Santora," *Advance*, May 23, 1924, 10.

24. "General Executive Board in Session," *Advance*, August 8, 1924, 7; Nina Asher, "Dorothy Jacobs Bellanca: Feminist Trade Unionist, 1894–1946" (PhD diss., Binghamton University, 1980), 145. The labels *Women's Bureau* and *Women's Department* were used interchangeably in ACWA literature during the thirteen months of its existence.

25. *Proceedings of the Seventh Biennial ACWA Convention*, 1926, 376; Asher, "Dorothy Jacobs Bellanca," 138–40.

26. Asher, "Dorothy Jacobs Bellanca," 142; Dorothy Jacobs Bellanca to Mary Anderson, February 3, 1925, ACWA Papers, Box 28, Folder 17.

27. *Advance*, December 5, 1924, 1, quoted in Asher, "Dorothy Jacobs Bellanca," 142–45.

28. Asher, "Dorothy Jacobs Bellanca," 146, 218; Ann Washington Craton, "Women's Share in Union Work," *Advance*, October 13, 1922, 10–11; "Why the Discrimination against Women in Our Organization?" *Advance*, April 8, 1927, 6; Dorothy Sue Cobble, "Rethinking Troubled Relations between Women and Unions: Craft Unionism and Female Activism," *Feminist Studies* 16, no. 3 (Autumn, 1990), 519–48.

29. "Yes, Women Are Discriminated Against: But What of It?" *Advance*, May 6, 1927, 4–6; "Another Letter on Discrimination against Women Members," *Advance*, October 29, 1926, 8.

30. Theresa Wolfson, "Equal Rights in the Union," *Survey*, February 15, 1927, 629–30; Louis Silverstein, "Can Women Be Organized?" *Advance*, October 19, 1926, 6.

31. "Amalgamated Women Demand Attention and What They May Get," *Advance*, September 3, 1926, 3; "Yes, Women Are Discriminated Against: But What of It?" *Advance*, May 6, 1927, 6; Paul Blanshard, "Who Bosses the Women and Why," *Advance*, August 4, 1922, 10; Nancy F. Cott, *The Grounding of Modern American Feminism* (New Haven: Yale University Press, 1987), 237.

32. "Why the Discrimination against Women in Our Organization?" *Advance*, April 8, 1927, 6.

33. *Proceedings of the Eighth Biennial ACWA Convention*, 1928, 236–37.

34. Bessie Hillman's tone was clearly one of appreciation; however, the *Advance* reported that she complained bitterly that this was the first time she had been given the opportunity to speak. See *Proceedings of the Eighth Biennial ACWA Convention*, 1928, 273; "What Happened at Our Chicago Convention," *Advance*, May 25, 1928, 8.

35. *Proceedings of the Eighth Biennial ACWA Convention*, 1928, 273–74. Attesting to the amalgamation of the sexes within the ACWA is the fact that until 1947 the organization did not separately categorize its membership records by gender. See "List of Total Membership, 1947–57," ACWA Papers, Box 246, Folder 3.

36. Sidney Hillman to Bessie Hillman, April 1921, ACWA Papers, Box 113, Folder 11. At a Chicago memorial service for Bessie, General Secretary-Treasurer Frank Rosenblum emphasized that Hillman's marriage "in no way deflected her deep involvement with the Union." See Frank Rosenblum, "In Memory of Bessie Hillman" (Chicago, IL, April 18, 1971), private collection of Philoine Fried.

37. As quoted in Matthew Josephson, *Sidney Hillman: Statesman of American Labor* (New York: Doubleday, 1956), 153.

38. Andrew R. Heinze, *Adapting to Abundance: Jewish Immigrants, Mass Consumption, and the Search for American Identity* (New York: Columbia University Press, 1990), 106. The domestic expectations for women in Jewish life are embodied in the Hebrew concept of *baleboste*, for which there is no

equivalent English term; the closest translation means "owner of the home." Traditionally it implies a "perfect housewife."

39. ACWA, "Organizational Activities of the Chicago Joint Board," ACWA Fifth Biennial Convention, May 8–13, 1922, 7, in ACWA Scrapbook, vol. 1, Chicago Historical Society, Chicago, IL.

40. See *Proceedings of the Fourth Biennial ACWA Convention, 1922*, 304; *Advance,* June 14, 1922, 3; Agnes Nestor, *Woman's Labor Leader: The Autobiography of Agnes Nestor* (Rockford, IL: Bellevue Books, 1954), 131.

41. Philoine Fried, "At Home with the Hillmans," 1 (unpublished paper), private collection of Philoine Fried.

42. Bessie purchased all of the family's homes. Philoine Fried, interview with author, December 29, 1996; Fraser, *Labor Will Rule,* 234–35.

43. Philoine Fried, interview with author, September 20, 2004.

44. Jewish immigrant men usually considered their wives' working outside the home indicative of the husband's inability to support the family. Bessie performed all her activities on an unpaid basis while Sidney was alive. Elizabeth Ewen, *Immigrant Women in the Land of Dollars: Life and Culture on the Lower East Side, 1890–1925* (New York: Monthly Review Press, 1985), 230; Philoine Fried, interviews with author, December 29, 1996, and September 20, 2004.

45. Fried, "At Home with the Hillmans," 4.

46. Andrew R. Heinze, *Adapting to Abundance: Jewish Immigrants, Mass Consumption, and the Search for American Identity* (New York: Columbia University Press, 1990), 116, 127.

47. Jacob Potofsky, "Before the Sixth Biennial Convention," *Advance,* March 14, 1924, 7; Jesse Thomas Carpenter, *Competition and Collective Bargaining in the Needle Trades, 1910–1967* (Ithaca, NY: Cornell University Press, 1972), 548. See also "The Use and Abuse of Power," *Advance,* March 26, 1926, 4. Runaway shops also plagued the women's garment industry. For the ILGWU's Pennsylvania campaign, see Kenneth C. Wolensky, Nicole H. Wolensky, and Robert P. Wolensky, *Fighting for Union Label: The Women's Garment Industry and the ILGWU in Pennsylvania* (University Park: Pennsylvania State University Press, 2002).

48. Mamie Santora, "Women Workers and the Amalgamated," *Advance,* January 4, 1921, 5; Pennsylvania Joint Board, *A Chapter in Labor History: 1933–1958* (New York: ACWA, 1958), 2; *Proceedings of the Tenth Biennial ACWA Convention, 1934,* 62.

49. David L. Graham, "Subsidies for Rugged Individualists," *Virginia Quarterly Review* (1939): 412–13; Pennsylvania Joint Board, *A Chapter in Labor History,* 2; Pennsylvania Department of Labor and Industry, "Conditions in the Needle Trade Industry," *Monthly Bulletin* 20, no. 8 (August 1933): 1–8.

50. Cornelia Pinchot, "Radio Address by Mrs. Over WCAU," June 6, 1933, 3–4, Cornelia Bryce Pinchot Papers, Box 474, Library of Congress, Washington, DC; "Mrs. Pinchot Says Bankers to Blame for Depression," *Harrisburg Telegraph,* June 2, 1933, Cornelia Bryce Pinchot Papers, Box 474.

51. "Shirt Factory Pay as Low as $2 Found," *New York Times,* July 24, 1933, in Hillman Scrapbooks, vol. 5, 188, ACWA Papers; Connecticut State Board of Education, "Confidential Excerpt for Public Officials," to Mr. Joseph Tone, State Commissioner of Labor, June 10, 1933, private collection of Philoine Fried.

52. Alice Kessler-Harris, "The Autobiography of Ann Washington Craton," *Signs* (Summer 1976): 1021–22. Craton's ability to speak English was also an advantage.

53. "Shirt Factory Pay as Low as $2 Found," *New York Times,* July 24, 1933.

54. Pennsylvania Department of Labor and Industry, "Conditions in the Needle Trade Industry," *Monthly Bulletin* 20, no. 8 (August 1933): 8; Amalgamated Clothing Workers of America, *Bread and Roses: The Story of the Rise of the Shirtworkers, 1933–1934* (New York: ACWA, 1935), 14.

55. Mary Duffy, Overall Workers' Union, 1907, quoted in Harriot Stanton Blatch and Alma Lutz, *Challenging Years* (New York: G.P. Putnam & Sons, 1940), 96.

56. Jane Addams, "An Industrial Union with a Social Vision," undated, ACWA Papers, Box 229, Folder 4.

57. Landon R. Y. Storrs, *Civilizing Capitalism: The National Consumers' League, Women's Activism, and Labor Standards in the New Deal Era* (Chapel Hill: University of North Carolina Press, 2000), 120.

58. George Martin, *Madam Secretary: Frances Perkins* (Boston: Houghton Mifflin, 1976), 342–47; Ware, *Beyond Suffrage,* 102; Storrs, *Civilizing Capitalism,* 241–42.

59. Bessie Hillman, undated notes for speech, ACWA Papers, Box 189, Folder 8.

60. Hyman H. Bookbinder, *To Promote the General Welfare: The Story of the Amalgamated Clothing Workers of America* (New York: ACWA, 1950), 77, 91, 98–100; Addams, "An Industrial Union with a Social Vision," 29.

61. Hillman, undated notes for speech, ACWA Papers, Box 189, Folder 8.

62. Esther Peterson, interview with author, February 17, 1997; Esther Peterson, "You Can't Giddyup by Saying Whoa," in *Rocking the Boat: Union Women's Voices, 1915–1975,* ed. Brigid O'Farrell and Joyce L. Kornbluh, 71 (New Brunswick, NJ: Rutgers University Press, 1996).

Chapter 5: Enter Sister Hillman:
The Runaway Campaign Years (1933–1937)

1. Pennsylvania Joint Board, *A Chapter in Labor History: 1933–1958* (New York: ACWA, 1958), 1; Amalgamated Clothing Workers of America, *Bread and Roses: The Story of the Rise of the Shirtworkers, 1933–1934* (New York: ACWA, 1935), 9.

2. Robert H. Zieger and Gilbert J. Gall, *American Workers, American Unions: The Twentieth Century* (Baltimore: Johns Hopkins University Press, 2002), 80.

3. Irving Bernstein, *The Turbulent Years: A History of the American Worker, 1933–1941* (Boston: Houghton Mifflin, 1970), 90–92 and chaps. 2 and 3.

4. Susan Ware, *Beyond Suffrage: Women in the New Deal* (Cambridge, MA: Harvard University Press, 1981), 36.

5. Landon R. Y. Storrs, *Civilizing Capitalism: The National Consumers' League, Women's Activism, and Labor Standards in the New Deal Era* (Chapel Hill: University of North Carolina Press, 2000), 8–9, 38–39; Ware, *Beyond Suffrage,* 35.

6. Ware, *Beyond Suffrage,* 33–35.

7. Storrs, *Civilizing Capitalism*, 8–9, 184–85, 189–90.

8. Susan Ware offers a prosopography of twenty-eight Washington-based network women in *Beyond Suffrage.*

9. Ware, *Beyond Suffrage*, 137–41; Annelise Orleck, *Common Sense and a Little Fire: Women and Working-Class Politics in the United States, 1900–1965* (Chapel Hill: University of North Carolina Press, 1995), 160.

10. Ann Davis, "The Character of Social Feminism in the Thirties: Eleanor Roosevelt and Her Associates in the New Deal," in *FDR: The Man, the Myth, the Era, 1882–1945,* ed. Herbert D. Rosenbaum and Elizabeth Bartelme (New York: Greenwood Press, 1987), 290, 293, 298.

11. As quoted in Ware, *Beyond Suffrage,* 17.

12. Ware, *Beyond Suffrage,* 88–89. Other members of the Labor Advisory Board included Dr. Leo Wolman (professor of economics at Columbia), William Green (AFL), John L. Lewis (UMW), and Sidney Hillman (ACWA).

13. NRA, "Code of Fair Competition for the Men's Clothing Industry" (Washington, DC: Government Printing Office, 1933); Ware, *Beyond Suffrage,* 91–92; Storrs, *Civilizing Capitalism,* 102–9.

14. Ware, *Beyond Suffrage,* 91–92.

15. Lois MacDonald, Gladys Palmer, and Theresa Wolfson, *Labor and the NRA* (New York: Affiliated Schools for Workers, 1935), 27–38; NRA, "Code of Fair Competition for the Men's Clothing Industry" (Washington, DC: Government Printing Office, 1933); ACWA, *Bread and Roses,* 62.

16. Pennsylvania Joint Board, *A Chapter in Labor History,* 1.

17. New York Joint Board, *Book of the Amalgamated in New York* (New York: New York Joint Board, 1940), 33–34.

18. Alice Kessler-Harris, "The Autobiography of Ann Washington Craton," *Signs* (Summer 1976): 1021–22.

19. "Union Declares War on Clothing Makers in Philadelphia," *Philadelphia Record,* July 19, 1928, 1; "Clothing Workers to Strike in Quaker City," *(Philadelphia) New Leader,* July 28, 1928, 2; *Proceedings of the Eighth Biennial ACWA Convention,* 1930, 20–32, 19, 197–99; Amidon, "Styles in Strikes," in ACWA, *Documentary History* (May 1928), 4; Steven Fraser, *Labor Will Rule: Sidney Hillman and the Rise of American Labor* (New York: Free Press, 1991), 238–40; Philadelphia newspaper accounts found in Hillman Scrapbooks, vol. 4, 2, ACWA Papers, Kheel Labor-Management Documentation Center, Cornell University (hereafter "ACWA Papers").

20. Orleck, *Common Sense,* 139.

21. "The Out-of-Town Movement," *Advance,* April 16, 1926, 6.

22. *Proceedings of the Eighth Biennial ACWA Convention,* 1930, 25–26, 192; "Philadelphia Drive by ACWA Is Opened," *Daily News Record,* July 2, 1928; "Union Declares War on Clothing Makers in Philadelphia," *Philadelphia Record,* July 19, 1928; "Clothing Workers to Strike in Quaker City," *(Philadelphia) New Leader,* July 28, 1928.

23. "Philadelphia Drive by ACWA Is Opened," *Daily News Record,* July 2, 1928; "Union Declares War on Clothing Makers in Philadelphia," *Philadelphia Record,* July 19, 1928; Hillman Scrapbooks, vol. 4, 3, ACWA Papers.

24. C. W. Erwin, "Notes from the Philadelphia Front," *Advance,* September 20, 1929, 3; *Proceedings of the Eighth Biennial ACWA Convention,* 1930, 20.

25. Israel Mufson, "Amalgamated's Victory in Quaker City," *Labor Age*, October 1929, 15.

26. "Clothing Workers to Strike in Quaker City," *(Philadelphia) New Leader*, July 28, 1928, 2.

27. *Proceedings of the Eighth Biennial ACWA Convention*, 1930, 192; "Union Declares War on Clothing Makers in Philadelphia," *Philadelphia Record*, July 19, 1928; "Clothing Workers to Strike in Quaker City," *(Philadelphia) New Leader*, July 28, 1928.

28. *Proceedings of the Eighth Biennial ACWA Convention*, 1930, 192; "Union Declares War on Clothing Makers in Philadelphia," *Philadelphia Record*, July 19, 1928; "Clothing Workers to Strike in Quaker City," *(Philadelphia) New Leader*, July 28, 1928, 2.

29. Amidon, "Styles in Strikes," 4.

30. Amidon, "Styles in Strikes," 4.

31. "Hillman Says ACW Drive on Philadelphia Will Go On to Finish," *Daily News Record*, July 26, 1928; "They Have Joined the Fighting Ranks of the Amalgamated," *(New York) Forward*, August 10, 1929, 2 (picture); "Pacts with Eight More Small Shops Claimed by ACW," *Daily News Record*, September 9, 1929; *Proceedings of the Eighth Biennial ACWA Convention*, 1930, 23–24. Newspaper accounts and a sample agreement are contained in Hillman Scrapbooks, vol. 4, 3–5, ACWA Papers.

32. *Proceedings of the Eighth Biennial ACWA Convention*, 1930, 25–26.

33. "Garment Workers Hail Second Big Victory in Week," *Philadelphia Record*, August 29, 1929; "Injunction Quiz Pleases Union," *New York Evening Telegram*, September 17, 1929; "Clothing Employees Win Strike Fight: 550 to Work Again," *Philadelphia Record*, September 25, 1929; Mufson, "Amalgamated's Victory in Quaker City"; Hillman Scrapbooks, vol. 4, 4–10, ACWA Papers.

34. On August 8, 1929, the Philadelphia County Court of Common Pleas No. 5 issued a preliminary injunction against the Amalgamated. See Harry Daroff, Louis Daroff, Charles Daroff, Joseph Daroff, Samuel Daroff, and Michael Daroff, co-partners, trading as H. Daroff and Sons Complainants v. Amalgamated Clothing Workers of America, No. 12837 (Philadelphia County Common Pleas, June Term 1929). For information concerning the injunction (temporary restraining order), see Zander Co., a Pa. corporation; Louis Goldsmith, Inc., a Pa. corporation; The Middishade Company, Inc., a Pa. corporation; Pincus Brothers, Inc., a Pa. corporation v. Sidney Hillman, President of the Amalgamated Clothing Workers of America, and individually; Sidney Rissman, member of the General Executive Board of the Amalgamated Clothing Workers of America, and individually; Hyman Blumberg, member of the General Executive Board of the Amalgamated Clothing Workers of America, and others, Nos. 5383, 5384, 5385 (E.D. Pa. June 1929), Record Group 25, National Archives, Washington, DC.

35. U.S. Congress, Senate, Term 1929, *Congressional Record*, 1–2, Hillman Scrapbooks, vol. 6, 6–7, ACWA Papers.

36. "Inquiry Asked on Writ against Clothing Union," *Washington Herald Tribune*, September 17, 1929.

37. U.S. Senate, *Congressional Record*, 71st Congress, September 16, 1929; "LaFollette Denounces Order," *New York Times*, September 17, 1929; Hillman Scrapbooks, vol. 4, 7, ACWA Papers.

38. "Injunction Quiz Pleases Union," *New York Evening Telegram*, September 17, 1929; "Court Modifies Order Curbing Clothing Union," *Women's Wear Daily*, September 17, 1929; Hillman Scrapbooks, vol. 4, 7, ACWA Papers.

39. "Judge's Opinion Says ACW Methods Violate Common Law and Anti-Trust Act," *Daily News Record*, October 9, 1929; "A Blow at Labor," *Washington Daily News*, October 11, 1929; *Congressional Record Appendix*, October 11, 1929, "Injunction Against Amalgamated Clothing Workers," Remarks of Honorable Robert M. LaFollette; "Another Foolish Injunction," *New Republic*, September 25, 1929.

40. *Proceedings of the Eighth Biennial ACWA Convention*, 1930, 26–28.

41. *Proceedings of the Eighth Biennial ACWA Convention*, 1930, 29–32; "ACWA Wins Philadelphia," *Labor News*, October 19, 1929; "A Great Victory," *Milwaukee Leader*, October 25, 1929. Newspaper accounts are in Hillman Scrapbooks, vol. 4, 7–11, ACWA Papers.

42. George J. Hexter, "Maladies of the Needle Trades," *Daily News Record*, October 22 and 29, 1929; "ACWA Wins Philadelphia," *Labor News*, October 29, 1929.

43. "Mrs. Sidney Hillman Has Been Organizing Shirt Collar Employees," unidentified Albany newspaper, ACWA Microfilm Collection, Reel 24, Frame 925; Elden LaMar, *The Clothing Workers in Philadelphia: A History of Their Struggles for Union Security* (Philadelphia: Philadelphia Joint Board, 1940), 130–31.

44. "Notes from the Philadelphia Front," *Advance*, September 20, 1929, 5; "500 Shirt Workers Quit at Signal," *Daily Worker*, May 11, 1933. Latter account is in Hillman Scrapbooks, vol. 5, 187, ACWA Papers.

45. "Krzycki, Bessie Hillman Address Cutters," *Advance*, June 1937, 20.

46. "Philadelphia Activities," *Advance*, July 1937, 11, 20; "Wife of NRA Board Member Active in Union Work in Albany," *Albany Evening News*, September 28, 1934, ACWA Microfilm Collection, Reel 24, Frame 934.

47. In 1915, author Mildred Moore labeled the militant (exclusively) working-class women who belonged to the Women's Trade Union League "industrial feminists." Mildred Moore, "A History of the Women's Trade Union League of Chicago" (master's thesis, University of Chicago, 1915), as quoted in Orleck, *Common Sense*, 6.

48. "Philadelphia Activities," *Advance*, July 1937, 11, 20; "Philadelphia Joint Board Cites Many Achievements during 1937," *Advance*, January 1938, 26; *Proceedings of the Twelfth Biennial ACWA Convention*, 1938, 378–379.

49. Nina Asher, "Dorothy Jacobs Bellanca," in *A Needle, a Bobbin, a Strike: Women Needleworkers in America*, ed. Joan M. Jensen and Sue Davidson, 215 (Philadelphia: Temple University Press, 1984).

50. *Proceedings of the Twelfth Biennial ACWA Convention*, 1938, 367–368; Alice Kessler-Harris, *Women Have Always Worked: An Historical Overview* (Old Westbury, NY: Feminist Press, 1981), 139–41.

51. Dorothy Sue Cobble, *The Other Women's Movement: Workplace Justice and Social Rights in Modern America* (Princeton, NJ: Princeton University Press, 2004), 3–4.

52. Rose Schneiderman, "Women in the Industrial Crisis," *Advance*, July 1, 1921, 7, in ACWA Papers, Box 235, Folder 2.

53. Among the few documents evidencing that more than a professional relationship existed between Sidney Hillman and Tecia Davidson is a telegram dated November 30, 1930, from Sidney to Bessie, telling her when he will return to New York. It was charged to Tecia Davidson's hotel room. ACWA Papers, Box 112, Folder 21; Esther Peterson, interview with author, February 17, 1997. Despite the fact that the affair was common knowledge in labor circles, family members do not openly admit that the relationship ever existed. Tecia remained silent on her relationship with Sidney, whom she referred to exclusively as "Mr. Hillman" throughout her life.

54. ACWA, *Bread and Roses*, 9.

55. ACWA, *Bread and Roses*, 40.

56. Bessie Hillman's handwritten notes on the back of "Connecticut Employers" list, private collection of Philoine Fried. The notes indicate that Bessie planned to meet with Fathers Wepenchoski, Malley, and Troynar.

57. Reverend Francis Haas, "To Whom It May Concern," July 6, 1933, private collection of Philoine Fried.

58. For more on specific ethnicities, see Thomas Dublin, *When the Mines Closed: Stories of Struggles in Hard Times* (Ithaca, NY: Cornell University Press, 1998), 14–15; Donald Miller and Richard Sharpless, *Kingdom of Coal: Work, Enterprise and Ethnic Communities in the Mine Fields* (Philadelphia: University of Pennsylvania Press, 1985), 171–212; John Bodnar, *Anthracite People: Families, Unions, Work, 1900–1940* (Harrisburg: Pennsylvania Museum & Historical Commission, 1983).

59. Peter Swoboda, interview with author, January 16, 1997. Swoboda, who was a presser during the runaway campaign, became an assistant Pennsylvania Joint Board manager in the 1950s and eventually ACWA vice president.

60. Frieda Schwenkmeyer, *Oral History Interview with Frieda Schwenkmeyer, Amalgamated Clothing Workers of America by Bette Craig* (Ann Arbor, MI: Program on Women and Work, Institute of Labor and Industrial Relations, University of Michigan–Wayne State University, 1978), 24.

61. ACWA, *Bread and Roses*, 42.

62. Pennsylvania Joint Board, *A Chapter in Labor History*, 4.

63. "Children on Strike," *Survey*, June 1933, in Hillman Scrapbooks, vol. 5, ACWA Papers; J. Stanley Lemons, *The Woman Citizen: Social Feminism in the 1920s* (Urbana: University of Illinois Press, 1973), 144–47.

64. Pennsylvania Department of Labor and Industry, "Children Striking," *Monthly Bulletin* 22, no. 4 (April 1933): 2.

65. Pennsylvania Department of Labor and Industry, "Conditions in the Needle Trade Industry," *Monthly Bulletin* 20, no. 8 (August 1933): 1–8; Pennsylvania Joint Board, *A Chapter in Labor History*, 3.

66. Peter Swoboda, interview with author, January 16, 1997; ACWA, *Bread and Roses*, 16; Hollinger F. Barnard, *Outside the Magic Circle: The Autobiography of Virginia Foster Durr* (New York: Simon & Schuster, 1985), 135–36; "Strike Wire Hit by Mrs. Pinchot," unidentified local newspaper article, July 19, 1934, ACWA Papers, Box 31, Folder 466.

67. General Record of the Department of Labor Office of Secretary Frances Perkins, General Subject Files, 1933–41, Box 41, Record Group 174; Lemons, *The Woman Citizen*, 147.

68. Pennsylvania Department of Labor and Industry, "Children Striking," 2; Pennsylvania Joint Board, *A Chapter in Labor History*, 4.

69. "Menace of Sweatshop Faces Wrath of State and Public as Probes Loom into Evils That Approach Slavery," *Philadelphia Record*, April 23, 1933; "Children on Strike," *Survey*, June 1933; "Shirt Pay as Low as $2," *New York Times*, July 24, 1923.

70. ACWA, *Bread and Roses*, 42; Pennsylvania Joint Board, *A Chapter in Labor History*, 3–4.

71. Pennsylvania Joint Board, *A Chapter in Labor History*, 2; ACWA, *Bread and Roses*, 10.

72. Pennsylvania Department of Labor and Industry, "Conditions in the Needle Trade Industry," *Monthly Bulletin* 20, no. 8 (August 1933): 1–8. Hearings were held in Northampton on April 28, 1933; in Allentown on May 4, 1933; and in Bangor on May 16, 1933.

73. Pennsylvania Joint Board, *A Chapter in Labor History*, 10.

74. "The Dictator and the Proclamator," *Allentown Little Stick*, November 3, 1934; "The Garment Workers," *Allentown Little Stick*, November 17, 1934; "Mayor Cites Laws Supporting Edict on Mass Picketing," *Allentown Chronicle*, November 8, 1934; Hillman Scrapbooks, vol. 5, 203–4, ACWA Papers.

75. ACWA, *Bread and Roses*, 8, 16.

76. Bessie Hillman's personal "List of Shirtmakers in Connecticut," private collection of Philoine Fried; *Proceedings of Tenth Biennial ACWA Convention*, 1934, 52–53.

77. ACWA Papers, uncatalogued; ACWA, *Bread and Roses*, 16–17.

78. Esther Peterson with Winifred Conkling, *Restless: The Memoirs of Labor and Consumer Activist Esther Peterson* (Washington, DC: Caring Publishing, 1995), 56–59.

79. Quoted in Dublin, *When the Mines Closed*, 204–5.

80. Peter Swoboda, interview with author, January 16, 1997; Pennsylvania Joint Board, *A Chapter in Labor History*, 8.

81. "Miners Picket Shirt Factory during the Night," *Uniontown News*, August 23, 1933; "St. Clair Folks Hear Merits of Clothing Union Discussed," *Pottsville Journal*, August 19, 1933; "Garment Workers Receive Charter," *Hazleton Standard-Sentinel*, August 29, 1933. Articles contained in Hillman Scrapbooks, vol. 5, 190–94, ACWA Papers.

82. Charles W. Erwin, "A Short Saga of the Shirt Workers," *Advance*, July 1933, 21–22.

83. *Proceedings of the Tenth Biennial ACWA Convention*, 1934, 62; Donald L. Pratt, "Tension in Reading Easier, But Labor Problems Continue," *Reading Daily News Record*, September 1, 1933, in ACWA Papers, Box 120, Folder 4; "Highlights in the History of the Amalgamated," *Advance*, May 15, 1962, 16.

84. Philoine Fried, interview with author, September 20, 2004.

85. "Woes to Federal Conciliator Here," *Reading Times*, July 19, 1933, in Hillman Scrapbooks, vol. 5, 192, ACWA Papers.

86. Lebanon Shirt Company to Miss Charlotte Carr, July 19, 1934, General Record of the Department of Labor, Office of Secretary Frances Perkins, General Subject Files, 1933–41, Box 41, Record Group No. 174, National Archives,

Washington, DC; Cornelia Bryce Pinchot Papers, Box 474, Library of Congress, Washington, DC.

87. "Arbitrator Decides Shirt Mill Dispute," *Pottsville Journal*, July 1933, in Hillman Scrapbooks, vol. 5, 193, ACWA Papers.

88. Ibid.

89. Cora Thomas to Bessie Hillman, October 30, 1934, ACWA Microfilm Collection, Reel 24, Frame 938.

90. Bessie Hillman to Cora Thomas, November 2, 1934, ACWA Microfilm Collection, Reel 24, Frame 937.

91. "Mrs. Pinchot Spoke to Overflow Meeting at Local Hall Last Night," *Pottsville Journal*, August 8, 1933.

92. "Board of Arbitration Assumes Jurisdiction of Shirt Plant Issue," *Pottsville Evening Bulletin*, August 10, 1933; "Shirt Factory Disputes Ended by Labor Heads," *Pottsville Journal*, August 19, 1933; Hillman Scrapbooks, vol. 5, 197, ACWA Papers. The National Labor Board, predecessor to the National Labor Relations Board, was appointed by FDR on August 5, 1933. It had no direct enforcement powers. Zieger and Gall, *American Workers, American Unions*, 76–77.

93. ACWA, *Bread and Roses*, 20.

94. "Rotary Shirt Company Workers on Strike," *Albany Times Union*, June 22, 1934, 1; ACWA Microfilm Collection, Reel 31, Frames 446–47; Mary Hillyer, "Shirt Drive in New York Capital District," *Advance*, May 1934, 17.

95. Cornelia Bryce Pinchot, "The Fight of Shirt Workers for Their Rights," 1934 speech, Cornelia Bryce Pinchot Papers, Box 313; "Shirt and Collar Workers to Hear Wife of Pinchot," *Knickerbocker Press*, June 14, 1934, Cornelia Bryce Pinchot Papers, Box 313; "Shirt Plant Strikers Tell Their Story of Albany Row," *Albany Evening News*, June 28, 1934, in ACWA Papers, Box 124, Folder 4.

96. "Something New in Albany: Women Organize," *Knickerbocker Press*, June 17, 1934; ACWA Microfilm Collection, Reel 31, Frame 431.

97. "Strike Disorders Cause Shirt Factory to Close," unidentified Albany newspaper, ACWA Papers, Box 120, Folder 4.

98. Unidentified article, June 29, 1934, ACWA Papers, Box 120, Folder 4.

99. Unidentified article, ACWA Papers, Box 120, Folder 4; AFS (secretary to Cornelia Pinchot) to Miss Mary Hillyer, June 19, 1934, Cornelia Bryce Pinchot Papers, Box 313.

100. Bessie Hillman to Cornelia Pinchot, July 5, 1934, Cornelia Bryce Pinchot Papers, Box 313; "Wife of NRA Member Active in Union Work," *Albany Evening News*, September 28, 1934; ACWA Microfilm Collection, Reel 24, Frame 934.

101. Mary Hillyer, "Capital District Shirt Workers Move On," *Advance*, June 1934, 13.

102. "Employees Are to Return to Work Today; Wage Question Will Be Decided Later," *Kingston Daily Bulletin*, October 29, 1934, in Hillman Scrapbooks, vol. 5, 201, ACWA Papers.

103. "Women Get Recognition: Troy Local 196 Celebrates 25th Anniversary Dinner," *Advance*, November 1, 1958, 8; Rita Baker to Bessie Hillman, January 14, 1963, ACWA Papers, Box 112, Folder 13.

104. Reverend Francis Haas to Reverend Theobald Kalanaja, November 21, 1934, private collection of Philoine Fried.

105. See NLRB, "In the Matter of the Kaynee Company and Dora Magalski, et al., and the Cleveland Joint Board of the Amalgamated Clothing Workers of America," Case No. 357, Hearings October 9, 16, 17 and November 20, 1934, Record Group 25, National Archives, Washington, DC.

106. National Labor Relations Board, Office of Executive Secretary, "In the Matter of the Kaynee Company and Dora Magalski, et al. and Cleveland Joint Board of the ACWA," December 13, 1934, and "Employers Brief with Appendices 'A' and 'B,' Case Files with Some Exhibits and Briefs," Cases 187–191, Box 44, NLRB 1933–1934, Record Group 25, National Archives, Washington, DC. For the company's version, see Frankel and Frankel and Stanley and Smoyer, Attorneys for the Kaynee Company, "Respondents Affidavits as to Strike Called and Closing of Cleveland Plants after Hearing before Cleveland Regional Labor Relations Board," Case 357, Record Group 25, National Archives; "Kaynee Parley Fails as Firm Asks for Delay," unidentified Cleveland newspaper, November 1935, in ACWA Papers, Box 120, Folder 4.

107. "Strike Spirit in Cleveland," *Advance,* December 1934, 7.

108. Action by Common Pleas Court in Upper Sandusky against Beryl Peppercorn, Manager of the Cleveland Joint Board and twenty pickets, ACWA Papers, Box 120, Folder 4.

109. Jacob Potofsky to Bessie Hillman, January 25, 1935, ACWA Papers, Box 120, Folder 4.

110. *Cleveland Citizen,* 1934, in ACWA Papers, Box 120, Folder 4.

111. *Cleveland Citizen,* n.d., in ACWA Papers, Box 120, Folder 4.

112. Zieger and Gall, *American Workers, American Unions,* 69; National Labor Relations Board, "In the Matter of the Kaynee Company and Dora Magalski, et al., and Cleveland Joint Board of the ACWA," December 15, 1934, Case 189, Record Group 25, National Archives.

113. Sidney Hillman to Bessie Hillman, January 25, 1935, ACWA Papers, Box 120, Folder 4; Sidney Hillman to the Kaynee Company, January 10, 1935, Record Group 25, National Archives; Francis Biddle to George Wakefield, President of the Kaynee Company, February 12, 1935, Record Group 25, National Archives.

114. Philoine and Selma Hillman to Bessie Hillman, January 12, 1935, private collection of Philoine Fried. On the end of the strike, see National Labor Relations Board, "Immediate Release," December 17, 1934, Record Group 25, National Archives; Harry L. Davis, Mayor of Cleveland to Honorable Francis Biddle, January 8, 1935, Record Group 25, National Archives; "Kaynee Plant Workers Return to Jobs Singing," *Cleveland Citizen,* n.d., in ACWA Papers, Box 120, Folder 4; "Back to Work," *Cleveland Press,* January 11, 1935, in ACWA Papers, Box 120, Folder 3; and "Union Wins Kaynee Strike," *Advance,* February 1935, p. 7.

115. Mary Hillyer, "Shirt Drive in New York Capital District," *Advance,* May 1934, 17.

116. ACWA, *Bread and Roses,* 42; Cornelia Bryce Pinchot to Sidney Hillman, June 19, 1935, ACWA Papers, Box 82, Folder 13.

117. "Work in a Union Shop," in *I Am a Woman Worker: A Scrapbook of Autobiographies,* ed. Andria Taylor Hourwich and Gladys L. Palmer (New York: Affiliated Schools for Women Workers, 1936), 64.

118. Pennsylvania Joint Board, *A Chapter in Labor History,* 17–18.

119. "Strike Grows at Wide Awake," *Reading Labor Advocate,* August 9, 1935, in Hillman Scrapbooks, vol. 5, 207, ACWA Papers.

120. Mildred Jeffrey (Educational Director of the Pennsylvania Joint Board of Shirtworkers, 1935–1936), interview with author, January 8, 1997.

121. ACWA, *Bread and Roses,* 16.

122. *Proceedings of the Twelfth Biennial ACWA Convention,* 1938, 367.

123. According to Steven Fraser, union officials were worried that the Social Security Act might threaten the power the Amalgamated derived from union pension plans. See Fraser, *Labor Will Rule,* 336–37.

124. ACWA, *Bread and Roses,* 31.

125. JoAnn E. Argersinger, *Making the Amalgamated: Gender, Ethnicity, and Class in the Baltimore Clothing Industry, 1899–1939* (Baltimore: Johns Hopkins University Press, 1999), 171.

126. Argersinger, *Making the Amalgamated,* 173–74; "Which Will She Choose?" *Advance,* September 24, 1920. Evidence for Hillman's early political preferences is sparse; however, given her union loyalty and the push for women to support socialist candidates from the early 1920s, it can be safely assumed that Hillman voted in accordance with union wishes.

127. Argersinger, *Making the Amalgamated,* 119, 171–4.

128. Despite support from the ACWA and a number of other AFL affiliates, the CIO failed to live up to its promises to women, especially in regard to promoting them to leadership positions. Orleck, *Common Sense,* 267.

129. Philip M. Weightman to Bessie Hillman, 1962, ACWA Papers, Box 115A, Folder 10; Fraser, *Labor Will Rule,* xiii.

130. "Wife of NRA Board Member Active in Union Work in Albany," *Albany Evening News,* September 28, 1934, ACWA Microfilm Collection, Reel 24, Frame 934.

131. "Mrs. Hillman," *New York Herald Tribune,* August 25, 1941, in ACWA Papers, Folder 3; ACWA, *Bread and Roses,* 16; "Kaynee Strike Caused by Intimidation by Bosses," *Cleveland Citizen,* 1935, in ACWA Papers, Box 120, Folder 4.

132. Reverend Francis Haas, "To Whom It May Concern," July 6, 1933, private collection of Philoine Fried. Haas indicated that he wrote several letters introducing Bessie Hillman at Sidney Hillman's request. See also *Proceedings of the Twenty-Fifth Biennial ACWA Convention Proceedings,* 1956, 251–52. Bessie credited Sidney with giving her the confidence to carry on when the work got tough.

133. Philoine Fried, "At Home with the Hillmans," 6 (unpublished paper), private collection of Philoine Fried.

134. Bessie Hillman, notes for address to AFL–CIO State Federation of Labor convention, 1959, ACWA Papers, Box 189, Folder 8.

135. Cobble, *Other Women's Movement,* 4, 56.

136. Alice Kessler-Harris, *In Pursuit of Equity: Women, Men, and the Quest for Economic Citizenship in 20th Century America* (New York: Oxford University Press, 2001), 12–13.

137. Gerda Lerner, *Fireweed: A Political Autobiography* (Philadelphia: Temple University Press, 2002), 323–24.

Chapter 6: *The Power of Labor Feminism: Organizing the Laundry Workers and the Second World War (1937–1946)*

1. Dorothy Sue Cobble, *The Other Women's Movement: Workplace Justice and Social Rights in Modern America* (Princeton, NJ: Princeton University Press, 2004), 3.

2. Bill Fletcher, Jr., "Labor's Renewal? Listening to the 1920s and 1930s," *Labor: Studies in Working-Class History of the Americas* 1, no. 3 (Fall 2004): 17.

3. Philoine Fried, interview with author, July 10, 2005.

4. "Membership of the Amalgamated Clothing Workers of America," ACWA Papers, Box 246, Folder 2, Kheel Labor-Management Documentation Center, Cornell University (hereafter "ACWA Papers").

5. John Thomas McGuire, "Two Feminist Visions: Social Justice Feminism and Equal Rights, 1899–1940," *Pennsylvania History: A Journal of Mid-Atlantic Studies* 71, no. 4 (2004): 445–77; Susan Ware, *Holding Their Own: American Women in the 1930s* (Boston: Twayne Publishers, 1982), 91–94.

6. Jane Addams, "The Progressive Party and the Negro" (1912), in Christopher Lasch, *The Social Thought of Jane Addams* (New York: Bobbs-Merrill, 1965), 169.

7. Arwen P. Mohun, *Steam Laundries: Gender, Technology, and Work in the United States and Great Britain, 1880–1940* (Baltimore: Johns Hopkins University Press, 1998), 179–81.

8. Annelise Orleck, *Common Sense and a Little Fire: Women and Working-Class Politics in the United States, 1900–1965* (Chapel Hill: University of North Carolina Press, 1995), 160; U.S. Bureau of the Census, *Historical Statistics of the United States, Colonial Times to 1957* (Washington, DC: Government Printing Office, 1960), 76, Section D 123–572, "Detailed Occupation of the Economically Active Population: 1900 to 1950"; Laundry Workers Joint Board of Greater New York, "Facts about Your Union," Hillman Scrapbooks, vol. 6, 443, ACWA Papers.

9. U.S. Department of Commerce, *The Fifteenth Census of the United States, 1930: Population.* Vol. V, *General Report on Occupations* (Washington, DC: Government Printing Office, 1933), 582. The census further categorized the workers as follows: Native White—84,261 male and 105,095 female; Foreign-born White—24,530 male and 18,645 female; Negro—12,768 male and 47,842 female; and Other Races—13,179 male and 4,059 female.

10. "Economics and Organization of Laundry Industry," *Advance*, February 1939, 10. The racial breakdown of the laundry workers is not well documented by the union or other official sources.

11. Sylvia R. Weissbrodt, "Women in the Labor Force," *Annals of the American Academy of Political and Social Science*, May 1947. The number of women in the laundry industry was 167,967 and an additional 186,183 women were listed as employed by private families.

12. New York Division of Women in Industry and Minimum Wage, "Report of the Industrial Commissioner to the Laundry Minimum Wage Board Relating to Wages and Other Conditions of Employment of Women in the Laundry Industry" (New York: New York State, 1937); ACWA, "Index of Employment in Laundry Industry in New York City" (1937), ACWA Papers, Box 524, Folder 5.

13. U.S. Department of Commerce, *The Fifteenth Census of the United States, 1930: Manufacturers: Reports by Industries* (Washington, DC: Government Printing Office, 1933), 2:1397; Herbert R. Northrup, *Organized Labor and the Negro* (New York: Harper & Row, 1944), 132.

14. Charles Lionel Franklin, *The Negro Labor Unionist of New York: Problems and Conditions among Negroes in the Labor Unions in Manhattan with Special Reference to the NRA and Post-NRA Situations* (New York: Columbia University Press, 1936), 106, 180, 209, 302. Table XXV, "Total Membership in Miscellaneous International, National and Local Unions, Manhattan, 1935," indicates that Local 280, numbering 800 members, contained 400 (50 percent) Negro workers and Local 290, numbering 250 members, contained 150 (60 percent) Negro workers.

15. Northrup, *Organized Labor and the Negro*, 132. By 1925 the laundry industry began to use trucks for delivery. U.S. Department of Commerce, *The Fifteenth Census of the United States, 1930: Population.* Vol. IV, *Occupations, by States* (Washington, DC: Government Printing Office, 1933), 4:1132, 4:1134. The census listed 4,281 Native white women, 2,664 Foreign-born women, 4,701 Native white men, 5,720 Foreign-born men, and 1,716 Negro men employed in New York City laundries.

16. As early as 1907, the WTUL had attempted but consistently failed to organize women laundry workers in New York. Nancy Schrom Dye, *As Equals and as Sisters: Feminism, Unionism, and the Women's Trade Union League of New York* (Columbia: University of Missouri Press, 1980), 43–44, 64–65, 101–2. Northrup mentions isolated efforts by the YWCA to organize women laundry workers in the 1920s. Northrup, *Organized Labor and the Negro*, 132.

17. Franklin, *The Negro Labor Unionist*, 106; Jean Collier Brown, "The Negro Woman Worker," *Bulletin of the Women's Bureau*, U.S. Department of Labor No. 165 (Washington, DC: Government Printing Office, 1938), 4–5; "A Job in a Laundry," in *I Am a Woman Worker: A Scrapbook of Autobiographies*, ed. Andria Taylor Hourwich and Gladys L. Palmer (New York: Affiliated Schools for Women Workers, 1936), 43.

18. Jane Filley and Therese Mitchell, *Consider the Laundry Workers* (New York: League of Women Shoppers, 1937), 48, 55.

19. Filley and Mitchell, *Consider the Laundry Workers*, 47–48.

20. Brown, "The Negro Woman Worker," 4–5; Franklin, *The Negro Labor Unionist*, 106.

21. Hyman H. Bookbinder, *To Promote the General Welfare: The Story of the Amalgamated Clothing Workers of America* (New York: ACWA, 1950), 60–63.

22. Dollie Lowther Robinson, *Oral History Interview with Dollie Lowther Robinson, Amalgamated Clothing Workers of America by Bette Craig* (Ann Arbor, MI: Program on Women and Work, Institute of Labor and Industrial Relations, University of Michigan–Wayne State University, 1978), 2 [microfiche].

23. Sam Levin, *Proceedings of the Thirteenth Biennial ACWA Convention, 1940*, 566.

24. Mohun, *Steam Laundries*, 138–39.

25. For a detailed analysis of racial and gender issues, see Mohun, *Steam Laundries*, especially chaps. 7 and 10; Rose Schneiderman and Lucy Goldthwaite, *All*

for One (New York: Paul Eriksson, 1967), 210, 217; Scheiderman quoted in Orleck, *Common Sense*, 165.

26. Cobble, *Other Women's Movement*, 51; Orleck, *Common Sense*, 160–61; Yvette Richards, *Maida Springer: Pan-Africanist and International Labor Leader* (Pittsburgh: University of Pittsburgh Press, 2000), 66–69; Yvette Richards, *Conversations with Maida Springer: A Personal History of Labor, Race, and International Relations* (Pittsburgh: University of Pittsburgh Press, 2004), 121–22.

27. "Meeting Minutes," March 5, 1934, New York Women's Trade Union League Papers, Reel 3, Frame 619; Karen Linn Fernia, *Cornelia B. Pinchot: Biographical Note* (Washington, DC: Library of Congress Manuscript Division, 1988), 2; Robinson, *Oral History Interview*, 2.

28. "Memorandum on Violations of Contract," February 23, 1934, NYWTUL Papers, Reel 3, Frames 603–5; "Organization Report," March 5, 1934, NYWTUL Papers, Reel 3, Frames 615–18.

29. "Organization Report," March 5, 1934, NYWTUL Papers, Reel 3, Frame 620; Franklin, *The Negro Labor Unionist*, 106.

30. U.S. Department of Labor, "Job Histories of Women at the Summer Schools," *Women's Bureau Bulletin*, no. 174 (Washington, DC: Government Printing Office, 1939): 4; Robinson, *Oral History Interview*, 2–4.

31. "Workman's Ghetto," *Daily Jewish Courier*, October 17, 1913, 2, Chicago Foreign Language Press Survey, WPA, Chicago Public Library.

32. Mohun, *Steam Laundries*, 220; Orleck, *Common Sense*, 153–54, 164–65. The NRA codes were rarely properly enforced and were struck down with the NIRA in June 1935; the New York State minimum wage law was overturned within a year.

33. A number of women organizers, including ILGWU official Maida Springer, credit Charlotte Adelmond as being "the moving force behind organizing the laundry workers." Richards, *Conversations with Maida Springer*, 121–22. (Adelmond is often spelled Adelman.)

34. Bessie Hillman, *Proceedings of the Thirteenth Biennial ACWA Convention*, 1940, 566.

35. Laundry Workers of Greater New York, "Facts about Your Union," 1937, ACWA Pamphlet Collection, Hillman Scrapbooks, vol. 6, 443, ACWA Papers; Robinson, *Oral History Interview*, 2; "Minutes of the Executive Board Meeting," May 27, 1937, NYWTUL Papers, Reel 4, Frame 121.

36. Rose Schneiderman to Jacob Potofsky, July 30, 1936, ACWA Papers, Box 127, Folder 8.

37. Statement on S. 653 Submitted to the Senate Committee on Labor and Public Welfare by Dr. Vera Miller, Research Associate, Amalgamated Clothing Workers of America (CIO), Laundry Division, April 13, 1949.

38. Richards, *Maida Springer*, 70; Robert H. Zieger and Gilbert J. Gall, *American Workers, American Unions: The Twentieth Century* (Baltimore: Johns Hopkins University Press, 2002), 82–87.

39. Robinson, *Oral History Interview*, 2–4; Brigid O'Farrell and Joyce Kornbluh, eds., *Rocking the Boat: Union Women's Voices, 1915–1975* (New Brunswick, NJ: Rutgers University Press, 1996), 287n5.

40. Franklin, *The Negro Labor Unionist*, p. 301.

41. Schneiderman and Goldthwaite, *All for One*, 216–17; Franklin, *The Negro Labor Unionist*, 301; "Report of Organizer," June-September 1937, NYWTUL Papers, Reel 4, Frame 167.

42. Northrup, *Organized Labor and the Negro*, 134.

43. "Minutes of Regular Meeting," September 13, 1937, NYWTUL Papers, Reel 4, Frames 155–67.

44. Laundry Workers of Greater New York, "Facts about Your Union," 1937, Hillman Scrapbooks, vol. 6, 443, ACWA Papers.

45. Mohun, *Steam Laundries*, 229.

46. Northrup, *Organized Labor and the Negro*, 133.

47. Northrup, *Organized Labor and the Negro*, 135; Helen Blanchard, "Report of Organizer," April 1937, NYWTUL Papers, Reel 4, Frames 101–02; ACWA Research Department, "New York Laundry Worker Gains Since Affiliating with the Amalgamated in 1937," ACWA Papers, Box 524, Folder 4.

48. Fair Labor Standards Act Amendments of 1949, *Hearings before the Subcommittee of the Committee on Labor and Public Welfare, United States Senate, 81st Congress, 1st Session, on S. 58, S. 67, S. 92, S. 105, S. 190, S. 248 and S. 653, April 11–14 and 18–22, 1949* (Washington, DC: Government Printing Office, 1949). The minimum-wage provision of the FLSA raised the laundry workers' minimum wage to 75 cents an hour.

49. Laundry workers were finally covered under the FLSA in 1966. Joseph E. Kalet, *Primer on FLSA and Other Wage and Hour Laws* (Washington, DC: Bureau of National Affairs, 1994), 15–17.

50. Mohun, *Steam Laundries*, 180, 222, 228; Brown, "The Negro Woman Worker," 15.

51. "Resolution on Race Tolerance," in *Proceedings of the Twelfth Biennial ACWA Convention*, 1938, 362; "A Laundry Worker's Creed," *Advance*, November 1938, 14; "15,000 Win Rise in Laundry Pay by Arbitration," *Herald Tribune*, November 8, 1937, 2.

52. *Proceedings of the Twelfth Biennial ACWA Convention*, 1938, 253–58; Linda Kline, *Hatpin Bessie* (New York: ACWA Laundry Workers of America, 1939), Act III, Scene 3.

53. "Ten Thousand Laundry Workers Get ACWA Contract," *Advance*, September 1937, 19.

54. ACWA, "Laundry Workers Win!" (New York: Laundry Workers Joint Board, 1939), ACWA Papers, Box 524, Folder 4; ACWA Research Department, "New York Laundry Workers Gains Since Affiliation with Amalgamated in 1937," ACWA Papers, Box 524, Folder 4.

55. ACWA Research Department, "Changes in Minimum Wages of Time Workers in the Laundry Industry and New York City," October 30, 1945; ACWA, "Family and Wholesale Divisions Contract," November 5, 1942, both in ACWA Papers, Box 524, Folder 4.

56. "Biographical Sketch of Mrs. Bessie Hillman, Vice President, Amalgamated Clothing Workers of America," May 3, 1949, ACWA Papers, Folder 160, Box 8.

57. "Gus Strebel Heads New York Laundry Workers Union," *Advance*, June 1939, 24; Mohun, *Steam Laundries*, 237.

58. Marie McGowan, "Mrs. Hillman, O.P.M. 'Widow,' Is Busy on Her Union Job Here," *New York Herald Tribune*, August 25, 1941, 1.

59. Northrup, *Organized Labor and the Negro*, 135. Only scant evidence exists to indicate rates of participation by race or gender. *Advance* photographs are among the only sources to provide insight into racial composition of the Amalgamated.

60. "Accomplishments of Laundry Workers' Organization Committee," *Advance*, May 1938, 15; Bessie Hillman, "A Life for the Workers," 1952 speech, private collection of Philoine Fried; ACWA, *Twenty-Fifth Anniversary ACWA Convention Documentary History*, 1938–1940, 63–64; *Proceedings of the Sixteenth Biennial ACWA Convention*, 1948, 279.

61. "Dolly Lowther Gets Honor from Hudson Shore Labor School," *Advance*, September 1940, 19.

62. McGowan, "Mrs. Hillman, O.P.M. 'Widow.'"

63. Bessie Hillman, "A Life for the Workers"; "Biographical Sketch of Mrs. Bessie Hillman," May 3, 1949, ACWA Papers.

64. O'Farrell and Kornbluh, *Rocking the Boat*, 287n2; National Women's Trade Union League, "School for Active Workers in the Labor Movement" (Chicago, 1915?), Pamphlet 58–3026, State Historical Society of Wisconsin; "Summer Schools," *Advance*, March 1, 1929; "Training Women to Be Leaders," *Advance*, February 7, 1930.

65. Daniel L. Katz, "A Union of Many Cultures: Yiddish Socialism and Interracial Organizing in the ILGWU, 1913–1941" (PhD diss., Rutgers University, 2003), 109.

66. Like Hillman, Cohn tried to keep workers' education out of the political arena, but the male leadership rebuffed her efforts after a membership increase in 1933. Daniel Katz, "Race, Gender, and Labor Education: ILGWU Locals 22 and 91, 1933–1937," *Labor's Heritage* 11, no. 1 (2000): 4–19.

67. Orleck, *Common Sense*, 185–86; Richards, *Conversations with Maida Springer*, 64; Alice Kessler-Harris, *Out to Work: A History of Wage-Earning Women in the United States* (New York: Oxford University Press, 1982), 243–44.

68. Katz, "Race, Gender, and Labor Education," 16–17.

69. Sara Fredgant, *Oral History Interview with Sara Fredgant, Amalgamated Clothing Workers of America by Bette Craig* (Ann Arbor, MI: Program on Women and Work, Institute of Labor and Industrial Relations, University of Michigan–Wayne State University, 1978), 77 [microfiche, 140–8], Kheel Labor-Management Documentation Center, Cornell University.

70. "Educational Activities Start Now," *Advance*, October 1938; Bessie Hillman, "Educational Department," *Advance*, December 1938; "Three LWJB Members in Broadway Hit Show," *Advance*, February 1940; "Laundry Workers Plan for 1940 Educational Season," *Advance*, September 1940; "New York Laundry Workers Ready Cultural Program," *Advance*, October 1941.

71. "Three LWJB Members in Broadway Hit Show," *Advance*, January 1940, 21; "Pins and Needles," *Advance*, January 1939, 21. The latter article covers the play *Pins and Needles* and mentions using "talkies" for the purpose of worker education.

72. Bessie Hillman, "A Life for the Workers"; "Biographical Sketch of Mrs. Bessie Hillman," May 3, 1949, ACWA Papers. Eleanor Roosevelt was also a sponsor of the Laundry Workers' Union. See Eleanor Roosevelt to Bessie Hillman, March 5, 1942, Eleanor Roosevelt Papers, Series 20.1, Box 23, Franklin

Delano Roosevelt Presidential Library, Hyde Park, New York; Robinson, *Oral History Interview*, 49.

73. Fredgant, *Oral History Interview*, 103.

74. "Sing over National Station," *Advance*, May 1940, 23.

75. Bookbinder, *To Promote the General Welfare*.

76. *Proceedings of the Fourteenth Biennial ACWA Convention*, 1944, 57–58.

77. Fredgant, *Oral History Interview*, 80.

78. "What Is the Department of Cultural Activities?" *Advance*, November 1937, 31; "DCA Regional Conference Arouses Wide Interest," *Advance*, November 1938, 20.

79. O'Farrell and Kornbluh, *Rocking the Boat*, 285n7; Robert Joseph Schaefer, "Educational Activities of the Garment Unions, 1890–1948: A Study in Workers' Education in the International Ladies Garment Workers' Union and the Amalgamated Clothing Workers of America in New York City" (PhD diss., Columbia University, 1951), 150, 177, 197; Richard J. Altenbaugh, *Education for Struggle: The American Labor Colleges of the 1920s and 1930s* (Philadelphia: Temple University Press, 1990), 32.

80. "Women in Majority in Rand Summer Class," *Advance*, July 26, 1918.

81. Quoted in Stephen Fraser, *Labor Will Rule: Sidney Hillman and the Rise of American Labor* (New York: Free Press, 1991), 439–40.

82. Fraser, *Labor Will Rule*, 439–40; Youngsoo Bae, *Labor in Retreat: Class and Community among Men's Clothing Workers of Chicago, 1871–1929* (Albany: State University of New York Press, 2001), chap. 6.

83. Bookbinder, *To Promote the General Welfare*, 144.

84. Altenbaugh, *Education for Struggle*, 32.

85. Katz, "A Union of Many Cultures," 107, 316.

86. *Report of the General Executive Board and Proceedings of the Twelfth Biennial ACWA Convention*, 1938, 75–84.

87. Esther Peterson, "You Can't Giddyup by Saying Whoa," in *Rocking the Boat: Union Women's Voices, 1915–1975*, ed. Brigid O'Farrell and Joyce L. Kornbluh, 59–83 (New Brunswick, NJ: Rutgers University Press, 1996).

88. U.S. Department of Labor, "The Summer Schools for Women Workers," *Women's Bureau Bulletin*, no. 174.

89. Margaret "Peggy" Wood (Director Hudson Shore Labor School) to Bessie Hillman, April 10, 1946 and June 6, 1948, ACWA Papers, Box 113, Folder 14; *The Women of Summer—The Bryn Mawr Summer School for Women Workers, 1912–1938*, produced by Suzanne Bauman and Rita Heller (Filmmakers Library, 1986).

90. Robinson, *Oral History Interview*, 20; Alice Hanson Cook, *A Lifetime of Labor: The Autobiography of Alice H. Cook* (New York: Feminist Press, 1990), 50–52.

91. Philoine Fried, interview with author, December 28, 1997.

92. "Department of War Activities," *Advance*, June 15, 1944; "Department of War Activities," *Advance*, June 15, 1945.

93. Bessie Hillman, "A Life for the Workers"; "Democracy Programs," *Advance*, April 1939, 7. To attract black workers, the laundry workers' union designed a radio series, entitled "Democracy Programs," in 1939–1940.

94. "Bessie Hillman," March 19, 1964, ACWA Papers, Box 161, Folder 3; *New York Daily News,* December 15, 1961, in ACWA Papers, Box 242, Folder 10; *Proceedings of the Seventeenth Biennial ACWA Convention,* 1950, 53.

95. Announcement of 1945 discussion, ACWA Papers, Box 114, Folder 10.

96. Jane Addams tried unsuccessfully to have a civil rights plank included in the 1912 Progressive Party platform. Jane Addams, "The Progressive Party and the Negro" (1912), in Christopher Lasch, *The Social Thought of Jane Addams* (New York: Bobbs-Merrill, 1965), 168–70; Hasia R. Diner, *In the Almost Promised Land: American Jews and Blacks, 1915–1935* (Westport, CT: Greenwood Press, 1977), 133.

97. "Dolly Lowther Gets Honor from Hudson Shore Labor School," *Advance,* September 1940, 19; Robinson, *Oral History Interview,* 4.

98. Robinson, *Oral History Interview,* 4–6.

99. "Dollie Robinson's Eulogy Reprinted as a Tribute to Bessie Hillman," *Advance,* February 5, 1971, 5; Dollie Robinson, "Report on Problems of Negro Women," October 1963, Katherine P. Ellickson Collection, Box 95, File 31, Franklin Delano Roosevelt Presidential Library, Hyde Park, New York; Arthur Goldberg, Secretary, U.S. Department of Labor, Press Release, March 4, 1961, ACWA Papers, Box 115, Folder 10. For correspondence between Hillman and Robinson, see ACWA Papers, Box 115, Folder 10; ACWA Microfilm Collection, Reel 24, Frame 485.

100. Bessie Hillman to Marc Karson (Education Director) and students at the Amalgamated Summer Institute, July 8, 1963, ACWA Microfilm Collection, Reel 23, Frame 578.

101. Robinson, "Report on Problems of Negro Women"; Goldberg, U.S. Department of Labor, Press Release.

102. Robinson, *Oral History Interview,* 10; Northrup, *Organized Labor and the Negro,* 135; ACWA Papers, Box 114, Folder 10.

103. U.S. Department of Labor, "Women Workers in Some Expanding Wartime Industries: New Jersey, 1942," *Women's Bureau Bulletin* no. 197 (Washington, DC: Government Printing Office, 1943): 10.

104. Ibid.; U.S. Department of Commerce, Bureau of the Census, *Sixteenth Census of the United States, 1940. Population,* vol. III, *The Labor Force,* Part I, Table 58, "United States Summary." According to the 1940 Census on Occupations, in both the men's apparel and laundry industries approximately 78 percent of the workers were women.

105. Mary Anderson, "Women Wartime Workers and Their Wages in Wartime," radio show transcript, Station WTOL, Toledo, Ohio, March 28, 1944, in Records of the Women's Bureau, U.S. Department of Labor, 1918–1965: Part II, Women in World War II, Series B, Subject Correspondence Files on War Industries, Reel 18, Frame 216.

106. Philoine Fried, interview with author, January 13, 2003.

107. Philoine Fried, interview with author, February 9, 2005. Tecia Davidson also accompanied Hillman to Washington.

108. "Amalgamated Civilian Defense Committee," *Advance,* October 15, 1943, 14; ACWA Papers, Box 115, Folder 5 (includes OPA Complaint Form); "Amalgamated Civilian Defense Committee," *Advance,* November 1, 1943, 3; Esther Peterson to Sidney Hillman, Memo on Civilian Defense Meeting,

December 21, 1942, ACWA Papers, Box 82, Folder 9; "Department of War Activities," *Advance*, April 15, 1944, 2; Esther Peterson, interview with author, February 17, 1997.

109. Philoine Fried, interview with author, February 9, 2005.

110. Philoine Fried, interview with author, April 21, 2005.

111. Suzanne A. Wunder, "When Mothers Have War Jobs," *Churchwoman* (Hinsdale, IL, February 1943), Women's Bureau Microfilm, Reel 23, Frames 324–29, Series B; Frances Perkins to Katherine Lenroot, June 6, 1942, "Children's Bureau File," Secretary Perkins's General Subject File, 1940–1944, Record Group 174, National Archives, Washington, DC; Philip Foner, *Women and the American Labor Movement: From the First Trade Unions to the Present* (New York: Free Press, 1982), 351–53.

112. Maureen Honey, *Creating Rosie the Riveter: Class, Gender, and Propaganda during World War II* (Amherst: University of Massachusetts Press, 1984), 27; Foner, *Women in the American Labor Movement*, 352–54.

113. Irving Salert (National CIO War Relief Committee) to Jacob Potofsky, October 16, 1943, ACWA Microfilm Collection, Reel 24, Frame 772; Wunder, "When Mothers Have War Jobs"; "Workers and Allies: Female Participation in the American Trade Union Movement, 1824–1976," exhibition organized by Judith O'Sullivan, Smithsonian Institution Traveling Exhibition Service (Washington, DC: Smithsonian Institution Press, 1975); *The National Cyclopedia of American Biography*, vol. 56 (Clifton, NJ: James White, 1975), s.v. "Bessie Abramowitz Hillman."

114. "Resolution on Women Workers," *Proceedings of the Twenty-Fifth Biennial ACWA Convention*, 1966, 288–90; Eileen Boris and Sonya Michel, "Social Citizenship and Women's Right to Work in Postwar America," in *Women's Rights and Human Rights: International Historical Perspectives*, ed. Patricia Grimshaw, Katie Holmes, and Marilyn Lake (Chippenham, Wiltshire, UK: Palgrave, 2001), 209; "ACWA First Union in Country to Initiate Child-care Center," *Advance*, May 15, 1968, 4.

115. Bessie Hillman to PFC Jerry MacKay, April 1945, ACWA Papers, Box 114, Folder 15.

116. For correspondence between Bessie Hillman and Dorothy Jacobs Bellanca, see ACWA Papers, Box 30, Folder 14.

117. David K. Niles to Grace Tully (FDR's secretary), May 19, 1942, President's Personal File (ACWA), Container 3585, Franklin Roosevelt Papers, Franklin Delano Roosevelt Presidential Library, Hyde Park, New York; Fraser, *Labor Will Rule*, 490–91.

118. "Mrs. Hillman Now in CDVO," *Advance*, November 1, 1942, 11. With many relatives still residing in Europe, the Hillmans had a very personal stake as well as a public interest in the outcome of the war.

119. "Department of War Activities," *Advance*, May 15, 1944, 21.

120. Robinson, *Oral History Interview*, 5; Judi Miller, *Women Who Changed America* (New York: Manor Books, 1976), 142.

121. David Stebenne, *Arthur J. Goldberg: The New Deal Liberal* (New York: Oxford University Press, 1996), 144–46; "Erase Intolerance with Education, Says Mrs. FDR," *Baltimore Jewish Times*, 1941, in Hillman Scrapbooks, vol. 8, 256, ACWA Papers. For a discussion of support of black rights by Jews, see

Diner, *In the Almost Promised Land.* On civil rights in the workplace, see Eleanor Roosevelt to Sidney Hillman, 1942–1944, Eleanor Roosevelt Papers, Reel
10, Frames 437–89, Roosevelt Library; Eileen Boris, "'You Wouldn't Want One
of 'Em Dancing with Your Wife': Racialized Bodies on the Job in World War II,"
American Quarterly 50, no. 1 (March 1998): 77–108.

122. Richards, *Maida Springer,* 66; Stebenne, *Arthur Goldberg,* 144–45.

123. Peterson, "You Can't Giddyup by Saying Whoa," 71.

124. Fannie Allen Neal, "Confronting Prejudice and Discrimination: Personal Recollections and Observations," in *Opening Doors: Perspectives on
Race Relations in Contemporary America,* ed. Harry J. Knopke, Robert J. Nor-
rell, and Ronald W. Rogers (Tuscaloosa: University of Alabama Press, 1991), 32;
Northrup, *Organized Labor and the Negro,* 129–35.

125. Fannie Allen Neal, *Oral History Interview with Fannie Allen Neal by
Maureen Rickard* (Ann Arbor, MI: Program on Women and Work, Institute of
Labor and Industrial Relations, University of Michigan–Wayne State Univer-
sity, 1978), 23–26.

126. Cobble, *Other Women's Movement,* 14.

127. Eileen Boris, "'The Right to Work Is the Right to Live! Fair Employment
and the Quest for Social Citizenship," in *Two Cultures of Rights: The Quest
for Inclusion and Participation in Modern America and Germany,* ed. Manfred Berg and Martin H. Geyer, 121–41 (Cambridge, UK: Cambridge University
Press, 2002); Eileen Boris, "Black Workers, Trade Unions, and Labor Standards:
The Wartime FEPC," in *Historical Roots of the Urban Crisis: African Americans in the Industrial City, 1900–1950,* ed. Henry Louis Taylor, Jr., and Walter
Hill, 251–73 (New York: Garland, 2000).

128. Foner, *Women and the American Labor Movement,* 395.

129. Women's Trade Union League, "Action Needed: Post-War Jobs for
Women" (Washington, DC: National WTUL of America, 1944); Katheryn
Blood, "Women's Wartime Role in Industry" (1944), Records of the Women's
Bureau, Part II, Women in World War II, Series B, Reel 23, Frames 917–19; U.S.
Department of Labor, "Women Workers after VJ-Day in One Community:
Bridgeport, Connecticut," *Women's Bureau Bulletin* no. 216 (Washington, DC:
Government Printing Office, 1946): 4; U.S. Bureau of Labor Statistics Division
of Employment Statistics, "Women in Factories: October 1939–December 1945"
(Washington, DC: Government Printing Office, 1946), 13 (Table 4, "Number of
Women per 100 Production Workers in Manufacturing Industries and Groups,"
indicates that more than 70 percent of workers involved in the production of
men's clothing were women); Robinson, *Oral History Interview,* 61.

130. Nancy Gabin, *Feminism in the Labor Movement: Women and the
United Auto Workers, 1935–1975* (Ithaca, NY: Cornell University Press, 1990),
47–48.

131. M. C. Fisch, "When Sam Came Back," *Advance,* July 25, 1930, 5.

132. Philoine Fried, interview with author, January 13, 2003; "Mrs. Hyman
Blumberg, 78, Dies," *New York Times,* November 1, 1965, 42.

133. By the time Bessie assumed the vice presidency of the union, she had enlisted in the Democrats for Reform movement, largely because of her admiration for Eleanor Roosevelt. Philoine Fried, interview with author, December 29,
1996; "ACWA Memories of Mrs. Roosevelt," *Advance,* November 15, 1962, 1.

134. Cobble, *Other Women's Movement*, 51.

135. ACWA Papers, Box 231, Folder 9; Dorothy J. Bellanca to Bessie Hillman, July 31, 1936, ACWA Papers, Box 30, Folder 6; Jacob Potofsky to Bessie Hillman, December 27, 1940, private collection of Philoine Fried; "After Leaving A.L.P. Group," *New York Sun*, 1946, in ACWA Papers, Box 120, Folder 4.

136. "League of Women Voters Offers Course in Democracy," *Advance*, May 15, 1944, 21; "Special Women Voters' Edition," *Advance*, October 27, 1944, 1; Bessie Hillman on FDR, ACWA Papers, Box 134, Folder 6.

137. "ACWA Women Hear Hollander and Bellanca at Political Rally," *Advance* (Special Women Voters' Edition), 1. The PAC was formed in 1942.

138. As quoted in Schaefer, "Educational Activities of the Garment Unions," 66.

139. Undocumented newspaper photograph from late 1940s titled "U.S. Reunion," picturing Bessie Hillman welcoming her niece, Luba Atin (sic), from Poland; Philoine Fried, interview with author, January 13, 2003.

140. Hillman invitation to Roosevelt inaugural, n.d., ACWA Papers, Box 231, Folder 4; Judi Miller, "Bessie Hillman: Early Labor Leader," in *Women Who Changed America* (New York: Manor Books, 1976), 172–73.

141. A power struggle accounts for the factional division in the ACWA after Hillman's death. Hillman's biographer Steven Fraser neglects this particular fracture in the union hierarchy, but recounts an incident in the early years of the union suggesting that Rosenblum had a history of divisive behavior in Fraser, *Labor Will Rule*, 97–98. Esther Peterson also refers to the factions in Peterson, "You Can't Giddyup by Saying Whoa," 78–79.

142. Philoine Fried, interviews with author, January 29, 1997 and January 13, 2003; Delia Gottlieb (Jacob Potofsky's daughter), interview with author, January 29, 1997. According to Gottlieb, Potofsky was the only one all the General Executive Board members could agree on. Fried mentioned the hard feelings that Rosenblum had against Bessie Hillman from that period forward.

143. "New Appointment Made to General Executive Board," *Advance*, September 1, 1946, 2; *Proceedings of the Sixteenth Biennial ACWA Convention*, 1948, x. The General Executive Board chose Bessie Hillman, Anthony Froise, and August Bellanca to fill the vacancies caused by the deaths of vice presidents Joseph Catalanotti and Dorothy Jacobs Bellanca, and by the election of Frank Rosenblum to the post of General Secretary-Treasurer. The only other female GEB member at the time was Gladys Dickason, who had earned her place among the leaders during the runaway strikes of the 1930s. Gladys Dickason was married but never had children.

Chapter 7: Union Women in the Postwar Years: Separate but Not Equal (1946–1961)

1. "New Appointment Made to General Executive Board," *Advance*, September 1, 1946, 2; *Proceedings of the Sixteenth Biennial ACWA Convention*, 1948, x. Sidney's estate was so small that after his death it was necessary for Bessie to work. Philoine Fried, interview with author, December 29, 1996. With the possible exception of her year of service to the GEB in 1915–1916, this was the

first paid position Bessie had held in the union, as the Hillmans firmly believed that only one of them should draw a union salary.

2. Lillian Poses to Bessie Hillman, August 30, 1946, ACWA Papers, Box 115, Folder 5, Kheel Labor-Management Documentation Center, Cornell University (hereafter "ACWA Papers").

3. Bessie Hillman to Pauline Newman, August 8, 1946, Pauline Newman Papers, MC 324, Reel 10, Frame 168, Schlesinger Library, Radcliffe University.

4. Bessie Hillman to Josephine Guest, November 20, 1962, ACWA Microfilm Collection, Reel 22, Frame 915; *Proceedings of the Sixteenth Biennial ACWA Convention,* 1948, 152–53; Philoine Fried, interview with author, December 29, 1997.

5. Sara Fredgant, *Oral History Interview with Sara Fredgant, Amalgamated Clothing Workers of America by Bette Craig* (Ann Arbor, MI: Program on Women and Work, Institute of Labor and Industrial Relations, University of Michigan–Wayne State University, 1978), 23.

6. Picture of Gladys Dickason and Bessie Hillman discussing union business. *Advance,* June 1, 1952, 6; Alice Kessler-Harris, "Problems of Coalition Building: Women and Trade Unionism in the 1920s," in *Women, Work and Protest: A Century of U. S. Women's Labor History,* ed. Ruth Milkman, 110–32 (New York: Routledge & Kegan Paul, 1987). Dorothy Jacobs Bellanca and Mamie Santora were the only other female vice presidents to serve on the GEB for the first thirty-five years of the union's existence.

7. Philoine Fried, interview with author, January 13, 2003; Esther Peterson, "You Can't Giddyup by Saying Whoa," in *Rocking the Boat: Union Women's Voices, 1915–1975,* ed. Brigid O'Farrell and Joyce L. Kornbluh, 78–79 (New Brunswick, NJ: Rutgers University Press, 1996).

8. Philoine Fried, interviews with author, December 29, 1997, and April 16, 2000. Fried implied that the restrictions Bessie encountered resulted at least partially from Rosenblum's resentment of her support of Potofsky for the ACWA presidential post.

9. Bessie Abramowitz Hillman, "Gifted Women in the Trade Unions," in *American Women: The Changing Image,* ed. Beverly Benner Cassara, 104 (Boston: Beacon Press, 1962); Dollie Lowther Robinson, *Oral History Interview with Dollie Lowther Robinson, Amalgamated Clothing Workers of America by Bette Craig* (Ann Arbor, MI: Program on Women and Work, Institute of Labor and Industrial Relations, University of Michigan–Wayne State University, 1978), 57; Alice Kessler-Harris, *In Pursuit of Equity: Women, Men, and the Quest for Economic Citizenship in 20th Century America* (New York: Oxford University Press, 2001), 207.

10. George Silver to Bessie Hillman, September 9, 1947, private collection of Philoine Fried; Alice Hanson Cook, *A Lifetime of Labor: The Autobiography of Alice H. Cook* (New York: Feminist Press, 1990), 102–6.

11. *Proceedings of the Twenty-First Biennial ACWA Convention,* 1958, 274; Philoine Fried, interview with author, January 13, 2003; correspondence (dated 1949–1951) with Claude Pepper, U.S. Senator, Florida, regarding the Rutenburgs, ACWA Papers, Box 115, Folder 1.

12. Golda Myerson (Meir) to Bessie Hillman, June 27, 1949, ACWA Papers, Box 114, Folder 14; "Hall and Museum at Amalgamated School Named after

Sidney Hillman," ACWA Microfilm Collection, Reel 23, Frames 320 and 332;
Meir speech, ACWA Papers, Box 113, Folder 8.

13. "Speech by Mrs. Hillman at Opening of Hillman Museum and Amalgamated School," 1952, ACWA Papers, Box 113, Folder 18; Ann Schofield, *"to do
and to be": Portraits of Four Women Activists, 1893–1986* (Boston: Northeastern University Press, 1997), 110–11; Hugo Hertz to Bessie Hillman, September
20, 1946, ACWA Papers, Box 113, Folder 10.

14. Fredgant, *Oral History Interview*, 42.

15. Letty Cottin Pogrebin, *Deborah, Golda, and Me: Being Female and Jewish in America* (New York: Crown, 1991), 237–40; Alice Kessler-Harris, "Organizing the Unorganizable: Three Jewish Women and Their Union," *Labor
History* 17 (Winter 1976): 8–9.

16. Bessie was also a lifetime member of a Jewish labor organization, His-
tadrut Haordim–General Federation of Labor, in Israel. See "Attending His-
tadrut Dinner," *Advance*, March 15, 1964, 5; Bessie Hillman to Benjamin
Abrams, April 3, 1951, ACWA Papers, Box 112, Folder 7.

17. George Marshall to Bessie Hillman, July 12, 1951, ACWA Microfilm Collection, Reel 28, Frame 751.

18. Bessie Hillman to Leora Barfield (Manager, North Georgia Joint Board),
March 11, 1952, ACWA Papers, Box 112, Folder 9.

19. Bessie Hillman to Captain Evelyn J. Blewett (Office of the Assistant Secretary of Defense), December 3, 1951, ACWA Papers, Box 118, Folder 2; "Parade,
Rallies Open Drive to Recruit Women," *New York Herald Tribune*, November
14, 1951, in ACWA Papers, Box 118, Folder 2.

20. Bessie Hillman to Mrs. Y. Saradatsky, July 9, 1951, ACWA Papers, Box
115, Folder 2.

21. Bessie Hillman to Dr. John Hannah (Assistant Secretary of Defense),
March 11, 1954, ACWA Papers, Box 118, Folder 5.

22. Quentin Sheean to Bessie Hillman, October 15, 1945, ACWA Papers, Box
114, Folder 15.

23. *Proceedings of the Fifteenth Biennial ACWA Convention*, 1946, 114–15;
Hyman H. Bookbinder, *To Promote the General Welfare: The Story of the Amal-
gamated Clothing Workers of America* (New York: ACWA, 1950), 44; Mary
Frederickson, "'I Know Which Side I'm On': Southern Women in the Labor
Movement in the Twentieth Century," in *Women, Work and Protest: A Cen-
tury of U.S. Women's Labor History*, ed. Ruth Milkman, 172–75 (New York:
Routledge & Kegan Paul, 1987).

24. Jacqueline Jones, *Labor of Love, Labor of Sorrow: Black Women, Work
and the Family, from Slavery to the Present* (New York: Vintage Books, 1985),
134–36.

25. U.S. Bureau of Commerce, *U.S. Census of Population 1950*. Vol. II, *Char-
acteristics of Population, Part 1, U.S. Summary* (Washington, DC: Government Printing Office, 1953), 2:1–2:410.

26. Jones, *Labor of Love*, 252.

27. Ray Marshall, *Labor in the South* (Cambridge, MA: Harvard University
Press, 1967), 175–76.

28. Steven Fraser, *Labor Will Rule: Sidney Hillman and the Rise of American Labor* (New York: Free Press, 1991), 386–401. The WTUL began to organize

women in the southern textile industry as early as 1925. See Frederickson, "I Know Which Side I'm On," 169–72.

29. *Proceedings of the Sixteenth Biennial ACWA Convention,* 1948, 209.

30. U.S. Department of Labor, Bureau of Labor Statistics, *Report Number 82,* "Wage Structure, Cotton Textiles," November 1954 (Washington, DC: Government Printing Office, 1954), 1–4.

31. Harry Reed (Director, Committee to Abolish Discrimination) to Bessie Hillman, March 22, 1951, ACWA Microfilm Collection, Reel 27, Frame 814; *Proceedings of the Twenty-Fifth Biennial ACWA Convention,* 1966, 299; ACWA Papers, Box 117, Folders 1–3; Roy Wilkins (Administrator, National Association for the Advancement of Colored People) to Bessie Hillman, October 19, 1951, ACWA Microfilm Collection, Reel 27, Frame 826.

32. Jacob Potofsky and Frank Rosenblum to Bessie Hillman, November 29, 1951, private collection of Philoine Fried; Bessie Hillman, "Union Label Speech—To Union Members," March 5, 1953, ACWA Microfilm Collection, Reel 24, Frame 972.

33. Fred Sard to Bessie Hillman, June 1, 1950, ACWA Microfilm Collection, Reel 25, Frame 152; "Immediate Program," ACWA Microfilm Collection, Reel 24, Frame 964; Jacob Potofsky and Frank Rosenblum to Bessie Hillman, November 29, 1951, private collection of Philoine Fried.

34. Landon R. Y. Storrs, *Civilizing Capitalism: The National Consumers' League, Women's Activism, and Labor Standards in the New Deal Era* (Chapel Hill: University of North Carolina Press, 2000), 18–23.

35. Bessie Hillman, "Notes for an Address at the Mississippi State AFL-CIO Convention, April 7, 1959," ACWA Papers, Box 189, Folder 8; Bessie Hillman to Hazel Bankston, November 22, 1951, ACWA Microfilm Collection, Reel 24, Box 961.

36. Annie Belle Swaney to Bessie Hillman, June 1, 1950, ACWA Papers, Box 115, Folder 21.

37. Barbara S. Griffith, *The Crisis of American Labor: Operation Dixie and the Defeat of the C.I.O.* (Philadelphia: Temple University Press, 1988), xiv–xv. The only other union to hire women organizers was the United Textile Workers of America.

38. Hillman, "Notes for an Address at the Mississippi State AFL–CIO Convention, April 7, 1959," ACWA Papers, Box 189, Folder 8.

39. Isabelle Jones to Bessie Hillman, June 1948, ACWA Papers, Box 114, Folder 2; Len DeCaux, *Labor Radical: From the Wobblies to the CIO* (Boston: Beacon Press, 1970), 330. DeCaux also criticized the male domination of the Amalgamated's leadership.

40. Dollie Robinson to Bessie Hillman, April 25, 1951, ACWA Papers, Box 115, Folder 10.

41. Hazel Bankston to Bessie Hillman, May 2, 1951, ACWA Papers, Box 112, Folder 8; Bessie Hillman to Hazel Bankston, September 14, 1951, ACWA Papers, Box 112, Folder 8.

42. "Civil Rights in ACWA Cited by Bessie Hillman," *Advance,* August 1, 1957, 4.

43. Victoria Byerly, *Hard Times Cotton Mill Girls: Personal Histories of Womanhood and Poverty in the South* (Ithaca, NY: ILR Press, 1986), 126, 149.

44. "Civil Rights in ACWA Cited by Bessie Hillman," *Advance,* August 1, 1957, 4.

45. Fannie Allen Neal, *Oral History Interview with Fannie Allen Neal by Maureen Rickard* (Ann Arbor, MI: Program on Women and Work, Institute of Labor and Industrial Relations, University of Michigan–Wayne State University, 1978), 36; Eula McGill, *Oral History Interview with Eula McGill by Jacquelyn Hall* (Ann Arbor, MI: Program on Women and Work, Institute of Labor and Industrial Relations, University of Michigan–Wayne State University, 1978), 118.

46. As late as 1960, only 15 percent of all southern textile workers were covered by union contracts, as compared to 93 percent of textile workers in New England. U.S. Department of Labor, Bureau of Labor Statistics, *Report Number 184,* "Wage Structure: Cotton Textiles," August 1960 (Washington, DC: Government Printing Office, 1960), 3.

47. *Proceedings of the Nineteenth Biennial ACWA Convention,* 1954, 85.

48. Griffith, *The Crisis of American Labor,* 38.

49. Ray Marshall, "The Negro in Southern Unions," in *The Negro and the American Labor Movement,* ed. Julius Jacobson (New York: Doubleday, 1968), 149–50.

50. William Chapman, "Labor Leader's Widow Attacks Eisenhower Team in Talk Here," n.d., ACWA Papers, Box 120, Folder 4.

51. U.S. Department of Labor, Bureau of Labor Statistics, *Report No. 184,* 3.

52. Ray Marshall, *The Negro Worker* (New York: Random House, 1967), 28; "She's Been in the Front Lines of the Labor Movement 58 Years," *Miami Herald,* May 29, 1968; Boris Shishkin (Director of the Department of Civil Rights) to Bessie Hillman, June 12, 1957 and October 21, 1957, ACWA Papers, Box 115, Folder 22.

53. Bessie Hillman, "Notes for an Address to the Mississippi State AFL-CIO Convention, 1959," ACWA Papers, Box 189, Folder 8.

54. "Statement by the AFL-CIO Executive Council on the Situation in Little Rock," September 24, 1957, ACWA Microfilm Collection, Reel 27, Frame 749.

55. Mary McLeod Bethune to Bessie Hillman, November 30, 1949, ACWA Papers, Box 112, Folder 11; Fleur Cowles to Bessie Hillman, March 10, 1949, ACWA Papers, Box 112, Folder 19; George Weaver (Director of the Civil Rights Committee) to Bessie Hillman, July 3, 1953, ACWA Papers, Box 117, Folder 3.

56. Jones, *Labor of Love,* 263–66.

57. Esther Peterson to Bessie Hillman, March 5, 1951, ACWA Microfilm Collection, Reel 24, Frame 231.

58. "Union in Politics," ACWA Papers, Box 189, Folder 8. Bessie Hillman was the first chair of the CIO's PAC.

59. Storrs, *Civilizing Capitalism,* 196–97.

60. Bessie Hillman to Harry S Truman, April 28, 1947, ACWA Papers, Box 115A, Folder 1; Charles Alexander, *Holding the Line: The Eisenhower Era, 1952–1961* (Bloomington: Indiana University Press, 1975), 112.

61. Coordinating Committee of Independent Democrats, "What Is the Committee's Purpose?" ACWA Microfilm Collection, Reel 23, Frame 167.

62. *Proceedings of the Seventeenth Biennial ACWA Convention,* 1950, 227–29.

63. Ibid.; Bessie Hillman to Messrs. Charlie Garrahan and Roy Gregware, November 13, 1950, ACWA Microfilm Collection, Reel 23, Frame 161.

64. "Bessie Hillman Scores Threat to American Civil Liberties," *Advance,* February 1, 1954, 3; "Conference Deals with Dangers to Civil Liberties," *Advance,* February 1, 1954, 4.

65. Esther Murray to Bessie Hillman, June 12, 1952 and November 9, 1953, ACWA Papers, Box 114, Folder 16.

66. Alexander, *Holding the Line,* 24.

67. "Bessie Hillman Scores Threat to American Civil Liberties," *Advance,* February 1, 1954, 3; "Conference Deals with Dangers to Civil Liberties," *Advance,* February 1, 1954, 4; Bessie Hillman to Mary Weston, March 6, 1952, ACWA Microfilm Collection, Reel 24, Frame 963.

68. Thomas K. Finletter and Anna M. Rosenberg (Co-chairmen, New York Committee for Stevenson and Kefauver) to Bessie Hillman, September 5, 1956, ACWA Microfilm Collection, Reel 24, Frame 695.

69. Alexander, *Holding the Line,* 182.

70. "Proposed Statement of the Democratic Advisory Committee on Labor Policy," ACWA Papers, Box 119, Folder 1.

71. William Chapman, "Labor Leader's Widow Attacks Eisenhower Team in Talk Here," n.d., ACWA Papers, Box 120, Folder 4; Bessie Hillman, 1960 speech, private collection of Philoine Fried; Elinore Herrick (Editor, *New York Herald Tribune*) to Bessie Hillman, December 10, 1960, ACWA Papers, Box 113, Folder 9.

72. Chester Bowles to Bessie Hillman, June 3, 1960, ACWA Papers, Box 112, Folder 13.

73. Kessler-Harris, *In Pursuit of Equity,* 213.

74. Elinore Herrick to Bessie Hillman, December 1960, ACWA Papers, Box 113, Folder 9; Carl M. Marcy (Chief of Staff, Senate Foreign Relations Committee), interview by Donald A. Richie, October 12, 1983, U.S. Senate Historical Office Oral History Project, 13, 127, www.senate.gov.

75. Elaine Tyler May, *Homeward Bound: American Families in the Cold War* (New York: Basic Books, 1999), 65–67.

76. Dorothy Sue Cobble, "Recapturing Working-Class Feminism," in *Not June Cleaver: Women and Gender in Postwar America, 1945–1960,* ed. Joanne Meyerowitz (Philadelphia: Temple University Press, 1994), 59.

77. Ruth Milkman, *Gender at Work: The Dynamics of Job Segregation by Sex during World War II* (Urbana: University of Illinois Press, 1987), 99–100.

78. Women's Bureau, *Conference of Trade Union Women and Women's Bureau* (Washington, DC: Government Printing Office, April 19–20, 1945), 32; Robinson, *Oral History Interview,* 57.

79. Alice Kessler-Harris, *Out to Work: A History of Wage-Earning Women in the United States* (New York: Oxford University Press, 1982), 277, 300–301; Kessler-Harris, *In Pursuit of Equity,* 205; May, *Homeward Bound,* 65–67.

80. Cobble, "Recapturing Working-Class Feminism," 60; Dorothy Sue Cobble, *The Other Women's Movement: Workplace Justice and Social Rights in Modern America* (Princeton, NJ: Princeton University Press, 2004), 17; "Total Membership," ACWA Papers, Box 246, Folder 3.

81. Dorothy Sue Cobble, "Lost Visions of Equality: The Labor Origins of the Next Women's Movement," *Labor's Heritage* 12, no. 1 (Winter/Spring 2003), 20–23.

82. *Proceedings of the Sixteenth Biennial ACWA Convention*, 1948, 246–47.

83. May, *Homeward Bound*, 16–17, 66–67.

84. Bessie Hillman, "Tribute to Rose Schneiderman," June 1949, ACWA Microfilm Collection, Reel 24, Frame 686; *Proceedings of the Sixteenth Biennial ACWA Convention*, 1948, 246–47.

85. Nancy Gabin, *Feminism in the Labor Movement: Women and the United Auto Workers, 1935–1975* (Ithaca, NY: Cornell University Press, 1990), 230–31.

86. Cobble, *Other Women's Movement*, 3, 56–58.

87. Kessler-Harris, *Out to Work*, 296.

88. Annelise Orleck, *Common Sense and a Little Fire: Women and Working-Class Politics in the United States, 1900–1965* (Chapel Hill: University of North Carolina Press, 1995), 30.

89. "State Protective Laws Still Needed for Women," *Advance*, May 15, 1967, 9; Ulla Wilkander, Alice Kessler-Harris, and Jane Lewis, eds., *Protecting Women: Labor Legislation in Europe, the United States, and Australia, 1880–1920* (Urbana: University of Illinois Press, 1995).

90. Kessler-Harris, *In Pursuit of Equity*, 42, 69.

91. Alice H. Cook, *The Working Mother: A Survey of Problems and Programs in Nine Countries* (Ithaca, NY: New York State School of Industrial Relations, 1978), x–xi; Sonya Michel, "The Limits of Maternalism: Policies Toward American Wage-Earning Mothers during the Progressive Era," in *Mothers of a New World: Maternalist Politics and the Origins of Welfare States*, ed. Seth Koven and Sonya Michel, 307–8 (New York: Routledge, 1993); Orleck, *Common Sense*, 125.

92. Kopelov, "Equal Pay for Women Bill Backed by ACWA," *Advance*, May 15, 1962, 6; "Are We Wasting Womenpower?" *Advance*, September 1, 1957, 15–16; Gabin, *Feminism in the Labor Movement*, 68.

93. Cobble, "Lost Visions of Equality," 17.

94. AFL-CIO, *Problems of Working Women: Summary Report of a Conference Sponsored by the Industrial Union Department of the AFL-CIO*, June 12–14, 1961, Publication No. 43, 49–50, ACWA Papers, Box 120, Folder 1; "Women Urged to Greater Union Role by Bessie Hillman," *Advance*, April 15, 1956, 9.

95. Bessie Hillman, "Minutes of the Committee on Protective Labor Legislation," President's Commission on the Status of Women, February 6, 1963, Reel 12, Frame 364, Binghamton University, Microfilm Edition 2248.

96. *Proceedings of the Sixteenth Biennial ACWA Convention*, 1948, 246.

97. Cobble, *Other Women's Movement*, 6–8.

98. Cobble, "Recapturing Working-Class Feminism," 71.

99. *Proceedings of the Sixteenth Biennial ACWA Convention*, 1948, 246–47.

100. Cobble, *Other Women's Movement*, 6–8. Works evidencing labor feminism in various unions include Gabin, *Feminism in the Labor Movement*, passim; Dennis A. Deslippe, *"Rights, Not Roses": Unions and the Rise of Working-Class Feminism, 1945–1980* (Urbana: University of Illinois Press, 2000); Milkman, *Gender at Work*; Alice Kessler-Harris, *Out to Work: A History*

of Wage-Earning Women in the United States (New York: Oxford University Press, 1982).

101. Deslippe, *"Rights Not Roses,"* 3.

102. *Proceedings of the Sixteenth Biennial ACWA Convention,* 1948, 246–47; Cobble, "Recapturing Working-Class Feminism," 69.

103. Kessler-Harris, *Out to Work,* 189; Kessler-Harris, *In Pursuit of Equity,* 207–9.

104. Kessler-Harris, *In Pursuit of Equity,* 208–9.

105. Cobble, *Other Women's Movement,* 8, 186–87.

106. Cobble, "Lost Visions of Equality," 18; Cobble, *Other Women's Movement,* 9, 98–99.

107. For a comprehensive account of equal pay history, see Kessler-Harris, *Out to Work,* 262; Kessler-Harris, *A Woman's Wage: Historical Meanings and Social Consequences* (Lexington: University of Kentucky Press, 1990), 81–112.

108. Storrs, *Civilizing Capitalism,* 196–97.

109. Cobble, *Other Women's Movement,* 96.

110. Rose Schneiderman to Joseph Schlossberg, December 9, 1938, ACWA Papers, Box 145, Folder 12; Cobble, "Recapturing Working-Class Feminism," 66.

111. Cobble, *Other Women's Movement,* 97, 105.

112. Cobble, *Other Women's Movement,* 54; Kessler-Harris, *Out to Work,* 306; Kessler-Harris, *In Pursuit of Equity,* 214.

113. The New York branch of the WTUL survived until 1954. Bessie continued to serve as a delegate at its conventions until at least 1947. See "Credential to the Thirteenth Convention (Deferred Triennial) of the National Women's Trade Union League of America," 1947, private collection of Philoine Fried.

114. Orleck, *Common Sense,* 265–66; Cobble, *Other Women's Movement,* 52, 55.

115. Cobble, *Other Women's Movement,* 56.

116. Cobble, "Recapturing Working-Class Feminism," 61; Gabin, *Feminism in the Labor Movement,* passim; Kessler-Harris, *In Pursuit of Equity,* 208.

117. Cobble, "Recapturing Working-Class Feminism," 61–62, 71–72.

118. Kessler-Harris, *Out to Work,* 310–11.

119. Bookbinder, *To Promote the General Welfare,* 117, 120, 133.

120. Deslippe, *"Rights, Not Roses,"* 43; Cobble, *Other Women's Movement,* 147. Cobble asserts that immediately after the AFL-CIO merger, the labor feminist agenda made some progress, but "women's rising expectations outpaced the ability or willingness of the male-led movement to respond" by the late 1950s.

121. "ACW Education Work to Be Commenced Soon," *Advance,* September 24, 1920, 1–2; *Proceedings of the Sixteenth Biennial ACWA Convention,* 1948, 246–47.

122. Mary M. Francis to Bessie Hillman, September 26, 1957, ACWA Papers, Box 113, Folder 4; *Proceedings of the Sixteenth Biennial ACWA Convention,* 1948, 246–47.

123. "Women Urged to Greater Union Role by Bessie Hillman," *Advance,* April 15, 1956, 9.

124. "Problems of Women Workers Discussed by Bessie Hillman," *Advance,* June 15, 1956, 7.

125. Maurice Neufeld to Bessie Hillman, December 12, 1957, ACWA Papers, Box 114, Folder 18.

126. Mary M. Francis to Bessie Hillman, September 26, 1957, ACWA Papers, Box 113, Folder 4.

127. Kessler-Harris, *In Pursuit of Equity,* 208; Gabin, *Feminism in the Labor Movement,* 93–94; Cobble, *Other Women's Movement,* 50–56.

128. AFL-CIO, *Problems of Working Women,* 49–50; "Women Urged to Greater Union Role by Bessie Hillman," *Advance,* April 15, 1956, 9.

129. AFL-CIO, *Problems of Working Women,* 49–50; "Women Urged to Greater Union Role by Bessie Hillman," *Advance,* April 15, 1956, 9.

130. *Proceedings of the Sixteenth Biennial ACWA Convention,* 1948, 246–47. See Deslippe, *"Rights, Not Roses,"* 7–8, for analysis of various feminist approaches by other unions.

131. Cobble, *Other Women's Movement,* 3–4.

132. Pauli Murray, *The Autobiography of a Black Activist, Feminist, Lawyer, Priest, and Poet* (Knoxville: University of Tennessee Press, 1987), 75; Linda Gordon, "What's New in Women's History," in *Feminist Studies* (Bloomington: Indiana University Press, 1986), 29–30; Kathryn Kish Sklar and Thomas Dublin, "Feminism and Mainstream Narratives in American History, 1780–2000," *OAH Magazine of History* 19, no. 2 (March 2005): 25.

133. Cobble, *Other Women's Movement,* 61.

134. Alice Hamilton as quoted in Cobble, *Other Women's Movement,* 61.

135. Gladys Dickason, "Women in Labor Unions," *Annals of the American Academy of Political and Social Sciences* (May 1947): 70–78.

136. Cobble, *Other Women's Movement,* 4, 7, 60–62.

137. Neal, *Oral History Interview,* 36; Barbara M. Wertheimer and Anne H. Nelson, *Trade Union Women: A Study of Their Participation in New York City Locals* (New York: Praeger Publishers, 1975), 85.

138. Gabin, *Feminism in the Labor Movement,* 5, 92–100. In 1944 the UAW established its own Women's Bureau.

139. *Proceedings of the Sixteenth Biennial ACWA Convention,* 1948, 247.

140. Dickason, "Women in Labor Unions," 75–76.

141. Cobble, *Other Women's Movement,* 13, 57–58; Kessler-Harris, *In Pursuit of Equity,* 208.

142. Cobble, *Other Women's Movement,* 9; Carol Nackenoff, "Jane Addams's Legacy for American Citizenship and for the Contemporary Feminist Ethic of Care Debate," paper presented at "Exploring Jane Addams" Conference, 29th Annual Richard R. Baker Colloquium in Philosophy, University of Dayton, November 8–9, 2002.

Chapter 8: Creating "A Sort of Revolution" (1961–1970)

1. As quoted in Alice Kessler-Harris, *Out to Work: A History of Wage-Earning Women in the United States* (New York: Oxford University Press, 1982), 308–10.

2. Kessler-Harris, *Out to Work,* 310.

3. See Katherine Pollack Ellickson, "The President's Commission on the Status of Women: Its Formation, Functioning, and Contribution," 1981, 9,

Caroline F. Ware Papers, File 1, Franklin Delano Roosevelt Presidential Library, Hyde Park, New York (hereafter "Caroline F. Ware Papers").

4. Dennis A. Deslippe, *"Rights, Not Roses": Unions and the Rise of Working-Class Feminism, 1945–1980* (Urbana: University of Illinois Press, 2000), 41; Nancy Gabin, *Feminism in the Labor Movement: Women and the United Auto Workers, 1935–1975* (Ithaca, NY: Cornell University Press, 1990), 57, 93.

5. Dorothy Sue Cobble, *The Other Women's Movement: Workplace Justice and Social Rights in Modern America* (Princeton, NJ: Princeton University Press, 2004), 157.

6. AFL-CIO, *Problems of Working Women: Summary Report of a Conference Sponsored by the Industrial Union Department of the AFL-CIO,* June 12–14, 1961, Publication No. 43, 49–50, ACWA Papers, Box 120, Folder 1, Kheel Labor-Management Documentation Center, Cornell University (hereafter "ACWA Papers"). Hillman pointed out that Peterson was "picked" because Arthur Goldberg recommended her to Kennedy.

7. AFL-CIO, *Problems of Working Women,* 49–50.

8. Isabelle Shelton, "Take to the Hills, Chairman Advises," *Washington Evening Star,* June 15, 1961, in ACWA Microfilm Collection, Reel 24, Frames 262–63.

9. Ibid.; Marie Smith, "Women Blame Own Labor Bosses," *Washington Post,* June 15, 1961, C19, in ACWA Microfilm Collection, Reel 24, Frame 258; Emily Hickman, Chair of the Committee on Women in World Affairs, "A Statement to Secretary of State Byrnes," December 31, 1946, ACWA Microfilm Collection, Reel 25, Frame 246; "IUD Conference Concludes: Working Women Still Have a Long Row to Hoe," *Advance,* July 1, 1961, 12.

10. Mary Anderson to Bessie Hillman, note on copy of *Washington Evening Star* article, ACWA Microfilm Collection, Reel 24, Frame 262; Shelton, "Take to the Hills"; Smith, "Women Blame Own Bosses"; Dollie Robinson to Bessie Hillman, June 22, 1961, ACWA Papers, Box 115, Folder 10.

11. "IUD Conference Concludes," 12.

12. Cobble, *Other Women's Movement,* 159.

13. Nelson Lichtenstein, *State of the Union: A Century of American Labor* (Princeton, NJ: Princeton University Press, 2002), 164–71.

14. Cobble, *Other Women's Movement,* 16.

15. Kessler-Harris, *Out to Work,* 289; Gabin, *Feminism in the Labor Movement,* 63–64.

16. Kessler-Harris, *Out to Work,* 289; Steven Fraser, *Labor Will Rule: Sidney Hillman and the Rise of American Labor* (New York: Free Press, 1991), 507–9.

17. Deslippe, *"Rights, Not Roses,"* passim; Gabin, *Feminism in the Labor Movement,* 229–36.

18. Frances Lide, "Esther Peterson Is Sworn In," *Washington Evening Star,* August 17, 1961, C4–C5, in ACWA Microfilm Collection, Reel 24, Frame 255; Robinson, undated note, ACWA Microfilm Collection, Reel 24, Frame 259.

19. "IUD Conference Concludes," 12; Deslippe, *"Rights, Not Roses,"* 41.

20. Cobble, *Other Women's Movement,* 62–68; *Proceedings of the Sixteenth Biennial ACWA Convention,* 1948, 246–47.

21. Esther Peterson with Winifred Conkling, *Restless: The Memoirs of Labor and Consumer Activist Esther Peterson* (Washington, DC: Caring Publishing, 1995), 64–65.

22. Mrs. Thomas Braden and Jacqueline Kennedy to Bessie Hillman, September 29, 1960, ACWA Papers, Box 114, Folder 4. The Women's Committee for New Frontiers included Frances Perkins, Eleanor Roosevelt, Anna Rosenberg, Agnes Meyer, Eugenie Anderson, and Bessie Hillman.

23. Peterson, *Restless*, 96–98.

24. Quoted in David Stebenne, *Arthur J. Goldberg: The New Deal Liberal* (New York: Oxford University Press, 1996), 251.

25. Kessler-Harris, *Out to Work*, 313.

26. "Meeting of Trade Union Women," February 28, 1961, Esther Peterson Papers, Box 41, Folder 833, and Katherine P. Ellickson Papers, Box 90, Folder 31, Franklin Delano Roosevelt Presidential Library, Hyde Park, New York.

27. Esther Peterson to Arthur Goldberg, March 28, 1961, Esther Peterson Papers, Box 41, Folder 833; Arthur Goldberg to John F. Kennedy, March 29, 1961, Esther Peterson Papers, Box 41, Folder 833; John F. Kennedy to Esther Peterson, April 5, 1961, Esther Peterson Papers, Box 41, Folder 833.

28. Esther Peterson to Arthur Goldberg, June 2, 1961, Esther Peterson Papers, Box 41, Folder 833.

29. Alice Kessler-Harris, *In Pursuit of Equity: Women, Men, and the Quest for Economic Citizenship in 20th Century America* (New York: Oxford University Press, 2001), 214, 229–32.

30. Peterson, *Restless*, 117.

31. Anna Margolis to Leah Eisenberg, April 14, 1961, ACWA Papers, Box 113, Folder 1.

32. Peterson, *Restless*, 106–7; Kessler-Harris, *In Pursuit of Equity*, 216–18.

33. Eleanor Roosevelt to Bessie Hillman, April 15, 1962, ACWA Papers, Box 119, Folder 2.

34. "Members of Women's Committee for New Frontiers," ACWA Microfilm Collection, Reel 23, Frame 463.

35. Ellickson, "The President's Commission on the Status of Women," 4.

36. Mary Callahan, in *Rocking the Boat: Union Women's Voices, 1915–1975*, ed. Brigid O'Farrell and Joyce Kornbluh (New Brunswick, NJ: Rutgers University Press, 1996), 127.

37. Cobble, *Other Women's Movement*, 171; Kessler-Harris, *Out to Work*, 305. The Women's Bureau withdrew its formal opposition to the ERA in 1954, but it was later reasserted in the 1960s under Peterson and Keyserling.

38. Lichtenstein, *State of the Union*, 94–95.

39. Roger Sheldon, press release regarding "Committee Appointed to Study Protective Labor Laws for Women," May 27, 1962, ACWA Papers, Box 119, Folder 2; Ellickson, "The President's Commission on the Status of Women," 4.

40. Women's Bureau, U.S. Department of Labor, "Highlights, 1920–1960," ACWA Microfilm Collection, Reel 30, Frame 2; Deslippe, *"Rights, Not Roses,"* 20; Elaine Tyler May, "Cold War Warm Hearth: Politics and the Family in Postwar America," in *The Rise and Fall of the New Deal Order, 1930–1980*, ed. Steven Fraser and Gary Gerstle (Princeton, 1989), 159.

41. PCSW, *Report of the Committee on Protective Labor Legislation to the President's Commission on the Status of Women* (Washington, DC: U.S. Government Printing Office, October 1963), iii, 30; Reverend Addie Wyatt, interview with author, March 27, 2002. Other members of the Committee on Protective Labor Legislation were Margaret F. Ackroyd, Chief, Division of Women and Children, Rhode Island State Department of Labor; Doris Boyle, Professor of Economics, Loyola College; Henry David, President, New School for Social Research; Mrs. Paul McClellan Jones, Vice President, National Board, Young Women's Christian Association; Mary Dublin Keyserling, Associate Director, Conference on Economic Progress; Carl McPeak, Special Representative on State AFL-CIO; Clarence R. Thornbrough, Commissioner, Arkansas Department of Labor; S. A. Wesolowski, Assistant to President, Brookshire Knitting Mills, Inc.; and Ella C. Ketchin, who served as technical secretary for the committee.

42. Carolyn F. Ware, "The President's Commission on the Status of Women, 1961–1963," 14, Carolyn F. Ware Papers, Folder 1; PCSW, "Inquiry Committee on Protective Labor Legislation," ACWA Papers, Box 119, Folder 5; Cobble, *Other Women's Movement*, 171.

43. "President's Commission on the Status of Women," microfilm ed., Binghamton University, Series 2248, Reel 12, Frame 64, and Reel 12, Frame 274.

44. PCSW, *Report of the Committee on Protective Labor Legislation, Appendix C*, 31.

45. "President's Commission on the Status of Women," microfilm ed., Binghamton University, Series 2248, Reel 12, Frame 125, and Reel 12, Frame 152.

46. "Statement of Dolly Lowther, Laundry Workers' Division of the Amalgamated Clothing Workers Unit, CIO, Representing the Greater New York Area," Fair Labor Standards Act Amendments of 1949, Hearings before the Subcommittee of the Committee on Labor and Public Welfare, United States Senate, 81st Congress, Session 1, April 11–14 and 18–22, 1949 (Washington, DC: Government Printing Office, 1949); William G. Whittaker, *The Fair Labor Standards Act* (New York: Novinka Books, 2003), 8.

47. Bessie Hillman, notes for speech to the AFL-CIO Mississippi State Federation of Labor Convention, April 1959, ACWA Papers, Box 189, Folder 8.

48. Bessie Hillman to the members of Huntingdon, Tennessee Local 525, October 30, 1961, ACWA Papers, Box 112, Folder 7. A 1961 amendment to the FLSA promised to raise the minimum wage to $1.25 by 1965.

49. Cobble, *Other Women's Movement*, 162–63.

50. Cobble, *Other Women's Movement*, 162–63; PCSW, *Report of the Committee on Protective Labor Legislation*, 22, 36; "President's Commission on the Status of Women," microfilm ed., Reel 12, Frame 152.

51. "President's Commission on the Status of Women," microfilm ed., Reel 12, Frame 192.

52. Rachel Carson, Mary Dublin Keyserling, and Helen Hill Miller, "Report of the Women's Committee on New Frontiers," 1960, ACWA Microfilm Collection, Reel 23, Frame 478.

53. Cobble, *Other Women's Movement*, 137–38.

54. "President's Commission on the Status of Women," microfilm ed., Reel 12, Frames 529–39.

55. "President's Commission on the Status of Women," microfilm ed., Reel 12, Frames 261 and 265.

56. PCSW, *Report of the Committee on Protective Labor Legislation,* 1; Ware, "The President's Commission on the Status of Women," 14; PCSW, "Inquiry Committee on Protective Labor Legislation," ACWA Papers, Box 119, Folder 5; Committee on Protective Labor Legislation, "Substance of Recommendation," February 8, 1963, Caroline F. Ware Papers, Box 157, Folder 3; Committee on Protective Labor Legislation, "Redraft Outline: Preliminary Report of Subcommittee of Committee on Protective Labor Legislation," March 14, 1963, Caroline F. Ware Papers, Box 157, Folder 2; Committee on Protective Labor Legislation, "Summary Report and Recommendations," March 26, 1963, Caroline F. Ware Papers, Box 157, Folder 2. The U.S. Department of Labor and the American Labor Education Service furnished statistics and information for the Committee on Protective Labor Legislation.

57. "Notes from Meeting of the President's Commission on the Status of Women," February 5, 1962, Katherine P. Ellickson Papers, Box 90, Folder 23; Dorothy Sue Cobble, "Lost Visions of Equality: The Labor Origins of the Next Women's Movement," *Labor's Heritage* 12, no. 1 (Winter/Spring 2003), 21; Cobble, *Other Women's Movement,* 172.

58. Cobble, *Other Women's Movement,* 177–78.

59. As quoted in "American Women, 1963–1968," in *Women's Issues: PCSW 1961–1968,* 20, Citizen's Advisory Council (1968), Caroline F. Ware Papers, NOW, Box 157.

60. "President's Commission on the Status of Women," microfilm ed., Reel 12, Frame 369.

61. PCSW, *American Women* (Washington, DC: Government Printing Office, 1963).

62. Kessler-Harris, *Out to Work,* 313–14.

63. Kessler-Harris, *In Pursuit of Equity,* 232–33; Kathleen A. Laughlin, *Women's Work and Public Policy: A History of the Women's Bureau, U.S. Department of Labor, 1945–1975* (Boston: Northeastern University Press, 2000), 93.

64. Katherine Pollack Ellickson, "AFL-CIO Meeting Notes," February 5, 1962, Katherine P. Ellickson Papers, Box 90, Folder 23.

65. Peterson, *Restless,* 113.

66. Cobble, *Other Women's Movement,* 146.

67. Kessler-Harris, *In Pursuit of Equity,* 233–34.

68. "President's Commission on the Status of Women," microfilm ed., Reel 12, Frames 34–36.

69. "Notes from Meeting of the President's Commission on the Status of Women," February 5, 1962, Katherine P. Ellickson Papers, Box 90, Folder 23; Mary Dublin Keyserling to Bessie Hillman, March 18, 1964, ACWA Papers, Box 114, Folder 6; summary of the first "Meeting of Committee on Protective Labor Legislation," June 6, 1962, ACWA Papers, Box 119, Folder 2.

70. Mary Dublin Keyserling to Bessie Hillman, March 18, 1964, ACWA Papers, Box 114, Folder 6; PCSW, *American Women.*

71. Kathleen A. Laughlin, "How Did State Commissions on the Status of Women Overcome Historic Antagonisms Between Equal Rights and Labor Feminists to Create a New Feminist Mainstream?" Document 8: Agnes M.

Douty to Mary Dublin Keyserling, August 20, 1964 on Women and Social Movements in the United States, 1600–2000, http://www.alexanderstreet6 .com (accessed June 6, 2006); Cobble, *Other Women's Movement*, 183.

72. Kessler-Harris, *In Pursuit of Equity*, 264–65; Cobble, *Other Women's Movement*, 183, 186.

73. Cobble, *Other Women's Movement*, 174.

74. Cobble, *Other Women's Movement*, 43.

75. Reverend Addie Wyatt, interview with author, March 27, 2002; Cobble, *Other Women's Movement*, 34, 89, 128–29.

76. Callahan, in *Rocking the Boat*, 132.

77. Callahan, in *Rocking the Boat*, 132.

78. Peterson, *Restless*, 104–5.

79. Kessler-Harris, *Out to Work*, 313–14.

80. Helen Blanchard quoted in Deslippe, *"Rights, Not Roses,"* 47.

81. "Equal Pay for Women Bill Backed by ACWA," *Advance*, May 15, 1963, 6.

82. Cobble, *Other Women's Movement*, 174; Kessler-Harris, *Out to Work*, 313, 319; Kessler-Harris, *In Pursuit of Equity*, 234–35; Alice Kessler-Harris, *A Woman's Wage: Historical Meanings and Social Consequences* (Lexington: University of Kentucky Press, 1990), 103; Sybil Lipschultz, "Hours and Wages: The Gendering of Labor Standards in America," *Journal of Women's History* (Spring 1996): 114–25; Nancy Seifer, *Nobody Speaks for Me: Self-Portraits of American Working-Class Women* (New York: Simon & Schuster, 1976), 30.

83. Peterson, *Restless*, 110; Kessler-Harris, *A Woman's Wage*, 111–12.

84. Cobble, *Other Women's Movement*, 178; Whittaker, *The Fair Labor Standards Act*.

85. Cynthia Harrison, *On Account of Sex: The Politics of Women's Issues, 1945–1968* (Berkeley: University of California Press, 1988), 104–5; Gabin, *Feminism in the Labor Movement*, 189.

86. Bessie Abramowitz Hillman, "Gifted Women in the Trade Unions," in *American Women: The Changing Image*, ed. Beverly Benner Cassara (Boston: Beacon Press, 1962).

87. American Labor Education Service, "Statistical Reflections for a Discussion of Women's Problems," 1961, 2, ACWA Papers, Box 112, Folder 20.

88. AFL-CIO, *Problems of Working Women*, 49–50.

89. Fredgant, *Oral History Interview*, 23; McGill, *Oral History Interview*, 125.

90. AFL-CIO, *Problems of Working Women*.

91. Lichtenstein, *State of the Union*, 141. Chapter 4, "Erosion of the Union Idea," details the reasons for labor's decline.

92. "14th Summer School 'Rolls the Union On,'" *Advance*, August 1, 1962, 8.

93. *Proceedings of the Twenty-Fifth Biennial ACWA Convention*, 1966, 290; Lichtenstein, *State of the Union*, 94.

94. Cobble, *Other Women's Movement*, 9.

95. Neal, *Oral History Interview*, 36; Barbara Mayer Wertheimer and Anne H. Nelson, *Trade Union Women: A Study of Their Participation in New York City Locals* (New York: Praeger Publishers, 1975), 121–22; Bessie Hillman to George Arlook Company, December 14, 1951, ACWA Papers, Box 112, Folder 7.

96. Fredgant, *Oral History Interview*, 60; Robinson, *Oral History Interview*, 57; Annelise Orleck, *Common Sense and a Little Fire: Women and Working-*

Class Politics in the United States, 1900–1965 (Chapel Hill: University of North Carolina Press, 1995), 279, 297.

97. Fredgant, *Oral History Interview*, 33.

98. Robinson, *Oral History Interview*, 36.

99. Philoine Fried, interview with author, January 29, 1997.

100. Peterson, *Restless*, 56–59.

101. Regina Urdaneta, *Oral History Interview with Regina Urdaneta, Amalgamated Clothing Workers of America by Enid Valle* (Ann Arbor, MI: Program on Women and Work, Institute of Labor and Industrial Relations, University of Michigan–Wayne State University, 1978), p. 20.

102. Urdaneta, *Oral History Inverview*, 20.

103. Frieda Schwenkmeyer, *Oral History Interview with Frieda Schwenkmeyer, Amalgamated Clothing Workers of America by Bette Craig* (Ann Arbor, MI: Program on Women and Work, Institute of Labor and Industrial Relations, University of Michigan–Wayne State University, 1978), 24; Jacob Sheinkman (Hillman's attorney) to B. Altman Company, March 1, 1950, ACWA Papers, Box 112, Folder 13.

104. Arthur M. Schlesinger, Jr., *A Thousand Days: John F. Kennedy in the White House* (Boston: Houghton Mifflin, 1965), 972–73; Todd Gitlin, *The Sixties: Years of Hope, Days of Rage* (New York: Bantam Books, 1987), 144–45; UNITE History—"Time Line," www.ilr.cornell.edu (accessed September 5, 2005).

105. Callahan, in *Rocking the Boat*, 128.

106. Peterson, *Restless*, 114.

107. "Continue Full Protection for All Women Workers," *Advance*, June 1, 1967, 4; "State Protective Laws Still Needed for Working Women," *Advance*, May 15, 1968, 9; Jacob Potofsky and ACWA Research Department, "A Reevaluation of State Protective Legislation for Women Workers," March 9, 1970, Esther Peterson Papers, Box 71, Folder 1399.

108. Deslippe, *"Rights, Not Roses,"* 118.

109. "Title VII of the Civil Rights Act of 1964," Sections 705 (a), Section 706, and Section 709 [42 U.S.C. 2000e], in *Statutory Supplement to Employment Discrimination Law: Cases and Materials on Equality in the Workplace*, ed. Robert Belton and Dianne Avery (St. Paul, MN: 1999), 9–36; Kessler-Harris, *In Pursuit of Equity*, 277.

110. *Proceedings of the Twenty-Fifth Biennial ACWA Convention, 1966*, 290.

111. Gabin, *Feminism in the Labor Movement*, 192–93.

112. Deslippe, *"Rights, Not Roses,"* 124–25.

113. Gabin, *Feminism in the Labor Movement*, 137.

114. Deslippe, *"Rights, Not Roses,"* 140.

115. Lichtenstein, *State of the Union*, 148–49, 188, 270.

116. American Labor Education Service, "Statistical Reflections for a Discussion of Women's Problems," 2; "The Ladies Are Gaining in Union Memberships," *Advance*, October 1, 1966.

117. Milton Steward (Administrative Assistant to the Governor) to Bessie Hillman, January 17, 1955, ACWA Papers, Box 115, Folder 21; Pauline Newman to Bessie Hillman, November 1967, ACWA Papers, Box 114, Folder 17.

118. Bessie Hillman, "Rose Schneiderman: A Tribute [upon retirement from the NYWTUL], 1949," ACWA Microfilm Collection, Reel 24, Frame 686.

119. Pauline Newman to Bessie Hillman, November 1967, ACWA Papers, Box 114, Folder 17; Elisabeth Christman to Bessie Hillman, 1946–1967, ACWA Papers, Box 112, Folder 15; Bessie Hillman to Mary Anderson, August 21, 1952, ACWA Papers, Box 112, Folder 6.

120. Mary Anderson to Bessie Hillman, 1962, ACWA Papers, Box 112, Folder 6.

121. Robinson, *Oral History Interview,* 5; Agnes Murphy, "At Home with Mrs. Sidney Hillman," *New York Post,* August 19, 1962, reprinted in *Advance,* September 1, 1962, 5; Bessie Hillman to Josephine Guest, November 1962, ACWA Papers, Box 113, Folder 7; Joyce Miller, interview with author, March 3, 2001.

122. "Mrs. Hillman Is a Delegate of ICFTU at United Nations," *Advance,* May 1, 1963, 4; "Mrs. Hillman Helps Study the Role of Women," *Advance,* May 1, 1962, 5; Margaret K. Bruce (Chief, Section on the Status of Women) to Bessie Hillman, October 17, 1966, ACWA Papers, Box 113, Folder 17; Harm Buiter, General Secretary, "Women in ICFTU Resolution," July 30, 1969, Esther Peterson Papers, Box 73, Folder 1446.

123. Billie Luisi-Potts, interview with author, August 25, 2005; Philoine Fried, interview with author, October 28, 2005; Howard D. Samuel, *Amalgamated Panorama* (New York: ACWA, 1960), 104.

124. Bessie Hillman to Ethel Reilly, October 9, 1969, ACWA Microfilm Collection, Reel 24, Frames 418–19.

125. Maria Moreno to Bessie Hillman, 1962, ACWA Papers, Box 114, Folder 16.

126. "Record Enrollment Set for Summer Institute," *Advance,* July 1, 1961, 12.

127. ACWA Papers, Box 114, Folder 7; Bessie Hillman to Mortimer C. Ritter, 1952, ACWA Microfilm Collection, Reel 24, Frame 644.

128. Bessie Hillman to Polly Buttrick, April 25, 1950, ACWA Microfilm Collection, Reel 24, Frame 649; "A Better Tomorrow for America's Youth," *Advance,* January 15, 1951, 6; "Resolution on Amalgamated Education Program," by Education Committee Chairperson, Bessie Hillman, *Proceedings of the Twenty-Fifth Biennial ACWA Convention,* 1966, 242–43.

129. *Proceedings of the Twenty-Fifth Biennial ACWA Convention,* 1966, 242–44; *Proceedings of the Twenty-Seventh Biennial ACWA Convention,* 1970, 388–91.

130. Sara Evans, *Personal Politics: The Roots of Women's Liberation in the Civil Rights and New Left* (New York: Vintage Books, 1980), 15.

131. Theodore H. White, *The Making of a President, 1964* (New York: Atheneum, 1965), 391.

132. Bessie Hillman to the Honorable John E. Beck, March 2, 1946, ACWA Microfilm Collection, Reel 23, Frame 880; Bessie Hillman to the Honorable Seymour Brener, n.d., ACWA Microfilm Collection, Reel 23, Frame 883; John Sparkman to Bessie Hillman, April 4, 1949, ACWA Microfilm Collection, Reel 24, Frame 806; William Hassett to Bessie Hillman, March 24, 1951, ACWA Microfilm Collection, Reel 23, Frame 78; Senator Manfred Ohrenstein to Bessie Hillman, November 17, 1964, ACWA Microfilm Collection, Reel 24, Frame 182; Bessie Hillman, "Thirtieth Kingston Anniversary Speech, 1964," private collection of Philoine Fried.

133. Dollie Lowther Robinson to Bessie Hillman, May 18, 1967, private collection of Philoine Fried.

134. "Proposed Statement of Democratic Advisory Committee on Labor Policy," ACWA Papers, Box 119, Folder 1; "Josephine Telesco Heads New York City COPE Women's Committee," unidentified article, ACWA Papers, Box 120, Folder 4; "Southeastern Board Steps Up Register-Vote Campaign," ACWA Papers, Box 120, Folder 4; Bessie Hillman, "Kingston Thirtieth Anniversary Speech, 1964," private collection of Philoine Fried.

135. Lichtenstein, *State of the Union*, 188.

136. "ACWA Leaders Pay Tribute to Dr. King," *Advance*, May 1, 1968, 3.

137. Bessie Hillman to Ben Josephson, March 26, 1969, ACWA Microfilm Collection, Reel 23, Frame 431.

138. *Proceedings of the Twenty-Seventh Biennial ACWA Convention*, 1970, 391.

139. Deslippe, *"Rights, Not Roses,"* 123–24.

140. AFL-CIO Department of Civil Rights, Discrimination Case Files, 1947–1984, Record Group 9, Series 1, Box 4, Folders 20, 21, 24, 27, 28, 30–33, and 36–38, National Labor College Archives.

141. Cobble, *Other Women's Movement*, 184–85.

142. Cobble, *Other Women's Movement*, 70.

143. Cobble, *Other Women's Movement*, 178; Whittaker, *The Fair Labor Standards Act*; Adele Simmons, et al., *Exploitation from 9 to 5: Report of the Twentieth Century Fund Task Force on Women and Employment* (Lexington, MA: Lexington Books, 1975), 87–88.

144. *Proceedings of the Twenty-Fifth Biennial ACWA Convention*, 1966, 288–89; Deslippe, *"Rights, Not Roses,"* 118–19.

145. American Labor Education Service, "Statistical Reflections for a Discussion of Women's Problems," 3.

146. Lichtenstein, *State of the Union*, 187.

147. Maya Pines, "Someone to Mind the Baby," *New York Times*, January 7, 1968; "Salute to Bessie Hillman," *AFL-CIO News* 31, no. 33 (August 16, 1986): 1; "ACW Backs Bill to Allow Employer Aid to Union Scholarship, Child Care Centers," *Advance*, March 1, 1968, 12; "House Passes Bill to Permit Scholarship, Daycare Funds," *Advance*, September 15, 1968, 4; *Proceedings of the Twenty-Sixth Biennial ACWA Convention*, 1968, 322–23; "ACWA First Union in the Country to Initiate Child Care Center," *Advance*, May 15, 1968, 4.

148. "Chartering of a New Local Marks Unification of N.Y. Glove Workers," *Advance*, November 1, 1969, 3; "$2.50 Floor in 3 Years Urged by ACW Leader," *Advance*, March 5, 1970, 9.

149. "10–million Package for 4,000 at Xerox in Rochester Won by Amalgamated," *Advance*, April 15, 1970, 20; Peter McColough (President, Xerox Corporation) to Jacob Potofsky (upon the death of Bessie Hillman), January 5, 1971, private collection of Philoine Fried.

150. *"Movimento organizador continua,"* *Advance*, March 15, 1969, 10.

151. "SHF Award for Public Service Presented to David A. Morse," *Advance*, October 1, 1969.

152. Nell Womack Evans, "Mrs. Sidney Hillman, True Union Wife, Carries on Husband's Work," *Labor's Daily*, May 11, 1956, in ACWA Papers, Box 120, Folder 3; "Sidney Hillman Foundation Award for Public Service Presented to

David A. Morse," *Advance,* October 1, 1969, 5; "ACW Sees Women Rights Imperiled by Amendment," *Advance,* May 15, 1970, 12; "Women Unionists Protest Rights Amendment Minus Protection of Labor Laws," *Advance,* July 1970, 4; "ACW Resolution of Women's Rights," *Advance,* July 1970, 17; "ACWA Presses Fight on 'Equal Rights' Amendment," *Advance,* October 1, 1970, 11; "Platform Photo," *Advance,* June 15, 1970, 16.

153. Hillman, "Gifted Women in Trade Unions," 114–15.

154. Ibid.

155. Esther Peterson to Congresswoman Martha Griffiths, October 12, 1971, Esther Peterson Papers, Box 54, Folder 1061. Finally comfortable with existing labor standards, Peterson relented, stating, "After much soul searching, I have come to the conclusion that the time for waiting for court action is past and the enactment of an equal rights amendment would be a constructive step."

156. "GEB: Strengthen Laws for Women Workers," *Advance,* March 1, 1968.

157. Callahan, in *Rocking the Boat,* 127.

158. Philoine Fried, interview with author, December 29, 1997.

159. Philoine Fried, interview with author, January 13, 2003.

160. Leo Perlis to Jacob Potofsky, December 28, 1970, private collection of Philoine Fried.

Epilogue: Lifting Their Spirits

1. David Montgomery, "Labor Reform in the Long Shadow of the Hull-House," Legacies of Hull-House Conference, University of Illinois at Chicago, September 18, 1999.

2. "Is Hull House Doomed?" *Advance,* March 15, 1961, 16 (this article reprints the full text of Bessie Hillman's letter to Mayor Daley).

3. "ACWA Helped Save Hull House from Axe," *Advance,* July 7, 1961, 7; "A House of Labor," *Advance,* September 15, 1963, 12. Both articles refer to Hull-House as the birthplace of the Amalgamated.

4. Historians of women are calling for an inclusive approach to the historical study of twentieth-century feminism that considers the continuity of the movement and working women's place in it. Dorothy Sue Cobble, "Lost Visions of Equality: The Labor Origins of the Next Women's Movement," *Labor History* 12, no. 1 (Winter/Spring 2003): 23; Kate Weigand and Daniel Horowitz, "Dorothy Kenyon: Feminist Organizing, 1919–1963," *Journal of Women's History* (Summer 2002): 126–31.

5. Nancy Gabin, *Feminism in the Labor Movement: Women and the United Auto Workers, 1935–1975* (Ithaca, NY: Cornell University Press, 1990), 138.

6. Susan Glenn, *Daughters of the Shtetl: Life and Labor in the Immigrant Generation* (Ithaca, NY: Cornell University Press, 1990), 209–16.

7. Theresa S. Malkiel, *Diary of a Shirtwaist Striker* (Ithaca, NY: Cornell University Press, 1990); Annelise Orleck, *Common Sense and a Little Fire: Women and Working-Class Politics in the United States, 1900–1965* (Chapel Hill: University of North Carolina Press, 1995).

8. Philoine Fried, interview with author, February 8, 2005.

9. As quoted in Steven Fraser, *Labor Will Rule: Sidney Hillman and the Rise*

of American Labor (New York: Free Press, 1991), 98; Joyce Miller, interview with author, March 3, 2001.

10. Esther Peterson, interview with author, February 17, 1997. Esther Peterson held the post of Director of the ACWA Education Department in the late 1930s, and by the 1940s she served as the union's legislative representative in Washington.

11. Dorothy Sue Cobble, *The Other Women's Movement: Workplace Justice and Social Rights in Modern America* (Princeton, NJ: Princeton University Press, 2004), 4.

12. Potofsky, "Resolution on Bessie Hillman," March 4, 1971, private collection of Philoine Fried.

13. Esther Peterson to Philoine Fried and Selma Kraft, December 30, 1970, private collection of Philoine Fried.

14. Most women who would be considered ardent feminists by today's standards did not "think in those terms in those days." See Esther Peterson, "You Can't Giddyup by Saying Whoa," in *Rocking the Boat: Union Women's Voices, 1915–1975*, ed. Brigid O'Farrell and Joyce L. Kornbluh, 64 (New Brunswick, NJ: Rutgers University Press, 1996); "Women Unionists Protest Rights Amendment Minus Protection of Labor Laws," *Advance*, July 1970, 4; AFL-CIO, *Problems of Working Women: Summary Report of a Conference Sponsored by the Industrial Union Department of the AFL-CIO*, June 12–14, 1961, Publication No. 43, ACWA Papers, Box 120, Folder 1, Kheel Labor-Management Documentation Center, Cornell University (hereafter "ACWA Papers"); Bessie Abramowitz Hillman, "Gifted Women in the Trade Unions," in *American Women: The Changing Image*, ed. Beverly Benner Cassara, 103 (Boston: Beacon Press, 1962).

15. Hillman, "Gifted Women in Trade Unions," 112–14.

16. Dollie Robinson to Bessie Hillman, April 25, 1951, ACWA Papers, Box 115, Folder 10.

17. Dorothy Haener, *Oral History Interview with Dorothy Haener, United Auto Workers by Lyn Goldfarb* (Ann Arbor, MI: Program on Women and Work, Institute of Labor and Industrial Relations, University of Michigan–Wayne State University, 1978), 59–62.

18. Dollie Lowther Robinson, *Oral History Interview with Dollie Lowther Robinson, Amalgamated Clothing Workers of America by Bette Craig* (Ann Arbor, MI: Program on Women and Work, Institute of Labor and Industrial Relations, University of Michigan–Wayne State University, 1978), 46–47 [microfiche].

19. Sara Fredgant, *Oral History Interview with Sara Fredgant, Amalgamated Clothing Workers of America by Bette Craig* (Ann Arbor, MI: Program on Women and Work, Institute of Labor and Industrial Relations, University of Michigan–Wayne State University, 1978), 23; Katherine Pollack Ellickson, "The President's Commission on the Status of Women: Its Formation, Functioning, and Contribution," 1981, 8–9, Caroline F. Ware Papers, File 1, Franklin Delano Roosevelt Presidential Library, Hyde Park, New York; "Membership Reelects Officers," *Advance*, October 15, 1956, 3. Votes for Bessie Hillman totaled 115,518 and against 2,019.

20. David Stebenne, *Arthur J. Goldberg: The New Deal Liberal* (New York: Oxford University Press, 1996), 484n84.

21. "1910 Commemorated," *Advance,* November 15, 1960, 11–12.

22. Jacqueline Dowd Hall, "O. Delight Smith's Progressive Era: Labor, Feminism, and Reform in the Urban South," in *Visible Women: New Essays on American Activism,* ed. Nancy Hewitt and Suzanne Lebsock (Urbana: University of Illinois Press, 1993), 5.

23. Coalition of Labor Union Women, "Statement of Purpose,"adopted at the founding conference, March 23–24, 1974. Miller was one of the "new generation of women leaders" who, following her graduation from the University of Chicago in 1962, began her work with the ACWA, assuming the directorship of the Education and Social Service Department of the union; later she was the first woman appointed to the Executive Board of the AFL-CIO. Miller was elected to the vice presidency of the CLUW in 1977. ACWA Papers, Box 110, Coalition of Labor Union Women [CLUW] Folder; Joyce Miller, interview with author, March 3, 2001; CLUW, First Biennial Convention Program, September 13–16, 1979, 22, in ACWA Papers, Box 110, CLUW Folder; Gabin, *Feminism in the Labor Movement,* 226.

24. UNITE, "A Union Born," http://www.uniteunion.org/whatisunite/history/unionisborn.html, pp. 5–6.

25. Robert J. S. Ross, *Slaves to Fashion: Poverty and Abuse in the New Sweatshops* (Ann Arbor: University of Michigan Press, 2004), 198, 274–80, 298; Priscilla Murolo and A. B. Chitty, *From the Folks Who Brought You the Weekend: A Short, Illustrated History of Labor in the United States* (New York: Free Press, 2001), 318; Michael Zweig, *The Working Class Majority: America's Best Kept Secret* (Ithaca, NY: ILR Press, 2000), 147.

26. Carl Proper (UNITE Research Department), interview with author, January 12, 2001; UNITE, "A Union Born," http://www.uniteunion.org/whatisunite/history/unionisborn.html.

27. Dennis Delippe argues that by the 1970s, service-sector employees began to unionize and feminists turned their attention to improving women's lot in female-dominated jobs rather than to confronting sex-segregated occupational hierarchies. See Dennis A. Deslippe, *"Rights, Not Roses": Unions and the Rise of Working-Class Feminism, 1945–1980* (Urbana: University of Illinois Press, 2000), 195–96.

28. Cobble, *Other Women's Movement,* 206–7.

29. U.S. Department of Labor, Women's Bureau Website, www.dol.gov/wb.

30. U.S. Department of Labor, Bureau of Labor Statistics, "BLS Data on Unions, Women in the Labor Force: A Databook," Table 38, "Union affiliation of employed wage and salary workers by sex, annual averages, 1983–2004," www.bls.gov.

31. U.S. Department of Labor, Women's Bureau Website, www.dol.gov/wb.

32. Anonymous former Women's Bureau regional administrator, interview with author, April 2, 2006.

33. U.S. Department of Labor, Bureau of Labor Statistics, "BLS Data on Unions," Table 38, www.bls.gov. The figure for the male rate of union membership is only approximately a percentage point higher.

34. At present, only 20 percent of workers receive paid family leave (based on the individual employer's discretion). See Miriam Peskowitz, author of *The Truth Behind the Mommy Wars: Who Decides What Makes a Good Mother?* Virginia Festival of Books, March 24, 2006, aired on Book TV, April 1, 2006.

INDEX

Abbott, Grace, 49–51, 61
Abramowitz, Emanuel, 1
Abramowitz, Celia, 11
Abramowitz, Pauline, 11
Abramowitz, Sarah Rabinowitz, 1
activists: women in Russia, 7, 13;
    women in United States, 13, 19,
    40, 43, 52, 56, 62, 73, 79, 101, 129,
    136, 149; black women as, 173, 175,
    178–79, 187; Jewish women as, 21,
    194. *See also* labor feminists
Addams, Jane, 11; founding of Hull-
    House, 13; as advocate for working
    women, 18, 20, 22, 137; and WTUL,
    20–22; during 1910 Chicago strike,
    27–28, 33; and Amalga- mated
    Clothing Workers of America, 38,
    47, 71–72; and Bessie Abramowitz
    Hillman, 38, 42, 84–85, 105–06,
    191; in 1915 Chicago strike, 48–49;
    and social feminism, 53; useful
    citizenship, 62
Adelmond, Charlotte, 110–11, 179
Advance: on women, 50, 53, 55, 65–66
African-Americans: workers, 107–08,
    113, 117, 121, 127–28, 138, 140,
    142, 144; organization of, 106–08,
    128, 140; discrimination against,

107–08, 111, 113–14, 128, 138–39,
    142–43, 147, 152, 174, 177, 181,
    186–87, 196; Bessie Hillman's
    work with, 122, 139–41, 144, 173;
    women, during World War II, 127;
    President's Commission on the
    Status of Women recommendations
    on, 172. *See also* civil rights
Alabama, 128, 142
Albany, New York, 86, 94–97, 180
Alexander II, 3
Allentown, Pennsylvania, 86–89, 99
Amalgamated Clothing Workers of
    America (ACWA): foundations
    of at Hull-House, 38; founding,
    45–46; appointment of Sidney
    Hillman as president, 44–45; Bessie
    Abramowitz at First Biennial
    Convention, 46; Chicago District
    Number 6 (Chicago Joint Board),46,
    48; influenced by Jane Addams, 38,
    47, 71–72; new unionism, 47–48;
    Second Biennial Convention, 50;
    women organizers, 50, 63, 66, 71,
    77–79, 83, 98–99, 115, 117, 134, 140,
    163, 196; women's participation in,
    51, 53, 63–65, 127, 134, 140, 148,
    151, 177, 180; unionization of New

KAREN PASTORELLO is an associate professor of history and chair of Women and Gender Studies at Tompkins Cortland Community College in Dryden, New York. She is a contributor to *Women Building Chicago, 1790–1990: A Biographical Dictionary* (Indiana University Press, 1996); *The Encyclopedia of U.S. Labor and Working Class History* (Routledge, 2006); and *Jane Addams and the Practice of Democracy: Multidisciplinary Perspectives on Theory and Practice* (University of Illinois Press, forthcoming).

The University of Illinois Press
is a founding member of the
Association of American University Presses.

Composed in 9.5/12.5 Trump Mediaeval
by BookComp, Inc.
for the University of Illinois Press
Manufactured by Thomson-Shore, Inc.

University of Illinois Press
1325 South Oak Street
Champaign, IL 61820-6903
www.press.uillinois.edu